Miskwabik

Metal of Ritual

Miskwabik means "copper"
in the Native American language
of the Ojibwa tribe.

Miskwabik

Metal of Ritual

Metallurgy in Precontact Eastern North America

Amelia M. Trevelyan

The University Press of Kentucky

Publication of this volume has been aided by a grant from the Millard Meiss Publication Fund of the College Art Association.

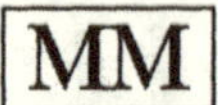

Scholarly publisher for the Commonwealth,
serving Bellarmine University, Berea College, Centre College of Kentucky, Eastern Kentucky University, The Filson Historical Society, Georgetown College, Kentucky Historical Society, Kentucky State University, Morehead State University, Murray State University, Northern Kentucky University, Transylvania University, University of Kentucky, University of Louisville, and Western Kentucky University.

Editorial and Sales Offices: The University Press of Kentucky
663 South Limestone Street, Lexington, Kentucky 40508–4008
http://www.kentuckypress.com

08 07 06 05 04   5 4 3 2 1

Library of Congress Cataloging-in-Publication Data

Trevelyan, Amelia M.
Miskwabik, metal of ritual : metallurgy in precontact Eastern North America / Amelia M. Trevelyan
p. cm.
Includes bibliographical references and index.
ISBN 0-8131-2272-4 (alk. paper)
1. Indian copperwork—East (U.S.) 2. Indians of North America—East (U.S.) —Rites and ceremonies. 3. Indian metal-work—East (U.S.) 4. Indian copperwork —Canada, Eastern. 5. Indians of North America—Canada, Eastern—Rites and ceremonies. 6. Indian metal-work—Canada, Eastern. I. Title.
E98.C76T74 2003
739.2'089'97—dc21   2003005795

This book is printed on acid-free recycled paper meeting the requirements of the American National Standard for Permanence of Paper for Printed Library Materials.

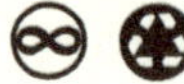

Manufactured in the United States of America

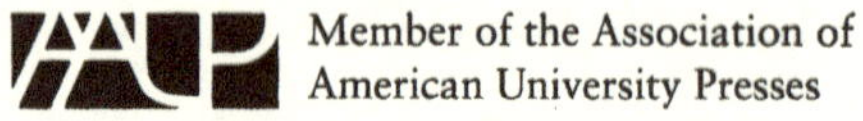

This volume is dedicated to my students, who have helped me learn as I teach; to my children, Whitney and Devon, for providing the joy and inspiration to roll on; and to Arnold Rubin, friend and mentor, whose brilliant intellect and deep humanity helped guide me here.

Contents

Maps

Tables

Figures

Plates

Acknowledgments

This project could not have been completed without the assistance of dozens of individuals, from the individuals charged with the care of the art works that are the subject of this study, to the scholars who first collected and analyzed them, to my colleagues in the field. Most important, of course, are the indigenous societies of North America who made and used these magnificent objects.

In addition to preserving the works and sharing them with me, the institutions who own these art works have been most generous in granting permission to illustrate them, as well as providing some of the images. They include: The American Museum of Natural History, New York; Etowah Indian Mounds State Historic Site Museum, Cartersville, Georgia; The Field Museum, Chicago; Florida Division of Historical Resources, Tallahassee; Frank H. McClung Museum, University of Tennessee, Knoxville; Illinois State Museum, Dickson Mounds, Lewiston; Illinois State Museum, Springfield; Milwaukee Public Museum; Missouri Archaeological Society, Columbia; Mound City Group National Monument, Ohio; Ohio Historical Society, Columbus; Ohio State Museum, Newark; Oklahoma State Historical Society Museum, Oklahoma City; Pictures of Record, Inc.; Smithsonian National Museum of the American Indian, Washington, D.C.; Smithsonian National Museum of Natural History, Department of Anthropology, Washington, D.C.; Southern Illinois University Center for Archaeological Investigations, Carbondale; The Thomas Gilcrease Institute of American History and Art, Tulsa, Oklahoma; University of Alabama Archaeological Collections, Tuscaloosa; University of Alabama Archaeological Collections, Moundville; University Museum, University of Arkansas, Fayetteville; University of Georgia Archaeological Collections, Athens; The Spurlock Museum, University of Illinois, Urbana; University of Michigan Archaeological Collections, Ann Arbor; University of West Georgia Archaeological Collections, Carrollton; Washington University Gallery of Art, St. Louis, Missouri; Woolaroc Museum, Bartlesville, Oklahoma; W.S. Webb Museum of Anthropology, University of Kentucky, Lexington. The collections of the Robert S. Peabody Museum of Archaeology, Phillips Academy, Andover, Massachusetts; Peabody Museum of Archaeology and Ethnology; and Sam Noble Oklahoma Museum of Natural History, The University of Oklahoma, Norman were also useful.

Introduction

Art objects designed for use in ritual are sometimes all that remain to bear witness to the complexity of the societies that peopled the Americas before Europeans arrived. Despite their beauty and technical sophistication, these artworks present forms, uses, and ideas that are so foreign to today's urbane modes and perceptions that it is all but impossible to link them to much that is familiar in today's materialistic, media-driven world. This difficulty is especially true of artworks from pre-Columbian North America.

Few of the conventional markers of civilization survive from this period. Without remnants of a written language to provide clues, and in the absence of much in the way of monumental stone architecture, for a long time it was difficult for Euro-Americans to recognize the basic humanity of these peoples, much less think of their cultural manifestations as "civilizations." But civilizations they were. Political and economic priorities were clearly different from those of modern Europe, but language, thought, models, and perceptions of reality were no less complex, though they had developed from very different perspectives.

The spectacular metallurgy of northeastern North America bears clear witness to that complexity. To begin to see the civilized sophistication of the tradition of metallurgy and to understand why it must be considered as such, we need to examine the beauty and intricacy of this corpus of objects in its entirety. We must also explore how the tradition developed and understand its relationship to indigenous cultural systems today, as well as to certain universals in the nature and function of art in all human societies.

Native copper was the most important ritual medium in use throughout eastern North America in prehistoric times. Hundreds of tons of it were mined and worked into ceremonial paraphernalia millennia before Europeans arrived in the New World. The specialized use of exotic materials such as copper was pervasive in the precontact arts of the Americas. Often the sources for those materials were hundreds and even thousands of miles away from the areas in which they were used. Means and methods for procuring such exotica were arduous, and the objects made were rarely functional in any literal sense. These challenges notwithstanding, thousands of pounds of these special materials were extracted and fashioned into elaborate ritual artwork.

What was the initial impetus for their use? How did these exotic materials and the objects fashioned from them function, and what was their significance? Why were they so highly valued? How did they move across such vast distances, and do so for millennia? What were the mechanisms developed for that movement and how did they change? Scholars have puzzled over these issues for more than a century.

Examination of the entire copper tradition in eastern North America, from the earliest objects produced through the time of European contact, reveals patterns of use and significance that help to answer these questions with a clarity that does not emerge in more circumscribed analysis. When copper artifacts appear in the eastern United States in their largest numbers, for example, it is always in conjunction with major ceremonial fluorescences such as the Hopewellian and so-called Southeastern Ceremonial Complex episodes. Also, increases in copperwork production consistently accompany significant changes in settlement and subsistence patterns as well as shifts in climate.[1]

Subject matter in the designs applied to copperwork often reflects those changes. Many aspects of the use of copper in ritual art are remarkably consistent across thousands of years, throughout much of the region. Looking at that continuity in detail makes possible seeing at least the outlines of the rich meaning and significance of these ancient objects. Comparing the ritual artwork and its archaeological contexts with references to ceremony and paraphernalia described in early ethnographic sources offers important details to help fill in the picture of vibrant and sophisticated societies. The continuity in use and iconography over millennia becomes clear through this process and validates such an approach (see Appendix, Section I).

The most spectacular and technically sophisticated examples of work were produced in connection with elaborate ritual practices, almost always associated with burial. In fact, the combination of complex earthworks and paraphernalia, very often fashioned of copper, identifies all of the most complex pre-Columbian ritual traditions in northeastern North America. Cultural manifestations dubbed "Adena," "Hopewell," "the Southeastern Ceremonial Complex," etc., by archaeologists are both defined and differentiated, in part, according to the specific characteristics of ritual artwork.

Both the ritual objects and the ceremonial traditions themselves developed in response to a variety of circumstances. Each period of significant production, in both quality and quantity, was accompanied by important changes in demographics and subsistence strategies. Both chronological and regional differences in use and the iconography associated with the artwork reflect social and cultural tensions likely to have accompanied significant changes in subsistence and demographics, as well as the meteorological conditions that may have occasioned both. That is not to say that a simple one-to-one relationship existed between these factors and the iconography of the copperwork, any more than to say that a simple cause/effect relationship existed between these external developments and the social and cultural responses of the peoples involved. The coincidence of these phenomena is undeniable, nonetheless.

It is clear that, when produced in quantity, copperwork was an integral element in traditional ways of dealing with social and ecological stress throughout the Eastern Woodlands. Even the geographical areas most frequently and severely affected by such crises appear to be those characterized by the greatest concentrations of copper-working activity.[2] In most human societies, art production blossoms in response to the tensions that arise when groups undergo significant ideological and cultural transitions. Under such circumstances art tends to fill the gaps that develop between ideology and experience, and the production of artwork increases in quantity and complexity until revisions in ideology, experience, or both close the gaps. Societies that produce very little art tend to be relatively stable and quite content with the status quo. When that changes, levels of art production inevitably rise and remain at a high level until a new socio-cultural equilibrium is reached. This phenomenon does not occur quickly, however. Like most fundamental shifts in culture, these changes take place very slowly, over generations. Art created in response to those changes tends to develop in advance of the general social consciousness of the changes and fades in significance once the transition is made by society at large.[3]

The relatively uniform ecology of eastern North America indicates that conditions likely to challenge the cultural status quo or force major changes in basic subsistence modes would undoubtedly have been felt widely. The archaeological record shows that clear similarities existed in the ceremonial responses of many peoples of the region to these periods of change and the conditions that brought them on. The similarities were also a function of consistencies in beliefs, behavior, and other broad patterns of culture—as much as they were a function of the unified character of the conditions precipitating the crises. Heightened interaction between affected groups was undoubtedly a significant element in the similarity as well.

The central importance of copper in so many of these developments—and for such a long time—indicates that the medium itself was an important factor in defining both the kind of ceremonial activity it was used in and the nature and degree of interaction between the participant groups. Early in the tradition, as well as at the time of its demise, unworked nuggets and undecorated objects were as common as more elaborate copperwork. This is another indication that the medium itself was as important to function as form and motif.

Many other reasons for the remarkable continuity in the ritual use of copper become apparent and comprehensible through examination of the entire tradition. The evolution of form and iconography in the corpus as a whole suggests that the beliefs upon which form and iconography were based were part of a widely shared body of religious tradition that was established very early in the prehistory of the region and that almost always involved copper. As time passed, more and more elaborate decoration was applied to copper metallurgy, until, soon after the arrival of Europeans, it ceased to be important in ritual.

Information from a broad range of written sources and texts is necessary to develop a viable context for the study of an art tradition produced by ancient, non-literate cultures. Art historical analysis of the pre-Columbian societies of northeastern North America has been meager. Literature on copper use by traditional societies outside North America offers insight into the sacred nature of both mining and metallurgical practices and the crucial importance of the medium itself in similarly organized groups. Early Historic Period documents can also provide a sense of the cosmological significance of copperwork, as well as clarify the nature of the ritual contexts in which the objects functioned. Linguistic studies—as well as ethnographic, archaeological, historical, and even geological ones—offer other clues to copper use and iconography. Native leaders and religious specialists from the region and ritual practices that are still part of the traditional round of ceremonies also offer crucial insights. Relevant data tends to appear only in small bits though, here and there.

The specific role copper played becomes clear only in the accumulated evidence of all these sources, just as the significance of the complex itself emerges only through consideration of the phenomenon as a whole. Scarcity of relevant data is hardly the only difficulty encountered in analysis of the relevant literature. The nature of the role copper played is also difficult to define because, in Western culture, the significance of exotic metals is traditionally viewed as primarily economic in nature. In fact, ethnocentric assumptions about values and motives often present the most persistent obstacles to a clear understanding of the copper tradition as a whole.

Since the early days of this project in the late 1970s, the field has begun to relinquish this kind of simplistic and essentially ethnocentric approach to the analysis of material culture. This development has resulted in increasingly clear impressions of the peoples that created these objects. These new attitudes are typified in the work of S. Terry Childs, who identified and articulated the need for such a re-orientation to material culture in the analysis of early metallurgy in Africa (1991:57–58).

Nevertheless, most studies of the copper complex have approached an analysis in economic rather than ritual terms, and have established elaborate models for the movement of trade goods.[4] Examination of widespread native ceremonial developments after the arrival of Europeans suggests that an exclusively economic definition of the use of copper omits much that was crucial to the tradition. The increased interaction and exchange between groups which participated in widespread prehistoric ceremonial movements was paralleled in many ways during Historic times. In those post-contact developments, the role of exotica was almost never economic in its emphasis.

Analysis of large-scale ceremonial movements in Historic times has led to the revision of a number of theories regarding precontact ritual structures. For the most part, recent scholarship rejects earlier notions about the monolithic nature of such movements in prehistoric times. The regional and even local character of certain aspects of the prehistoric traditions is clear. A similarly parochial quality is also apparent in Historic movements. The data that have led to rethinking the nature of these ritual manifestations, both before and after the arrival of Europeans, are significant.

However, the simultaneous occurrence of those ceremonial responses to crisis, and the other important similarities that occasioned earlier assumptions about the monolithic and messianic qualities of the responses, cannot be denied. As usual, an accurate evaluation of these phenomena lies somewhere between the two extremes. The central importance of individual religious specialists within all native North American ritual almost certainly accounts for the messianic qualities apparent in these developments, as well as for important differences from group to group. On the other hand, long-standing similarities in world view, shared perceptions regarding the nature and function of ritual, and roughly similar climatic and ecological conditions throughout eastern North America may explain why at certain periods both crisis situations and ceremonial responses to them were similar.

In large-scale Historic Period ceremonial developments, clearly the exchange between the groups and the individuals involved was primarily of ideological, not economic, significance. Available data on prehistoric ceremonial complexes involving copper suggests that, at least in this regard, these early manifestations were very similar to their historical counterparts. Thus, the ritual role of copperwork was probably more central to its importance than any economic significance it may have had.

The traditional norms of Western culture have also obscured the ritual basis for the political power wielded by members of native ceremonial elites—

those who used, possessed, and probably produced the copperwork. The historical record indicates that the power base of individual leaders associated with these kinds of ceremonial developments was essentially spiritual. Although their economic and political status was considerable, in most cases that status derived ultimately from their spiritual primacy. In previous studies of the copper complex, the elite status of individuals buried with copperwork is usually regarded as primarily economic and political. The religio-ceremonial role of those individuals and of copper is generally either ignored or only mentioned briefly.

This attitude almost certainly derives from a posture of methodological rigor which seeks to deal only with the material evidence and to avoid assumptions regarding belief systems and states of mind. However, given what is reliably known of the use of native copper in prehistoric and Early Historic times, such conservatism risks significant misinterpretation of the nature of the copper complex and the factors that gave rise to and supported it. The fact that copperwork from the prehistoric Eastern Woodlands has been discovered almost exclusively in special, burial-related contexts indicates that its importance was more ritual than utilitarian. Because copper appears so consistently as ceremonial paraphernalia, a proper understanding of its importance to the societies that used it must focus primarily on its role in ceremony. In fact, it would be difficult to develop an accurate picture of any aspect of the copper complex without first establishing how and why it was used ceremonially.

An economically based interpretation of the copper complex also risks attributing a political and economic orientation to these conventions that is utterly out of character with the fundamental structures of the societies in question. This is not to say that pre-Columbian native North Americans were incapable of developing complex and sophisticated structures in the political and economic spheres of their lives. They almost always did. Nevertheless, models of Native American political and economic structure based primarily upon economic or political analyses infer an essentially materialistic and accumulative orientation that is, in many respects, alien to native North American cultures, and far more akin to the lifeways of present-day Euro-American societies.

The radical difference between the values and lifeways of early native North American societies and those of Euro-American groups is perhaps most obvious in the tendency of Native Americans to bury extremely valuable items with certain of their dead. This practice was intimately associated with the copper complex. Archaeological and anthropological scholarship has generally treated this phenomenon as a puzzling anomaly. Notwithstanding occasional speculation regarding reasons for such behavior, the issue of the fundamentally ritual orientation of prehistoric copperwork is generally sidestepped. I am not alone in finding fault with such approaches. Polly Weissner (1989:56) has very clearly delineated the fallacies involved in ignoring anomalous evidence. She points out that such evidence should be "treated seriously as indicators that additional factors may need to be considered" in order to develop valid conclusions.

Since the tendency to bury exotic ceremonial goods with the dead is so pervasive in the Americas (and among so-called primitive societies generally), a more useful approach might be to assume that such cultural proclivities reflect some significant and probably basic aspect of the belief systems of the groups involved. Such practices may not be anomalies—the aberrant practices of societies that are essentially like our own or, at least, assumed to be like our own. Rather, the occasional similarities perceived between early Native American groups and present-day Euro-American society may be the anomalies, and practices such as the one described above may represent a norm in the value systems of groups whose social, political, and economic paradigms were fundamentally different from ours. Having established this premise, one may proceed to analyze these cultures as a whole, less distorted by modern cultural biases.

Irving Hallowell (1975:143) has proposed such an approach to what he calls "ethno-metaphysics." He insists that "human beings in whatever culture are provided with positive orientation to a cosmos; there is 'order' and 'reason' rather than chaos." He points out that "the actions of persons [like the burial of valuables with the dead] provide the major key to their world view," and that they are based upon and represent the same kinds of order and reason unique to and imbedded in every human cultural system. This study proceeds from the same premises.

A focus on the ritual importance of prehistoric native North American copperwork also offers important insights into the basic cultural structures and ideologies of the groups that produced it. Religious symbols are especially rich sources for clues to both ontological and cosmological convictions.[5] Since virtually all the artifacts included in the copper complex seem to consist of ritually significant paraphernalia and incorporate religious symbols, they represent a major source of information in these areas of belief and behavior.

Examination of ceremonial elements embodied in the copperwork also offers insight into an important and often misunderstood aspect of much of the art produced by traditional societies. The issue is raised by Raymond Firth (1966:15) when he questions "how far the arts are in fact regarded by the people engaged in them as a contribution to subsistence." Like the tendency to attribute exclusively economic significance to exotic metals, current conventional attitudes and ideas about the arts and their relative importance are of almost no help in working through this question as it applies to metallurgy in pre-Columbian North America. However, both the query and its answer are crucial to a clear understanding of the copper complex. Whether copperwork was buried with the dead or used by the living, as unworked raw material or a finely crafted work of art, the degree to which prehistoric Native Americans were convinced that copperwork contributed to their own subsistence and survival seems to have determined the nature and content of prehistoric artistry in copper and its significance to the cultures that used it.

1

A Long, Consistent History

Copper was central to five major ritual manifestations in eastern North America, dubbed by scholars: the Old Copper Culture; the Adena, Hopewell, and Copena peoples; and the Southeastern Ceremonial Complex. The Old Copper Culture was a Middle to Late Archaic development that lasted from about 3000–1000 B.C. and was focused primarily in the upper Great Lakes region. Adena was a Late Archaic to Early Woodland manifestation that thrived circa 1500 B.C. to 200 B.C. While major Adena centers were farther south, in what is now Ohio, Kentucky, and West Virginia, some overlapped with the development of Hopewell traditions. The latter, generally dated between 300 B.C. and A.D. 300, is a Middle Woodland phenomenon, centered in present-day Ohio and Illinois. Hopewell's southern counterpart, Copena, evolved slightly later and lasted longer, with major centers in Georgia and Alabama. Elaborate copperwork and associated ritual nearly disappeared after the demise of the Hopewell and Copena manifestations. The next five hundred years show little evidence of copper mining and metallurgy. Then, about A.D. 1000, copper activity burst forth again, first in the Midwest and later in the large ceremonial centers of the Southeast, in what has since been called the Southeastern Ceremonial Complex.

Each fluorescence was characterized by a plethora of localized developments that shared relatively few traits beyond apparent similarities in cosmological models and worldview, a focus on mortuary ritual—and remarkably similar approaches to the use and disposition of copper within those contexts. Little or no evidence suggests that the ritual traditions involved were monolithic or pan-regional in any but these and other very generalized ways, but the widespread influence of each is clear from the far-flung appearance of characteristic examples of copper artistry throughout the region.

The labels, Old Copper Culture, Adena, Hopewell, Copena, and Southeastern Ceremonial Complex, were applied to sites and materials found fairly early in the archaeological history of the eastern United States. At that time interest focused almost exclusively on the ritual remains of the groups involved. Consistency in the design and use of the ceremonial material recovered made it easy to apply these labels to peoples throughout the region, whether or not they had anything else in common. Because more recent evidence has demonstrated that the various groups that participated in these ceremonial complexes were often very diverse, these labels have become all but obsolete. However, because this study focuses on a single material used almost exclusively within ceremonial contexts (as opposed to the more varied cultural manifestations of the groups involved), these older, less specific designations are still useful.

Copper Sources and Mining Methods

For over a century, scholars and dilettantes alike speculated about the source of the copper used in all five traditions. For many years, scholars as well as laymen were unwilling to believe that Native American groups could have found and exploited deposits of native copper; nor were they convinced of the ability of native peoples to produce the copperwork excavated throughout eastern North America (e.g., Rickard 1932:225). Such attitudes, although not universal, ignored ample evidence and retarded systematic inquiry. As early as 1852, there was clear evidence that native groups living in the Lake Superior region at the time of European contact knew of the copper mines there and worked them, but kept these operations secret from the French (Drier and Du Temple 1961:49). Those mines had been the primary source of native copper for over three thousand years.

The origin of any piece of native copper can usually be determined through analysis of trace elements, the small amounts of chemicals present in addition to the pure copper. The identity and relative quantity of these elements indicate the source. However, only within the last two or three decades have techniques of metallurgical analysis been sufficiently refined to positively identify specific source areas for the raw material used in prehistoric copperwork.[1]

It is generally agreed that the Lake Superior mines were the source of native copper used by Early and Middle Woodland metal workers as well as by those of the Late Archaic. The Lake Superior mines were still being worked during Late Woodland and early contact times (Thwaites 1896 vol. 50:265–67). Late Woodland artifacts have been found in mining areas on Isle Royale (Griffin 1961:13).

The general topography of Isle Royale and the often treacherous trip across Lake Superior to reach the island make it unlikely that Native American groups would have gone there without the incentive provided by rich deposits of native copper and whatever special significance that metal may have had for them. The reports of several early explorers that Native American groups located hundreds of miles from the northern copper sources were familiar with that country and its raw materials suggest that those sources were still being exploited at that time.[2] Even Native Americans as far south as the mouth of the Mississippi River apparently knew of the Lake Superior deposits. They told early French and Spanish explorers that the copper they possessed came from far away, near "huge seas of fresh water" (Drier and Du Temple 1961:175).

The Jesuits Dablon and Allouez, reporting on their own activities in the Great Lakes region, also mention the copper area and various myths and legends connected with it (Thwaites 1896 vol. 50:265–67). Allouez says that the Native Americans with whom he had contact had no traditions regarding mining operations, past or present, in the area. However, Dablon's narrative suggests that the groups in question were simply unwilling to divulge this information; he found it "necessary to use artifice" to elicit whatever limited data he managed to obtain regarding the copper mines (Thwaites 1896 vol. 54:153).

Over a century after the Jesuits wrote, other chroniclers met with a large group of Native Americans who said that they were traveling to the Lake Superior region to obtain copper, a tradition they had kept for generations (Blue 1894:63). According to the account in question, this group was also reluctant to share information about the precise location of the mining sites with interested Europeans. Even twentieth-century tribes in the Lake Superior area used local copper.[3]

Identifying sources for native copper from the beginning of the Late Woodland Period until European contact becomes more difficult, as there were a number of copper-bearing regions in the eastern United States other than the Lake Superior area deposits—but all were very small by comparison. The size and nature of the sources outside the Lake Superior core area were such that for many years they were not believed to have been exploited by Native Americans at all (Goad 1978:46). This conclusion was reinforced by the fact that evidence of prehistoric mining activity has never been discovered in conjunction with any of these smaller deposits.

Nevertheless, more recent research, as well as a few Early Historic references, indicate that many sources other than those near Lake Superior were quite extensively exploited prehistorically.[4] These sources dot the Appalachian Piedmont from Frederick, Maryland, south to Anniston, Alabama, with major deposits in Madison and Fairfax Counties, Virginia; Ash and Pearson Counties, North Carolina; Polk County, Tennessee (Ducktown); and Fannin and White Counties, Georgia (Goad 1978:52–53). Because no evidence of precontact mining has been discovered in these areas, methods of removal by prehistoric miners are a matter of speculation. What is clear is that the size of the deposits as well as of the individual nuggets of copper available at those sites is very small compared to the copper resources of the Lake Superior region. Other sources for raw copper also existed.

Long before prehistoric miners first traveled to the Lake Superior region, glacial activity ripped chunks of copper from exposed veins and pushed them as far south as Illinois and Missouri and as far east as New Jersey and Connecticut (Aitchison 1960:414). Later, as the glaciers melted, many of these pieces of Lake Superior copper moved even farther from their source in the runoff. This "float copper," as it is called, was also an important source of native copper for precontact Americans. Its close association with water was an important influence in the development of ceremonial traditions surrounding the material.

The phenomenon of float copper raises important questions about scattered examples of Old Copper Culture and Adena-related copperwork, discovered in the New England area and farther south in New Jersey, Maryland, and Virginia. It is difficult to determine whether these pieces found their way to these remote locations through trade with core areas farther north and west, or whether they were fashioned from float copper found locally. The answers to such questions must be based on stylistic analysis.

Hundreds of prehistoric mining sites have been identified in the Lake Superior region, concentrated on the Keweenaw Peninsula and Isle Royale in Michigan, and along the eastern end of Lake Superior above the Saint Mary's River in Ontario. Estimates of the amount of copper removed from these prehistoric mines vary from 5.6 million to 2 billion pounds, based on the size of the prehistoric excavations and on the amounts of native copper removed from adjacent areas by modern copper miners (Drier and Du Temple 1961:17, 158, 171).

Because of the severe winters in the region, it is unlikely these mines were worked year round. Precontact miners may have been active in the area only three to four months each year. The historical depth of mining activity in the Lake Superior area is made impressively clear by the extraction of so much copper while using primitive techniques and under difficult conditions.

Native copper in the Lake Superior region deposits occurred in a wide range of forms, from small flakes to huge boulders weighing several tons. The copper was almost pure metal and had only to be separated from the surrounding matrix. This task was frequently difficult since that matrix was often solid rock, although occasionally the copper could be found among strata of gravel.[5]

Native American miners worked every productive vein of copper in the Lake Superior area, many of which were not exposed at the surface (Drier and Du Temple 1961:21). Their uncanny skill in locating and following the veins continues to baffle mining engineers. The prehistoric miners showed similar skill in locating native copper in deposits of drift gravel and chloritic rock, despite the fact that in such deposits it appears randomly rather than in traceable veins (Griffin 1961:52, 60). Prehistoric mines on the Keweenaw Peninsula dot an area referred to as the "trap range," to a length of almost one hundred miles through three Michigan counties.[6]

The most common tools used in mining operations were large stone mauls weighing from five to forty pounds (Griffin 1961:48). Thousands of tons of these mauls were put to use during prehistoric mining operations. Broken mauls litter the mining areas, as well as the pits themselves.[7] Maul types vary from site to site, although mauls found in any single mine site tend to be similar.[8] This suggests very strongly that peoples of different cultural traditions mined neighboring sites and that, in some cases, the mining occurred during the same time periods.

Extracting the copper was seldom easy. Sometimes pit shafts had to be sunk through solid rock up to fifty feet deep (Drier and Du Temple 1961:21). Drainage is so poor on Isle Royale that many excavations probably filled with water almost as soon as they were dug. The arrangement and depth of individual excavations for the extraction of the copper show that prehistoric miners were familiar with and allowed for this problem. Systems of drainage trenches have been discovered in conjunction with the ancient mines, bark-lined in some places and cut into the surrounding rock in others. Other drainage systems were entirely subterranean. Wood and birchbark containers, up to three feet in diameter, have been found at the bottom of several mines. These were probably used to bail water from the pits as the miners worked.

In some cases, the copper was separated from its stone matrix by heating both to a high temperature and then quenching the copper with cold water. The sides of many ancient mining pits still showed discoloration when excavated in modern times, probably the result of this extraction method. Other sites show no evidence of exposure to fire.[9] Once cracked, the broken rock surrounding deposits of native copper was shoveled from the pit. Several shovels made of cedar, resembling canoe paddles but clearly used as shovels, have been found in the bottoms of ancient mines (Griffin 1961:53).[10]

The Native American miners showed considerable skill and foresight in their excavations. In one instance, part of the copper vein itself (four feet thick) was left intact to support subsequent digging (Griffin 1961:52). Other prehistoric mines were timbered with wood or with large boulders, weighing up to four hundred pounds (Drier and Du Temple 1961:85).

Some blocks of stone, dislodged and removed from mine pits, weighed even more, up to two or three tons (Griffin 1961:52). Occasionally, even larger masses of pure metal were also excavated. An eighteen-ton mass was discovered during nineteenth-century mining operations by Euro-Americans, sections of which had obviously been removed by their prehistoric counterparts (Drier and Du Temple 1961:156). In another ancient mine, the miners had separated a boulder of copper weighing six tons and raised it five feet on a platform of oak logs, six to eight inches in diameter. Like the eighteen-ton mass, the surface had been worked smooth (Griffin 1961:63).

The amount of material removed from the Lake Superior area mines in precontact times by these primitive means is staggering. A modern engineer estimated that under precontact conditions it would have taken about ten thousand miners a thousand years to have removed the amounts of material displaced in the Lake Superior mine regions alone (Drier and Du Temple 1961:16, 21).

Metallurgy in the Late Archaic Period

Copper mining was well under way in the Lake Superior area by about 3000 B.C. and perhaps even earlier. The beginnings of mining activity in this region represent the earliest known use of metals in the Americas, and they probably preceded central Siberian metal traditions as well (Griffin 1961:132).

During the Archaic Periods, copper use and trade was primarily confined to northern portions of eastern North America, but with some important exceptions. For example, copper is among the exotica found at the Archaic Poverty Point Site in Louisiana. Still, approximately twenty thousand Late Archaic artifacts have been found in the Great Lakes region compared to fewer than twenty-five in the Southeast (Goad 1978:93).

These totals may not be entirely accurate. Relatively few of these objects have been subjected to metallurgical analysis, rather they have been identified primarily on the basis of stylistic criteria. A large proportion of the examples in museum collections, perhaps even the majority, were not discovered through excavation, even by amateurs.[11] Nevertheless, the largest concentrations of objects discovered from this period and the greatest variety of object types found occur in and around the copper sources. Generally speaking, the greater the distance from these sources, the fewer are the objects fashioned from copper that are found and the less utilitarian are the forms (Goad 1980:6).

Evidence of this earliest use and exchange of copper is referred to as the Old Copper Culture in much of the archaeological literature, although today the term refers only to the use of copper and actually includes many quite different groups throughout the Northeast. That is, as well as being less well known, the generic term, Old Copper Culture, also refers to the use of copper by various groups in a primarily ritual/mortuary context, rather than to use by a culture in any real sense. This is also true of the terms

Adena, Hopewell, and Southeastern Ceremonial Complex, but less so than the designation Old Copper Culture. Like those other manifestations, however, local groups participated to a greater or lesser degree, depending on their specific needs and orientations (Mason 1981:196–98). Many of the objects involved were very similar, as were the technological processes used to manufacture them and the ways in which the final products were utilized.

Metallurgical testing and observation indicate that native copper was primarily cold-worked in precontact times and forged rather than cast. However, because the temperatures necessary for melting as well as smelting copper are comparatively low, the latter was probably a technical possibility.

In addition, the prehistoric native metallurgists were accomplished at annealing technology. Native copper is very soft and quickly becomes brittle and unworkable if it is merely cold-hammered into shape. Archaic coppersmiths knew just when to stop hammering, when to heat the metal, and when to plunge it into water before continuing to beat the object into its final shape. This process alters the molecular structure of the copper and makes it possible to create complex forms that are stronger as a result of having been annealed and cold-hammered repeatedly.

The oldest examples of Old Copper Culture metallurgy appear about 3000 B.C. and continue to be evident at some sites in the Great Lakes region until about two thousand years ago. However, most evidence of Old Copper Culture activity disappears by 1000 B.C. (Map I). Three type sites constitute the bulk of what is known about the ritual complex: the Osceola, Oconto, and Reigh sites in Wisconsin, which date between 2590 B.C. (± 400 years) and 1500 B.C. (Mason 1981:190–93). All are cemeteries located on waterways, a pattern typical of almost all mortuary traditions in the copper complex for over three thousand years. The Riverside Site in Michigan is somewhat later (1100 B.C.–A.D. 1) and has been defined as a transition group, a cultural bridge between the Late Archaic and Woodland Periods (1981:227). Most societies participating in Old Copper Culture mortuary ritual were active in the Lake Superior Basin until 1000 B.C. Judging from the complexity of their material remains, they reached their height of participation about 1500 B.C. (Griffin 1961:129).

The estimated number of copper artifacts produced in connection with this Late Archaic tradition is impressive, some twenty thousand. Three facts help to put these numbers into better perspective. First, the longevity of the tradition itself, two thousand to three thousand years, is many times longer than any of the other manifestations participating in the copper complex. Spread over three millennia, the number of objects created is less staggering. Second, participants in the Old Copper Culture lived very near, even adjacent to, the mining areas. Old Copper Culture metallurgists were spared the considerable investment of time and energy that was necessary for later users to transport the copper from the mines to their homes. They could expend that time and energy creating more copperwork and apparently did. Third, except for stone objects, items of copper easily outlasted virtually all other remains of participants in Old Copper Culture ritual. Furthermore, as important ceremonial paraphernalia, copper objects were undoubtedly curated more carefully than other elements of material culture. Old Copper Culture copper artwork exists in quantities today that certainly outstrip the percentage of material culture it comprised when it was in use.

From very early on, exchange was an integral part of the tradition, even before the characteristics of the mortuary complex were firmly established. By 2500 B.C., marine shell was being transported into the Great Lakes region and copper began to be carried south as well. Eventually, this Late Archaic trade in copper moved as far south as Tennessee (Chapman 1985:51) and appears to have reached Poverty Point in Louisiana. Evidence indicates that it was a reciprocal exchange network, probably between specific individuals in each society, as opposed to the redistributive type. This kind of network usually focuses on the exchange of ritual and ceremonial goods, although the structure itself may have developed to solidify more utilitarian structures for exchange between the groups involved (Goad 1980:7).

Undoubtedly, the mortuary ritual associated with the objects moved through the Eastern Woodlands in much the same way. A number of Late Archaic groups used copper and participated in the exchange networks, as well as in related mortuary practices. These groups include Laurentian in the Northeast, Glacial Kame and Red Ocher in the Northeast and Midwest, and Indian Knoll farther south. Each group developed its own version of the ritual, however, that reflected unique aspects of form and function. All have the use of copper in common, and many utilized natural knolls or kames to bury individuals with special treatment and burial goods. A few even built burial mounds. Within the traditions of every group, it is clear that the significance of the copperwork in the graves went well beyond the utilitarian, regardless of the form of the objects involved (e.g., Mason 1981:198). All these patterns and structures, including the unique character of individual sites, are very similar to later manifestations of the copper complex.

The widespread and ritual nature of the Old Copper Culture mortuary complex and related ones is clear. Less clear are the reasons that the tradition developed when it did and in the way that it did. There are a number of clues, however. According to Cleland, during the Middle Archaic Period human populations on the fringes of the receding glaciers underwent "environmental trauma," a long period of forced subsistence readjustment (Cleland 1976:69). During this time, increasing numbers of local plants were exploited, as well as smaller animals. Population density was extremely low. In the early Late Archaic, the subsistence adjustment Cleland refers to was probably complete, but the success of those adjustments may have resulted in population growth that outstripped the new subsistence strategies. Evidence of this is not only apparent in larger population figures, but in the fact that during the Late Archaic Period the domestication of local cultigens begins in eastern North America and the first of the important tropical cultigens (squash) is introduced from Mexico. The remains of the latter have been identified at the Late Archaic Carlston Annis Site, an Indian Knoll Phase group in Kentucky (Chomko and Crawford 1978:407).

Indian Knoll societies present an interesting case study. Burial remains from these sites show evidence of severe population pressure and related stress. Obvious dietary limitations and the increasing importance of cultigens in their subsistence patterns add another important ingredient (Perzigian 1977:106). Both factors would tend to restrict mobility, a crucial element in the development of the social complexity that gives rise to ritual elaboration, according to Price and Brown (1985:437). Not surprisingly, these sites also have an unusually large quantity of copper burial material, particularly given their distance from the mining areas (Goad 1980:9). The usual explanation for such anomalies is geographical, with speculation that the high levels of ritual paraphernalia may be due to a strategic location along important trade routes. However, the evidence cited above suggests that other factors may have been more important. One factor, virtually never considered, is the evolution of oral traditions and the ontological and cosmological concepts and explanations imbedded within them.

Oral traditions undoubtedly became increasingly out of touch with the changes in flora and fauna and related shifts in subsistence strategies and demographics discussed above. All these important shifts would have required radical, though gradual, alteration of age-old ideas about the nature of things. Oral histories would have had to have been altered to reflect the new status quo. Such concepts tend to change even more slowly than subsistence strategies since the needs involved are less directly tied to survival. Nevertheless, making those kinds of intellectual and spiritual adjustments are fully as stressful for human populations as the more obvious ones affecting subsistence. The simultaneous conjunction of all these important shifts, both physical and intellectual, probably accounts for the rather sudden blossoming of distinct and increasingly elaborate ritual traditions throughout the Eastern Woodlands in the Late Archaic. The wide variations in response evident from group to group is to be expected, depending on the specific circumstances of each. Indian Knoll offers an extreme example of the kinds of problems facing many Late Archaic societies, problems that gave rise to the Old Copper Culture and related ritual traditions utilizing copper.

The vast majority of objects fashioned from copper during this period were tools—adzes, axes, awls, points, hooks, knives, etc.—although whether their function was entirely utilitarian is questionable. Axes and adzes tend to be heavy, rugged tool forms, often crudely made and ranging from a few inches to well over a foot in length. Two types of adze existed. Some were essentially rectangular and others were quite sophisticated in form, with a heavy socket for the attachment of a haft and often secured with a small copper rivet.[12]

Awls were another important category of objects produced by Late Archaic coppersmiths (see Appendix, Sections II.1.a. and II.2.a.). Awls or pins of copper were made during every period of precontact copper usage and are one of the largest categories of copper items found in prehistoric remains. Almost invariably, when only a few examples of finished copperwork are discovered at a given site, an awl will be among them, regardless of culture or date. Late Archaic versions range from one-half inch to three feet in length; but most are between six and ten inches long, are altered in a huge variety of ways, and are clearly designed for specific purposes.

Old Copper Culture peoples made hundreds of knives, also in two basic styles: one with an essentially straight-edged blade similar to a modern steak knife; and the other with a crescent-shaped blade, similar to the Inuit *ulu* or woman's knife. Both types include a substantial copper tang or socket that was apparently fitted with a wooden handle. With the one known exception of an elaborate Adena piece, carefully crafted copper knives ceased to be made after the Late Archaic Period.

Old Copper Culture tanged and socketed copper points were also made from the earliest periods of copper-working activity. Many are arrow points from one to four inches long, but most are over four inches long. They probably served as spearheads or, at least, were large enough to be used in killing large animals (Fig. 1). Most Archaic points are beautifully designed and worked, although many are in an advanced state of deterioration. Several different types of both large and small points seem to be generally well defined—almost standardized—and most examples conform very closely to a particular type-configuration. Point forms evolved through the years; indeed different types may represent different chronological positions within the corpus (Wittry and Ritzenthaler 1957).[13]

Most Old Copper Culture implements were probably only marginally effective tools. Some obviously could not have functioned in any utilitarian way, due to their construction. An excellent example is the double axe in Plate 14 that is very similar to bannerstones made during the same period and is clearly symbolic rather than primarily utilitarian in significance.

Late Archaic coppersmiths also made a number of objects that are obviously not implements even in a symbolic sense, and therefore appear to be essentially decorative or ornamental. These represent only a tiny fraction of

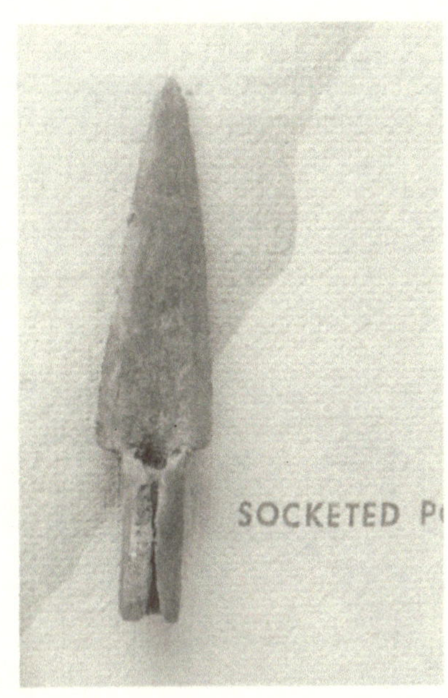

Figure 1. "Old Copper Culture" Socketed Spear Point, Middle to Late Archaic. University of Michigan Archaeological Collections, Ann Arbor. Menominee Co., Michigan. Ca. 3 3/4" long.

the Archaic copper corpus, however. The peoples of the Archaic Old Copper, Glacial Kame, and Red Ocher cultures all made copper beads. The beads vary in construction, from crudely drilled nuggets to matched strings of beautifully formed, rolled beads that diminish in size from the center of the string to the ends. Precontact Native American coppersmiths from every period produced both crude and refined examples of the rolled variety. A large majority of the beads were constructed of overlapping rolled strips of copper that range in thickness from very thin sheet copper (usually used for tubular beads) to strips three-eighths of an inch thick. The more carefully finished beads were shaped and ground off in such a way that the overlapping is hardly visible. Almost none of the beads were decorated with designs of any kind. As might be expected, copper beads were strung for use as necklaces, bracelets, and anklets.

There are scattered examples of copper rings from every period of precontact history in the eastern United States, but they are relatively rare, except at Adena sites.[14] Bracelets, usually constructed of solid copper rods bent into a C-shape, are far more common at Archaic sites. A few bracelets made of thin bands of copper with a longitudinal row of punctate bosses along them have also been found with Old Copper Culture material. This rudimentary form of metalwork decoration continues to be the norm in the Great Lakes area well into Middle Woodland times. Even copperwork associated with Hopewell-type ritual practice was decorated in this way, but only rarely so outside of this region.

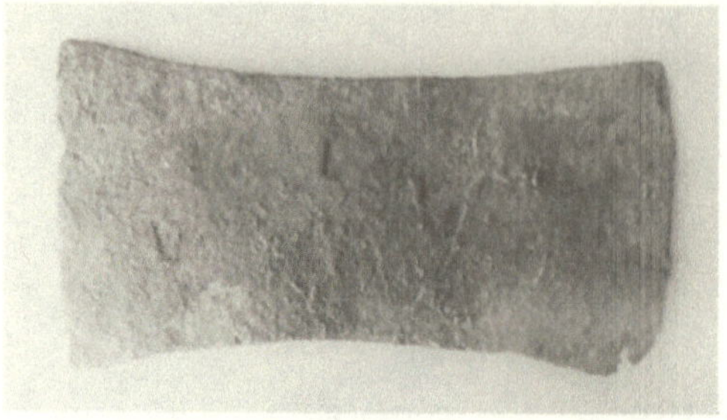

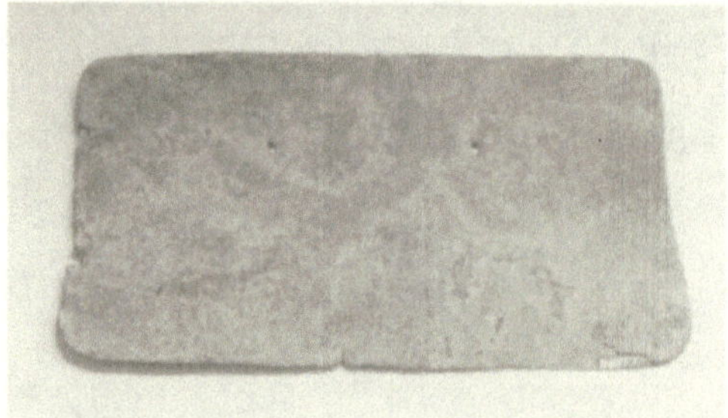

Figure 2a and 2b. A: Red Ocher Culture Breastplate, Late Archaic. The Spurlock Museum, University of Illinois at Urbana-Champagne. Morton Mounds, bu. 3, Fulton Co., Illinois. Ca. 8" long; B: Hopewell Style Breastplate, Middle Woodland. The Field Museum, Chicago, #56077. Hopewell Mounds, Ross Co., Ohio. Ca. 9" long.

Late Archaic metallurgists created several types of objects that, although unusual in the Archaic corpus, would later become basic items for many groups that used copper. Copper breastplates are one such item (see Appendix, Section II.1.b.). They are extremely rare in this early horizon. The lone example found in the collections inventoried for this study is a roughly rectangular piece from a burial in the Morton Mound Group in Ohio, a Red Ocher site (Fig. 2a). Its design mimics many similarly shaped ground stone objects from the same era that were often placed on the chest in burials. The existence of this piece presents a significant pattern within the copper corpus, one that bears witness to its remarkable continuity in use and design (Fig. 2b and Plate 2). Within each major period of copper-working activity there are a few anomalous pieces, object types and designs that are typical of earlier or later manifestations of the complex, rather than the period in which they were apparently created. As such, these anomalous pieces seem to be either remarkable early precursors of or strange throwbacks to stylistic traditions from another era. In this case, the Morton Mound breastplate provides an important stylistic and functional precedent for hundreds more that will be produced by Adena and Hopewell coppersmiths in subsequent centuries.

Copper tinkling cones, such as the metal tinklers in common use throughout the Eastern Woodlands in the Historic Periods, are in the same category. Tinklers are made of roughly triangular pieces of metal rolled to form small hollow cones. When hung in groups from clothing or bags, they jingle; hence the name. These, too, were apparently introduced to the region by Old Copper Culture peoples. A lone tinkler, in near perfect condition, was found at the Riverside Site.[15]

Only one example of cut copper sheet with a roughly recognizable form was found in the collections of Late Archaic copperwork examined. It is a tiny but precisely formed pendant in the shape of a raptor's beak or claw. This is yet another unique example of subject matter introduced in the Archaic Period that will become central to the iconography of copper later on. In the later manifestations of the copper complex, spectacular headdresses were also constructed using elaborately decorated copper elements. This use, too, was introduced in a unique piece from Wisconsin (see Appendix, Sections II.1.c. and II.2.b.). Several pieces of cut copper sheet were attached to a fur cap found in an Old Copper Culture burial at the Reigh Site in Wisconsin. Thin tapered strips of copper were placed vertically along the front and sides of this early headdress (Baerreis et al 1957:251).

Other than these two pieces, Archaic coppersmiths produced only a few simple designs fashioned out of thin copper sheet, primarily pierced disks and crescents.[16] All are very small, never more than an inch or two in length or diameter. Several more unusual examples were taken from Archaic sites in Kentucky. Some are roughly triangular; others are shaped like "expanded center bar gorgets," another Archaic form usually found in stone. In general, the application of designs to Late Archaic copperwork was rare. Circular motifs compose about 25 percent of the very limited designs that were used (Table VI). Most examples are simply flattened rings of heavy copper wire. Similar simple and often crude circular forms continued to be important in northern areas during Middle and Late Woodland times among societies that appear to have been largely unaffected by the religio-political developments of Hopewell-related and Mississippian groups farther south. Simple spiral forms have a similar history in the upper Great Lakes. Like the circles, they are made from copper wire, wound into a spiral and then flattened. Most are rather crude, but a few are quite beautifully made.[17]

Copper and the objects made from it were given special treatment by virtually every group that used the metal, including Old Copper Culture peoples. Even unworked nuggets of the material are generally found only in ritual contexts. Copper is virtually never recovered from habitation sites or middens. Only in the copper mining areas is this general rule violated with any consistency. Chunks of raw or only slightly worked copper appear fairly often there, apparently dropped at random at some mining sites but not elsewhere (see Appendix, Sections II.1.d. and II.2.c.).

The preponderance of implement forms produced in the Late Archaic Period has led many to believe that at that time the copper complex was primarily utilitarian in emphasis. Indeed, this was the assumption made at the outset of this study. Provenience data from Late Archaic burial sites indicate otherwise, however, as does other evidence. Even in the Archaic Periods, the structures surrounding the use of copper were primarily ritual in their significance. The insistence that Old Copper Culture implement forms were merely utilitarian objects is based in part on old assumptions about social and religious complexity among hunter-gatherer societies, peoples without agriculture or sedentary living arrangements. It was assumed that their lifestyle prevented the development of complex social structure and ritual, hence the relatively sparse nature of their material remains.

Much of this thinking has been appropriately revised (e.g., Price and Brown 1985). It has become increasingly clear that the development of material culture and subsistence strategies are essentially independent variables, although frequently related. Details surrounding the use and manufacture of copperwork in the Late Archaic Period point to similar conclusions. Although Late Archaic peoples in the Lake Superior area had a very different lifestyle than their later counterparts in the copper complex, their utilization of copper material and the structures surrounding that use were very similar and essentially ceremonial. In fact, it appears that basic ideas about the material and its significance in ritual were developed in those early periods and remained fundamental to its use from then on.

Despite the active interest in metallurgy demonstrated by some Late Archaic societies, many apparently did not use or trade in copper at all, even though they lived in close proximity to copper-using groups (Quimby 1960:44). This pattern was typical of every phase of the native North American copper complex, from these earliest manifestations to the time of contact with Europeans. This disparity in use within a given region also suggests functions and meanings for copper artifacts beyond the practical. Merely utilitarian advantage in the use of metal, rather than stone or bone, for implements would have been generally acknowledged as a significant technological improvement and would eventually have been adopted by all to whom the new materials were available, just as were the horse and gun after the arrival of Europeans. This was never the case with copper despite the massive amounts of the material available and the millennia spanned by its mining and use in the region.

Furthermore, the vast majority of Old Copper Culture implements are spear points, most useful in the taking of large animals, yet introduced at a time when that subsistence mode was increasingly obsolete in those regions. If the manufacture and use of copper implements was an outgrowth of specific ritual activities, it would not matter that the type of point made most often corresponded to an obsolete hunting mode. Given the stresses involved with the shifts in subsistence modes discussed above, the careful manufacture of ritually important but obsolete hunting gear seems a very reasonable response. As a matter of ritual rather than utilitarian advantage, the use of copper would be expected to have been less uniformly widespread. And, indeed, that was the case. This scenario is the one suggested by the bulk of the archaeological evidence.

While it is true that most of the copper objects produced in the Late Archaic Period were obviously implement forms, few of them show much evidence of having been utilized as weapons or tools. The only clear exceptions are those apparently used in the mines. Relatively few have been found in that context, however.[18] Many examples of Late Archaic metallurgy are in an advanced state of deterioration. This fact also suggests that they were not used as tools. If Old Copper Culture implements were primarily utilitarian, resharpening would have been a necessity since native copper is extremely soft and would have required reworking after any heavy use. The annealing and grinding processes necessary for resharpening copper implements would have rendered them less susceptible to this kind of deterioration.

The most convincing evidence of the ritual significance of Old Copper Culture material comes from archaeological provenience data, although it is limited. Many examples of Old Copper tool forms have been discovered in caches without other associations, but the majority of the implements collected have been isolated finds, often in gravel formations and frequently near important northern water routes. Unfortunately, virtually no reliable provenience data for most of these discoveries exists. Most well-documented Late Archaic copperwork has been discovered in burial contexts.

Human-made burial mounds, frequent repositories for copper artifacts in later periods, were not generally in use although cemeteries and individual burials were often located on or within natural knolls during the Archaic Periods. Patterns of use within these very early burials are almost identical to those occurring later in the copper complex. That is, burial with copper was reserved for a small percentage of the population and usually associated with only the most elaborate graves. That members of both sexes and all ages were included in this elite group forms another pattern that remains constant throughout the history of the complex. In general, the most highly refined and decorative examples of Old Copper Culture metallurgy were used exclusively as burial accompaniments (for example, at the Riverside Site in Michigan and the Reigh Site in Wisconsin). More typical implement forms were also included in those graves, but, again, with only a few individuals. Most members of Late Archaic societies whose cemeteries have been subjected to analysis were not buried with copper.

Still, the vast majority of the copperwork associated with the Old Copper Complex has been found in relatively isolated contexts without any hint of human remains. Regardless of what one may believe regarding the significance of these objects, the fact that most of them seem to have been disposed of at random is difficult to understand. There is a plausible explanation, however. In addition to the few Old Copper Culture cemeteries that have been discovered, several other facts suggest that despite their apparently random dispersal, these very early manifestations of the copper complex were as important as burial furniture in Archaic times as they were later on. Isolated finds of Old Copper-type implements and implement caches are almost always discovered near major rivers or lakes, usually in strata of gravel or clay, as though placed there by the action of water.

As the glaciers retreated, huge new lakes and river channels were formed by the run-off. When the melting was complete, the land surface in the upper Great Lakes buckled, up to five hundred feet. These phenomena took place over many hundreds of years and repeatedly effected enormous changes in lake and river levels in the region. At the same time, native peoples were moving into the area and mining the copper there. The mythology surrounding the copper mining area suggests that the native people in the region were aware of these changes.

Isle Royale, a major location for many prehistoric mines, is described in some myths as a floating island. Certainly the native people knew as well as we that islands do not float. However, the significant geological changes in the region very likely radically altered the distances between the island and the mainland over the centuries, making the island seem to float. If the place was important in oral tradition—which it must have been, given its early importance in the copper complex—myths and tales involving that place would have to account for the wide variations in the distance of the island from the shores of Lake Superior. Calling it a floating island would have solved the problem.

This would not have been the first time such an adjustment was made in the oral history of a ritually important locale. The island of Delos in the Mediterranean Sea, a place as sacred to the Greeks as Isle Royale was to the peoples of northeastern North America, was also defined as a floating island in oral history and myth. In both cases, the time depth of the traditions involved stretches across at least two or three millennia. It seems clear that these two ritually important places were described as floating islands for precisely the same reasons, to account for changes in the distance between the island and the mainland. Studies have shown that oral traditions can be historically accurate across hundreds of years. The designation of Isle Royale as a floating island within this tradition very likely points to prehistoric awareness of the changes in the depth and shoreline of the Great Lakes during those centuries when the copper complex had its inception.

Other related and very important implications are suggested by the more recent geological history of the copper mining regions. If the peoples of the area buried their dead near water courses, as did virtually every other group that utilized copper in mortuary ritual, most of those burial grounds would have been altered repeatedly or even eradicated as radical alteration of water levels and shorelines proceeded.

Bone material and other relatively lightweight perishables would have deteriorated and washed away. Heavy copper implements, on the other hand, would have settled to the bottom. They would have been gradually covered by layers of clay, silt, and gravel, just as the majority of the implements found during the last century were situated. In the thousands of years since, many of the lakes and rivers that caused the disappearance of those cemeteries have themselves disappeared or radically altered their levels and courses, leaving all that remains of most Old Copper Culture burial grounds—thousands of copper implements—reburied, although not necessarily under water. These bits and pieces of evidence not only account quite nicely for the curious disposition of most Old Copper Culture copperwork, but they also imply that the possession of copper for use in burial ceremony was as central to ritual in Old Copper Culture times as it was later on.

Thus, both the methods for the procurement of native copper and the basic parameters surrounding its ritual use were well established by the end of the Late Archaic Period. Old Copper Culture peoples and their contemporaries developed the foundation of a ceremonial and technological tradition that would remain viable for at least three thousand years.

The Woodland Periods

The burial rituals of many Woodland Period societies were based squarely upon those of the Late Archaic peoples involved in the Old Copper Culture and related traditions. These groups developed increasingly elaborate mortuary complexes within which a significant portion of the population was given special treatment. Many were interred in carefully prepared graves, surrounded by beautifully crafted works of art. There does not seem to have been any consistent restriction with regard to the age or sex of individuals given this special treatment. Men and women, the elderly, infants, adolescents—both sexes and all age levels—are amply represented. Their special status was almost always signified by burial in a small hillock or knoll with grave goods that far exceeded those buried with the average person. In the richest burials, those special grave goods almost always included copper.

From the outset, exchange was an important factor among these groups, and so was a tendency toward individualized practice within the general parameters of the tradition. No two sites are ever identical. The individualism reflected within the mortuary complex extended beyond it as well. In the Woodland Periods, as in the Late Archaic and every subsequent precontact period, there were many societies in the Eastern Woodlands that show no evidence of having participated in the mortuary tradition at all. In addition to these consistent patterns, there were important new developments in the copper complex as a whole.

As the Late Archaic gave way to Woodland Period times, many changes were under way in eastern North America. The characteristics of the Old Copper Culture and related traditions began to fade by 1000 B.C., and interest in copper and its use waned for a time. When copper becomes central to ritual again, approximately five hundred years later, the core area for the tradition shifts to the south, a development that would be repeated in subsequent eras. In the Woodland Periods a distinct shift is also apparent in the kinds of ritual objects made from copper. Variety is far greater and the refined and elaborate nature of many pieces makes the ceremonial significance of Woodland copperwork more obvious than it was in the Late Archaic. Variety in object types and iconography also reflects increased complexity within many of the societies that used copper.

Burial ceremony continued to become more elaborate. In the North, ceramic technology was introduced for the first time. This innovation may have migrated there from the Southeast, where pottery developed somewhat earlier. Ideas about the use and creation of ceramics, as well as the need for them, probably moved north along the same routes and within the same structures that supported Late Archaic exchanges of exotica and ritual tradition. Local cultigens, as well as those introduced earlier from Mexico (just squash at the outset), were increasingly important to subsistence during this period as well. Most of these changes either caused or resulted in decreased mobility on the part of the societies involved. This was an important factor in the development of sedentism and increased social complexity.

These shifts also point to important changes in the social fabric of many Woodland Period societies. Both early horticulture and ceramic technologies are usually associated with women. The time and energy demanded for increased reliance upon cultigens in the diet and the manufacture of the textile and ceramic equipment necessary to harvest and prepare those foods must have effected fundamental changes in female lifestyles, as did increased sedentism.

The concomitant reduction in the importance of hunting to subsistence would also have altered traditional male lifeways significantly. Such fundamental social shifts almost always produce high levels of tension in human societies and are likely to have been a primary factor in the spectacular ritual and artistic energy displayed in the remains of these groups. In fact, the evolving iconography of ritual copperwork produced during this time suggests that elaborate ceremonies celebrating both hunter and prey may have been a response to the dwindling importance of hunting in the real economy of these groups.

Archaeologists have divided the Woodland Period into three sections, Early, Middle, and Late. The dates for the Early Woodland Period vary according to the source consulted, but most would agree that it spans the years between about 1500 and 200 B.C.[19] In the first centuries of the Early Woodland Period, from 1500 to 1000 B.C., important climate shifts took place and undoubtedly affected the cultural changes noted above. The so-called Algoma Stage, an abnormally cold period, chilled the entire region around 1000 B.C. (Quimby 1960:26). Today most scholars agree that changes in the environment are rarely, if ever, the only agents in developing cultural complexity. Still, the coincidence of this major climate shift with significant changes in the cultures of the eastern area suggests that there were probably important, if not complex, relationships between the two.

Despite the changes that separate the Archaic and Woodland Periods, the clear evidence of continuity between them is, in many ways, more significant to an understanding of the copper complex. Adena, Copena, and Hopewell are the generic terms for the major ritual traditions of the Woodland Periods. In all three, copper continued to be a central element in burial ceremony. Participation in and intensification of the exchange networks established in the Late Archaic were also characteristic. More and more exotica (copper, mica, galena, grizzly bear and alligator canines, obsidian, sharks' teeth, etc.) were included in this trade as time went on.

One of the most important and widespread Woodland cultural developments with roots in the Archaic past was the consistent use of artificial burial mounds for the dead. This approach to mortuary elaboration also tended to limit the mobility of the societies involved. The elaborate mortuary complexes built in Woodland times must have provided a considerable incentive for the increased sedentism that usually precedes the development of cultural complexity.

The early appearance of burial mounds in northeastern North America is central to the definition and understanding of the copper complex in several ways. Since most Early Woodland copperwork has been excavated from mound burials, this practice offers another significant element of continuity between Late Archaic burial ritual and subsequent developments in the complex. As noted above, Late Archaic peoples often placed individuals buried with copper in natural knolls and kames.

The Elizabeth Site in Illinois is an excellent and undeniable example of this continuity. Late Archaic burials at Elizabeth were placed on the surface of a natural knoll. The same knoll was enlarged as time went on to include burials from the Woodland Periods, becoming more an artificial mound than a natural feature of the landscape (Charles et al 1988:28). In fact, the mortuary complex at Elizabeth represents five thousand years of linked traditions in burial ritual, several of which involved copper.

Finally, the Early Woodland introduction of the use of burial mounds precedes many comparable traditions in Mexico. The chronology of these developments is important to analysis of the copper complex because it has often been proposed that the mound complexes of Mexico were the source of the ideas behind such practices farther north. Scholars have also suggested that Mexico was the source for many of the designs found on copperwork from the Eastern Woodlands. The early introduction of burial mounds in North America and their obvious continuity with much older traditions in the region indicate that these developments were indigenous ones, not imported. This is undoubtedly true of the artistic tradition as well.

Adena

Adena is the most important Early Woodland mortuary complex that utilized copper. Like later groups involved in the North American copper complex, the specific societies labeled "Adena" are not as homogeneous as this generic label implies. The Adena peoples were a number of quite diverse groups that shared certain traits labeled "Adena," one of which was copperwork. In fact, of all the Woodland Period ceremonial manifestations, Adena is the most diverse. Many Adena-related sites have little in common beyond a few ritual traits.

The focus of Adena cultural development was in the Ohio River valley, particularly in southern Ohio and Kentucky. The concentration of sites in this area and the unusual amounts of copper in the burials of Late Archaic Indian Knoll groups represent a significant coincidence. Indian Knoll societies in the Green River Valley of Kentucky, not far from the Adena core area, developed an unusually elaborate burial tradition and use of copper. Whatever factors were responsible for the importance of copper metallurgy in Late Archaic developments in Kentucky were probably also significant in the timing and locus of Adena tradition, as well as in determining many of its characteristics.

Adena influence eventually spread north into New England, east to Pennsylvania and West Virginia, and south into Maryland, Georgia, and Alabama (Webb and Baby 1957:77–82). Full-blown expression of Adena-type ceremonialism, including burial mound complexes, did not materialize until approximately 500 B.C., but associated patterns of behavior, from subsistence to ritual and material culture, had been fully established in the preceding centuries. Yet, despite the extensive influence of Adena, many peoples in the region did not participate in the copper complex at all. This was another pattern established much earlier in the Late Archaic.

The most striking aspect of the Adena copper corpus is the emphasis upon what appear to be items of personal adornment. There are hundreds of Adena copper bracelets, more than were produced by any other precontact group (see Appendix, Section II.3.c.). Size and quality vary widely, even among offerings within a single burial. This suggests that the metallurgists were less craft specialists than they were members of a ritual elite, producing ceremonial material for their own use and that of their family or clan. It may also indicate that some bracelets were passed down from generation to generation before being deposited in burials. Adena coppersmiths also produced more copper rings than any other group participant in the complex (see Appendix, Section II.3.e.). Beads were another important category of Adena copperwork (see Appendix, Section II.3.b.). Like most Woodland Period copper beads, they were often finely crafted and some were arranged in strands carefully graduated in size, with smaller ones at each end and the largest in the middle.

A formal anomaly in the Adena copper corpus is important. Unlike any other pre-Columbian group in northeastern North America, not a single example in any major collection of Adena copperwork is circular in form or decorated with circular motifs. A parallel anomaly, the obvious and unique centrality of bracelets and rings, is probably related. All the latter include a circular or oval design that was basic to their function as rings and bracelets. Given the importance of the circle in the copper complex as a whole, it is likely that the circular form of these pieces was as symbolic as it was functional.

A similar layering of significance that links form, function, and symbolic meaning was undoubtedly fundamental to the utilitarian forms of Archaic metallurgy as well. This is another point of continuity between the two traditions. Also, the circular form of Adena rings and bracelets probably held a symbolic significance comparable, at least in part, to the circular forms and designs used by every other group in the copper complex. The same is probably also true of the unique spiral rings made by Adena coppersmiths.

Adena copper breastplates are common (see Appendix, Section II.3.d.). All are relatively small and the quality of workmanship varies widely, just as it does for Adena bracelets, and probably for the same reasons. Some are elegant, carefully finished forms. Most resemble the Red Ocher example from the Morton Mound cited above, with two slightly concave or convex sides, although most are "reel-shaped," with four concave sides. No two are exactly alike, and a few even have a crescent shape. As with most copper breastplates from the Archaic and Woodland Periods, the crescent ones have double perforations centered on the longitudinal axis and were found in the chest area of burials.

A crescent headdress was recovered from the Wright Mounds in Kentucky (Webb 1940a:43). The only other example of an Adena copper headdress is a pair of sheet copper deer antlers from the Fisher Site, also in Kentucky (Webb and Haag 1947a:65). The antlers are life-sized, although small, and each is notched on both sides at the bottom, most likely for attaching to a headdress. They had been tightly folded into a small bundle. Though unique in the Adena corpus, these two headdresses provide important precedents in the ritual and symbolic use of copper that will become increasingly important in later periods. The one example of a copper knife in the Adena collections examined represents a similar point of continuity, but one that harks back to Archaic copper tradition and signals the end, rather than the beginning, of a genre of copper metallurgy. It was taken from the Drake Mound, Fayette County, Kentucky—a large, carefully wrought example (Webb 1941:177). Fragments of its wooden handle, preserved by copper salts, still cling to the metal.

Adena coppersmiths produced many other idiosyncratic examples of copper metallurgy. More examples of these exist than in the Late Archaic, and they also tend to be larger. Most are very thin copper cut in elongated rectangular, oval, or triangular shapes and they usually have a single perforation. Like their Archaic counterparts, Adena artists also made copper versions of forms that were more common in stone.[20] Copper weapons and tools were important items too, although most of the types made in the Archaic Periods were no longer of importance. There are a few Adena copper points cut from thin sheet copper—clearly more ceremonial than functional—with the same kind of variation in shape and quality of workmanship that is typical of most Adena metallurgy.

The Adena peoples continued to make copper awls and axes but in fewer numbers than before (see Appendix, Section II.3.a.). A few objects resemble axes but were never tapered to form a blade. Some have suggested that these pieces were blanks, incomplete objects that would eventually have been sharpened except for some unknown circumstance that caused them to remain unfinished. This seems a plausible assumption, but it leaves unanswered the question of why unfinished copperwork would have been placed in graves along with obviously completed examples.

It may be that the explanation lies in the central importance of the material itself. It could be that the finished implement forms were made in the early years of Adena ritual and kept as heirlooms, and that the blanks were manufactured later. If so, perhaps the waning importance of implements in the symbolic vocabulary of the tradition made it unnecessary to finish these newer objects. The importance of highly refined implements in later Hopewell tradition would indicate a reversal of this general trend later on, however.

Another plausible explanation for these unfinished axes might be that they represent items traded to relative newcomers to copper-related mortuary tradition. Given the shrinking importance of implement forms in ceremony, new converts without direct connections to Late Archaic copper ritual may have been more interested in the exotic nature of the material and its symbolic associations within the mortuary complex than in the specific form of the object, especially a ritually obsolete one. Under those circumstances, it may well have made no difference whether a rectangular chunk of copper was or was not a finished axe. Native use of and interest in metals just after the arrival of Europeans indicate similar variations in the relative significance of the material and its form to different groups and reflect attitudes that were clearly formulated before the invaders arrived.

The mortuary tradition established in the Early Archaic undoubtedly provided the foundation for Adena burial ritual and metallurgy, but significant changes in the details of both developed in the centuries between the two traditions. This combination of strong structural continuity with important variation in the specifics associated with both symbol and practice is characteristic of the copper complex as a whole.

HOPEWELL

In terms of its metallurgy, Hopewell was the most widespread and complex of the mortuary traditions in the prehistoric Eastern Woodlands. Many links are obvious between Hopewell and Adena, as Adena material shows up fairly often in early Hopewell sites. The Hopewell version of the copper complex dominated the Middle Woodland Period, from approximately 300 B.C. to A.D. 300.[21] The peoples involved used massive amounts of copper and other exotic raw materials: marine shell, mica, meteoric iron, gold, chlorite, galena, silver, obsidian, and chalcedony, to name a few. The products made from these exotica were deposited in earth mounds, usually in conjunction with human burials, although some caches of objects and materials are without associated human remains. The mounds were often arranged in geometric patterns and combined with other earthworks to form large ceremonial complexes.[22]

Again, many neighboring peoples do not appear to have participated in Hopewellian ritual. In some cases, evidence exists of exchange in raw materials between Hopewellian groups and these others without any clear participation in the mortuary complex. The elaborate nature of the mound complexes undoubtedly formed a ritual focus for the groups involved and further encouraged the gradual move toward sedentism begun in Adena times. At many Middle Woodland sites there is clear evidence of population growth, both in terms of simple numbers and relative density.

Although Hopewell tradition obviously had its roots in the earlier mortuary complexes of the Eastern Woodlands, this new version of mortuary tradition was far more complex. The Hopewellians extended the trade networks that were established in the Late Archaic and that intensified in the Early Woodland Period until they spread throughout eastern North America and, in some cases, as far west as the Rocky Mountains. The volume and variety of goods that moved through those networks also seems to have multiplied several times. The volume of copper use and exchange reached its peak, and both the material and the rituals associated with it spread throughout the region. The variety of approaches to the practice of the Hopewellian ritual, from the construction of mounds and mound complexes, to individual burial practices, to the relative importance and use of specific objects and materials, is almost bewildering. The centrality of copper in the mortuary tradition provides an important element of continuity, although copper was clearly utilized in a rich variety of ways.

Subsistence strategies gradually became more complex, too. Most groups continued to use a variety of local cultigens as well as squash. Maize was introduced into the region for the first time.[23] Middle Woodland peoples remained hunter-gatherers, combining the gardening of local and tropical cultigens with hunting as their subsistence base. The production of cultivated foods very gradually became more complex and sophisticated, nevertheless. This was also true on the hunting side of the subsistence pattern. The bow and arrow were introduced into the area in the latter years of the Middle Woodland Period. But these developments were very gradual and do not significantly alter subsistence strategies until much later. The causes for the development of elaborate Hopewell ritual must be sought elsewhere.

Hopewell is the name given to the dominant cultural manifestation in the Middle Woodland, but there were many important regional variations.[24] In each case, relationships to the core areas are obvious, but it is clear that local tradition deeply colored each group's approach to the ritual and was frequently the dominant influence. The differences in approach among Hopewellians were determined by many factors, such as: social complexity and organization, ecological advantages and limitations, access to important raw materials, and population density.

Ritual approaches probably depended upon less tangible factors, as well: prior tradition, the reputation and power of those who introduced the ritual, and the degree to which the pressures that gave rise to the tradition in the first place were felt within each society (some elements in this category must have been widely shared, given the similarities observed and the broad regional adoption of the ritual). For most of the groups involved, mound burial, the use of exotica like copper in mortuary ritual, and a shared but limited vocabulary of designs that were applied to burial goods are the only elements of Hopewellian tradition that are shared consistently. Many other threads of continuity exist, but they only provide links among a few groups, never among all those involved. These secondary threads form the complex tapestry of connections that comprise what has been called the Hopewell interaction sphere.

The copperwork of Hopewell-related cultures continued the general trend evident in Adena—away from implement forms and toward designs of more apparent ritual significance. Nevertheless, finely worked implements also constitute a significant portion of Hopewell-related copperwork. Hopewell ceremonial weapons are much more standardized in size and detail than those from the earlier periods of copper use, although no two are exactly the same. The utilitarian orientation of Late Archaic ritual metallurgy is apparent in complex forms such as the socketed adze. Hopewell adzes and other implements are far less complex. Their graceful shape and careful finish indicate a more aesthetic orientation to the production of copper tools (see Appendix, Section II.4.b.). For example, most Middle Woodland adzes have a delicately curved, flaring blade and are beautifully finished overall. The degree of refinement goes far beyond utilitarian needs. Some do show clear evidence of having been hafted,[25] but Hopewell tools seldom show any signs of use.[26]

Hopewell coppersmiths also made awls that were mostly small and refined like those from Adena sites. Others reflect the evolution of the copper tradition away from utilitarian forms and toward complex ritual paraphernalia[27] (see Appendix, Section II.4.a.). Loss of interest in copper arrow points after the Late Archaic seems to have become a permanent exclusion from the corpus.[28]

Hopewellian coppersmiths, no doubt in conjunction with ritual specialists (if, indeed, any distinction existed between the two), introduced a form that would be central to all subsequent peoples involved in the copper complex—the copper earpiece. Thousands of copper earpieces were made during the Woodland Periods and thereafter.[29] The size and general design of Hopewellian earpieces is extremely complex, yet they are remarkably standardized from the outset (Figs. 3a and 3b). They are always circular spool-shapes with a basically concentric design that centers on that portion of the piece that joins two cymbal-shaped sides. Almost always two concentric circles or ridges are worked into the surface of each side of the piece. Manufacturing techniques also show a remarkable degree of consistency, especially when they are compared to other types of copperwork from the period.[30]

This consistency in quality and design represents a significant departure from the nature of Adena metallurgy, with its wide variations in both, and probably indicates the introduction of some degree of artistic specialization. Each earpiece required from two to five (most commonly) separate pieces of copper for its construction. This standard type of copper earpiece is found throughout the eastern United States at most Hopewell-related sites. Not surprisingly, earpieces from sites far away from the Hopewell core area

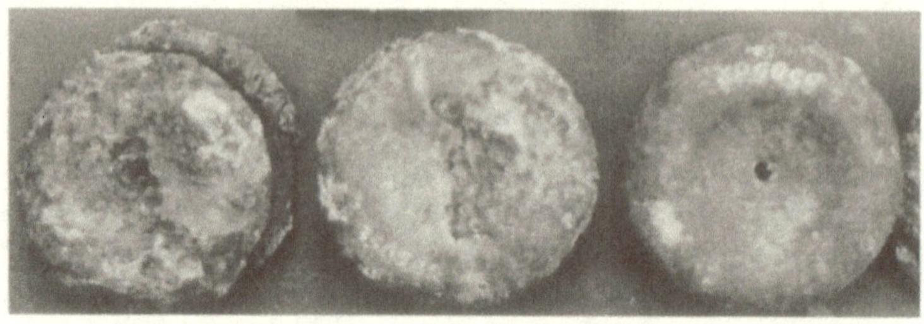

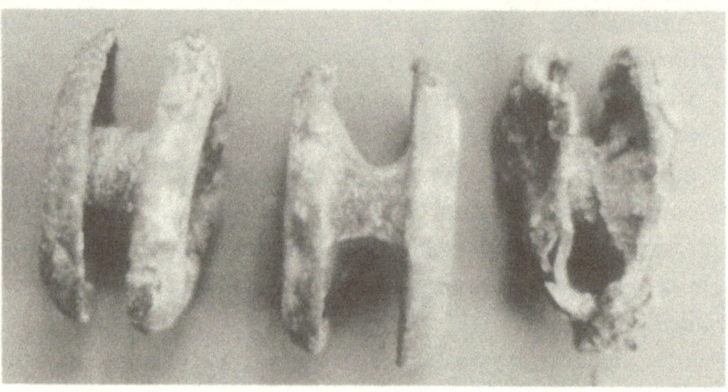

Figure 3a and 3b. Hopewell Style Earpieces (top and side views), Middle Woodland. Catalogue No.#350582, Department of Anthropology, Smithsonian Institution, Washington, D.C. Porter Mounds, Mound 15, Ross Co., Ohio. Each ca. 1 3/4" in diameter.

in Ohio show the most technical variation. However, usually examples of this "standard" form are found at those sites, too, in addition to local versions (see Appendix, Section II.4.g.).

The consistency in design and distribution of copper earpieces suggests that they were probably central items of exchange and ceremony, manufactured in the core area and exported along with the specifics of the ritual. Huge numbers were recovered from the Hopewell type-site, which has more than any other site. Generally speaking, the farther that sites are removed from the core area, the fewer of these items appear in burials. A distinct pattern is established here. Several other sites seem to be the centers for certain other types of copper objects, usually items that also appear to have been central to the ritual during various periods. These include breastplates, plummets, and panpipes of copper as well as stone pipes, frequently elaborated with metal. Most sites have at least a few examples of each type of object, but one or two sites seem to have specialized in particular aspects of

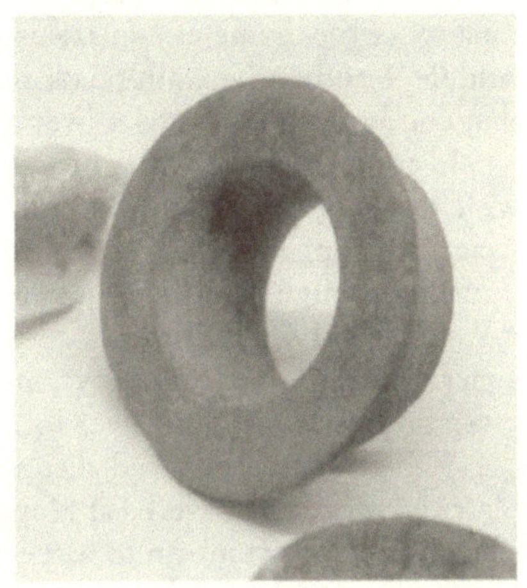

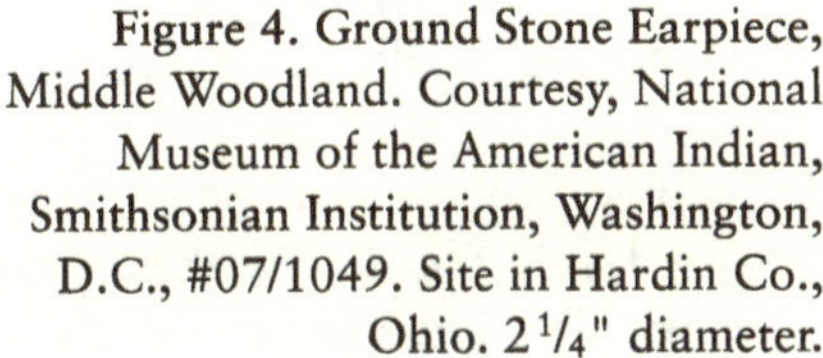

Figure 4. Ground Stone Earpiece, Middle Woodland. Courtesy, National Museum of the American Indian, Smithsonian Institution, Washington, D.C., #07/1049. Site in Hardin Co., Ohio. 2 1/4" diameter.

the ritual and include far more examples of such objects in their burial remains, relative to the overall size of the site.

After the Woodland Periods, copper earpieces continued to be important in burial ritual, but the form of the object changed considerably, both in size and method of manufacture. Nevertheless, connections between Hopewellian versions of these objects and later Southeastern Ceremonial Complex copper earpieces (see below) are apparent in a few examples. The form is somewhat anomalous within each of the traditions individually, but is shared by both. The existence of these objects (though they are not numerous) is another link in the chain of undeniable relationships between the two versions of the mortuary complex, although hundreds of years pass between the demise of one and the advent of the other. Four of these earpieces resemble small Mississippian pulley-type ones (e.g., Fig. 63). However, they were made and used by Middle Woodland peoples.[31]

Another remarkable similarity between Middle Woodland and Southeastern Ceremonial Complex earpiece designs is apparent in a second group of earpieces. These are also related to the pulley type, but with important differences in overall design. These objects are open rings of either copper or stone with a curved upper surface (Fig. 4). The upper surface of the stone examples has a copper overlay. Like the earpieces discussed above, they were found in both Southeastern Ceremonial Complex and Woodland contexts.

Middle Woodland metallurgists produced more copper beads than any other group in precontact history. Strings of them were worn as necklaces and bracelets, often in conjunction with freshwater pearls. About 60 percent are globular or barrel-shaped, and most are very precisely formed and finely finished. A few are covered with a thin overlay of silver or meteoric iron, as earpieces occasionally were. The rest are tubular with the length at least twice the diameter and are usually made of much thinner copper sheet. Middle Woodland metallurgists also made a few spherical and ovoid beads that combined copper sheet over a wood or stone core.

In addition to elaborate beads, Hopewellian coppersmiths introduced a wide range of other highly complex objects previously unknown in Native American copperwork. They refined many others. Interest in bracelets continued, although Middle Woodland artists made fewer of them (see Appendix, Section II.4.c.). They are constructed of thick copper sheeting and are generally very large, very heavy, and very beautifully made. Some have been given an overlay of thin silver foil.

Well over one hundred distinctively Middle Woodland copper breastplates have been discovered at Hopewell-related sites (Fig. 2b). With very few exceptions, they conform to a specific range of sizes and shapes, closely related to earlier breastplate forms, yet distinctive. Like earlier breastplates, most Middle Woodland examples have two perforations whose relative spacing and placement is as consistent throughout the Middle Woodland copper corpus as it was earlier. However, the typical Hopewell breastplate is considerably larger than those of earlier periods, and most have a trapezoidal shape, rather than a simple rectangular or reel form (see Appendix, Section II.4.d.). Both Adena and Copena breastplates tend to be smaller and more graceful. In this respect, Hopewell breastplates seem to have had more in common with the Archaic copper tradition than with its closer contemporaries.

A few breastplates more characteristic of Adena culture and many characteristic of Copena culture (see below) have also been recovered from Hopewell-related sites—evidence of significant, albeit unclear, links among all three traditions. Also important are a few variations on the basic Hopewell breastplate form within the Middle Woodland corpus. Unusual examples found within the core areas of Ohio usually exhibit the typical size and shape of the basic breastplate form, but various and always unique designs have been cut from each piece. At the Seip Mound Site, several standard Hopewell breastplates have elegant scroll forms cut from one corner (Plate 3). At Mound City, a grave distinguished by several examples of copperwork with representational bird imagery, included two breastplates decorated with abstract bird motifs. One was worked in a repoussé technique and the other in an elaborate openwork design (Plate 4, Fig. 5).[32]

Only a few of the breastplates from Hopewell groups in Wisconsin approximate the typical Hopewellian size and shape, although the placement and spacing of the perforations is consistent with typical Hopewell examples. All of the Wisconsin breastplates are decorated with punctate rather than cut-out or repoussé designs and include the only conventional point-shaped motif in all of the Middle Woodland copper material examined.[33] The punc-

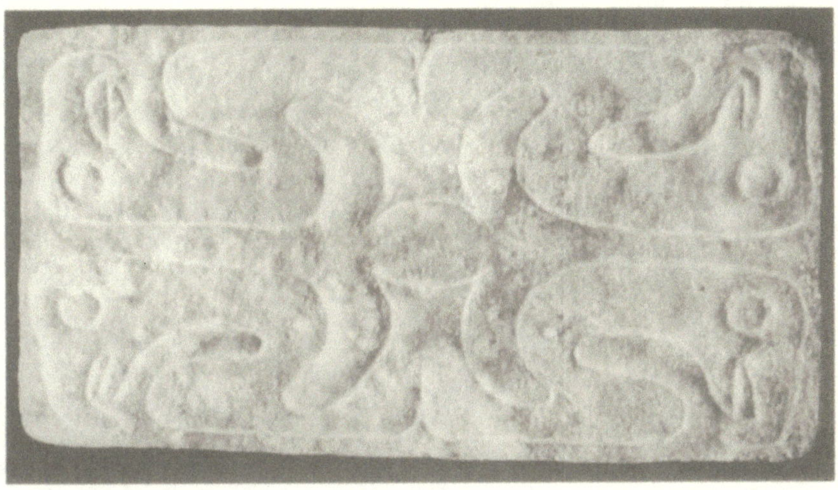

Figure 5. Repoussé Breastplate with Four Raptor Heads, Middle Woodland. Ohio Historical Society, Columbus, #260/22. Mound City Mounds, Ross Co., Ohio. Ca. 10" long.

tate design consists of parallel rows of small dots. This is a decorative technique also found on some Old Copper Culture spear points and is an important design element in the metallurgical tradition of the Wisconsin area from that point on.[34]

Hopewell peoples also extended earlier precedents in their regular use of copper headdresses to the extent that the form becomes an almost diagnostic piece of ritual gear in the Ohio core area. The most common type was a carefully worked, roughly rectangular piece of heavy, concavo-convex sheet copper that was occasionally elaborated with openwork, repoussé design or various appendages (Plate 5, Figs. 6, 7, and 8). It was curved to fit the contours of the human head and frequently was tapered slightly from one end to the other. Each piece appears to have been designed specifically for the individual who used it or who, at least, wore it in death. At any rate, no two are exactly alike in size or shape, and they were often decorated with openwork designs carefully adjusted to the basic form. The range of proportions and degrees of concavo-convexity is also fairly wide, and alterations to the basic rectangular shape range from slight variations to complete transformation. The head, legs, and tail of a bear were appended to one example (Fig. 7). Another was cut to represent a headless human body (Fig. 8). Others were fitted with horns or antlers. Several sets of copper antlers were taken from Hopewell-related sites (Plate 8, Fig. 66) (see Ap-

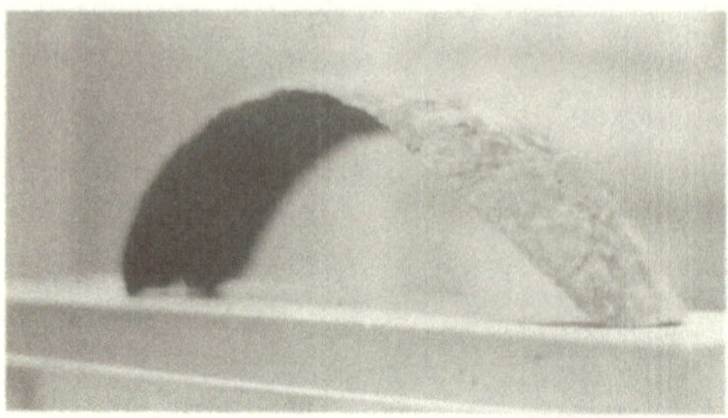

Figure 6. Hopewell Style Headplate, Middle Woodland. Ohio Historical Society, Columbus, #260/33. Mound City Mounds, Ross Co., Ohio. 11" across.

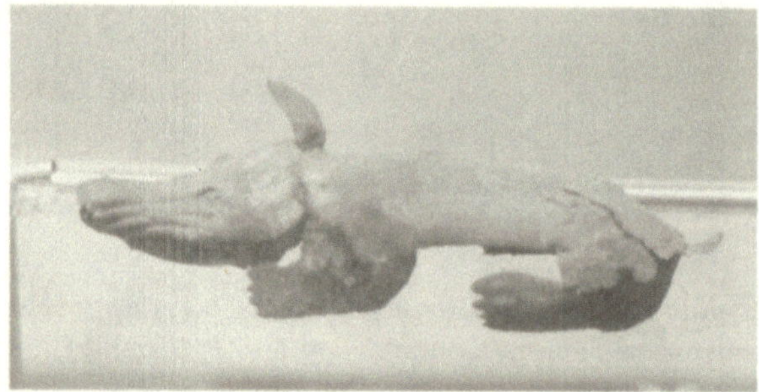

Figure 7. Bear Headdress (with moving parts), Middle Woodland. Ohio Historical Society, Columbus, #260/59. Mound City Mounds, Ross Co., Ohio. Ca. 9" long.

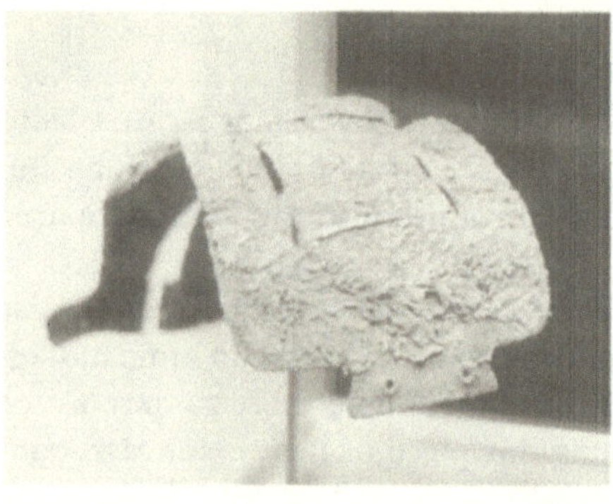

Figure 8. Headplate (shaped like a headless human body), Middle Woodland. Ohio Historical Society, Columbus, #260/142. Mound City Mounds, Ross Co., Ohio. Ca. 9" long.

pendix, Section II.4.h.). All are fairly small but life-sized and have tabs or perforations for attachment, presumably to headdresses.

Copper panpipes represent another essentially diagnostic category of copperwork found in the later excavation levels at Hopewell sites (Fig. 9). These are a uniquely Middle Woodland manifestation; at least one set has been found at every major Hopewell-related site (see Appendix, Section II.4.j.). Distribution patterns suggest that panpipes may well have been introduced into the ritual from the Southeast. Very few sites have more than a few examples, and most have only one. At the Tunacunnhee Site in Georgia, however, ten to twelve panpipes were interred with the dead. This was a

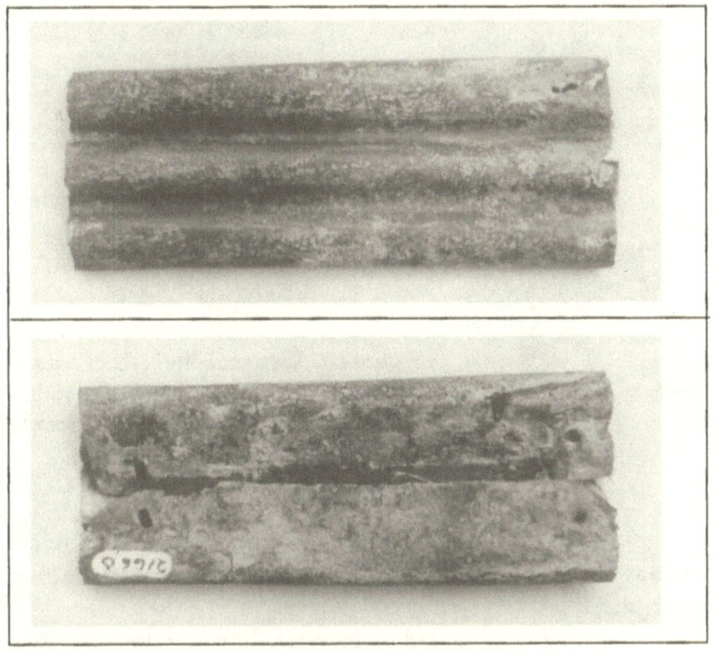

Figures 9a and 9b. Hopewell Style Panpipe (front and back views), Middle Woodland. By Permission of the Department of Anthropology, University of Georgia, Athens, #21660. Tunacunnhee Site, bu. 17, Dade Co., Georgia. 4 1/2" long.

radical deviation from the norm, given the overall size of the site. Perhaps an important religious specialist from this area introduced this element of the ritual and it spread like the distinctive five-part earpieces throughout other participant groups.

Hopewellian coppersmiths also introduced another unique bit of copper paraphernalia into the corpus, the copper "plummet." Like panpipes, these items appear to be a southern introduction. They are dubbed "plummets" because they seem to be weights. Some are shaped roughly like a modern plumb bob, although there is a fairly wide range of sizes and shapes. Similar objects occur earlier, but are always made of stone or shell. Plummets have been found in burials according to essentially the same pattern as panpipes. Rarely is more than one at any single site, but they are distributed throughout the areas occupied by Hopewellian peoples. The one exception to this rule is the Crystal River Site in Florida. A single burial mound at that site contained twelve of these objects interred with various individuals. Once

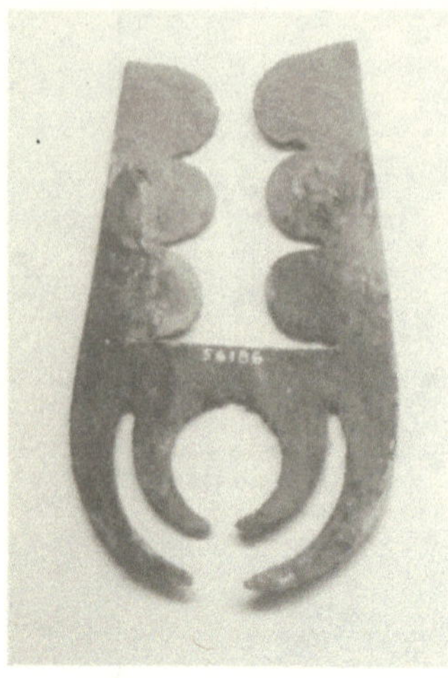

Figure 10. Abstract Silhouette of a Raptor's Claw (one of a pair), Middle Woodland. The Field Museum, Chicago, #56186. Hopewell Mounds, Ross Co., Ohio. Ca. 4" long.

again, interest in this item of paraphernalia (and, presumably, related ritual) appears to have been centered in Florida and introduced into the Hopewellian sphere from there.

Another unique form created by Hopewellian metallurgists was the copper clad "button," a label given to it in the archaeological literature. It was a small hemisphere of stone, clay, or wood covered with copper sheet and ranging in size from $^{3}/_{8}$" to 1$^{1}/_{2}$" in diameter (see Appendix, Section II.4.e.). The construction and placement of buttons in graves indicates they were primarily decorative, sewn to the outer surface of garments or blankets in rows and in other more complex patterns. A few have an overlay of silver or meteoric iron. Copper "tinklers" were probably used in much the same way as these buttons as decorative elements applied to items of wearing apparel. That is how metal tinklers functioned and continued to function after the arrival of Europeans (see Appendix, Section II.4.e.).

Without question, the most spectacular examples of Hopewellian metallurgical art are flat, two-dimensional pieces. They are the hundreds of complex geometric designs cut from heavy sheet copper that include virtually every category of subject matter used in the Hopewellian corpus (e.g., Plates 6–8, Figs. 10 and 12). Most were produced in pairs and the designs themselves are usually bilaterally symmetrical. Tiny holes along the edges of most examples suggest they were fastened to other materials, probably textiles or wood (see Appendix, Section II.4.f.). The largest cache of these objects, some 250 pieces, includes spectacularly complicated forms as well as much simpler ones, a combination that suggests that they may have been components in a complex, mural-like construction.

Less complex cut-out designs are common, as well. Copper crescents

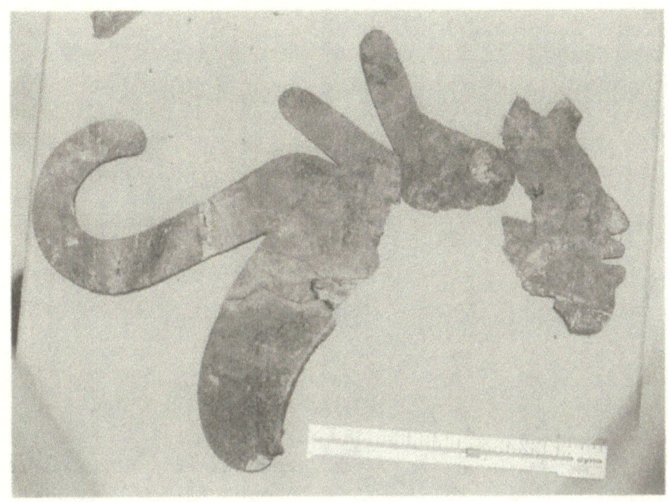

Figure 11. Human Profile (with typical facial features and elaborate headdress), Middle Woodland. Ohio Historical Society, Columbus, #283/350. Hopewell Mounds, Ross Co., Ohio. Ca. 1' across.

appear quite frequently in Hopewell burials. In fact, all the geometric designs most common in the copper complex as a whole, appear in cut sheet copper within the Hopewellian corpus. Motifs that were common in earlier periods remain so. On the other hand, the equal-armed cross, which will be central in Southeastern Ceremonial Complex copperwork, is rare (see Appendix, Section II.4.m.). Like the cross, several relatively rare designs in the Hopewellian corpus will become central to copper metallurgy later on and provide another consistent pattern in the complex as a whole.

Perhaps the most striking of these designs is that of avian imagery. Hopewellian coppersmiths were the first to introduce bird imagery since the lone bird claw/beak deposited in a Late Archaic burial. Hopewellian versions are rare but spectacular, and they usually reference specific species, such as the peregrine falcon that is also identified specifically in much Southeastern Ceremonial Complex copperwork (Plate 15). The Hopewell examples come from only three sites in Ohio and one in Illinois (see Appendix, Section II.4.l.). The peregrines were found at Mound City in Ohio, two from the same grave (Burial 9, Mound 7).

Hopewell coppersmiths were the first to introduce human imagery into the copper complex (see Appendix, Section II.4.n.). Like cruciform and bird motifs, human imagery is as rare in Middle Woodland copperwork as it will

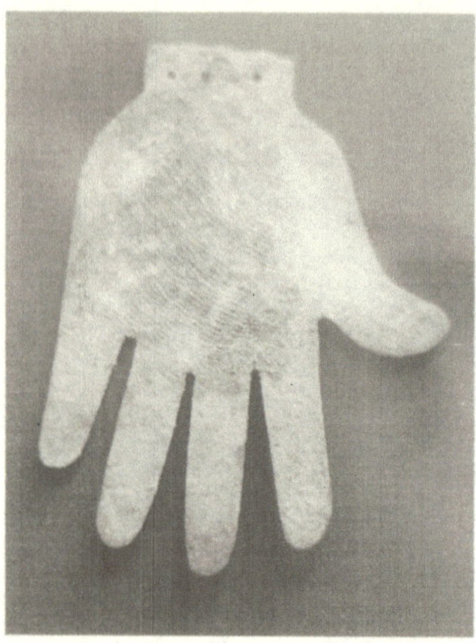

Figure 12. Human Hand (one of a pair), Middle Woodland. Ohio Historical Society, Columbus, #260/62. Mound City Mounds, Ross Co., Ohio. Ca. 4".

be basic to the iconography of copper in the Southeastern Ceremonial Complex. The entire human figure never appears, but there are two heads, a pair of hands, and a torso, including upper arms and thighs (Figs. 8, 11, and 12).

There are also designs in copper that are unique to the Hopewell tradition. The repeated use of certain complex designs on copperwork, produced over long periods of time, in widely separated areas, and among groups which almost undoubtedly shared no common language, suggests not only a body of shared ritual but also a widely shared symbolic vocabulary. Hopewell copperwork in this category includes the earpieces and breastplates already discussed. The formal qualities of other objects in this category are more complicated and combine design elements that appear across the whole region (in some cases, the entire complex) on an individual basis, but in a combinations that are unique to Hopewell. These more complex configurations probably embody a symbolic distillation of the core concepts of the ideology that was the basis for Hopewellian ritual as well as for the use of copperwork in its celebration. The same sets of complicated abstract symbols are used repeatedly and were apparently read and understood by culturally diverse units throughout the entire eastern United States.[35]

In Hopewell copperwork, these composite designs seem to be based on a fairly limited vocabulary of stylized forms, most of which appear to be derived from sources in nature. Apparently the individual components of the design were important, not the order in which they were combined, a common phenomenon in Native American art. The presence of those elements alone probably identified and elaborated the subject matter. Design components that recur most frequently are:

1. curved claw or canine tooth forms, usually depicted in pairs but occasionally occurring in groups of five;
2. comma or nostril forms—the importance of this motif was also noted by Myron (1954a:11).
3. a loop or circle and dot combination, with the dot sometimes enclosed within the loop, sometimes not;
4. a rounded *M* shape;
5. rounded ear forms which seem to be related as well to the loop/dot configuration.

The naturalistic basis for most of these design elements is clear when they are compared with representational imagery in copper and other media. Generally, representational motifs are less complex than the composite designs and are unquestionably less stylized. Many of the individual elements that comprise the composite designs are easy to recognize within that more naturalistic context, a factor that makes their identification fairly certain. The preponderance of naturalistic references, even in more esoteric composite designs, suggests that a preoccupation with certain creatures and ceremonies associated with them probably formed the core of Hopewellian ritual. The specific implications of that interest will be discussed at length in subsequent chapters. For now, the focus will be on the animals involved.

Specific and undeniable reference to mammals is very common. Interest in mammal motifs within the copper complex as a whole reaches its peak in the Middle Woodland Period.[36] Deer were important, as indicated by the life-sized copper deer antlers found at Hopewell sites. One headdress even appears to represent the female of the species.[37]

The beast of primary interest, however, was the bear. Like the deer, the bear was generally represented by specific parts of its anatomy and rarely in its entirety. In fact, the only complete rendering of a bear in copper is the headdress mentioned above (Fig. 7). The most common form of bear-related imagery is copper grizzly bear canine teeth.[38] The objects have a wide distribution throughout the eastern United States.[39] Many unique and far more complex examples of bear imagery are also included in the Hopewellian copper corpus (see Appendix, Section II.4.k.).

Among the most complex designs in copper are two objects that are generally identified as birds, but the attribution is not convincing. One object, a fragment unavailable for close examination, was found in an ash bed in a mound of the Harness group in Ohio.[40] The other object is even more

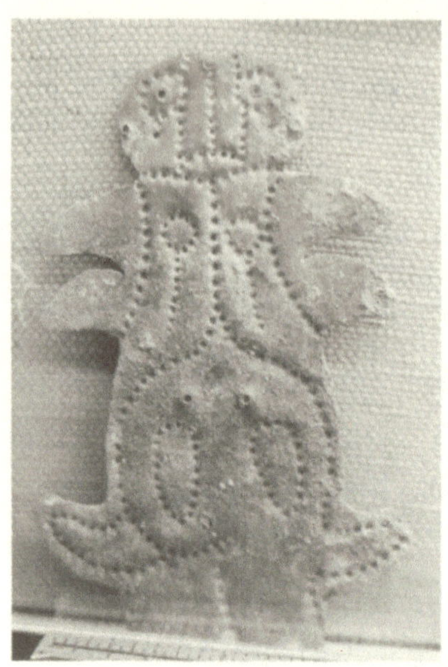

Figure 13. Composite Figure with Punctate Designs, Middle Woodland. The Thomas Gilcrease Institute of American History and Art, Tulsa, Oklahoma. Bedford Mounds, Pike Co., Illinois. Ca. 7" long.

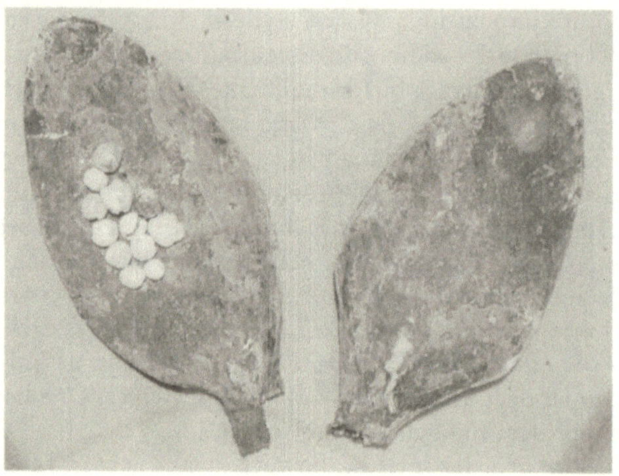

Figure 14. Deer Ears (part of an elaborate headdress), Middle Woodland. Ohio Historical Society, Columbus. #283/104. Hopewell Mounds, Ross Co., Ohio. Each, ca. 10" long.

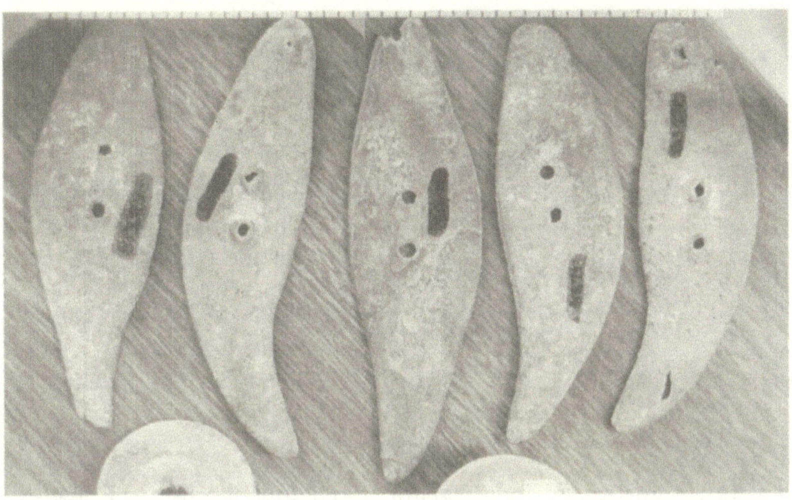

Figure 15. Life-Sized Grizzly Bear Teeth, Middle Woodland. Illinois State Museum, Dickson Mounds, Lewiston. Liverpool Site, Fulton Co., Illinois. Each ca. 4" long.

certainly not an example of avian imagery, although it has been said to represent a bird (e.g., Seeman 1979:316). It was found in the Bedford Mounds, a Middle Woodland site in Illinois, and is a crude but excellent example of composite symbolism in Hopewell art (Fig. 13). It combines several basic Hopewellian motifs in its abstract punctate design, but only a few bear any demonstrable relationship to other Hopewellian bird imagery in copper. The Bedford Mound piece has far more in common with a much better known piece that also has been misidentified and that is another example of Hopewell composite symbolism. Although crude, the Bedford Mound piece mimics the combination of motifs so closely that it may represent an instance of long distance pairing of objects between Hopewellian sites, such as are seen in other media.

Much of the archaeological literature suggests that this piece, one of the most spectacular in the Hopewell corpus, represents the head of a serpent (Plate 6). This identification was never certain, but has been generally, albeit erroneously, accepted.[41] The abstract vocabulary of the "serpent head" and the Bedford Mound piece, as well as their design and structure, have far more in common with the complex imagery on Adena stone tablets produced in the preceding era than with other examples of unique Hopewell imagery. The Adena tablets often combined bird and mammal imagery in a field divided into quadrants. These two objects do the same and, with a handful of others, seem to be holdovers from older Adena ritual and very

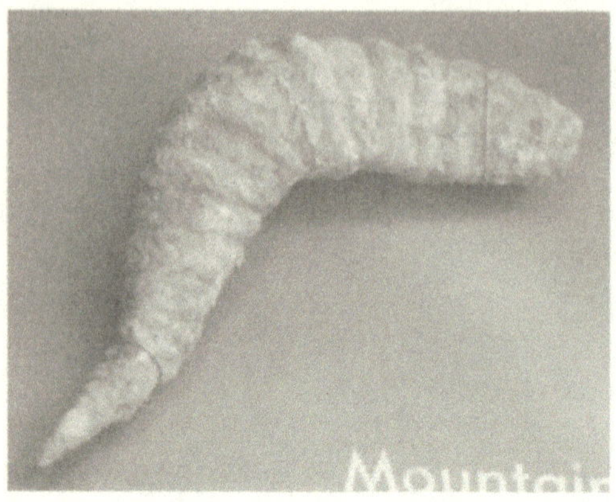

Figure 16. Mountain Goat Horn, Middle Woodland. Ohio Historical Society, Mound City Group National Monument, Chillicothe, Ohio, #260/41. Mound City Mounds, Ross Co., Ohio. Ca. 6" tall.

likely from within a single ancestral line of religious specialists. Hopewellian copper artists obviously shared some of the same basic Adena interest in subject matter and design, but only rarely did their work display such a clear relationship to Adena form. Thus, it seems far more likely, given the relationships between Hopewell and Adena and the nature of Hopewellian design in general, that these objects represent similarly complex composite imagery and not a snake.[42]

Although snakes were not represented in copper, Middle Woodland artists were the first to create imagery in copper that represented animals other than mammals or birds, as well as a number of creatures that were not indigenous to the Eastern Woodlands, such as the grizzly (see Appendix, Section II.4.o.). In almost every case, the conception is highly representational, with naturalistic details. This is another argument against the identification of the pieces discussed above as either snakes or birds. The most common subject matter of Middle Woodland artists is the turtle.

One of the most unusual examples of this genre is a single mountain goat horn found in Mound 7 at Mound City (Fig. 16).[43] The obviously realistic approach to the form is consistent with the construction and scale of Hopewellian deer antlers. However, neither mountain goats nor grizzly bears lived in Ohio. The source for both grizzly teeth and mountain goat horn was probably the same, the Rocky Mountains. Apparently, Hopewellian religious specialists were less impressed with the horned creatures of the West than they were with the impressive carnivores there, since this is the only reference to the latter species. An exotic creature with spectacular teeth from another region was also represented in Hopewellian burial tradition. Many alligator teeth found their way to Ohio from the Southeast.[44]

Although Hopewellian artists made relatively few three dimensional objects from metal, they were fine sculptors. Copper was applied to many

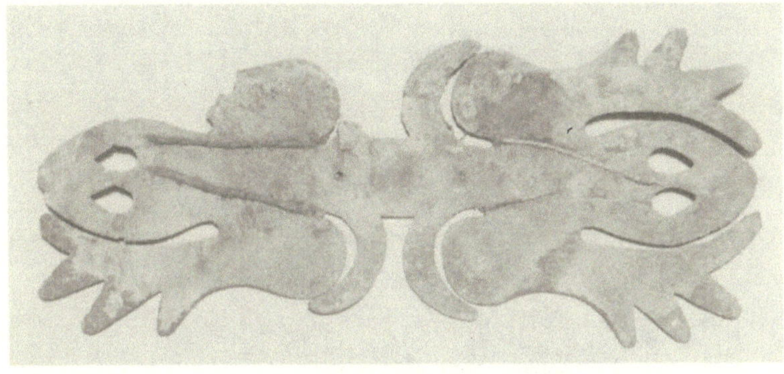

Figure 17. Abstract Design, Middle Woodland. Ohio Historical Society, Columbus. Rutherford Mound 1, Illinois. 6 1/2" long.

of the exquisite stone pipes found in Hopewellian graves. Like so many important objects in the Hopewell corpus, most examples of stone pipes come from a limited number of sites, Mound City and Tremper in Ohio. All are classic Hopewell platform pipes, sculpted from stone, with a short, often curved, rectangular platform that serves as the pipe stem. On most pipes is a figure sculpted in the center of the platform, usually a bird or an animal (humans are rare). The animal's eye sockets are often filled with small nuggets of copper.

Several pipes are in the form of the head, shoulders, and forepaws of bears, with emphasis on claws and canine teeth (Figs. 18a and 18b). Except for this anatomical abbreviation, the pipes tend to be very naturalistic in concept. In addition to the copper in the eye sockets, two of the bear pipes are also elaborated with an engraved circumocular marking that is usually associated with raptorial birds and is never found on bears in nature.

Other mammal pipes with copper eyes include raccoons, beavers, otters, and (rarely) pumas. Many of these also have the same unnatural circumocular markings seen on the bear pipes and found only on birds and raccoons in nature. Given the strongly naturalistic quality of these works, this obvious departure is intriguing. The formal (and, most likely, symbolic) linkage suggested between eyes, raptors, and copper will be central to copper design and symbolism in the Southeastern Ceremonial Complex. Apparently this link was already developed to some degree in Middle Woodland times, although its nature and significance remains unclear. Several of the pipes with copper eyes represent raptors (Fig. 19). The peregrine falcon appears several times as well as crows, quail, and various water birds.

Additional copper elaboration on pipes, although unique, provides fur-

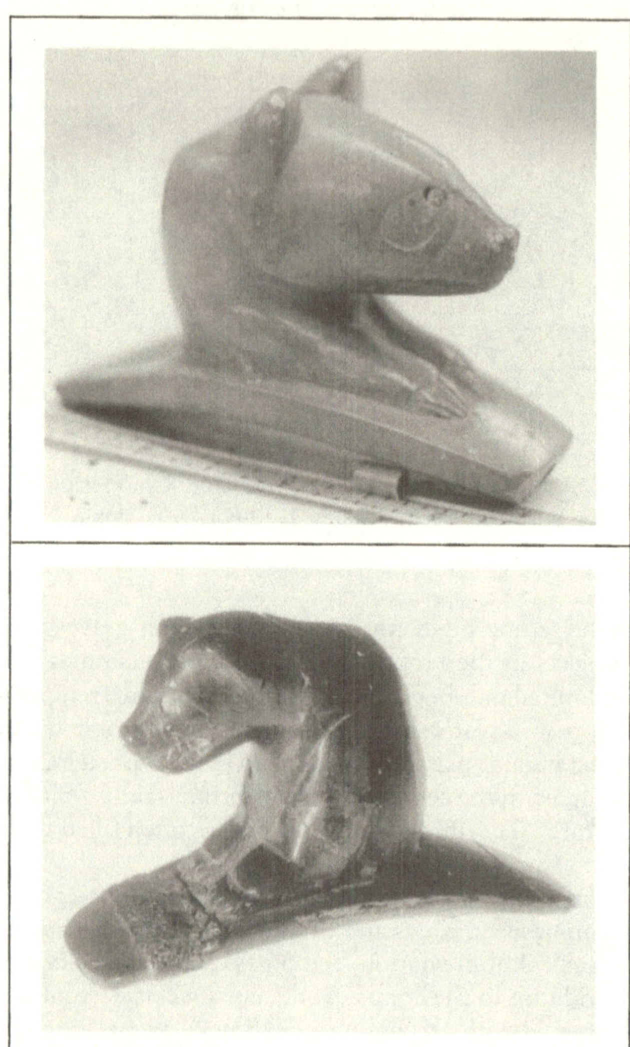

Figures 18a and 18b. a: Stone Platform Pipe, Bear (with copper eyes), Middle Woodland. Courtesy of the Center for Archaeological Investigations, Southern Illinois University, Carbondale, #54.48/43. Wilson Mounds, White Co., Illinois. Ca. 2 1/2" x 4 1/2"; b: Stone Platform Pipe, Bear (with copper band repair), Middle Woodland. Ohio Historical Society, 125/?. Tremper Mound, Scioto Co., Ohio. Ca. 2 1/2" x 4 1/2".

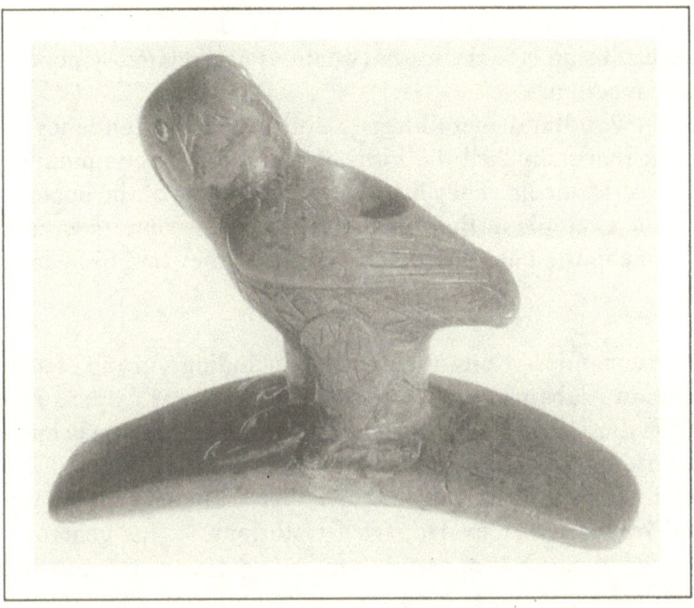

Figure 19. Stone Platform Pipe, Peregrine Falcon, Middle Woodland. Ohio Historical Society, Columbus, 125/19. Tremper Mound, Scioto Co., Ohio. Ca. 2 1/2" x 4"

ther insight into the significance of the medium itself. A beaver pipe from the Elizabeth Mound in Illinois is fitted with a copper nose. One of the Tremper pipes depicting an otter not only has copper eyes, but also an essentially unworked lump of copper that is set in the bottom of the platform directly below the bowl area. Perhaps whoever sculpted the otter ground the bowl of the pipe a bit too deep and plugged the resulting hole in the platform with copper as a way to repair the damage. The use of copper on other pipes suggests the purpose of this placement. Several broken pipes, usually without copper eyes, appear to have been repaired with bands of copper before being buried in the mounds. One of the Mound City pipes was so badly broken that it had been entirely encased in copper (Squier and Davis 1848:273).

A few unbroken pipes also have copper bands attached, but in the vast majority, any copper other than in the eye sockets was used to repair breakage. Some archaeologists believe that these pipes were important early in the development of Hopewell ritual and then fell out of use (most have been found in large caches in burial mounds). Perhaps the addition of copper to so many of them was a way of updating an earlier smoking tradition and integrating it into new Hopewellian ritual, as well as reconsecrating or ritually reactivating damaged pipes. Whatever the details of use may be in this context, the allusion is to the special qualities and related symbolic associations of the medium.

Middle Woodland metallurgists continued the tendency to create copperwork that mimicked the form of objects more commonly found in other, less exotic, media. They made several versions of the boatstone, such as the unique example in the Adena corpus. These objects were normally made of stone in the Late Woodland Period, as they had been earlier.

Copena

The southern manifestations of Hopewell, including a group of about thirty related sites in Alabama and Tennessee (referred to as Copena rather than Hopewell in the archaeological literature) were comparatively late in developing, according to carbon dating of site materials (Walthall 1972:137–41). Archaeologists disagree as to whether Copena peoples were more influenced by Adena or by Hopewell traditions.[45] This general disagreement is fueled in part by copperwork from Copena sites that includes some forms and designs similar to Hopewell work and some that clearly show an affinity with Adena metallurgy. Except for the importance of copper earpieces, however, Copena copperwork certainly had more in common with Adena work. Copena copper bracelets are very similar to Adena ones in size, shape, quality, and apparent method of manufacture. Copena breastplates are also much closer to Adena ones in form. They are among the most numerous Copena copper objects produced—graceful attenuated versions of the Adena reel form (Plate 2). Several appear to have been mutilated prior to burial, but most are highly refined works of art. Many have been found in Hopewell burials farther north.

Like Adena peoples and unlike Hopewellian groups, Copena metallurgists made virtually no elaborate designs from cut sheet copper. A few blocky rectangular pieces have been found in burials, but little else of a decorative nature exists. Nor are there examples of representational imagery. Stone pipes carved by Copena peoples were generally much larger than Hopewellian ones and never included applied copper elaboration. Several have been found in northern Hopewell burials, nevertheless.

On the other hand, Copena axes combine some Early Woodland characteristics with those more typical of Middle Woodland versions and are similar to Hopewell axes in size and shape. Other axes are very irregular like those from earlier periods. Unlike their Adena predecessors, over half of all copper designs on Copena copperwork are circular in design and consist almost entirely of concentric designs on copper earpieces rather than on bracelets and rings. Adena-related peoples did not make copper earpieces. Copena ones are often heavier and somewhat cruder than standard Hopewellian forms, and

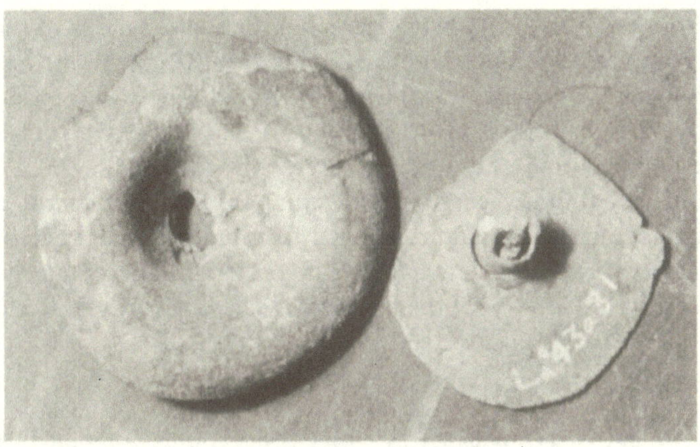

Figure 20. Copena Style Earpiece, Middle Woodland. University of Alabama Archaeological Collections, Moundville, #a31. Terry Site, Lawrence Co., Alabama. Ca. 1 3/4" dia.

generally used only three or four pieces of copper in their construction (as opposed to the five-piece construction of many northern Hopewell examples). They usually have only a flat square or circular plate on one side of the spool, opposite a more typical cymbal form (Fig. 20). None of the Copena earpieces examined were elaborated with metal overlays or other decoration.

These construction methods required considerably less copper and may reflect the relative distance of these groups from the copper sources as much as a different approach to design. The interiors of the cymbals on many Copena earpieces were also filled with galena, a practice apparently unique to these groups. They also produced large numbers of copper beads.

The widespread and distinctive cultural traits identified with Hopewell gradually died out or began to evolve into new ones during the beginning of the Late Woodland Period, between ca. A.D. 400 and 600. The entire era, which continued until around A.D. 1000, was one of transition and change. Perhaps the most significant development in eastern North American during this time was the increasing importance of agriculture in subsistence patterns. A very likely concomitant development for the groups that began to embrace intensive agriculture as their primary mode of subsistence was a shift from patrilineal to matrilineal social organization. So radical a shift within traditional societies probably took many generations. The steady increases in sedentism and growing importance of local cultigens, as well as of squash and some maize in Middle Woodland times, suggests that those important cultural shifts were already under way and may well have been significant factors in the development of Hopewellian ritual. In fact, the demise of the ritual tradition may signal that the social aspects of the transition were complete and that the more complex groups in the region had settled into a new gardening/agricultural lifestyle with related social patterns that were relatively free of the tensions that gave rise to Hopewellian tradition.

Some copper trade and manufacture persisted in the Late Woodland Period, but the volume is very small compared to that at the apex of Hopewellian activity. It would be almost five hundred years before elaborate burial ritual and associated art in copper would once again become a central element in the lives of the peoples of eastern North America.

The Mississippian Periods

The last vestiges of Hopewellian-related ritual and copperwork died out between A.D. 500 and 600. Use and manufacture of copper paraphernalia never died out completely in those centuries, but only a few examples exist from that period. It is clear, however, that neither mining techniques nor those required to produce refined metallurgy were lost. When copperwork became ritually important once again, no need for a gradual redevelopment of the necessary skills was apparent. Even the earliest examples from the Mississippian Periods exhibit highly refined craftsmanship in both the working of the metal and the application of designs. The focus of activity shifted to the south as it had with every previous manifestation of the complex.

The hiatus in the production of elaborate ceremonial art was long read as evidence of a kind of "Dark Age" in the Eastern Woodlands. In fact, it was a time of relative stability and increased interdependence and cohesiveness among households in village life.[46]

What caused the collapse of Hopewellian tradition is not clear. Theories abound, but few are completely satisfactory. What is clear is that between A.D. 700 and A.D. 900, many groups throughout eastern North America broke away completely from earlier hunter-gatherer subsistence strategies (which included an increasingly broad variety of local cultigens) to establish primarily agricultural economies with maize, squash, and beans at the center of their subsistence tradition. About this same time many groups must also have shifted from the patrilineal social organization characteristic of most hunter-gatherer societies to the matrilineal organization more typical of early agricultural groups and characteristic of Historic Period agriculturalists in the Eastern Woodlands. As noted above (and discussed in more detail below), much of the symbolism on Hopewellian copperwork suggests that the tensions generated by these changes in subsistence strategies and social organization were significant elements within the ceremonial tradition. Such tensions would also help to explain the difference between Hopewellian approaches to use and design in mortuary copper and the approach of Mississippian copper workers. In fact, the demise of Hopewellian ritual complexity (paralleled by simplification in many other aspects of culture in Late Woodland times) may well reflect the success of Hopewellian ritual in mediating those tensions and assuring its own disappearance.

Whatever the reasons for the significant changes that settled in throughout the Eastern Woodlands between A.D. 700 and 900 (the timing varies regionally), most recent scholarship on Mississippian developments tends to use these dates as the starting point for the various ritual traditions that eventually coalesce into what has been called the Southeastern Ceremonial Complex, the ceremonial fluorescence that produced the last extensive body of precontact ritual copperwork. Many characteristics of the Complex bear a distinctly Southeastern flavor from the outset.

There were significant differences in cultural development in the Southeast. The importance of shellfish in the diets of southeastern peoples and the tendency of edible species there to inhabit the same waters over many years led to repeated use of certain sites by relatively large human populations. Those sites are distinguished by very large deposits of shell. Ceramics first appeared in the Southeast, long before any such interest was apparent farther north (Sassman 1995). The first evidence of pottery emerges as early as 1700 B.C., although it does not come into general use until about a thousand years later. The earliest evidence of imported cultigens in North America was also discovered at southern sites.[47] Interest in cultigens may have been important in the early development of pottery in the Southeast.

Spectacular earthworks are also important at a few southern sites very early, centuries before northern groups began to build them. The complex mounds at Poverty Point in Louisiana were constructed just after 1300 B.C. This tendency toward the monumental in constructing earthworks is a distinctively Southeastern trait. Despite the early interest in mound building and the eventual continuation of some of the distinctive aspects of this site, earth mounds, like ceramics, do not become a regular feature of ritual tradition in the Southeast until much later, about 300 B.C.

Another difference in the mound-building approach of Southeasterners is important. As at Poverty Point, in the later periods of prehistory in the Southeast, mounds were not used primarily for burial as they were farther north. They were used more often as raised settings for politically and ritually significant architecture, although burial mounds were important as well.

The more complex social developments represented by these early developments in the Southeast (the Poverty Point, Tchula, and Tchefuncte sites, e.g.) gave way to simpler manifestations in the Woodland Periods, exhibiting a pattern of waxing and waning cultural complexity that is less apparent farther north. Still, connections among Southeastern ceremonialism, Middle Woodland, and even Archaic traditions are important. Exchange among the regions very early, especially in the crucial ritual materials, copper and marine shell, is evident.[48] Shell gorgets featuring bird motifs, an important marker for the Southeastern Ceremonial Complex, were found at the Hopewellian Mound City Site in Ohio (Philips and Brown 1978:157).

In some cases, differences in ritual among Middle Woodland groups present distinctly southeastern precedents that will flourish in Mississippian times.[49] Many sites in Florida with active Middle Woodland ritual traditions show continuous occupation through Mississippian times and clear participation in developments associated with Southeastern Ceremonial Complex ritual. This is true of the Spiro Site in Oklahoma as well, with evidence of occupation from the Late Archaic through the Late Mississippian Period.

Mississippian copperwork was created in connection with burial ritual identified generically as the Southeastern Ceremonial Complex. Interpretation of the Complex itself varies.[50] Detailed provenience data for Mississippian copperwork are sparse. Many of the major sites were excavated before the importance of recording details of mound construction and burial disposition was recognized. Other sites have been all but destroyed solely to extract collectible and/or salable artifacts. Records of provenience during such plunder were and are almost never made. Still other Mississippian locations have been properly excavated, but the data remains unpublished and, for the most part, inaccessible. Many areas with Mississippian materials have not yet been completely excavated.

At least one of the above-mentioned situations characterizes the archaeological history of each of the four major Mississippian sites: Moundville, Etowah, Spiro, and Cahokia. Thus, to develop even tentative attribution regarding use for many examples of Mississippian copperwork is difficult. Were it not for copious engravings on shell and much of the copperwork depicting regalia in use, the task would be all but impossible.

What is clear is that between A.D. 1100 and 1200 certain social and cultural phenomena occurred, giving rise to a rather abrupt increase in the production of material culture and earthworks throughout much of the Southeast. The ritual copperwork produced in conjunction with this fluorescence and for the next two centuries shows some remarkable areas of continuity, regardless of where it was found. Changes in design and symbolism on this artwork suggest at least two distinct phases in these developments.[51]

Climatic and demographic patterns between A.D. 1000 and 1500 were probably important factors in the stylistic and symbolic differences between the two phases and reinforce the conclusions drawn from the stylistic record (see, e.g., Bryson and Murray 1977:25). The initial flowering of the Complex at Cahokia coincides with a period of unusually warm weather around A.D. 1000 (Quimby 1960:7), while its demise is accompanied by a long period of unstable climatic conditions that began to affect the Mississippian

Valley about A.D. 1250. Very likely the increasingly severe weather and problematic patterns associated with the so-called Little Ice Age that peaked in the mid-fifteenth century were important as well. Obviously, the rise and fall of Cahokia and other Southeastern Ceremonial Complex centers were the result of an array of factors both human and otherwise, but the coincidence of these patterns and significant shifts in global and/or regional climate cannot be ignored, especially since all the peoples involved depended upon agriculture for survival.[52]

The chronology of the Southeastern Ceremonial Complex has been under discussion for many years with significant differences of opinion along the way. Most would agree that one of the earliest important sites exhibiting the complex social and cultural structures associated with the Complex was Cahokia in southern Illinois. It had emerged as a powerful regional presence by about A.D. 1000. At its peak, Cahokia's influence is clear throughout much of the Southeast, even as far away as Florida. By about A.D. 1250 it was in decline, however, and major Mississippian sites throughout the Southeast became more localized centers of power. Many were situated at the junctures of major physiographic provinces or ecosystems, and most, like Cahokia, were established on or near major water courses, especially the Mississippi and its tributaries. The precise dating of all of this is still under some dispute, but the main ceremonial centers and their approximate dates of ascendancy within the Complex are as follows:

Cahokia in southern Illinois—A.D. 1000–1300 or 1350
Moundville in Alabama—A.D. 1250–1500
Etowah in Georgia—A.D. 1250–1500
Ocmulgee in Georgia—A.D. 1000–1400
Mount Royale in Florida—A.D. 1100–1500
Lake Jackson in Florida—A.D. 1240–1476
Spiro in Oklahoma—A.D. 1350–1450

Sites in Tennessee, Louisiana, Arkansas, Indiana, and even Wisconsin also include material that is clearly related to aspects of the Complex.

Most of the major centers had ceased to function as such by the time Europeans arrived in the region. When de Soto passed through, Moundville and Etowah were still occupied but were abandoned like most others shortly thereafter.

Nevertheless, elements of ritual associated with the Southeastern Ceremonial Complex continued to be evident within the traditions of many societies in the Southeast. In fact, ritual response to the social and cultural tensions that resulted from the European invasion and the diseases that accompanied it may well have breathed new life into the remnants of the

Complex, although mound building had all but ceased by the end of the sixteenth century. Copper continued to be a central element in the rituals of many groups although, increasingly, European copper alloys and other metals were used in place of native copper.

From the outset, many characteristics of Southeastern Ceremonial Complex copper metallurgy were significantly different from those of the Middle Woodland corpus. The amount of copper in individual pieces is generally reduced, although the objects themselves do not diminish in size, and in some cases they become considerably larger. Complex metallurgical techniques (e.g., as seen in the construction of Hopewellian earpieces) generally give way to elaborate design in repoussé on thin copper sheeting. Copper is used increasingly in conjunction with other materials (wood, stone, shell, bone, and clay) as a thin overlay or applied decoration. Even celts and awls become thinner and more attenuated in design. Utilitarian pieces constitute a very small portion of the total Mississippian copper corpus. Thus, the general trend apparent in the copper complex from earliest times continued, away from obviously utilitarian forms to those more clearly ceremonial in significance.

As was also the case during earlier periods, in Mississippian times culture groups utilizing copper and participating in the Southeastern Ceremonial Complex existed alongside other groups that seemed to have had no interest in participation. This is particularly true in northern areas, many of which retain Late Woodland cultural patterns until after contact with Europeans. Other northern groups developed their own variations of the Southeastern Ceremonial Complex and its later manifestations, much as southern groups redefined certain aspects of Hopewell during the Middle Woodland Period.

There was a drastic reduction in the number of copper objects produced after the height of Southeastern Ceremonial Complex activity around A.D. 1450. Because copperwork from Late Mississippian through Early Historic times (just after the arrival of Europeans) differs sufficiently from that of the main centers of the Southeastern Ceremonial Complex, it warrants a separate designation. The amount of copperwork in this category from individual sites is generally modest and will be referred to in this study as "Post-Mississippian."[53]

Important shifts in design as well as in use and preferred technique in copper metallurgy occurred during Mississippian times. Nearly half of all copper objects were elaborated with applied decoration. Similar increases in the use of decorative motifs is characteristic of each phase of the copper complex as a whole.[54] Mississippian metallurgists made many of the same items for ritual use as did their Middle Woodland counterparts, but almost always with distinctive variations in form. Copper awls and pins tended to be considerably larger and more elongated and delicate than Archaic ones, and few show any evidence of having been fitted with handles as most

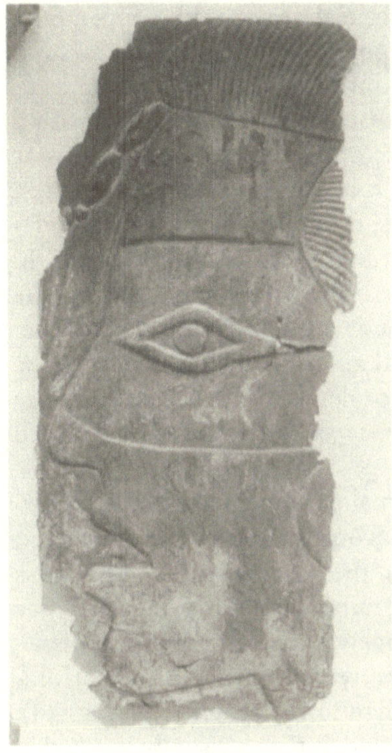

Figure 21. Copper Repoussé Portrait Plate, Mississippian. Courtesy, National Museum of the American Indian, Smithsonian Institution, Washington, D.C., #20/699. Spiro Site, LeFlore Co., Oklahoma. Ca. 10" tall.

Hopewellian examples were (see Appendix, Section II.5.a.). Mississippian awls and pins are usually identified as hair pins or parts of headdresses in the archaeological literature. A few have copper designs shaped like rattlesnake rattles fastened to one end.

Mississippian axes vary even further from Middle Woodland norms. They are more elongated in shape and tend to be quite thin and less finely finished. Earlier axes were usually substantial enough to have been used as tools (although few show any evidence of such use). Almost all Mississippian examples are so thin that their function must have been exclusively ceremonial, although several show evidence of hafting, as fragments of their wooden hafts still cling to the copper (see Appendix, Section II.5.b.).

Mississippian Period sites have yielded far fewer beads and beadlike objects than were found in Middle Woodland contexts. And those that have been found were not made in the same way that most earlier copper beads had been (see Appendix, Section II.5.c.). The context in which the heads were used is often different, too. Many appear to have been used in the hair or on the ears. Engravings on shell and some copper repoussé work show beads strung on a lock of hair and hung down on the forehead as a part of certain ritual regalia (Fig. 21).

Unlike the myriad of Hopewellian pipes elaborated with copper, only two Mississippian Period pipes have any copper associated with them. Both are small clay elbow pipes (excavated at Grant Mound in Florida), undecorated except for a small rectangular plate of copper lashed to each with a piece of cord (Moore 1894–1896:480). Each plate has a five-pointed star shape cut out of the center and each of the four corners of the plate.

The broad range of designs cut from sheet copper have distinct relationships to other categories of copperwork in the Mississippian corpus. In general, the Mississippian shapes are more standardized than the Middle Woodland examples and almost always include interior designs in repoussé. Some types, usually quite small, and several almost identical, tended to be buried together in groups in a single burial or deposit (Figs. 22 and 23) (see Appendix, Section II.5.e.). Others, somewhat larger, were worked over carved wooden plaques.

Copper breastplates were important ritual paraphernalia in the Mississippian Periods just as they were in Middle Woodland times (see Appendix, Section II.1.d.). Like Hopewell breastplates, the general form and design is consistent throughout, although there are minor variations in detail (see Appendix, Section II.5.d.). Unlike their Hopewellian counterparts, Mississippian breastplates are circular rather than rectangular, and the perforations are near the top of the piece rather than in the center (e.g., Fig. 24). Also, most breastplates carry some surface design that is usually worked in a repoussé technique. Scholars can only conjecture how the Hopewellian pieces may have been worn, but we have visual evidence of the way Mississippian copper breastplates were worn and in what contexts. Circular gorgets depicted on dancing figures in many shell engravings clearly represent copper breastplates.

Like their Middle Woodland predecessors, Mississippian copper workers produced hundreds of earpieces.[55] Their earpieces also are almost always circular and usually have concentric designs, but are never of solid copper. Instead, thin copper sheet is used as an overlay on the face of an object that is made of another material (see Appendix, Section II.5.f.). There are two basic types of Mississippian earpiece. One is almost always a copper/wood combination, approximately the same size as Woodland versions (1"–2" in diameter), but consisting of a single pierced and, usually, decorated wooden disk covered with copper sheet (Fig. 25).[56]

The second basic type of Mississippian earpiece is a pulley wheel shape. Most examples are made from stone and copper, although some are also bone, shell, and wood (Plate 9 and Fig. 26). Usually both sides are quite flat, with only one side decorated and covered with the copper overlay. Most of these earpieces are much larger than the first type: 2½"–3" in diameter and ½"–¾" thick.

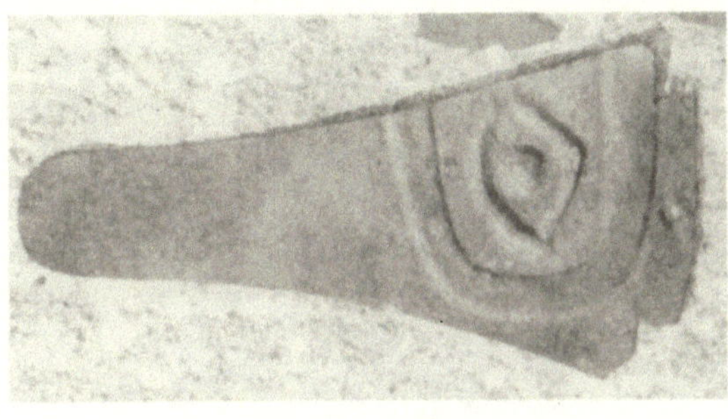

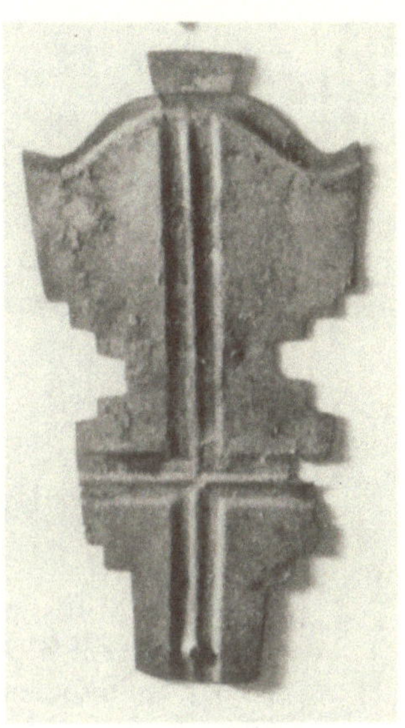

(Above) Figure 22. Copper Repoussé Pendant (one of several found together), Mississippian. University of Alabama Archaeological Collections, Moundville, #a78. Koger's Island Site, bu. 23, Lauterdale Co., Alabama. Ca. 3" long. (Right) Figure 23. Copper Repoussé Pendant (mace-shaped, one of several found together), Mississippian. Florida Division of Historical Resources, Department of State, Tallahassee, #96.115.14.1. Lake Jackson Site, Florida. Ca. 4" long.

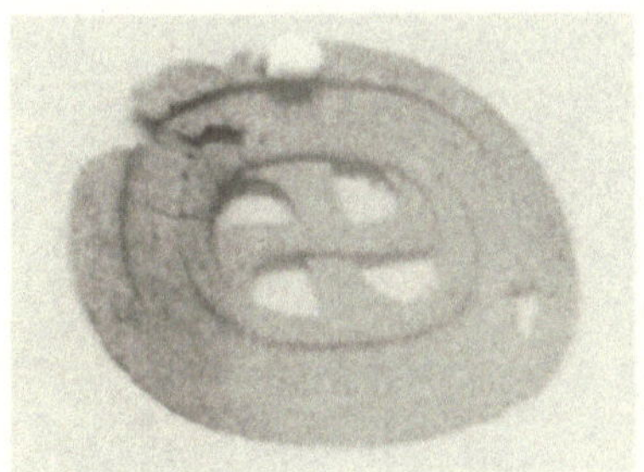

Figure 24. Small Openwork Repoussé Breastplate (with freshwater pearl), Mississippian. Courtesy, National Museum of the American Indian, Smithsonian Institution, Washington, D.C., #17/0168. Moundville, Hale Co., Alabama. Ca. 2" dia.

A number of Mississippian copper earpieces conform to neither basic type. The small copper masquettes, called "long-nosed god masks" in the archaeological literature, are an important example. The name derives from their size, shape, and the fact that they always occur in pairs (Fig. 27). In addition, a large stone pipe from Spiro (the so-called "Big Boy") has pieces of similar design hanging from the ears (Fig. 28). Rarely is more than a single pair of these little masquettes discovered at any one site, but they are found throughout the regions affected by the Southeastern Ceremonial Complex.

Another kind of Mississippian earpiece has a similarly wide, if sparse, distribution. Formally this kind is very different from other earpieces in the Mississippian corpus. Each earpiece consists of two pointed cones carved of

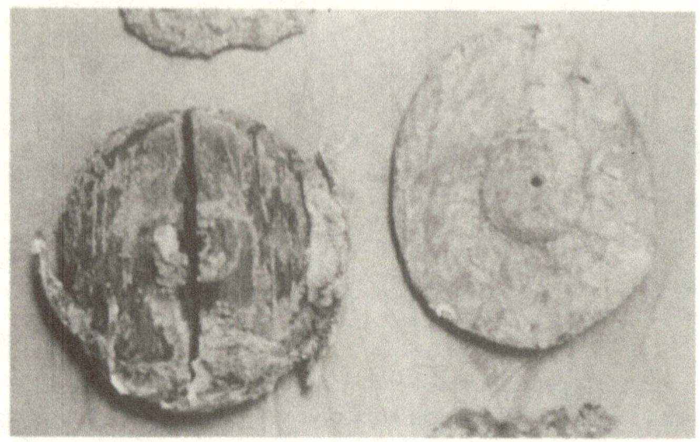

Figure 25. Mississippian Style Wood/Copper Earpieces. Catalogue Nos. #38/4991 and #38/4992, Department of Anthropology, Smithsonian Institution, Washington, D.C. Peach Tree Site, Cherokee Co., North Carolina. Ca. 1 1/2" dia.

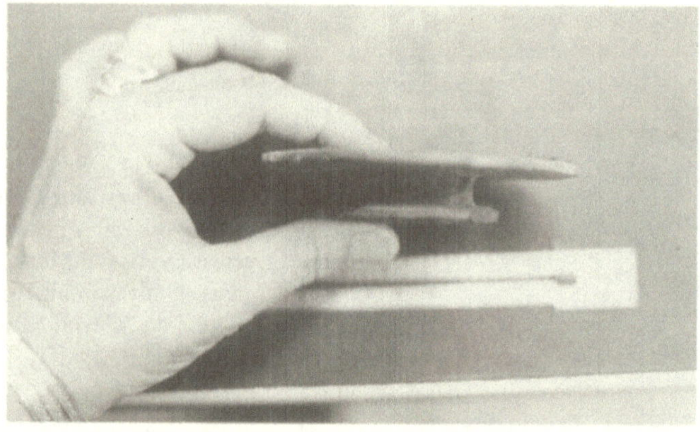

Figure 26. Mississippian Style Stone/Copper Earpiece. Catalogue No. 33/4337, Department of Anthropology, Smithsonian Institution, Washington, D.C. Veasy Mound 2., Pecan Island, Vermillion Parish, Louisiana. 3 1/2" dia.

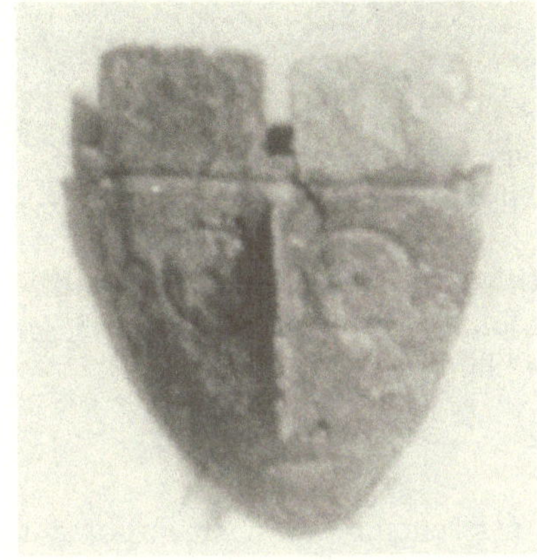

Figure 27. Small Masquette Earpiece, Mississippian. Courtesy, National Museum of the American Indian, Smithsonian Institution, Washington, D.C., #17/0197. Photo by Carmelo Guadagno. Grant Mound, Duval Co., Florida. Ca. 2 1/2" tall.

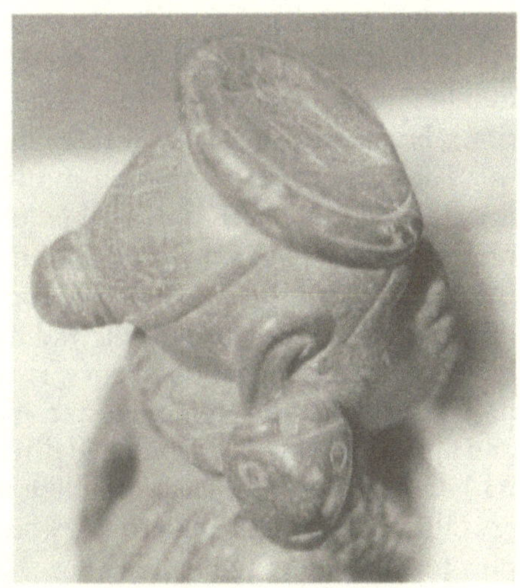

Figure 28. Large Stone Figurine/ Pipe, Mississippian. University Museum, University of Arkansas, Fayetteville. Spiro Site, LeFlore Co., Oklahoma. Ca. 11" tall.

wood and covered with copper (Fig. 29). The dowel and one cone were carved as a single piece, with the end of the dowel fitting snugly into a hole at the base of the other cone.[57]

In addition to earpieces, Mississippian coppersmiths made a wide variety of objects used as headdress elements (see Appendix, Section II.1.c.). Sheet copper cut-outs in many sizes and shapes were either fastened to large headdresses made of organic materials (leather, fur, feathers, etc.) or placed directly in the hair. Cut-outs used for the latter purpose were attached to flat wood, bone, shell, or horn pins. The most common motifs found on these headdress elements are bird-related (Fig. 30) (see Appendix, Section II.5.g.). References to mammals on Mississippian copper headdresses are rare, as they are in Mississippian copperwork in general. Most were appar-

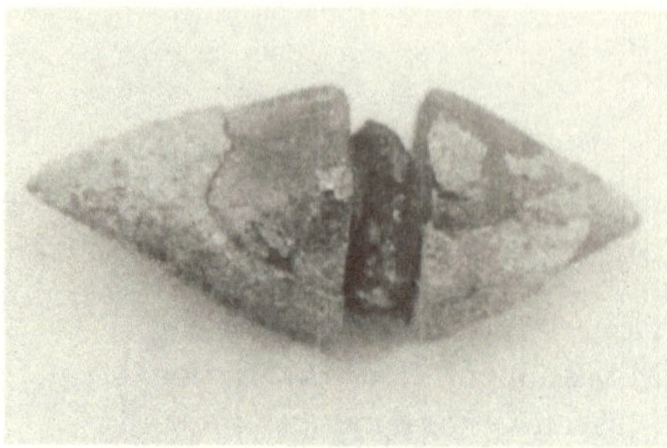

Figure 29. Wood/Copper Earpiece, Mississippian. The Spurlock Museum, University of Illinois at Urbana-Champagne, #5/5. Powell Mound, Madison Co., Illinois. 3"–4" long, ca. 1" dia.

ently masks, either antlered (probably in reference to deer, an important link to Middle Woodland usage) or feline. Middle Woodland interest in bears also appears in the Mississippian corpus, but only occasionally. Copper-covered wooden bear teeth were found in a Mississippian "headdress bundle" (catalogue note, Museum of the American Indian, Heye Foundation). Fragments suggest that there may have been other examples as well.

The second most common motif on this type of Mississippian headdress element is referred to as the "bi-lobed arrow" (Fig. 31). It is a complex symbol associated with the Southeastern Ceremonial Complex alone. Nothing similar appears in the iconography of earlier times and the symbol disappears completely with the fading of the Complex. Another common motif, in much the same category, is the so-called "mace" form, named for its resemblance to ceremonial axe forms. Most examples are quite small and appear to have been attached directly to larger headdress elements (Fig. 23). Others are fairly large and, like the bi-lobed arrows and copper feathers (although far less numerous), were lashed to bone, wood, horn or shell pins for placement in the hair (Fig. 32).

Another type of Mississippian headpiece is a quite large (most are approximately one square foot) copper plate. Most are rectangular and always have designs worked in repoussé on the surface. They were generally placed either under or atop the head of the deceased in Mississippian burial mounds. Many are decorated with variations on the swastika motif that is commonly associated with Southeastern Ceremonial Complex material (Fig. 33). It is also common for human beings or portions of them to be depicted on this type of Mississippian headgear, often including avian attributes (see Appendix, Section II.5.g.). Depiction of a single human head in profile is most common. These are also quite large (about three-fourths life-size) and include details of physiognomy and facial paint that suggest that they could be portraits as well (Plates 1, 13, and 16 and Fig. 21).

An item of headgear traditionally called the "occipital hair knot" and included in many Mississippian depictions of humans in stone, shell, and

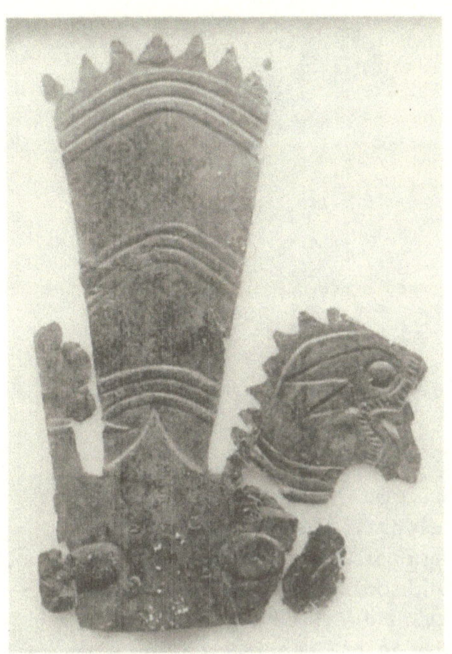

Figure 30. Repoussé Headpiece with Raptor Design, Mississippian. Etowah Indian Mounds State Historic Site Museum, Cartersville, Georgia. Etowah Mounds, Bartow Co., Georgia. Ca. 6" tall.

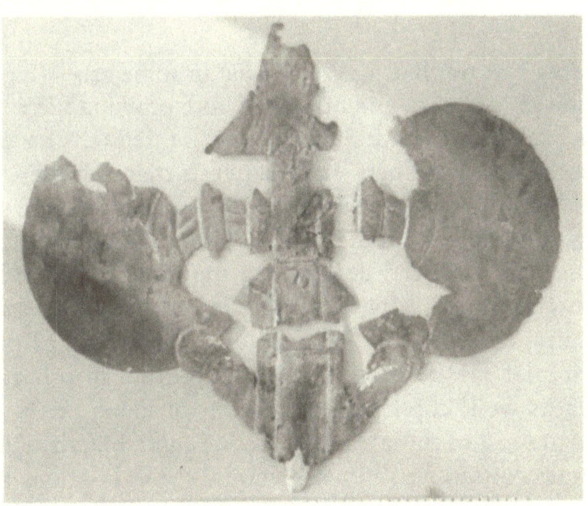

Figure 31. Repoussé Bi-Lobed Arrow Headpiece, Mississippian. Antonio J. Waring, Jr. Archaeological Laboratory, University of West Georgia, Carrollton. Etowah Mounds, Bartow Co., Georgia. Ca. 7" tall.

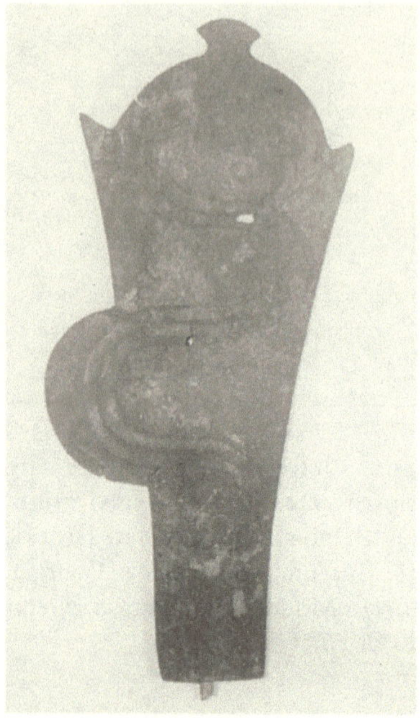

Figure 32. Mace-shaped Repoussé Headpiece, Mississippian. Courtesy, National Museum of the American Indian, Smithsonian Institution, Washington, D.C., #00/7960. Photo by Carmelo Guadagno. Site in Jackson Co., Alabama. Ca. 8" long.

copper probably was not hair at all, at least in some cases (Fig. 34). Several examples made of copper over a hollowed core of wood have been found in burials at the back of the head; they have perforated tabs for attachment to other headdress elements. Their shape suggests that they were not meant to depict hair, either. All are carved into a broad spiraling design with far more in common with snakes or animal horns than with hair.

Circles and circle-related designs are the most common motifs in the Mississippian corpus (e.g., Plates 9 and 10). As was the case in Middle Woodland times, this is partly because of the importance of copper earpieces, but circular motifs become more important in other categories of paraphernalia as well, copper breastplates, for example. Not only is the exterior form of most of these breastplates circular, but virtually all of them also incorporate concentric repoussé designs. Spiral designs are also common. Despite formal variations on the theme, all Mississippian spirals seem to be related symbolically because they occur in many of the same contexts, although the precise nature of that relationship remains obscure (see Appendix, Section II.5.p.).

Early use of spiral designs seems clearly connected to the whorls of the large marine shell (*fulgur* or *busycon perversum*) that figures so importantly in Mississippian art and ritual. Spiraling columella pendants removed from the outer layer of this shell were important aspects of paraphernalia de-

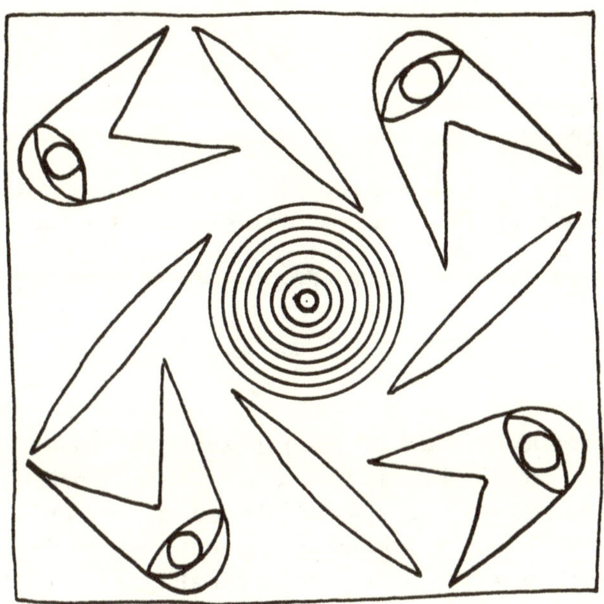

Figure 33. Large Repoussé Headpiece, Mississippian. Mount Royale Site, Putnam Co., Florida. Ca. 11" square. Drawing by A.M. Trevelyan.

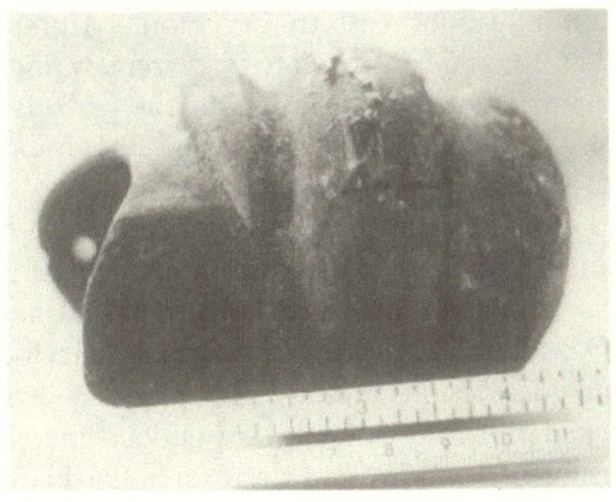

Figure 34. "Occipital Hair Knot" Headpiece (copper/wood), Mississippian. Antonio J. Waring, Jr. Archaeological Laboratory, University of West Georgia, Carrollton. Etowah Mounds, Bartow Co., Georgia. Ca. 4" tall.

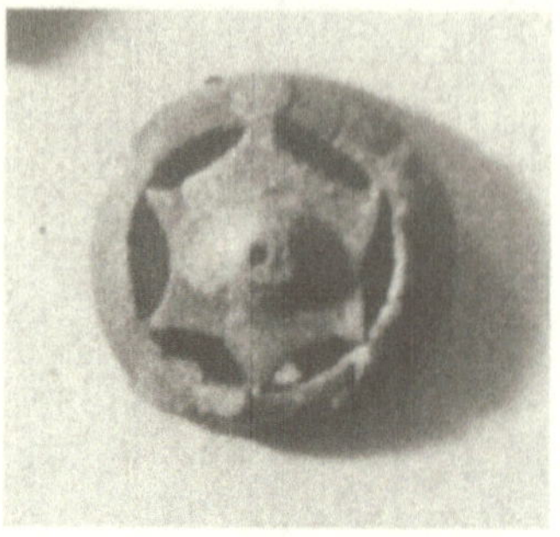

Figure 35. Small Openwork Copper/Wood Earpiece, Mississippian. Courtesy, National Museum of the American Indian, Smithsonian Institution, Washington, D.C., #15/8077. Citico Mound, Chattanooga, Tennessee. Ca. 1 1/2" dia.

picted in both copper and shell (probably the same pieces removed to create elaborately decorated shell cups). In several examples, smaller versions of the shells themselves were reproduced in wood and covered with copper sheet. The spiral form of the "occipital hair knot" may represent a similar but more abstracted version of this kind of spiral.

Mississippians used more sunburst designs in the decoration of copperwork than any other group in the prehistory of the Eastern Woodlands. Usually these designs appear on earpieces done in copper repoussé over stone, wood, and shell (e.g., Fig. 35) (see Appendix, Section II.5.q.). Crosses, almost never seen in Hopewellian copperwork, were a central motif in the design of Mississippian copper material. The cross was among the first of the most common Southeastern Ceremonial Complex designs to appear (Kneberg 1959:13) and continued to be extremely important in ritual art well into the Historic Periods. Throughout the periods of its use, the cross was consistently combined with circles, a fact that indicates an important symbolic relationship between the two forms.[58]

Like circles and crosses, crosses and swastikas seem to have been used quite interchangeably in much of Mississippian art (see Appendix, Section II.5.r.).[59] The form ranges from simple angular designs such as earlier (though very rare) Middle Woodland examples to extremely curvilinear, fluid versions. This range includes designs that are very precisely delineated as well as very subtly arranged motifs in which the swastika is merely suggested by the placement of design elements around a central point (Plate 10, Fig. 33).[60]

Mississippian coppersmiths applied more representational designs to their work than any other group of precontact metallurgists. They were the first to include implement forms within the context of more abstract imagery, although their use of implement-based designs per se is more limited than that of the earlier Eastern Woodlands groups using copper (see Appendix, Section II.5.m.).

The most common identifiable representational motifs found on Mississippian copperwork are bird-related. A few examples recall Middle Woodland bird forms, but most are uniquely Mississippian. Whole birds, their

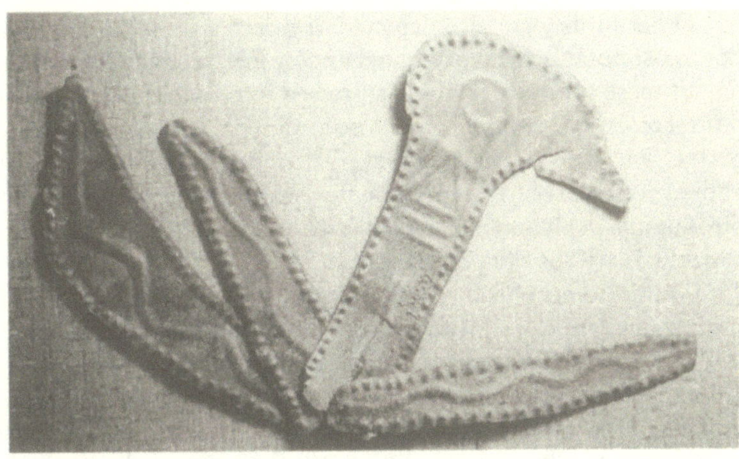

Figure 36. Bird with Punctate Designs, Mississippian. Courtesy, Frank H. McClung Museum, The University of Tennessee, Knoxville, #1599/41. Long Island, Roane Co., Tennessee. Ca. 9" long.

beaks, eyes, claws, feet, and feathers, all appear (see Appendix, Section II.5.I.). The most common references to birds are the feather headdress pieces fashioned out of thin copper sheet as mentioned above. Nearly all are graceful and beautifully stylized shapes. Most appear to be full-sized. Details are skillfully rendered in repoussé.

The species most commonly depicted was long assumed to be an eagle, but carefully rendered naturalistic markings indicate that again it is the peregrine falcon. These pieces are decorated in several regional styles and with varying degrees of skill, but with consistent reference to the specific markings and attributes noted on Hopewellian versions of the same species. Even the crudest example of this genre, a strange little piece from Tennessee, carefully represents the circumocular marking, neck rings, and a rudimentary but obvious attempt to show the scalloped wing markings (Fig. 36).

One of the most prominent designs found on material remains from the Southeastern Ceremonial Complex is the so-called forked or weeping eye design in its several variations. One version of it clearly depicts the natural circumocular marking of the peregrine falcon when at rest, while another version reflects the change in that same configuration when the bird is in flight. These designs are not associated exclusively with recognizable depictions of the peregrine, however. They are also found on human hands, in abstract feather configurations, and as an isolated motif applied to various items of paraphernalia (e.g., Fig. 33).[61]

Other birds were also depicted or referred to in the Mississippian corpus, most notably the ivory-billed and/or pileated woodpecker. The head of one of these spectacular birds is pressed into each quadrant defined by the central cross on a group of otherwise traditional Mississippian circular breastplates. The wooden hafts of several copper axes from Spiro (mentioned above) were carved to represent the head of this same bird. Some of the bird/human depictions suggest that the ivory-billed woodpecker was impersonated as well as the peregrine.

Anthropomorphic bird images, almost as numerous as those that depict birds alone, are closely allied to the latter, but the preponderance of birds, as opposed to bird/human combinations, in the iconographic record suggests that it was the bird and its attributes that were most important symbolically. The human impersonator—which these pieces almost certainly represent—may be said to have constituted a practical necessity for the performance of ritual (see Appendix, Section II.5.1.).

In the earliest examples, what distinguishes the humanized bird imagery from the copper birds (aside from the obvious human attributes) are the carefully detailed items of regalia. These include many important pieces of ritual material: bi-lobed arrow headdresses, "occipital hair knots," earpieces, forelock beads, breastplates, maces, bellows-shaped aprons, etc. Full-size examples of all but the last two of these items were made of copper (as well as some other materials) and have been found in many of the same burials as the repoussé figures. The individuals in those burials were apparently dressed as the copper plates depicted them prior to interment.

There are at least two distinct stylistic approaches to the depiction of humans with bird attributes. Earlier examples are usually in a very active, dancing posture and anatomical details are relatively naturalistic; depictions of paraphernalia are precise and very numerous (e.g., Plates 1 and 13, Figs. 37 and 68).[62] On later pieces the figure is much less animated, few examples of paraphernalia are included, and anatomy is more stylized (Plate 11, Fig. 38).

By the Late Historic Period and perhaps even earlier, references to the eagle begin to replace those to the falcon in much of Southeastern ritual metallurgy. Several traditional depictions of the peregrine in copper appear to have been altered to reflect this change (e.g., Plate 12). The head on these examples is clearly reworked or replaced to conform to clear distinctions between the two species. The smooth head of the peregrine is replaced with the feathered profile of the eagle. In these examples, repoussé details in the reworked area are far cruder than work on the body of the bird—clearly they were executed by a different, less skillful hand.

As the Hopewellian phase waned, so did interest in mammal imagery in copper. Relatively few examples of Mississippian copperwork make any clear reference to mammals. Mammals are only about half as common as

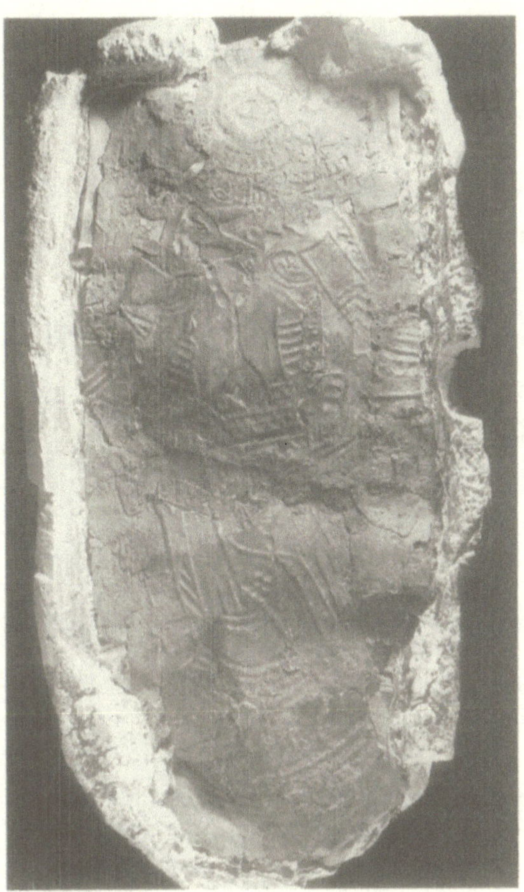

Figure 37. Large Repoussé Plaque, Mississippian. Florida Department of State, Archaeological Collections, Tallahassee, #96.115.35.10. Lake Jackson Site, Florida. Ca. 19" long. Drawing by A.M. Trevelyan.

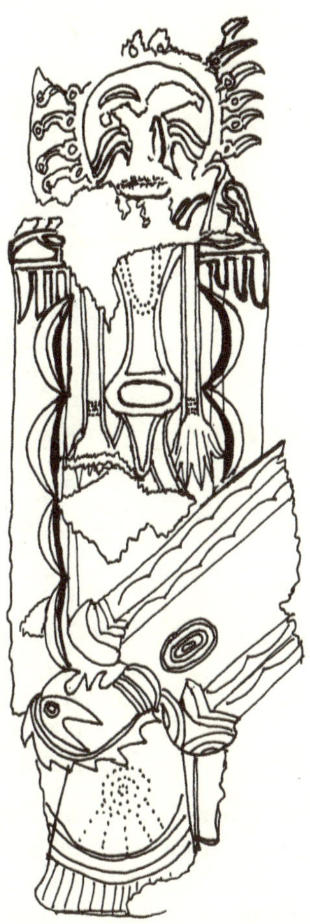

Figure 38. Large Repoussé Plaque, Mississippian. Florida Department of State, Archaeological Collections, Tallahassee, #96.115.85.1. Lake Jackson Site, Florida. Ca. 18" long. Drawing by A.M. Trevelyan.

they were in the Middle Woodland corpus. When mammals do appear, the designs refer to similar aspects of essentially the same species that interested Middle Woodland coppersmiths. That is, the designs refer to the teeth and claws of large carnivores (bears are the most numerous) and to antlered beasts (presumably deer).

Most common are copper teeth, probably replicating those of the black

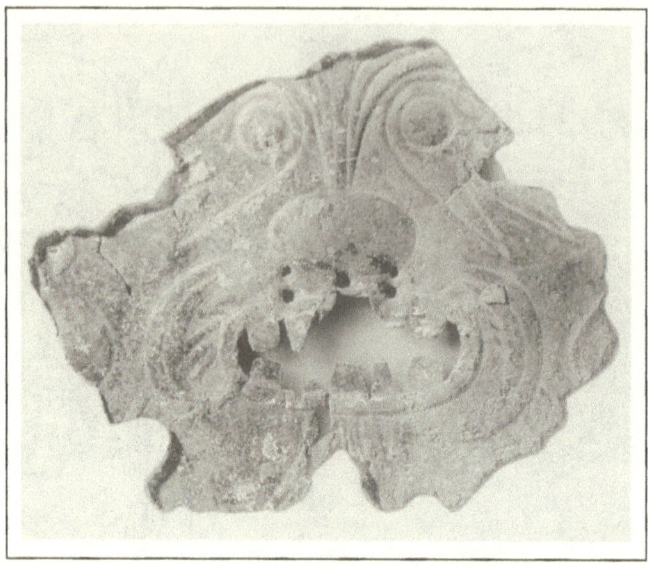

Figure 39. Fragment of a Repoussé Headpiece with Feline Design, Mississippian. Catalogue No. #135227, Department of Anthropology, Smithsonian Institution, Washington, D.C. Hollywood Mound, Richmond Co., Georgia. 5" across.

bear, *ursus americanus* (see Appendix, Section II.5.h.). It is possible that some of the teeth found were intended to represent those of the puma, or perhaps the wolf. Feline subjects are considerably more common in Southeastern copper than they were farther north.[63] The species represented is usually identified as *felis concolor,* the mountain lion. Each of two fragmentary headdresses of copper includes repoussé frontal renderings of a feline head (Fig. 39). The elaboration of the area around the eyes is identical to markings on many birds and animals in Middle Woodland art, as well as to markings on birds and humans depicted in Mississippian copperwork. The consistency with which this kind of elaboration appears, regardless of whether it occurs in nature, probably offers important clues to the symbolic vocabulary of all of the peoples involved in the copper complex. So far they remain indecipherable, however.

As was the case in Middle Woodland times, Mississippian coppersmiths evoked the image of deer almost exclusively through the representation of antlers.[64] Several antlered masks and masquettes, carved of wood and probably covered in sheet copper, have been found at Mississippian burial sites. Most have shell inlays to represent eyes, teeth, and sometimes earpieces. Copper-covered fragments from these sites suggest that there were many more antler sets (either with or without accompanying masks) that have not survived intact.

Other examples of Mississippian copperwork with feline subject matter include mountain lion jaws, cut from the skull and covered with sheet copper. In one case, a pair of corrugated copper ears was found with a similar set of mountain lion jaws, suggesting a sort of mask made of organic materials and elaborated with copper.

Reptiles, fish, and other lower life forms were also depicted in the Mississippian copper corpus. No copper imagery of this genre appears before Middle Woodland times, but the genre continues to be of some importance from that point on. Snakes, particularly rattlesnakes, were the reptile of greatest interest to Mississippian copper artists, although the use of snake motifs is limited and appears rather late.[65]

There are two clear references to snakes in the Mississippian corpus. Most such pieces involve rattlesnake rattles, either of cut sheet copper or carved in wood, and given a copper overlay (Moore 1894–1896:154). The others are thin copper rods bent into a series of serpentine curves and naturalistically tapered at each end. Each rod has a loop at one end to form the snake's head. Mississippian coppersmiths also crafted a few turtles, although they have not always been identified as such.[66] Also in the Mississippian copper corpus are a few copper-covered wooden shells (*busycon perversum*) and one spider (see Addendum, Section II.5.o.).

Copper salts have preserved a few examples of wooden sculpture, including a few small-scale representations of human beings that appear to have been covered originally in thin copper sheet. Some depict a squatting or seated human form. Several others are masquettes ranging from two to seven inches tall, generally too small to be worn as masks, although all are carefully hollowed out as though that was the intent (Fig. 40). The masquettes have shell inlay representing eyes, mouth, teeth, and earpieces in various combinations. A few have antlers, but most have only human attributes. A number of other copper and wood sculptures from Mississippian sites depict human heads and were apparently rattles like those carried by the dancers represented on some copper plates and mentioned above (Fig. 41).[67]

Perhaps the copper complex's most difficult motifs to decipher are the composite symbols apparently directly associated with the specifics of ritual. In many cases these symbols are unique to the period in which they were used and therefore have fewer links to design in other periods. Long and careful analysis of the use of design on copper throughout the millennia spanned by the complex indicates that the ways that Mississippian coppersmiths arrived at their most esoteric symbolic expressions were fundamentally different from approaches used by Middle Woodland coppersmiths. This is hardly surprising since the two cultural phenomena were very differ-

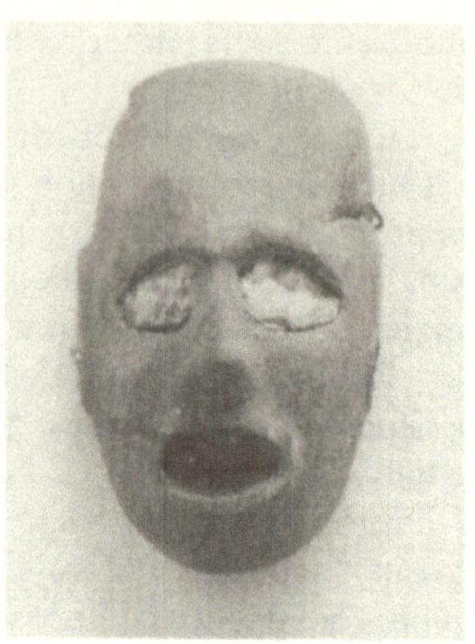

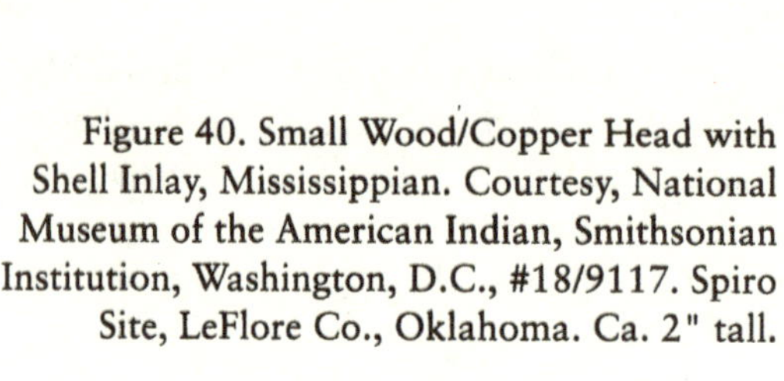

Figure 40. Small Wood/Copper Head with Shell Inlay, Mississippian. Courtesy, National Museum of the American Indian, Smithsonian Institution, Washington, D.C., #18/9117. Spiro Site, LeFlore Co., Oklahoma. Ca. 2" tall.

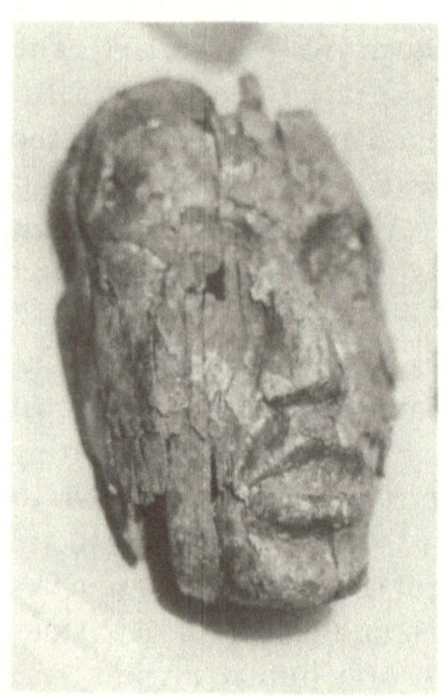

Figure 41. Human Head Rattle (copper/wood), Mississippian. Oklahoma Museum of History, Oklahoma Historical Society, Oklahoma City. Spiro Site, LeFlore Co., Oklahoma. Ca. 4½" tall.

ent and were separated by several centuries. Furthermore, the individuals responsible for the development of the complex symbolism of Hopewellian and Mississippian art almost certainly belonged to different linguistic groups and proceeded from very different conceptual bases, given the apparent and often radical differences in subsistence strategies and social organization. Still, all the pieces involved, whether Middle Woodland or Mississippian, are similar in that particular sets of symbols were in use and were apparently understood, at least in some degree, by cultural units throughout much of eastern North America.[68]

The origins of Mississippian composite symbols were, like Middle Woodland ones, probably based in nature. Unlike Hopewellian examples in which the presence of certain elements, not their order, was crucial; it was the overall shape of the piece that apparently conveyed the principal message in Mississippian composite symbol design. In fact, the overall shape of each item within the three basic types of Mississippian copperwork included in this category is almost always the same, although small details may vary. There seems to have been no mixing of essential elements in various combinations as there was in Hopewellian pieces of this genre. The three types are:

1. small, roughly triangular badges, found grouped in single burials throughout much of the Southeast (e.g., Fig. 22);
2. mace-shaped badges and headdress elements (Figs. 23 and 32);
3. the bi-lobed arrow symbol (Fig. 31).

Pieces of the first type, the triangular badges, are always approximately the same shape and almost always occur in groups. Interior designs vary slightly, however, including many designs of importance in the Mississippian cultural complex as a whole—particularly eye forms and swastikas. Some evidence suggests that this general shape has continued to enjoy a certain amount of popularity and perhaps even ceremonial significance among Southeastern groups in recent times.

The second type, the mace shape, is probably the most straightforwardly representational of these three motifs. Reference is always clear to an important item of regalia that was certainly a weapon or had been used as such at one time.

The third and last design in this category, the bi-lobed arrow, is clearly the most complex. Despite many slight variations, the basic form is always the same. Every bi-lobed arrow is bilaterally symmetrical, with a vertical central element flanked by two essentially crescent-shaped ones. The crescents are usually attached to the axis by two angular lines and the top of the design is usually point-shaped.

The arrival of Europeans brought the fairly quick demise of the copper complex as it had existed in eastern North America for millennia. With very few exceptions, the significance of the material and its central position in elaborate burial ritual seems to have been inalterably changed by the middle of the eighteenth century. That quick demise and its implications for the cultures involved, although imperfectly understood, are crucial to an understanding of the history of cultural interaction in North America. The analysis of material and motif in the following chapters, as well as the details and statistics provided in the appendix offer important insight into these and related issues.

2

Meaning and Significance in Design

Interpretation of the designs and symbols applied to ritual copper seems the most obvious route to understanding the role of this material, but it is hardly the only one. The medium used for the creation of ritual artwork is often as central to an understanding of function and significance as are form and motif. In ceremonial traditions, design and material are frequently interdependent in many other ways as well. Certain materials tend to be used in the creation of particular categories of objects. Likewise, specific shapes and designs tend to be reserved for objects made of particular mediums. This was certainly the case in the Eastern Woodlands prior to the arrival of Europeans. A satisfactory explanation of meaning in the design and function of the ritual copperwork produced in the Eastern Woodlands must reflect this interdependence between design and material.

Important data exist which may be utilized in interpreting symbolism in the range of designs used and the contexts in which the designs appear. Still, the analysis of symbolism in ritual art is always risky. An accurate reading of abstract symbols that are associated with specific ceremonial experiences and are only loosely tied to real world objects is very difficult to construct, even when the objects involved are products of one's own tradition. Problems multiply when the art comes from a non-western culture, especially a non-literate one. Add a prehistoric time frame to that complex of difficulties, and the task is truly daunting.

A fully interdisciplinary approach is another crucial element in the successful analysis of meaning. Because neither documents nor living informants are available, accurate interpretation of significance in the copper corpus requires the meticulous coordination of disparate data sets that include archaeological and ethnographic material as well as facts about the physical properties of the material and its procurement. None of these information categories provides sufficient evidence on its own; only fragmentary evidence is available from any one source. Clear patterns of use and significance begin to emerge only through the synthesis of all these scraps of data. Together they provide a clear picture of the belief structures and motives that supported the ritual use of copper in the prehistory of eastern North America.

The fundamental premise of this study is that discovering the meaning of symbolic and ritual material in prehistoric Native American art is possible, but only in the most general terms. Conventional methodologies of art history and anthropology are not very useful in the analysis of symbolism from such cultures. Traditional art history relies too thoroughly upon text and historical documentation for interpretation, and neither exists for the material in question. Also, the iconographical and iconological methodologies of art history were designed to interpret religious and cosmological structures that simply do not exist in much of Native American tradition. Understanding the nature and magnitude of these problems is essential to appreciating the kinds of symbolic interpretation that *are* possible for this material. Thus, examining traditional approaches to interpretation and the difficulties associated with each will be useful before attempting to analyze the designs themselves.

Scholars have used three basic approaches in their analysis of this material:

1. interpretation of prehistoric designs based on similar motifs used in ceremonial contexts by Historic Period Native Americans;
2. the assignment of meaning based upon beings and incidents that appear in the oral tradition of historic peoples that are from the same or contiguous regions;
3. and interpretation of individual motifs based upon the testimony of native informants.

Interpretation of Prehistoric Designs Based on Similar Motifs Used in Ceremonial Contexts by Historic Period Native Americans

This approach begins with the simple comparison of prehistoric and Historic ritual regalia. Cyrus Thomas (1884) and Charles Willoughby (1897) were among the first to apply this methodology. Both cite correspondences between certain aspects of precontact design and post-contact ritual among peoples that speak Muskogean languages. Henry Hamilton (1974) continues that tradition in his analysis of the material from Spiro. Many subsequent studies also use this approach to some extent.

Virtually all the designs that appear consistently on prehistoric copper are also found on ceremonial paraphernalia used by native North Americans in Historic times. Accordingly, specific meanings based on those Historic counterparts have been proposed for prehistoric designs. This methodology is seriously flawed. The very nature, form, and content of Native American religious beliefs and practices that generated artistic developments like the precontact copper complex tend to invalidate interpretation on this basis. In fact, categorical statements about the meaning of ritual symbols can rarely be considered accurate (except in the most general terms), even when the rituals and objects can be studied firsthand.

In his discussion of the Sun Dance among Plains groups, Spier (1921:503) notes considerable differences among origin myths connected with the ritual, even among groups with almost identical versions of the ceremony. Such important differences certainly resulted in varying interpretations of the symbolism involved although, superficially, both symbol and ritual might appear to be exactly the same. Spier (1921:512–16) also noted that individual initiative as well as problems in obtaining certain items of paraphernalia introduced new symbols and interpretations with almost every performance of the ceremony. These observations led him to conclude that the Sun Dance produced "a greater uniformity throughout the area in the distribution of regalia and behavior than of ideas, organizing and mythological, associated with them."

Other research on Native American religious developments supports this conclusion. Linton's analysis of nativistic/messianic movements (1943:233) points out that the symbols involved are always familiar ones with "new meanings . . . attached." Hittman (1973:249) states that since various tribes participated in such movements for different reasons—social, political, and economic—differing emphasis and interpretation of symbolism was inevitable.

The tremendous problems involved in attempting to assign specific categorical meanings to the symbols used in native North American ritual are also made very clear in Mooney's analysis of the Ghost Dance (1965:19): "each tribe has built a structure from its own mythology, and each apostle and believer has filled in the details according to his own additions as come to him from the trance. Some changes, also, have undoubtedly resulted from the transmission of the doctrine through the imperfect medium of sign language." The Ghost Dance was a unique manifestation in many ways, but so was every major Native American religious movement on record. In other words, individualized structure and personalized interpretation tend to be characteristic of all native North American religious revitalization movements.

In the same passage quoted above, Spier points out that since no difference exists between the character of borrowed or invented traits that are incorporated in the Sun Dance and those that are rejected, it follows that the determinants (and, therefore, the significance of those traits to each of the groups involved) must be sought in the conditions under which incorporation proceeds. That is, the significance of the various symbols and rituals each group may choose to include in any individual performance of the Sun Dance depends very much upon the reasons why that group chose to embrace the tradition in the first place, as well as upon additional motivations for proceeding with each subsequent performance of the ritual. Mooney (1965:19, 173, 201) notes similar patterns of behavior in connection with the Ghost Dance.

Despite these problems, there are clear relationships between these Historic Period ceremonies and prehistoric developments, ones that can offer considerable assistance in the interpretation of the latter. In many instances the Historic ceremonial movements represented an attempt on the part of the native peoples to reintroduce "the old ways." This conscious rejection of recent, detrimental influences was usually associated with the arrival of Europeans. Such conscious attempts to return to the practices of the past, coupled with the demonstrable accuracy of oral traditions among many Native American groups, suggests that the ritual structures developed in conjunction with these movements may well reflect precontact approaches to crisis resolution, despite the extraordinary circumstances that gave rise to those post-contact developments.

Generally, cultural material from the sites of groups utilizing copper in the eastern United States is so diverse as to suggest that the use of symbolism on ritual objects was at least as complex then as it was in the Historic Periods and perhaps even more so. Specific information regarding the reasons why prehistoric groups embraced those rituals and performed given ceremonies is simply not available, although identifying causal factors in general terms, such as major changes in climate, demographics, or technological development, may be possible. However, the sharing of precise interpretation of specific symbols, even among the groups known to have participated in particular religious movements, was unlikely. All the societies involved were non-literate, so specific symbolic information could only be transmitted orally, along with the paraphernalia. The virtual impossibility of sharing precise symbolic concepts under these conditions is particularly clear because these religious developments probably involved at least a few groups who spoke unrelated languages. In short, it is clearly impossible to attach specific meanings to the symbols involved with any presumption of accuracy, beyond the simple identification of clearly representational motifs.

There are other problems involved in the application of Historic Period meaning to precontact symbolism. An important problem peculiar to the copper complex is obvious in most of the ethnographic and historic material that I have examined in connection with this study. That is, many ceremonies and rituals practiced in the eastern United States after European contact were clearly related to precontact ceremonies and rituals. However,

Historic Period Native American ceremonies almost never involve copper. (Important exceptions to this general rule are discussed below.) This fact alone indicates that important changes had occurred in the ceremonies, and presumably in their significance, by the time European observers began to write about them.

Another problem with reliance upon Historic Period Native American belief and practice for the specific interpretation of precontact symbolism is the likelihood that certain practices outlasted their symbolic accoutrements. For example, the recurrent use of turtle imagery in Native American myth, as well as in precontact copperwork (often in the form of rattles), indicates that turtles were important ceremonially and suggests that the turtle shell had some symbolic significance. Howard (1968:90) notes that turtle shell rattles made from the shells of real turtles were considered an important element of the woman's costume at a 1965 performance of the Busk or Green Corn Ceremony by a group of Cherokee, but that those without turtle shell rattles wore condensed milk cans at their ankles. The turtle is particularly important in Cherokee myth, suggesting that the use of turtle shell rattles in crucial rituals like the Green Corn Ceremony originally had special symbolic significance. The substitution of tin cans for shells indicates that by 1965 the symbolic importance of turtle shell rattles had diminished to the point that the specific symbolic form was no longer regarded as essential. Approximation of the trappings of traditional ceremony, with little or no apparent connection to earlier symbolic associations, apparently sufficed.

That this substitution resulted from a shortage of turtles is possible, but regardless of the specific reasons for using cans instead of turtle shells, the symbolic significance of the rattles was clearly in transition. Such transitions probably occurred fairly often in the extremely long, slow development of prehistoric Native American ritual, particularly in view of the ecological changes brought on by migration and climatic shifts. The documentation of this phenomenon historically, again, casts considerable doubt on the validity of attempts to infer the meaning of prehistoric designs on the basis of historic usage.

The Assignment of Meaning Based upon Beings and Incidents that Appear in the Oral Tradition of Historic Peoples that are from the Same or Contiguous Regions

Interpretation of prehistoric designs based on symbolism in Native American myths is no more reliable than is the ethnographic analogy. A major problem with this second method lies in the fact that often a single tribal unit may have two very different myths to account for the same phenomenon. The expression of that phenomenon in artistic terms might well involve a single set of symbols, but the interpretation of each symbol would take on very different meanings, depending upon which myth was referred to (e.g., Swanton 1928a:207). In other instances, the same symbolic creature (a horned serpent, for example) may play completely different roles in the myths of different groups (e.g., Howard 1968:52), or two different symbolic creatures may play essentially the same role (Howard 1968:217). Again, it follows that the corresponding designs might vary considerably, as would an ad hoc interpretation of significance.

In addition, Boas (1940:447; 1928:353) demonstrated long ago that the content of myths and tales among Native Americans "does not by any means represent an old system, but has been assembled from many systems, partly from times gone by, partly quite recently." The tendency in all so-called primitive art, he says, is "to keep the chief cultural interests of the people." This being the case, the interpretation of any designs based on traditional myths is extremely difficult, even with the help of reliable native informants. The human tendency to develop myths and tales, as well as art work, *from* ancient ritual objects and practices themselves (instead of from the persons and circumstances to which the objects and practices originally referred) presents a similar problem, one that is particularly significant in the interpretation of prehistoric symbol systems.

The nature and existence of the biblical Apocrypha and the Golden Legend, as well as their role in Christian art and iconography, illustrate that this tendency is common even among literate peoples. In this case, both the art and the literature were created centuries after the originating events and individuals associated with the ritual had disappeared. These are stories about stories. They are narratives generated from ritual objects, ceremonies, and priestly discourse, *not* references to the historic or ceremonial realities that gave rise to the tradition initially. Most recent scholarship indicates that many of the objects associated with the copper complex were curated for many years and used ritually for numerous generations before being interred in burial mounds. If the specifics of Historic Period myths can ever be plausibly linked to these objects, it is far more likely that the object and related ritual generated those myths, rather than the other way around.

Thus, the recent attempt of Robert Hall to link the Winnebago Red Horn myth cycle to Southeastern Ceremonial Complex iconography, as intriguing as it may be, is extremely problematic. The hundreds of years between the creation of those objects and the twentieth-century myth makes any direct correlation extremely unlikely. If the two are related, it is far more likely that the myth cycle as recorded a few decades ago was constructed around the pictographs in Gottschalk cave (and loosely related ritual) rather than the other way around.

Even the most circumspect researchers frequently cannot resist the temptation to draw such intriguing, albeit highly implausible conclusions, even when their own research casts considerable doubt on those speculations (e.g., Howard 1968:45–47). Howard's suggestion that certain Southeastern Ceremonial Complex depictions from Georgia represent an aspect of an historic "eagle and calumet rite" is another such example. Attempts to associate prehistoric designs with historical mythologies are certainly futile, although not uncommon even among the most respectable scholars (e.g., Waring 1968:43–44).[1]

Interpretation of Individual Motifs Based upon the Testimony of Native Informants

That this basic approach to interpretation of precontact designs is the most obviously problematic is only partly true. The pitfalls of this approach as it is usually implemented were hinted at by Holmes (1906) in his study of the cross as a symbol. Data obtained by this most often utilized approach may be reliable only if the information is applied solely to designs in current use by the informant's own tribe. Unfortunately, the tendency has been to assume that the interpretations given by native informants were universal, and they were subsequently extended to similar configurations that were remote in time, distant in space, and without demonstrable ethnographical linkage.[2]

The justification for this methodology was based upon the assumption that the symbols involved were abstractions from nature. Scholars apparently reasoned that since natural forms visible to precontact Native Americans were essentially the same as those visible to their late nineteenth- and early-twentieth-century counterparts, the significance of symbols derived from those forms would be the same for both. This assumption has two major fallacies.

To begin with, symbols derived from natural forms will not necessarily be interpreted in the same way, even by contemporaries, much less by individuals from societies that flourished centuries apart. The cross as a symbol is a good case in point. Both the well-known Christian symbol and the similar one used to mark intersecting roads were derived from physical configurations. Yet, interpretation of the symbol by contemporaries today might differ as much as would interpretation by two individuals in Roman society living at the time of Christ. Clearly, the significance attributed to that symbol by an individual from each era would differ radically.

Even the premise that native North American symbols are derived from visual reality is faulty, according to Boas (1928:123, 128). "Sameness of form and . . . difference of meaning (on the part of native informants) are not due to a geometricization of realistic forms but to a reading of significance into old conventional patterns." In fact, "the form is constant, the interpretation variable, not only tribally, but individually."

Another problem with this approach to the interpretation of symbolism stems from linguistic differences between researcher and informant. Arguments about the identity of some bird motifs in Plains art provide a good example of the difficulties that can occur. Scholars often disagree as to whether certain abstract designs in Plains art represent the eagle or the hawk. The fact that many Plains peoples make no linguistic distinction between these two species indicates the question itself may be something less than significant to an understanding of the designs under analysis (Mooney 1965:185).

Similar basic differences between Native American systems of classification and the classification methods of modern scholarship are also apparent in Walker's discussion of Oglala Sioux metaphysics. In that worldview virtually all forms in nature (with the exception of the irregular forms of stones) are classified as circles or are at least believed to be vitally linked to other forms which are circular (1975:216). In that system, no distinction is made between "perfect circles and ovals, ellipses or even irregular but basically circular forms," suggesting perhaps that classification has more to do with what the form *does* (process) than what it looks like.[3]

In his discussion of the cross motif, Boas (1940:556–58) pointed out another facet of the problem of symbolic interpretation that all three of the traditional methods of analysis discussed above always ignore. Boas asserts that accurate interpretation of meaning in native North American designs is possible (but not automatic) only with the assistance of numerous qualified native informants, resources that are obviously not available to scholars examining designs on prehistoric material.

On the other hand, the longevity of linguistic patterns and the kinds of cultural and conceptual connections that are apparent in linguistic structure are invaluable in the interpretation of this material, such as in the instance just referred to above, regarding linguistic distinctions—or the lack thereof—between raptor types on the Plains. The importance of understanding such structures makes the participation of native informants and that kind of linguistic data essential to accurate assessment of symbolism, particularly if the individuals involved are from groups with demonstrable historic or ritual links to the material in question. Even if such links cannot be established, collaboration with contemporary native peoples also provides the non-native scholar with important data on epistemological and ontological structures that obtain throughout North America and that are often poorly developed in the academic literature, if indeed they are discussed at all. This kind of generalized information is crucial to the development of a viable methodology for the identification and classification of both object and symbol in historic contexts as well as in precontact ones.

Some investigators have tried to define meaning in Native American design according to yet other perspectives. In a few instances, symbolism in native North American art has been subjected to Freudian analysis (e.g., Anderson 1979). This approach does not seem to be any more valid than those mentioned so far. Results show that Freudian definitions of symbolic meaning for motifs used by historic Native Americans coincide with the opinions of native informants only about half the time (Anderson 1979:72). This suggests that the application of Freudian analysis to precontact motifs would not produce persuasive results.

The Need to Include a Broader Range of Data in the Analysis of Ancient Artwork

Not only do the methods discussed so far (with the exceptions noted) utilize faulty premises and inaccurate (or at least incomplete) information in their analysis of prehistoric design, they invariably raise questions of scope. All three approaches discussed above rely almost exclusively upon the external form of objects and symbols in their interpretation of significance. A convincing methodology may begin with the visual material but must continue to examine techniques of manufacture as well as basic subject matter. Likely sources for the raw material used must be located. The site of discovery of each piece must be considered, as well as available data regarding its specific disposition within the site. The relative numbers of each type of object found should be calculated, and the distributive and ceremonial relationships of the various types to one another must be examined.

In addition, great care must be taken to avoid making assumptions based upon the cultural biases of the investigator or the investigator's audience. Labels and descriptive terms are fraught with the considerable "ceremonial and ritual" implication of our own culture. Terms such as "God," "Deity," "idol," "effigy," "ornament," "prestige," "valuable," "utilitarian," "religious," "pragmatic," etc., should be used only with great care or avoided altogether. Another important consideration, often ignored in the interpretation of symbolism in Native American art, is the fact that the significance and meaning of symbols used in similar contexts were almost certainly interrelated. The relationships between motifs must be examined with as much care as the individual designs.[4]

Analysis of the visual material must focus on the details of representation and design and on the specific attributes given the subject. Edmund Leach (1973:223) emphasized this crucial requirement since "those messages which are quite specific to particular cultures . . . cannot be transmitted cross-culturally, but . . . messages that refer to some attribute or part of the human animal [or, presumably, other animals] as such are not culture bound." Each motif and its particular attributes must also be analyzed within the context of the typical art style and known cultural idiosyncracies of the group that produced it. Plausible conclusions are possible only if it is clear that the analysis cuts across cultural and tribal boundaries as well as temporal ones and is based on demonstrably valid generalizations, rather than on isolated details. Boas (1940:209, 449–50) has suggested that this kind of analysis is essential to the study of Native American myth.

Still, even if the data utilized are accurate, interpretation of even the most obvious representational motifs in Native American art presents the scholar with a difficult dilemma. On one hand, according to Native American worldviews, many animals and birds depicted in art were subject to radical and sudden changes of form under certain circumstances. A bear encountered in the forest, for example, might actually be a human sorcerer (e.g., Hallowell 1975:158–64). This is particularly true of creatures important in myth and ritual. Again, a direct relationship between a given form and its meaning in Native American ritual art can rarely, if ever, be assumed. To further complicate the matter, both linguistic and ethnographic evidence suggest that to many Native Americans, art forms and symbols are themselves living entities, with a life and identity that are related to, but not necessarily dependent upon, that which they represent.

Iroquois False Face masks, for example, usually represent one of two types of entities, the "humpbacked one" or one of the so-called "common" faces (Furst and Furst 1982:208–9). Specific sets of facial traits are associated with each. In general spiritual terms, the more powerful masks depict the "humpback" because that being is considered to be the more powerful. However, a newer "humpback" mask, without a history of successful ritual activity, may be used and regarded as a "common" face (despite its formal depiction of the facial characteristics of the "humpback") until its spiritual capacity and identity have been demonstrated in practical terms. On the other hand, a mask depicting one of the "common" faces but successfully utilized in several curing ceremonies may eventually be used and referred to as a "humpback" mask. These two aspects of Native American belief systems—the potential for metamorphosis and ambivalent form that is inconsistent with specific identification—obviously affect the relationship between symbolic form and meaning in Native American art. They are problems that rarely obtain in the study of iconographically more rigid "western" artistic traditions. Nevertheless, an appreciation of these two crucial problems in the interpretation of symbol in Native American art is central to achieving accurate results.

The importance of metamorphosis and transformation in so much of Native American ontology determines the framework within which every motif must be considered. Metamorphosis or transformation was accomplished at will by many animals and humans. Reference to any collection of or commentary upon Native American tales and myths will confirm the frequency and relative ease with which transformation from one form to another was thought to be accomplished. Metamorphosis is frequently reported in the lives and visions of Native Americans.[5] Indeed, one suspects that for most (if not all) traditional Native Americans, "outward appearance is only an incidental attribute of being"—as Hallowell (1975:159) has commented with regard to the thunderbird of Ojibwa tales.

This constant potential for change in physical form is also apparent in the languages of some Native American groups. The Wintu, for example, never speak of a "deer" or a "bear," but rather to the generic deerness or bearness of something. Such a practice implies the less than static entity of such beings (Lee 1960:15).

Clearly, the potential for changing form at will, without altering identity, presents a problem in the specific identification of meaning in representational motifs. Other factors compound the problem. Not only is transformation believed to be possible and frequent, but the individual transformed (a shaman assuming the "soul" of a bear, for example) may retain his human shape in one location while his "soul" wanders about elsewhere looking like a bear (Hallowell 1975:160–62). While the specifics of these examples may or may not have applied in prehistoric times, perceptions of reality that conform to such a model are sufficiently consistent in the ethnographic literature to suggest that prehistoric Native American ontological structures provided for similar phenomena.

To create an accurate visual expression of the bear shaman and his "soul" would present any artist with a tremendous conceptual challenge. The challenge to the art historian, however, is even greater. What would seem to be a clearly recognizable creature or individual to the modern observer may have represented something quite different to those whose perception of reality conforms to Native American tradition. Its significance to those privy to the esoteric dimension of the experience involved may have been different still.

Traditional Euro-American folklore provides an apt illustration of the way misconceptions regarding symbolic meaning might be spawned under these circumstances. Imagine some future scholars studying our culture, unfamiliar with the climax of a well-known fairy tale. They might well assume that a picture of a pretty girl kissing a frog depicts a strange frog-kissing ritual or, at the very least, an individual with a curious affinity for frogs—entirely missing the point regarding who and what the frog really is and why the girl is kissing it.

To propose that the pervasive interest in metamorphosis in much of native tradition may account, in part at least, for the composite imagery found in precontact art seems reasonable. This pervasive interest may also help to explain why Waring and Holder (1945:4) found that very different motifs, such as the eye and encircled cross that was used in the art of the Southeastern Ceremonial Complex, appeared interchangeably in certain contexts.

Levine (1957:960) discusses the other horn of the dilemma faced by scholars attempting to interpret native North American design. He asserts that among hunting and gathering peoples, a work of art frequently *is* the thing that it represents. That is, the kinds of distinctions made by members of industrialized societies between an object or a being and a depiction of that object or being were apparently not as clear among hunting and gathering peoples, if, indeed, those distinctions were made at all.

For the Algonkian, this kind of reasoning also applies to myths. Tales about sacred beings are themselves thought of as beings (Hallowell 1975:151). They live. In industrialized societies, the making of art is usually thought of in terms of additive and/or reductive processes that involve inanimate or, at least, unconscious matter. In a few cases, the process may include living entities (as in "happenings," film, video, and other newer art forms), and concepts such as "creation" and even "revelation" may be involved. Still, endowment or transference of animate being from artist to object is rarely, if ever, a factor.

On the other hand, if Levine is correct (and it appears that he is) for artists in hunting and gathering societies (and probably for other tribally organized peoples), the process by which myths as well as visual art forms were produced apparently includes aspects of animation—the formation of living entities—as well as of construction and representation. Rothenberg (1985:543, 563) cites a number of examples that lend support to this proposition.

Examination of Native American linguistic patterns and usages often helps to resolve these important conceptual differences between industrialized peoples and their tribally organized contemporaries. Certain verb forms in the language of the Wintu, for example, support what Levine has suggested about the nature of art objects among hunting and gathering peoples. In Wintu the word applied to the process of manufacture actually means to "transform" or "turn into" (Lee 1960:189). In this instance at least, the very act of making something from a raw material involves much more than simple construction or representation. It is transformation from one type of reality to another. The same sort of process is apparent in Choctaw words for "make," "transform," and "create" (Byington 1915).

Given this complex of difficulties, unless all available evidence regarding the use and construction of precontact artwork is examined and essential differences between the perceptual system of a subject culture and that of the investigator are carefully considered, attempts to accurately interpret motifs must fail. Even then, although significant interpretations may be achieved, often the cultural perceptions of subject and investigator are so alien to each other that the real impact various works had upon the peoples of the producing culture may never be appreciated.

Despite the problems and pitfalls of symbolic interpretation, much can be learned about meaning and significance in the designs on prehistoric copperwork. Research in the last four decades suggests that there are aspects of so-called "primitive art" in general and Native North American art in particular, that seem to be more or less constant (e.g., Pasztory 1982:7). Many characteristics of the copper complex reinforce those suggestions. Firth (1966:28) states that the abstracting process of the "primitive" artist is based upon selection and representation of those elements that best define the relationship of the subject, not to naturalistic space or visual reality, but to "the rest of a social structure." Levine (1957:960) draws similar conclusions in his analysis of the abstracting process. He states that "the selection reflected in the subject matter, depictive treatment, and compositional arrangement of the art is the clue to the selection which characterized the outlook of the ancient people." Such social structures, including social organization, must be understood as encompassing, and perhaps even as being based upon, each culture's deeply held ontological and cosmological convictions, convictions that are subject to only the most gradual and barely perceptible changes.

The most commonly recurring subjects chosen by precontact coppersmiths were almost always accorded important and usually interrelated cosmological significance in Historic times. Their cosmological grounding as well as their repeated use in ritual across millennia also indicate a relationship to aspects of individual and group survival that was the focus of attention for most so-called "primitive" artists. Artistic reference to such concerns is usually expressed in terms of subsistence needs, reproduction, and the society's dominance of or submission to other groups (Anderson 1979:196). Although the level of importance accorded these areas of interest remains consistently high in non-industrialized societies, the various ways that a crisis might arise within any of them varies. The kinds of challenges faced also vary, and vary widely.

Among Native Americans, the method for defining and implementing strategies to deal with crisis in the areas Anderson mentions was usually the dream or vision, a tradition grounded in the shamanic origins of virtually all Native North American religion.[6] Although those dreams and visions resulted in response to crises that were generally unique and thoroughly individualized, they also mirrored traditional and very ancient cultural values and patterns. As Boas (1928:157) has stated, in Native American ritual art "novelty consists generally in the combination of old pattern elements in new ways," usually through the medium of dreams or visions. This phenomenon accounts in large part for the persistence of certain aspects of Native American culture and tradition, even in the face of the enormous pressures of acculturation after the arrival of Europeans.

Consistency in motif and general artistic approach in the ritual art of practically all phases of the copper complex is remarkable. This pattern of consistency most likely proceeds from the nature of traditional Native American religion, which was based on and deviated only superficially from its roots in Archaic shamanic practices. The outward forms evolved and continue to evolve with relative rapidity; language changed, as did social and political organization. Even specific cosmological ideas may have shifted. The basic ontology, however, rooted in Archaic shamanism, seems to have undergone very little alteration. The symbols and, in a few cases, the beings associated with that ontology seem to have remained remarkably constant.

Furthermore, the remarkable consistency with which a certain few motifs are used in specific contexts throughout the thousands of years spanned by the copper complex is not unique. Such regularities and correspondences are to be found in many of the same combinations, and with what appears to be closely related significance, throughout the cultures of the Americas. Some reasonable explanation must exist for this consistency beyond the suggestions that these ideas diffused inch by inch across two continents or were carried directly to the hundreds of groups involved by the migration of a few artistically rich societies to their culturally impoverished neighbors. The explanation probably lies instead in that ancient and remarkably durable Native American ontology, one shared by cultures that were otherwise strikingly distinct. This is not to say that the symbols involved express very specific or easily definable concepts. Rather, they seem to provide links to basic forces and feelings, known from experience to exist but so basic to the process of daily life as to be difficult to identify, much less define.

Once again, the designs applied to precontact copperwork fall roughly into three categories. They are defined according to their appearance and to their generalized significance (the categories also correspond roughly to the distinct kinds of "signs" discussed by Richard Anderson[7]):

1. power symbols—abstract shapes; simple, essentially geometric forms with little or no obvious correlation to specific objects in the natural world;
2. representational forms—shapes that bear a clear resemblance to objects and beings from the natural world and that are often strongly conventionalized;
3. cult signs—complex, composite designs combining geometric

shapes with others that are apparently representational, although highly stylized.

Power Symbols

A fairly limited range of simple geometric motifs are designated "power symbols" for reasons discussed below. These designs are found on ceremonial material in use throughout the copper complex, as well as in the ceremonial arts of most Historic Native North American groups. As has been pointed out above, the fact that they were in such general use does not indicate that their specific significance was everywhere the same. In fact, definitions of meaning among Native American informants are rarely precisely alike. Still, as noted above, some aspects of meaning were shared, if only in very general terms.

Circles are the most common of the "power symbols" found in the copper complex. Circular designs were also of paramount importance in Early Historic times, particularly in metalwork.[8] Quimby (1966:9) notes that European metalsmiths, copying native gorget forms, manufactured circular silver gorgets specifically for trade with native peoples in the Great Lakes area and that these silver pieces were worn only by Native Americans. Farther south, circular copper plates were important elements in the annual Busk ceremonies of Tuchabachee, a Creek town (Pickett 1851:82). The symbolic importance of circles and their use as religious motifs continued even after the disappearance of copper as an integral element in ritual—in the Sun Dance and later in the Ghost Dance of Plains groups, as well as in Creek Busk ceremonies and in the Peyote ritual of present-day Native American religion.[9]

As implied in the earlier discussion of these designs, the circle is, in many ways, the most basic geometric shape. It holds this same position within the symbolic system of the Historic Period, representing generalized aspects of power and natural order. Circles are associated specifically with the cosmos, the sun, the sky and horizon, earth's boundaries, and sometimes water. Similar connections are noted by early commentators as well.[10]

The most succinct and probably the most generally accurate discussion of the significance of circular motifs and their implications in Native American ceremony and art was compiled by Clifford Geertz (1973:128) from data received from an Oglala Sioux informant. The circle, he says, is:

> a symbol whose meaning is intuitively sensed, not consciously interpreted. . . . But the power of the symbol, analyzed or not, really rests on its comprehensiveness, on its fruitfulness in ordering experience. Again and again the idea of a sacred circle, a natural form with a moral import, yields, when applied to the

> world within which the Oglala lives, new meanings; continually it connects together elements within their experience which would otherwise seem wholly disparate, incomprehensible. . . . The common roundness of a human body and plant stem, of a moon and a shield, a "tipi" and a camp circle give them this meaningful common element which, once extracted, can then be employed for ritual purposes.

It is significant that a part of the overall sense of the circle's significance rests on its relationship to things round. This is particularly true with regard to the apparent roundness of celestial bodies, the "dome" of the sky, and the circumferential appearance of the horizon. Nevertheless, it is not a descriptive form per se. This summary of associations with the circle as a symbol probably indicates the basic conceptual framework of most Native American groups. This kind of generalized but deeply significant set of basic meanings seems to be associated with most of the motifs commonly found on copperwork.

Like circular designs, crescentic ones continued to be of considerable importance in post-contact times. In fact, the reason that there are so few Post-Mississippian crescents in native copper probably lies in the fact that generous supplies of European metallic crescents were traded to native peoples in Early Historic times. Because the crescents were made of "trade" metal, not native copper, they have not been included in this study, however. Many scholars have noted instances of crescents in both copper and silver worn by members of Early Historic Period groups.[11] It is interesting that most of these were worn as breastplates, just as they apparently were in much earlier times.

Even after the disappearance of copper and other metals as central elements in Native American ritual, the crescent form has continued to play an important ceremonial role. Crescents were one of the most frequently used motifs in the tattooing of Historic Southeastern peoples (Swanton 1946:533). Among some Plains groups the altar within the Sun Dance Lodge was always crescentic (Spier 1921:471). In the rituals connected with the Peyote ceremony, still an integral part of worship in the Native American Church, use of a crescent-shaped altar is typical (La Barre 1938:7, 43, 46–47).

In Historic times, crescent and circle symbols were closely associated. Together, they were the shapes most often used by European and native craftsmen in the manufacture of silver breastplates for native use (Quimby 1966:9, 92). The two symbols are also linked in more recent ceremony. In the standard early Peyote ritual, the basic structures for its performance were the crescent altar mentioned above and a circular tipi (La Barre 1938:7) in which the altar was located.

Another crescent-like form important in the arts of Historic Native

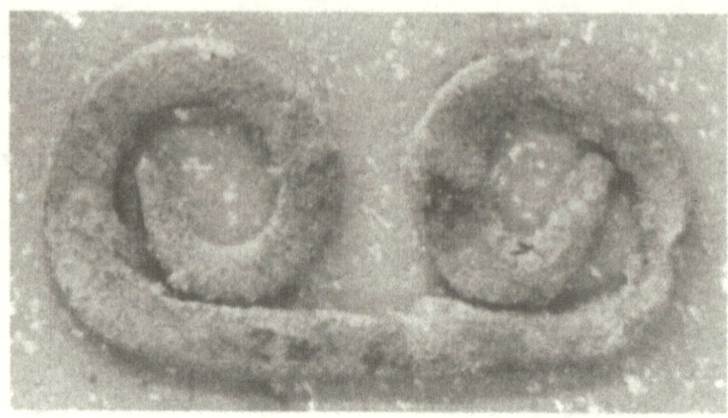

Figure 42. Hammered Copper Wire Double Spiral, Late Archaic. William S. Webb Museum of Anthropology, University of Kentucky, Lexington. Indian Knoll Site, Ohio Co., Kentucky. Ca. 1 3/4" long.

American groups, particularly in the Northeast, is the pervasive double curve. For the Iroquois, the double curve refers primarily to "celestial, geographical, and mythical phenomena," involving the "sky dome, world tree, scroll or helix, chief's horns and sun" (Speck 1914:8). For the Penobscot, the same motif also has a vaguely political significance, and in certain more complex arrangements on ceremonial clothing, may refer to "bonds of alliance in a general way," as well as in more specific terms (Speck 1914:4–5).

The importance of political implications in the range of meanings identified in these forms is significant. It suggests that political arrangements, from local leadership to intertribal treaties, were perceived as outgrowths of the natural order of things. Machiavellian pragmatism and other traditional "western" political concepts were probably entirely alien to Native American perceptions in this area, and as a result, their histories were very different.

The range of meanings associated with the double curve is closely related to many of the meanings for the circle and crescent. Double curve arrangements in Historic Native American art are also often reminiscent of both Archaic and Middle Woodland designs that incorporate spirals. This connection was noted as well by Quimby (see Figs. 10, 42, and 53 and Plates 3, 4–7, and 14).[12]

Star or sunburst motifs were also important symbolic designs in both precontact and Historic Native American art. The Jesuit priest Radisson noted that the ceremonial dress of certain Siouan groups in the Upper Peninsula of what is now Michigan, included earpieces in a star shape (Griffin 1961:38). Swanton (1946:497) says that "stars" were also a favorite design in the formal vocabulary of Historic Yuchi silversmiths and suggests that

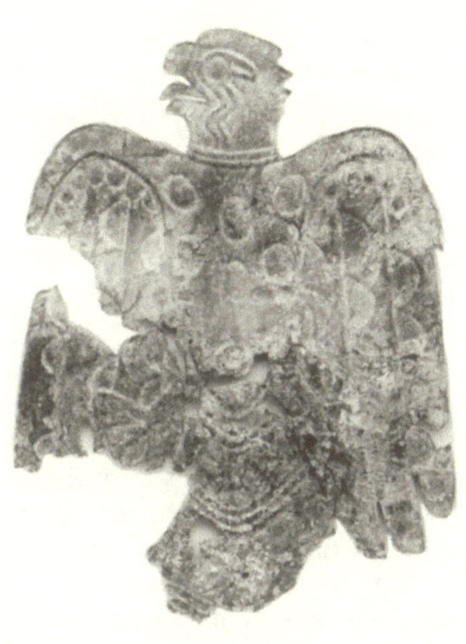

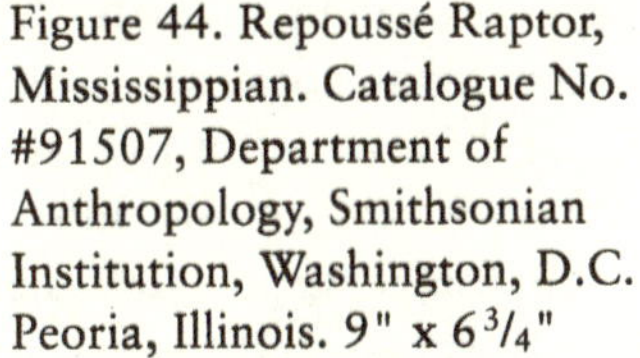

Figure 44. Repoussé Raptor, Mississippian. Catalogue No. #91507, Department of Anthropology, Smithsonian Institution, Washington, D.C. Peoria, Illinois. 9" x $6^{3}/_{4}$"

Figure 45. Elongated Copper Bird, Post-Mississippian Headpiece. Courtesy, National Museum of the American Indian, Smithsonian Institution, Washington, D.C., #17/214. Rose Mound, Cross Co., Arkansas. Ca. 1' 4" long.

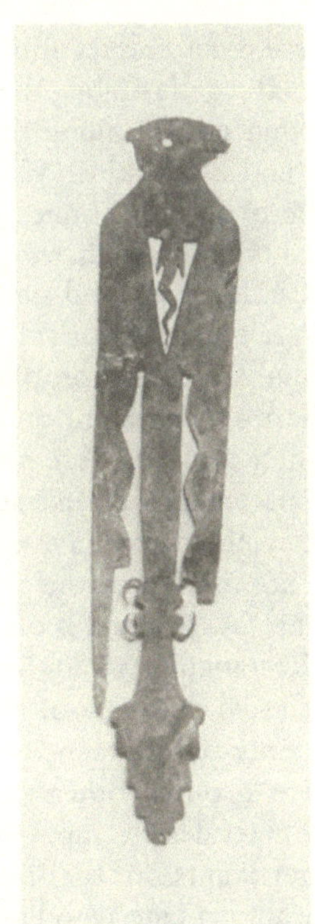

eastern native informants. They identified it most often as emblematic of the "Native religious system." Whatever the specific definition, cruciform symbolism (encircled or standing alone) is apparently always associated with the powerful ordering and organizational elements of the universe.

The longstanding significance of the cross motif in native North American ceremony, particularly in the Southeast, was probably a factor in the initially friendly reception accorded de Soto and other cross bearing European visitors. Crosses appear again and again on important ritual objects found with the remains of precontact Native American cultures. To Native Americans, the symbol clearly referred to important sources of power with both religious and political implications, just as the circle and crescent did. As a whole, these facts suggest that the multitude of European copper and silver crucifixes found in Early Historic Native American burials throughout the eastern United States is probably less an indication of the proselytizing abilities of the Europeans than it is a testimony to the persistence of native modes of thought and ritual—European intervention notwithstanding.

In formal terms, the encircled cross is also closely allied to the swastika. Like the cross and the circle, the swastika is frequently associated with the wind in Historic Native American symbolism.[14] From contact times until the late nineteenth century, swastikas were worn on certain important ceremonial regalia among the Sac, but an observer noted that the tradition was breaking down among the young who wore them for "luck" along with bear and otter skins (Wilson 1894:895). It is significant that despite the fading of specific connections with the form it continued to be associated with a type of beneficent power.

Circle, cross, and swastika motifs all seem to share a similar range of associations in historical Native American tradition. In Southeastern Ceremonial Complex paraphernalia, the circle, cross, and swastika also seem to share similar significance. That Waring and Holder (1945:4) found that the three symbols were used essentially interchangeably "on otherwise rigidly specialized objects" suggests once again that the general significance of these symbols may have persisted into contact and later Historic times. This does not imply that the specific meaning was identical, however, and keeping this fact in mind is crucial.

Rectangular symbolism in ethnological and historical literature is discussed less than any of the other motifs found in the copper complex. In fact, only one reference to the use of rectangular motifs, among historic eastern groups (other than Plains cultures) and in contexts similar to precontact designs, appeared in the literature examined (Painter 1971:84). Painter points out that rectangular symbolism was of considerable importance among Late Woodland peoples in the central Atlantic states—on smoking paraphernalia and ceramic work (including square breastplates)—but apparently not on metalwork. Painter offers no suggestions regarding the significance of these designs, however. This dearth of reference to use of rectangular motifs in the early contact periods coincides with the clear tendency away from the use of such designs apparent in the copper complex from early Mississippian times. Nor do rectangular symbols seem to have played any significant role in important post-contact revitalization movements.

With the exception of the examples mentioned in Painter, rectangular symbolism used in Historic times tends to be applied more to elements of architecture and village structure than to small items of paraphernalia. Nevertheless, all examples of rectangular symbolism from Historic times in eastern North America (discovered in the course of research for this study) were associated with the same kinds of concepts and ideas as were tied to circle and crescent motifs. For example, the "square ground" of the Creek, Seminole, Yuchi, and Cherokee is the ceremonial center of the village where the annual sacred fire (associated with the sun and constructed with four logs oriented to the four cardinal points) is kindled. Howard (1968:19) points out that this rectangular area is itself sometimes referred to as a "fire." In the Eastern Woodlands the same "square ground" where the Busk or Green Corn ceremony is celebrated is considered a "world symbol," as well as a reference to "the rainbow" (Witthoft 1949:69).

The statistical relationship between circle-related forms and rectangular forms within the copper complex reveals some intriguing trends, particularly when the relationship is examined in conjunction with the use of rectangular symbolism in Historic times. Three important aspects of the history of the copper complex have been noted in the preceding chapters. All three aspects developed at about the same rate. They are:

1. a clear shift from an obvious preference for rectangular designs in copperwork during early periods through Middle Woodland times, to a predilection for circular forms during the Mississippian Periods;
2. a parallel shift in representational subject matter from mammalian to avian;
3. and a gradual change in the kinds of objects made from copper. A heavy preponderance of implement forms gives way to more complex designs and representational motifs until full-scale implement forms are relatively rare, although they continue to appear as miniaturized weaponry or as designs on pieces devoted primarily to other subject matter.

These three developments coincide with the gradual change from hunting and gathering economies to the practice of intensive agriculture (discussed in detail below). It is tempting to believe that all three developments

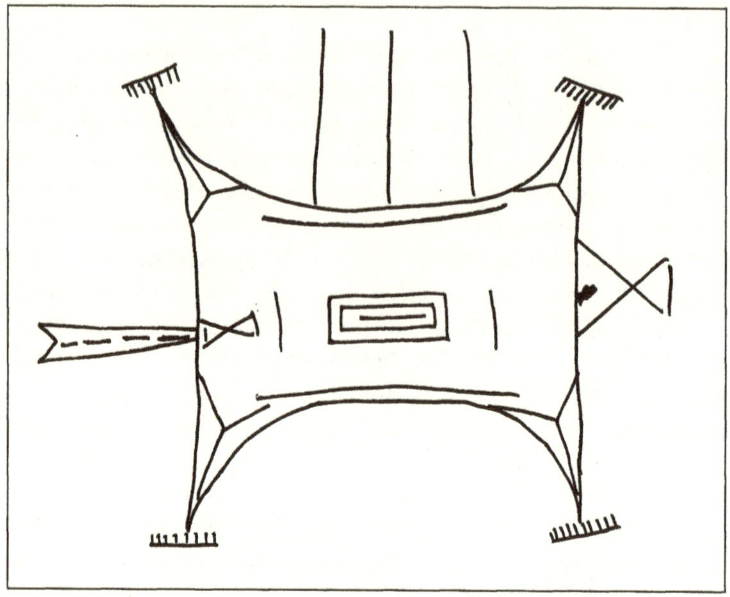

Figure 43. Buffalo Symbol, Plains Area, Historic Period. Drawing by A.M. Trevelyan (after Boas 1928, p. 119).

are directly related to this fundamental change in subsistence modes. If so, the symbolic associations of the rectangular symbolism of the "square ground" among Historic eastern groups may represent a survival of very old hunting symbolism that was respected as a crucial element of village structure but that was no longer a factor in living ceremonial tradition. That is, the symbolic associations may have no longer applied to individual items of ritual paraphernalia. The rectangular format of various long house ceremonies among Iroquoian groups may involve a similar survival.

In eastern North America, the only Historic native art tradition in which rectangular and other quadrilateral forms were in common use was that of the Plains groups (e.g., Fig. 43). This is particularly interesting since many of the eastern Plains groups that had been agriculturalists returned to a hunting and gathering economy and lifestyle (Haberland 1964:148).

In the previously cited historic and ethnographic literature, the range of meanings for the geometric designs used most often on copper suggests that all the meanings refer in some way to the elementary powers and ordering influences in the universe—those powers and influences that were believed to have formed and governed existence for native North Americans; hence the designation "power symbols." The same sources of power appear to have been appealed to regardless of the nature of the problems faced by the native groups. Rituals based upon distinctly different visions and in response to a wide range of difficulties involved paraphernalia decorated with many of the same symbols. Thus, the formal qualities of the symbols used to represent these sources of power changed much more gradually than their specific interpretations or associations.

Representational Forms

Like the power symbols just considered, most of the representational motifs on prehistoric Native American copperwork also continued to be important in ceremonial art through the time of European contact and, in some cases, continue in use today. These representational designs symbolized ideas and perceptions similar to those just discussed. Most refer to generalized concepts, connected particularly with the "natural order of things" and the powers and influences that preserve and/or disrupt that order.

Bird forms, particularly raptors like eagles and hawks, were important subjects for coppersmiths as early as Middle Woodland times and possibly even earlier. They are very common in Mississippian copperwork as well. The species depicted most consistently is the peregrine falcon or duck hawk.

Two factors suggest that the use of peregrine depictions on Mississippian copper material could have been a carryover from the Woodland tradition. First, it is clear that some Middle Woodland copper bird representations depict the peregrine, although they are extremely rare. The essential anatomy, eye, and feather markings are almost identical to Mississippian examples (Plates 1, 11, 12, and 15 and Fig. 44). Furthermore, Mississippian bird/human depictions on copper, incorporating these specific details of avian anatomy, are some of the earliest motifs associated with the Southeastern Ceremonial Complex.

Other birds are also depicted in the arts of both Middle Woodland and Mississippian peoples. The pileated woodpecker was one of the most important. Woodpecker depictions (usually limited to references to portions of the bird's anatomy) are often found in Mississippian copperwork. Moore (1907:400–401) concluded that many of the small triangular pieces, usually found in groups, probably represent the prominent and highly prized beak of that bird. He excavated many of these and assumed at first (as did many others) that they represented arrow points. Later, on the basis of their shape and the frequent inclusion of an eye motif on each piece, he revised his opinion, convinced that they were copper depictions of the beak of the ivory-billed woodpecker. This interpretation is probably correct for pieces of this type that Moore discovered at Moundville, but others are of different shape and may well represent arrow points (e.g., Fig. 22). Whether beak or point-shaped, all pieces are about the same size and occur in groups (often several were pierced at the larger end and joined by a copper pin),

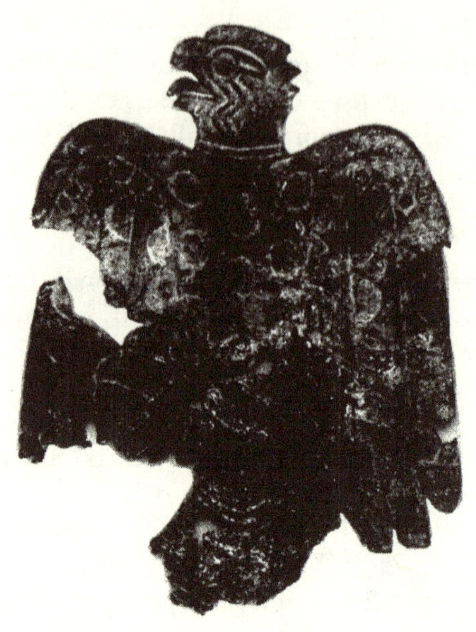

Figure 44. Repoussé Raptor, Mississippian. Catalogue No. #91507, Department of Anthropology, Smithsonian Institution, Washington, D.C. Peoria, Illinois. 9" x 6 3/4"

Figure 45. Elongated Copper Bird, Post-Mississippian Headpiece. Courtesy, National Museum of the American Indian, Smithsonian Institution, Washington, D.C., #17/214. Rose Mound, Cross Co., Arkansas. Ca. 1' 4" long.

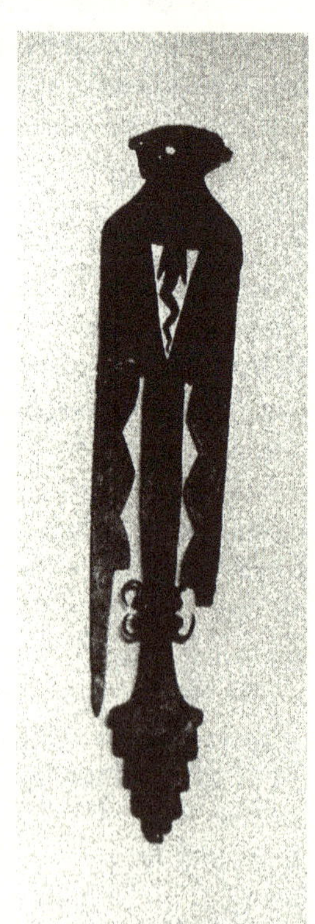

suggesting that the use and significance of the pieces was similar, despite differences in shape.

The way these pieces were usually joined formed a fan shape that suggests the tail of the wild turkey. Turkeys were also central to the iconography of the Southeastern Ceremonial Complex. If the intent in these pieces was, indeed, to reference the wild turkey, this is the only reference to that bird in Mississippian copper. It is interesting and perhaps significant that both woodpeckers and turkeys were associated with warriors in Historic times.

The spectacular hunting and flying abilities of raptors and their use as motifs on ceremonial paraphernalia in copper seem to be directly connected. With very few exceptions, non-raptors important in the ceremonial arts of Middle Woodland and Mississippian peoples (such as the roseate spoonbill and the turkey, respectively) are never depicted in copper. The ivory-billed woodpecker is the only notable exception to this rule. In addition to its connections with warriors, the spectacular size of that bird, its potentially vicious bill, and the special value of the bill itself may account for its depiction in copper.

In very Early Historic times, the ceremonial connection between raptors and copper was still important. For example, Swanton (1946:510) quotes an early writer who noted that the "Werowance of Rapahanna," an important religious and political leader, wore copper-covered bird claws in his ears. Copperwork at the Charlotte Thompson place in Alabama, a site with occupation levels from both before and after European arrivals, included an artifact of European manufacture depicting a spread eagle flanked by heraldic lions (Moore 1900:328). The piece was found in a context identical to that of many examples of precontact native copperwork with bird motifs. The design and material suggest that its significance to those who buried it was probably the same as it would have been for a more traditional piece made of native copper.

Several Historic Native American groups also associated raptors with war. A few tribes consistently included hawk skins in their "war bundles" (Howard 1968:45). The aggressive, predatory behavior of raptors in the wild may account for this fairly common tendency to think of these birds in connection with war. Another characteristic of the peregrine that may have been a factor in traditional war associations is the fact that, because its feet are weak, the peregrine falcon does not kill with its talons but rather by literally knocking its prey out of the sky. This unusual way for a bird to take its prey closely approximates human methods of warfare at the time, which emphasized handheld axes, maces, or clubs.

Howard mentions a number of Historic Southeastern traditions that also imply a strong connection between raptorial birds and human combat. He goes on to suggest that because maces and severed human heads appear so frequently in Mississippian art, the primary focus of the tradition is war-related, and that associated bird motifs must be symbols of war as well. This definition of bird imagery in the Southeastern Ceremonial Complex is far too specific. Limiting the significance of this motif to war-related contexts ignores important data and risks missing a crucial element in the significance of raptors throughout much of Native American art. Depictions of raptors appear in many of the same contexts as do representations of other creatures, with little, if any, association with war, suggesting that their significance probably extends well beyond a simple connection to warfare.

Furthermore, the traditional relationships between these other creatures (deer and bear, for example) and raptors in myth and ritual are crucial to an understanding of the importance of raptors as symbols in ceremonial art. If the interpretation of raptorial imagery is limited to its associations with war, these other relationships are obscured. Like the "power symbols" discussed in the preceding section, depictions of raptors in precontact as well as Historic Period ceremonial art refer to power sources in more general terms (this proposition will be discussed in detail below.) Thus, the relationship between symbol and meaning was almost certainly not one to one, such as bird to war. Rather, the powers associated with these bird species were utilized in dealing with a variety of problems, ranging from war to lovemaking.

Eagles and hawks (especially those with distinctively jagged circumocular eye markings like the peregrine) are frequently associated with rain, thunder, and lightning among Historic Period Native North American groups. Sometimes they are identified directly with the mythical "thunderbirds," supernatural beings that could assume a human form at will, either male or female (Hallowell 1975:155, 157). The "thunderbird" was a central motif in Sun Dance ritual on the Plains, a ceremony with only the most tenuous connections to war making, focusing instead on cosmic power and influence. The central pole of the Sun Dance Lodge almost always held a "bundle of brush," referred to as the thunderbirds' or eagles' nest (Spier 1921:467–69). In much Native American tradition, these same raptors are connected with cosmic forces that were believed to maintain control of the realm above the earth (e.g., Howard 1968:52). For many groups, the "thunderbirds" themselves are accorded these powers. For others, it appears the concept is more abstract.

Nevertheless, the raptor, as a motif in ceremonial art, was probably always associated with this kind of far-reaching and elemental power, providing some kind of link with that power which could, in turn, enhance human abilities in attempts to solve major problems. Although the particular problem addressed at certain times in the Mississippian Periods was war, the significance of the birds as symbols lies more in the reasons why they were appealed to than in any specific problems upon which their special powers were brought to bear.

The validity of a wider frame of reference for the interpretation of bird imagery in native North American ceremonial art is also apparent elsewhere in the literature. For example, raptors are frequently depicted on the "medicine bags" of several Great Lakes tribes (Phillips 1984:25). The power associated with these repositories for spiritually powerful objects could be used to destroy enemies, but they were equally important in curing ceremonies, for "locating" animals, and the casting of "spells of love." A "spotted eagle" was the town emblem of Coweta, a Creek settlement (Swanton 1928a:243). It was the symbol of a socio-political unit whether at war or peace. In some areas, hawks and eagles or parts of their anatomy played central roles in religious practices that, like the Sun Dance, had virtually nothing to do with war.

Hawks and, in some cases, woodpeckers were believed to be the messengers of the peyote in the early history of the Peyote Ceremony. In the same ritual, as practiced by some groups in the 1930s, the "Chief Peyote" was placed on an eagle feather. Novices received their first peyote on two more eagle feathers, used as a spoon (La Barre 1938:43). In some versions of the ritual, the "Peyote bird" was actually called the "sun-eagle" and his shape was formed of ceremonial ashes during the all-night ritual (La Barre 1938:69–71). Woodpecker feathers figure importantly in some other versions of the ceremony (La Barre 1938:71). Peregrine falcon and raven wing and tail feathers are also important components of the Potowatomi "Dog Dance Bundle," essential ritual paraphernalia for certain shamans. The peregrine feathers are worn during the casting of shamanic spells and are known as "Wiska's hair ornament," Wiska being the Potowatomi culture hero (Salzer 1974:114–18). Early chroniclers report that in the post-contact Southeast, the wings and skins of hawks were also important items of ceremonial paraphernalia and were usually worn as headdresses.[15] Feathers, particularly those of hawks, eagles, and crows, figured importantly in numerous other historic Native American dances and rituals that had little or nothing to do with war, but they clearly transcend the merely decorative. These included (and in some cases continue to include): Creek dance and ritual, including the annual Busk festival[16]; the ordination of new priests for the Ghost Dance Ceremony (Mooney 1965:167, 184, 187); the Great Feather Dance of the Iroquois Green Corn Festival (one of four ceremonies given by the "creator" and confirmed by Handsome Lake [Witthoft 1949:23]); and the Potowatomi "bear walker" shaman's bundle ceremonies (Salzer 1974:116).

Among some Native North American groups, the crow was apparently thought of as a power just below hawks and eagles. In the Ghost Dance ordination ceremony, for example, a hawk feather or a crow feather constituted the badge of priesthood, and was presented on ordination. Only one feather was required if hawk feathers were presented, while two were necessary if they were crow feathers (Mooney 1965:184). The special position of the crow, nonetheless, is suggested in the quite widespread northern tradition that corn came to the eastern United States in a crow's ear (Witthoft 1949:157). Certain traditional tales from the Southeast describe huge maneating raptors—crows, as well as hawks and eagles—again, without any reference to intertribal warfare (Howard 1968:43). It is interesting that the crow and woodpecker are occasionally included, along with eagles and hawks, in this group of birds with special powers and associations. Crows and woodpeckers appear on copperwork (*N.B.*, the copper crows found at the Hopewell Mound site in Ohio and the woodpecker references on small copper badges from Mississippian sites) in both Middle Woodland and Mississippian times, although less frequently than does the peregrine. Post-Mississippian associations among these birds, copper, and burial ritual continued. In one of the few burials with copper at the proto-historic Flynn Cemetery Site, a raven's skull was found along with a copper cross form in the area of the upper torso of one body (Bray 1961:16).

As controllers of the regions above the earth, raptors were often perceived to act in direct opposition to snakes and/or serpents, the controllers of the regions below the earth's surface (Rands 1954:79–80). Snakes comprise another important category of representational depiction on precontact copperwork. In his study of Southeastern Ceremonial Complex shell engravings, Duffield (1964:49) noted an interesting division of significance and symbolic interest between bird and snake imagery. He suggested they represented the two major "deities" worshiped by Mississippians. While this characterization probably does not accurately reflect Mississippian religious concepts, it certainly points out the quite central positions of those two species as controllers of power in their respective realms in the ritual and beliefs associated with the complex.

Early contact-period finds at Great Lakes area sites indicate that Mississippian interest in snakes and their association with metal continued to be important. "Snake effigy pendants made of copper" were recovered from the Anker Site in Illinois, and finds at Dumaw Creek (ca. A.D. 1600) in Michigan also included a copper snake-shaped pendant (Quimby 1963:30, 39). Later, in the same region, flintlock guns with "serpent shaped sideplates of brass . . . were made specifically for use by the Indians" (Quimby 1966:9).

Farther south the association of metals with snakes died out quickly. However, snakes continued to be important ceremonially and were clearly associated with extraordinary power. The fangs of certain snakes were used in scarification rites among some groups (Lawson 1860:363). Bartram

(1791:258–61) reported that southern native groups he visited in the eighteenth century would not kill snakes for fear that their spirit would enter a relative to avenge the injury. He also tells of a scratching ceremony he was subjected to among the Seminole when he killed a rattlesnake, to atone for the death and avoid inevitable misfortune (Bartram 1791:272–73). Swanton (1946:252) notes that in Virginia, shamans wore the skin of a rattlesnake as a headdress, as well as live green snakes. He also says that Creek town emblems, often carved from wood, included the snake, alligator, and gar fish (Swanton 1928a:243).

Snakes figure importantly in much of Native North American myth (e.g., Wallace 1969:98). Like raptors they and/or their attributes seem to embody and confer extraordinary power that is related to their traditional control of a particular section of the cosmos, the regions below ground level. Most often they seem to affect subsistence, whether in the form of weather phenomena or success in hunting. Among the Seminole, for example, quartz crystals believed to be fragments of the horns of horned serpents were used as hunting charms, since they were supposed to be irresistibly attractive to game animals (Howard 1968:52). In the Creek Corn origin myth, Corn Mother gives her son a headdress made of snakes and various birds, presumably to enhance his personal power in confronting the tasks ahead of him (Witthoft 1949:79).

In another Creek tale, a horned serpent was said to actually control the weather (Howard 1968:52). The final task in Hiawatha's unification of the Iroquois is usually referred to as "combing the snakes" from the hair of a particularly powerful and hostile shaman (Wallace 1969:98). Human/snake transformation is also fairly common in Native American myth and was believed to occur in actuality as well; in fact, Ojibwa sorcerers were believed capable of assuming the form of a snake (or a bear) at will (Hallowell 1975:175n.).

In some cases, snakes—specifically the rattlesnake—also enjoyed aspects of status reserved for human beings or a few creatures of similar reputation. This special status seems to stem from the position of snakes (with raptors and bears) as controllers of different levels of the universe. Among the Ojibwa, both the rattlesnake and the bear were referred to as "grandfather" (Hallowell 1926:46–47). Traditional lore of the Potowatomi offers another link between these two creatures. Potowatomi sorcerers are said to use the "virtue of the horned serpent" to effect the change in form from human to bear in transformation rituals (Salzer 1974:140). Rands's (1954:79–80) study of serpent imagery in Native American myth notes the frequent association of snakes with water, horns, and thunder. For the Yuchi, serpents have all these associations as well as some with storms in general, rainbows, lightning, and disease. Two of the myths Rands quotes concern a man who, through a series of unusual circumstances, is transformed into a serpent that causes destructive floods. Many of these attributes coincide with powers and abilities also associated with raptors.

Following contact with Europeans, the use of mammal imagery on copper ceremonial art underwent essentially the same changes already observed, with regard to bird and reptile motifs. That is, mammal imagery and anatomy continued to be important in art, but the use of copper as a medium for its expression died out very quickly. The application of mammal motifs to metal was still quite common at the time of contact, nevertheless. Early trade materials in the Great Lakes area included crescent gorgets of silver with animals, as well as birds, engraved on them (Quimby 1966:9). Swanton (1946:510–11) quotes an early writer who observed that Powhatan men in Virginia frequently wore bear and raccoon claws (as well as those of eagles and hawks) in their ears as alternatives to the more common copper and bone beads.

Sites occupied at contact or perhaps somewhat later have yielded miniature animals cut from the sides of brass and copper kettles. Most appear to come from the Cherokee region (Lewis 1946). Because they are from the historical period, analysis of the significance and design implications of these pieces are beyond the scope of this study. Nonetheless, their existence indicates a continuing connection between animal imagery and its ceremonial expression in metal, for a time at least.

In some ritual art produced by Historic Native North Americans, feline imagery and attributes are associated with great power and ceremonial significance. The very dangerous and much feared "underwater panther," for example, is a key actor in much of northern Algonkian myth as well as an important visual concept in the art of those peoples.[17] This beast had a long serpent-like tail and was frequently depicted with horns. These characteristics, its habitation below ground level, and the generally malevolent powers and activities attributed to it are reminiscent of tales of the horned serpent in the Southeast. These two mythical creatures apparently fulfilled essentially the same role in the cosmological structures of each region.

Bears were the third species in a sort of triangle of elemental powers represented by raptors and the horned serpent/underwater panther. Bears were apparently believed to wield considerable control at ground level (Salzer 1974:135). Hallowell's (1926) detailed study of bear ceremonialism among historic tribes indicates that the fascination with the head (especially the nose and canine teeth), paws, and claws of that beast, obvious in the precontact complex, continued to be a factor in historical art and ritual, despite the fact that copper played no role in later practices. Connections between these three (raptors, snakes/underwater panthers, and bears) are found throughout the myths and ceremonial traditions of the eastern area.

For example, it is significant that, among the Prairie Potowatomi, members of the bear clan are the caretakers of the medicine bundle used in tribal ceremonies connected with the underwater panther (Howard 1968:218) Also, given the persistent interest in noses apparent in some copperwork, it is interesting that Swanton quotes one version of the horned serpent stories, in which the monster was said to have lured animals to its watery lair to destroy them, but contented itself with eating only the tips of their noses (Swanton 1928a:494). In Salzer's (1974:122, 127) more recent analysis of Potowatomi shamanism (specifically "bear-walkers"), he states that both the claws and the canine teeth of the bear are important elements in essential bundles of powerful paraphernalia associated with those practices.

The special position accorded bears in most Native North American ceremony indicates that animal's general sphere of influence and suggests reasons why they were accorded so much attention in ceremonial art. Again, interest often centers on subsistence hopes and needs. Witthoft (1949:16) says that in the Eastern Woodlands the well-documented Green Corn or Busk Ceremony, a ceremony celebrating the corn harvest, was actually secondary in importance to the Bear Sacrifice Ceremony which occurred six months later. The latter ritual opened the hunting season and included observances that were very similar to those performed in connection with the corn harvest. In the Bear Sacrifice ceremony, corn was the primary item of sacrifice and was offered to the bear and the deer. By contrast, during the Green Corn ritual, bear meat was sacrificed to beings believed to be instrumental in the successful propagation of corn (Witthoft 1949:14).

The various versions of the Green Corn or Busk Ceremony, conducted in some form by virtually all the agriculturally active groups of the Eastern Woodlands, have been closely scrutinized in the ethnological literature, especially in connection with the Southeastern Ceremonial Complex. It is curious that relatively little attention has been paid to its bear sacrifice counterpart mentioned here. It may be that the success of agriculture in the Southeast caused the early demise of ceremonies with an emphasis on hunting ritual.

The visual evidence in the late prehistoric periods—that is, the shift away from the representation of animals which were directly important economically (such as deer and bear) to a preponderance of bird motifs—associated with agriculture, but not important as a food source, per se—certainly would support such a suggestion. In any case, there is clearly an important connection between the bear and success in hunting, just as there is a definite association between raptors and the weather phenomena that are crucial to success in agricultural pursuits.

This symmetry between the ceremony of hunting and agriculture, and symbol is quite common in Historic Period Native North American art and tradition and is probably a continuation of the significance of bird and bear motifs found in the ceremonial art of precontact times. Again, more is involved than a simple one-to-one relationship between the bear in ceremonial art and some kind of hunting magic. The ceremonial practices of Native Americans throughout the eastern region make this as clear regarding the significance of the bear as they do regarding raptor symbolism.

For example, among the native peoples of Virginia and other groups farther south, bear oil was used to dress men's hair in preparation for war.[18] Women's hair was dressed with bear oil before important ceremonial dances (Witthoft 1949:55). Fresh bear oil was also applied to the newly pierced ears of members of the Cherokee and Creek tribes. The opening was later bound into a crescent shape with brass or silver wire (Swanton 1946:512–13). Bear oil was also the major ingredient (along with red pigment) in a mixture used to paint the skulls of deceased Choctaw chiefs prior to their placement in the ossuary (Bushnell 1920:98). The South Carolina Santee used a similar mixture to dress the hair of deceased chiefs as they lay in state. The body was then placed under a canopy that was set atop a mound built especially for that purpose (Bushnell 1916:35). All these practices suggest that special properties and powers were imputed to the bear itself as well as to portions of its anatomy, much like the raptors discussed earlier.

As with raptors, a number of conceptual and mythological relationships exist between humans and bear. These may partly account for their consistent use as images on Native American ritual material in precontact times. These relationships probably contributed as well to the special position of bears in Native American belief structures later on. In his classic study of Bear Ceremonialism, Hallowell (1926:151) details a number of reasons why the bear may have enjoyed his special position in eastern North American ceremony. Most of these are also based upon strong similarities in behavior—and even anatomical appearance—between bears and humans. He goes on to note a number of essentially universal attitudes and practices regarding the treatment of bears among Native North Americans (Hallowell 1926:145). One is the very deferential approach of virtually all groups to killing bears that is apparently in recognition of the animal's controlling spirit, the source of his special powers.

Hallowell (1926:43–47) also discusses various honorific forms of address used for bears. Most are terms usually applied to humans, not animals; for example: "cousin" (St. Francis Abenaki); "grandfather" (Penobscot and Tête de Boule); "grandmother" or "grandfather," depending on sex (Montagnais-Naskapi); "four legged human" or "chief's son" (Plains Cree); "relative" (Ojibwa); "old man" (Sauk); "elder brother" (Menominee). After its death, the Montagnais-Naskapi referred to the hunted bear as "food of the fire," tying the bear to that important concept and symbol, as well (Hallowell 1926:45).

In the spiritual hierarchy of the Oglala Sioux, the bear ranks fifth in terms of power—below the sun, the sky, the earth, and rock, in that order (Walker 1975:214). Thus, the bear is accorded a level of power and status that associates him, like certain raptors, with cosmic and elemental forces. In Sioux tradition, the only animal who was invested with a comparable level of spiritual status and power was the buffalo, a horned creature of paramount economic importance.

Hallowell (1926:162) traces the existence of such ritual connections (between deer—horned beasts of economic importance—and bear) to ancient Boreal Archaic cultures, in which the reindeer and the bear were of primary ceremonial significance. Indeed, economic factors may account, in part at least, for the persistence of deer imagery in crucial rituals performed farther east, as well as for the continual appearance of deer-related imagery in precontact art.

At least part of the ceremonial significance of both deer and buffalo, however, is due to the fact that both have horns or antlers. Deer antlers, so common in the copper complex, remained important as headdress elements and symbols of power in post-contact times (e.g., Phillips 1984:51, n. 84) They held this position in both literal and conceptual contexts and often in situations where any specific subsistence-related significance is difficult to identify. For example, a Creek informant told Howard (1968:59) that in earlier times the wearing of antlers denoted high rank.

The antelope, another antlered creature of considerable economic importance, was a focal element in the Sun Dance rituals of all Plains groups, according to Spier (1921:463). Antlered creatures (deer in this case) are also important in the origin myths surrounding the Peyote religion (La Barre 1938:107). In addition, the Algonkian bear-walker shaman's bundle contains various items of deer anatomy because the bear-walker's messages are believed to be transmitted to the people by deer (Salzer 1974:120).

The persistent appearance of horns on "underwater panthers" and certain snakes also indicates that horns and antlers had a significance that was more than merely economic. As noted above, the power and significance of the horned serpent and the "underwater panther" seem to blend in Native American tales from the eastern area. Again, the ceremonial position of both creatures rests on their roles as controllers of the realm below the surface of the earth. The nature of the power wielded by underwater panthers and horned serpents (as well as their principal antagonists, the thunderbirds) was often characterized by the ability of each to produce thunder (Swanton 1928a:496) and is yet another example of the complex interrelationship of all these important motifs. In this connection, it is interesting that Salzer's (1974:110) Potowatomi informants always refused to discuss bear-related ritual and practice on days when thunderclouds were in the sky.

Howard (1968:59) suggests that the significance of horns and/or antlers in Native American tradition is essentially "chiefly or sacred." He notes a number of very specific Iroquoian references to antlers and horns in a political/power context (Howard 1968:49). A newly installed chief, for example, is referred to as "putting on the antlers"; a "fallen chief" is referred to as "dehorned." Certainly, the symbolic meaning of such motifs and costume elements include political dimensions. To equate the wearing of horns with possession or transfer of special powers would probably be more accurate, however. This interpretation coincides with many practices among Historic Native Americans. For example, Plains groups occasionally made horned headdresses for their horses although in myth and most art, horns were generally applied only to reptile and feline beings. One such horned headdress, formerly on display in the Museum of the American Indian, New York, displays a row of brass tacks along the length of each horn. Brass was often equated linguistically with copper in historic languages.

Virtually all depictions of humans in the copper complex include other symbolic attributes, primarily mammalian or avian. The combination of human and deer imagery in the Iroquois linguistic traditions discussed above is particularly interesting in light of this fact. The importance of transformation in so much of Native North American tradition suggests that prehistoric imagery combining human and animal attributes may have referred, at least in part, to ritual metamorphosis. In fact, according to many Native North American myths and ritual practices, all the birds and animals discussed so far had the ability to assume human form.

Transformation was clearly a part of historic ritual involving relationships between humans and bears. A bear is the form most often assumed by malevolent shamans and sorcerers among the Potowatomi and Ojibwa (Salzer 1974:129, 160). According to Walker (1975:215), crucial symbolic information was imparted to Oglala Sioux shamans by the bear. Walker does not indicate how this information was exchanged, but impersonation and/or transformation is frequently involved in shamanic communication with the spirit world. Aspects of transformation and impersonation were also part of historic ceremonial activity involving raptors. An early observer in the Southeast noted that there was an order of "venerable old Gentlemen" among the Choctaw who wore extremely long fingernails on the thumb, fore-, and middle fingers of each hand (Bushnell 1920:95–96). The task of these men was to strip the flesh from the bones of the deceased (who had lain in state for some time) in preparation for their disposition in the ossuary. The ossuary itself had a large sculpture of a "dove"—more likely a hawk—with outstretched wings on the roof.

Most raptors have three large talons on each foot and some prehistoric shell engravings depict human-like beings with such talons for hands and with other avian attributes. Probably this order of "venerable" old Choctaw gentlemen was impersonating raptors in the performance of their macabre duties. In fact, it may be that only through such ritual impersonation could an individual involve himself in so dangerous a task as manipulation of the remains of the dead. This is *not* to suggest that Mississippian shell engravings depict this same "order" observed in action centuries later. That is highly unlikely. All that can reliably be assumed to have remained constant was the appeal to and utilization of power believed to be under the control of certain raptors; as well as the general methodology for gaining access to that power—impersonation and/or transformation.

The impersonation of birds, primarily raptors, continued to be central in many important ceremonies in North America. Among some Plains groups, for example, individuals impersonating birds were responsible for the supernatural raising of the center pole for the Sun Dance Lodge (Spier 1921:470). Blasts on a bird bone whistle, an important element of the Peyote ritual, are said to imitate (or impersonate) the "water bird" (La Barre 1938:47).

As noted above, almost all human imagery found on copperwork is accompanied by references to nonhuman beings. This aspect of human imagery on copper is so consistent there might be some question regarding whether those depicted are actually humans or mythical, nonhuman composite beings. They probably represent both. Transformation, from human to other-than-human form, is a prominent feature within shamanically derived religions such as those of Native North America (Pasztory 1982:7). The metamorphosis is often achieved through impersonation, the donning of masks and other regalia symbolic of the spiritual entities involved. Properly purified and costumed participants "become" the entities they represent (e.g., Furst and Furst 1982:206). Thus, the depiction of a ritual in progress must also represent the spirit world made visible.

On the other hand, as noted above, a number of facts suggest that human depictions on copper do, in fact, show elaborately costumed human beings. Many full-scale items of copper paraphernalia have been found identical to those depicted in miniature on other pieces of copper ritual material. In addition, many Mississippian bird/human combinations show individuals with aspects of bird anatomy that appear to be masks or other costume elements (e.g., Plate 12) rather than anatomical features.

Many composite depictions on precontact copperwork combine abstract designs with motifs that are usually associated exclusively with humans. Several of the full figure depictions in copper are developed on a rectangular format. Costume elements and anatomical features almost always include circles and, frequently, crescents and sunbursts. The Mississippian "occipital hair knot" presents an excellent example of this combination of essentially abstract design and representational human imagery. It is a headdress element found only on human beings (composite and otherwise) in Mississippian art. It is also a variation of the spiral motif. A similar configuration is found on the knobs that protrude from the heads of Middle Woodland clay figurines found at the Turner Mounds in Ohio and the Knight Mounds in Illinois. Ringed knobs very reminiscent of these also appear on certain human-headed pipes from late precontact and Early Historic Iroquois sites (Mathews 1982: Figs. 11 and 15). Not only do they appear to be spirals, but many of these protrusions also look like truncated horns and often appear in a position on the head, either singly or in pairs, that reinforces this impression.

The implication of the motif seems to be the symbolic depiction of enhanced personal powers (Mathews 1982:322). Interpretation of more specific significance for these pieces is difficult since Mississippian depictions, at least, represent not merely some kind of conceptual notion but actual items of paraphernalia. "Occipital hair knot" headdress pieces from both Etowah and Spiro, made of wood with a copper coating, were examined during research for this study. It is likely that the copper as well as the spiral, horn-like design served to endow the headdress with special powers and thereby enhance the abilities of the individual who donned the piece.

Thus, human depictions appear to involve at least two levels of significance, reference to mortal people involved in ritual activity and allusions to extraordinary power. The miniaturized human depictions may also refer to supernatural beings that were imitated by those who were buried wearing virtually identical paraphernalia. Power associations are almost always present in the human imagery, but those elements are invariably derived from symbols and anatomical details borrowed from nonhuman sources. On the other hand, all nonhuman representations as well as abstract symbols commonly used on copperwork seem to refer directly to more or less self-contained sources of power.

This distinction between human imagery and the other design sources in the copper complex reflects the apparent relationship between the copperwork itself and the human populations that made and used it. That is, the copper material was believed to be a source of power utilized to enhance the potency of the individuals who possessed and manipulated it.

The meaning of representational implement forms and designs in the copper complex is perhaps the most difficult to unravel. The practical significance of native copper implements as usable tools is fairly clear, even when the forms are simply design motifs, spear and arrow points, hooks, axes, and adzes, etc. However, the kind of significance accorded virtually all other designs in common use on precontact copperwork—avian, reptilian, and mammalian, for example—suggests the importance of ceremonial implements and implement-shaped motifs probably went considerably beyond mundane utility.

Historical references to copper weaponry and/or related designs are few. The only reference from early contact times in the Southeast comes from the narrative of Garcilaso de la Vega (Swanton 1946:567). It offers little or no insight into the ceremonial significance of these shapes. Garcilaso describes the temple area of a Native American village, noting that it was guarded by six large wooden figures. One pair of figures carried wooden clubs with copper bands, and a second pair carried large pikes with copper heads. All six figures guarded what he describes as a veritable arsenal of copper weaponry that included pieces identical to those carried by the figures as well as hafted flint and copper axes. The flint blades of the former were held in place by copper bands.

Copper weapons similar to those described in this account have been found at various prehistoric sites in the eastern area. However, coppersmiths from the Old Copper Culture period in the Great Lakes region were the only ones that produced usable copper implements in quantity. No known archaeological or historical evidence suggests that an arsenal of copper weaponry on the scale described by Garcilaso ever existed in the Southeast; his account may be exaggerated. However, whether or not his estimates regarding the numbers of copper implements are accurate, the reference indicates that, at contact, at least one native group in the Southeast still possessed and presumably utilized copper weaponry. Furthermore, it is significant that the repository for these items was in the "temple" compound, a sacred area.

Early Historic Period data from the Northeast offers more insight into the actual significance of such objects. An intriguing reference from records of Dutch exploration along the Hudson River indicates Native Americans in that area tended to associate metal implement forms with ceremonial display rather than with more mundane uses. The Dutch apparently traded several metal hoes and axes to native peoples they encountered on their first trip up the river. They were highly amused a year later when they returned to the area and found that none of the implements was being used "properly." Instead, the native peoples chose to wear them as breastplates (Miller 1841:73–74). Among the Tuchabachee Creeks of the Southeast, some metal implements were also reserved for purely ritual use. The town of Tuchabachee possessed a number of copper plates in various shapes, including several axe-shaped ones. They were powerful and dangerous ceremonial pieces, used only with the greatest care in the most important of ceremonies (Pickett 1851:82–87).

Even in much later Historic times, certain types of weaponry which included aspects of design and use of copper that recalled prehistoric tradition were also used for exclusively ritual purposes. An iron tomahawk, formerly at the Museum of the American Indian in New York, provides a good example of such correspondence (Harrington 1920:56). Although iron, its shape and hafting method are reminiscent of Mississippian ceremonial axes. The wooden haft depicts an otter, an important creature in Middle Woodland art. The eyes of the otter are two copper cylinders hammered into the wood. Middle Woodland otters were usually stone, but most had inset copper eyes. According to Harrington, the axe was apparently not used as a weapon, but was instead used in important ceremonies as the principal element of a medicine bundle, the repository for many types of personal powers—all acquired supernaturally.

The importance of copper itself in prehistoric ritual, the elaborate nature of most burials including copper implements, and this Historic Period data suggest that copper implements played a significant role in ritual. The problem is to discover the process through which certain mundane objects could become powerful items of ritual gear. Clues may be found in certain native North American linguistic structures. As noted above, the place where the Cherokee "sacred fire" was kindled itself came to be referred to as the "fire" (Howard 1968:19), a single verbal concept, encompassing form, function, and location in ritual matters. Algonkian groups referred to certain tales about supernatural beings as "beings" themselves (Hallowell 1975:151). This tendency to ramify meaning, especially in ceremonial matters, is not uncommon among the peoples of eastern North America. It may be that the long tradition of ceremonial copper weaponry in the prehistory of the region, as well as other symbolic traditions regarding copper, were based upon ancient linguistic connections between words for copper, various forms of weaponry, and certain ritual and ceremonial ideas.

Considerable evidence in Historic Period literature refers to weaponry used in a ceremonial contexts.[19] An especially interesting reference involves a wooden knife carried by the leader of the Woman's Dance at a Cherokee Busk Ceremony attended by Howard (1968:90) in 1965. The blade was painted red and the handle green (colors of copper in various stages of oxidation). The woman indicated that a metal knife was used in earlier times. (This citation is particularly intriguing in view of the fact that ritual use of copper disappeared relatively quickly following the arrival of Europeans.) The informant also said that the green color was achieved by mixing spittle with clay. Glauconite, a clayey green substance often found in Southeastern burials containing copperwork, and an effective polishing agent for native copper (Dr. Joan Gardner, personal communication 1976), seems a likely choice for a clay-producing green pigment. Many pieces of Southeastern precontact copperwork have a "brushed" look that was probably the result of repeated polishing with such an agent. Native copper was virtually the only metal available in precontact times and trade copper continued to be in common use even after contact. Very likely, then, the original knife used in this dance was copper. The conditions that precipitated the shift from a copper to a wooden knife may also have caused the ceremonial practice of polishing with glauconite to evolve into a ritual painting with the same material.

Howard's (1968:90) discussion of this knife also hints at other aspects of the use and significance of implement forms and symbols in the copper complex. This wooden knife (which, again, the informant said had been metal in earlier times) was carried to "ward off evil spirits." For that, a wooden knife could conceivably have been just as effective as a metal one.

Such beliefs may help to explain one of the most puzzling aspects of the many implements in the copper complex: the fact that the implements rarely bear any evidence of use as tools. The hundreds of beautifully and carefully formed but obviously unused weapons found throughout the copper complex would presumably have maintained their flawless, unused appearance if they had been reserved for spiritual combat, even if they served that same function over many years before interment with those who wielded them.

The care with which most copper implements were fashioned suggests another avenue of investigation into the attempt to understand their significance in ceremonial terms, as well as how the tradition may have evolved from Archaic times. Copper is relatively soft in the native state and can only be hardened through repeated cold working, annealing, and reworking (Grosvenor 1962:561). Most Old Copper Culture points are carefully worked and refined implements. Because of their numbers and the isolated locations in which many were found, they may actually have been used in the hunt and for various woodworking activities at some level. To effectively serve those uses, repeated cold working and annealing would have been necessary. Probably, expertise in these copper-working processes was developed for that very purpose, to make more effective weapons and tools. On the other hand, a great many Old Copper Culture implements show deterioration due to weathering, but many that have not deteriorated show no more signs of use than Middle Woodland copper implements (e.g., Griffin 1961:67).

Most Middle Woodland axes and adzes are also carefully worked and most are highly refined forms. However, almost all have been found in burial contexts, and virtually none of them show any evidence of use. Their consistently flawless condition indicates that these implements were never utilized as woodworking tools or weapons. As suggested earlier, they may have been used to battle spiritual foes or to construct visionary edifices of some sort. It is virtually impossible to determine the precise nature or effect of such usage, except to assume that they would not have been nicked or scratched as a result. In any case, the careful working and reworking to which they must have been subjected certainly had nothing to do with making them into more effective utilitarian tools or weapons. Apparently by

Middle Woodland times, the ceremonial aspects of the copper working process had completely supplanted any vestiges of utilitarian function. However, the careful annealing and reworking processes apparent in the quality of Old Copper Culture pieces continued to be applied to Middle Woodland ones. It may be that in Middle Woodland times these annealing and reworking processes were repeated as a ritual necessity, without regard for (or perhaps even the knowledge of) the technical advantages they conferred upon the artifact.

In general, Mississippian copper implements do not show the same amount of refinement that Middle Woodland ones do. Nor would they have been very effective as woodworking tools or weapons. Nevertheless, the thin sheet copper Mississippian coppersmiths used for the majority of their work attests to their knowledge of the same annealing and reworking processes used by Old Copper Culture artists. Mississippians did not anneal and rework native copper objects in order to achieve a harder, more effective tool or weapon form; annealing and reworking techniques were used only minimally in the manufacture of copper implements. Rather, the most refined techniques were reserved for production of thin sheets of the metal for the fabrication of ritual paraphernalia.

These gradual changes in the relationship between technology and function in the manufacture of copper implements suggest that copper working techniques evolved from a relatively pragmatic development that was necessary to the production of effective weapons and tools to a ritualized procedure that was designed to enhance the spiritual power resident in the native material.

All the "power symbols" and "representational forms" discussed here appear repeatedly in the ritual art traditions of Historic Period native peoples in eastern North America. Use of the same symbol in essentially unrelated ceremonies (the Peyote ritual and the Ghost Dance, for example), even within the same tribal entities, implies at least two levels of meaning that are necessary in order to differentiate their respective significances:

1. one meaning specific to the ritual involved; and
2. one meaning that requires the use of key motifs in conjunction with virtually every important ceremony, configured to apply to a specific context.

For specificity, symbols must have been precisely defined and represented specific ideas associated either with the vision upon which the ritual was based or with current problems and their individual solutions. A good example of such specificity is the circular, crescentic, and star-shaped symbolism associated with the Ghost Dance and specifically interpreted in terms of the Paiute prophet's visions (see Mooney 1965). Similarly, the many variations in the significance attributed to the symbolism used in performance of the Sun Dance provide clear instances of the adjustment of the symbolic meaning of identical forms to fit specific needs (Spier 1921:512–16). Whether based upon a prophet's idiosyncratic vision or upon providing ad hoc solutions to problems, at this level the specific meaning of ritual symbolism cannot be discovered with any accuracy without the assistance of qualified native informants. It is virtually impossible, then, to determine the specific symbolic significance of such designs in precontact art.

Nevertheless, as indicated above, although Historic Period informants have offered fairly inconsistent interpretation for the designs found on precontact copperwork, most of the interpretations given seem to fall within a fairly narrow range of ideas. In Historic Period ritual, too, the significance of similar motifs falls into an equally narrow range of meanings.

These facts indicate the existence of the second level of significance, one that determines which symbols or generalized sources of power will be deployed in each set of ceremonies. The consistent use of these designs in ritual contexts both historically and before European contact implies that the more generalized level of significance was established very early and continued to be valid. An apparent degree of universality at this level of meaning would help to explain the apparent ease with which both prehistoric and post-contact groups that might have had little else in common were able to incorporate each other's ceremonies into their own traditional round of ritual practices.

Cult Signs

The specific significance of cult designs is apparently so complex as to make reconstruction of their meaning virtually impossible. All involve compound symbolism: incorporating elements of the other two design categories, "power symbols" and "representational forms." Thus, it may be assumed that aspects of the meanings associated with those motifs are inflected through juxtaposition in these more complex symbols. Unlike symbols in the other two categories, however, none of the "cult signs" appears in art traditions either before or after those traditions in which each kind of design was a central emblem. Thus, their complexity and especially their unique character suggest that designs in this category refer to specific concepts and ideas associated with the particular ceremonial tradition in which they were used, and that the significance of those symbols could be elucidated only through the testimony of native informants.

The "power symbols" and "representational forms" were probably understood in similar terms, but these motifs can also be appreciated on the more general level of significance that connects their meaning with more recent usage of similar designs. An exhaustive study of the entire known symbolism and practice of each ritual manifestation would probably be necessary to unravel the specific significance of the "cult signs," if, indeed, they can be interpreted at all. Such an undertaking is beyond the scope of this study.

Conclusion

In the prehistoric eastern United States, the motifs used most often on copperwork, the kinds of objects made from copper, the difficulties involved in obtaining the raw material, and the ways in which it was apparently used and distributed by the groups that possessed it indicate that copper must have functioned almost exclusively in ceremonial contexts. Similar forms in the art of Historic Period Native North Americans were also used ceremonially. In fact, most of the designs found on precontact copperwork continued to be of great ceremonial importance after European contact. All show complex interrelationships with one another and refer generally to the most basic aspects of nature and the power associated with them—particularly in terms of the ordering of nature's elements and functions. As such, those symbols and motifs not only suggest a fundamental consistency in the ceremonial arts of often disparate groups over thousands of years, they also embody the elements and forces in nature that those groups believed to be present in and essential to order and continuity in the natural realm.

As such, these motifs and the rituals in which they figured were probably most widely utilized at times when that natural order and continuity seemed, for whatever reason, to be breaking down. In the Historic Periods, at least, the ceremonies in which these symbols and motifs played an important part were often performed in celebration of the maintenance of a favorable order in nature (as in the Green Corn or Busk Ceremonies of the eastern area). However, the most spectacular use of these designs occurs in rituals designed to rectify apparent disorder in the natural realm, such as curing, control of bad weather, resurrection of the dead, and the return of game animals (as in the Ghost Dance).

In the Historic Periods, the specific roles imputed to animals and mythical beings with animal attributes vary from group to group, as do specific interpretations of geometric symbols and stylistic approaches. However, in ceremonial contexts, the general meaning of virtually all of them coincides with the generalized interpretations outlined above. Formal variation is apparent in prehistoric as well as Historic times. Styles and emphasis in design on copperwork varied from region to region and even between sites in the same general vicinity. These variations indicate that the cultural diversity of Historic Period groups in the eastern area also prevailed prehistorically. Such diversity is to be expected since "a particular art style is a product of a particular historical socio-cultural entity" (Levine 1957:956). At one level, the meaning of most images on prehistoric Native North American copperwork (still in use through much of the eastern United States in historic times) was apparently grounded in traditional ontological convictions that were themselves based on the shamanic origins of Native American religious practices. This unified undercurrent is apparent in the generalized concepts associated with the designs and motifs discussed above and may be seen in other basic structures of Native American societies.

This undercurrent should not, however, be taken to suggest the kind of homogeneity in culture that the term "Indian" has come to imply. There were and continue to be vast differences between languages and lifestyles, arts and subsistence modes among Native American cultures, including those in the eastern United States. Nevertheless, the apparent existence of this quite unified ontological outlook clearly indicates that, as Krieger (1945:490) puts it, the "depictions executed on . . . copper plates . . . are actually but the surface indication of certain mental patterns," patterns with very ancient roots and a remarkable ability to survive cultural crisis and change through many centuries.

3

Meaning and Significance in Material

Both archaeological and historical evidence indicate that the ceremonial and ritual importance of copper was based, in large part, on ideas and traditions associated with the metal itself. The nature of this evidence ranges from certain characteristics of the mineral and the ways it was utilized prehistorically, to observations on how it was used by Native North Americans just after contact with Europeans. Often the information amounts to little more than intriguing bits of data that suggest that copper was held in high esteem, even in its raw state. Taken as a whole, these inferences and intimations offer enough clues to develop a clear impression of the importance of copper to eastern groups during and just after prehistoric times.

Only a small percentage of pieces within the copper corpus was elaborated with designs. Most copperwork either mimics the form of artifacts made from more mundane substances or sheathes objects made primarily of another material. These facts alone imply that it was the copper, not the design of individual pieces of copperwork, that was of greatest importance. Many other facts support this suggestion. As noted above, prehistoric copperwork (whether in the form of unworked nuggets, beads and bracelets, adzes and awls, or elaborate designs worked in repoussé) is consistently found in elaborate burials within mounds or other situations of obvious ceremonial significance. Artifacts similar to those of copper, but made of more mundane materials, were not consistently afforded this kind of special treatment. Unlike most other materials utilized by these native groups, copper is almost never found scattered in village middens or otherwise casually disposed of.

The factors just discussed, the monumental problems involved in procurement of the raw material outlined in Chapter 1 and the complex technological processes connected with its fabrication, all point to the fact that copper was a highly prized and desirable commodity. There is general agreement on this point.

Disagreement centers on the nature of the value of copper to Native North Americans. Without careful consideration of all available evidence, the tendency is to view the significance of copper in primarily economic terms. It is all too easy to draw superficial parallels between prehistoric interest in copper and the position of precious metals in western European cultural traditions. Data gathered in connection with this study demonstrates that the primary importance of copper in Native North American prehistory was as a repository for spiritual rather than economic power. Much of that power was embodied in the nature of the material itself. Copper was believed to have and/or to confer special supernatural power. Examination of the material and the ways and contexts in which it was used both before and after contact all lead to this conclusion.

One characteristic of native copper that was undoubtedly of interest to Native North Americans was its red color. The word for copper in a number of Native American languages shows a clear association with the word for "red," indicating that the color of the metal was significant to those groups. This is especially apparent in vocabularies developed more recently (Trevelyan 1976:4–7). The color red, in general, has traditionally carried important symbolic connotations for many Native North American groups and has appeared very often in the art and ceremony of the eastern region. In many cases, those connotations involve symbols and concepts associated with the designs and beings represented on precontact copperwork.

For example, one of the two most powerful "medicines" of the Florida Seminole was a reddish powder, "the gift of thunder" (Greenlee 1944:325). Creek hunting charms, said to be fragments of broken horn from the "horned serpent," were also red (Swanton 1928a:494). Preparations for the Creek Busk festival included repainting an important ceremonial structure red (Witthoft 1949:53). Virtually all early contact Southeastern groups used various "red roots" in dressing their hair, particularly for war but in certain cases for burial as well.[1] Early observers also mention red most frequently in their descriptions of body paint in the Southeast (Swanton 1946:528).

This interest in the color red was not limited to Southeastern groups. The Yurok and Wiyot, displaced Algonkian speakers in northwestern California (most Native Americans that speak Algonkian languages are found in the northeastern United States, which suggests that these peoples may originally have come from the Northeast), made large ceremonial blades chipped from red and black obsidian for use in their most important rituals. The red blades were held to be of much greater value than the black ones (Taxay 1970:80). On the Plains, catlinite was the material preferred for pipes. It occurs in shades ranging from cherry red to buff, but red was preferred, according to Douglas and d'Harnoncourt (1941:132). Comments by Furst and Furst (1982:172) also support this suggestion. Red was also the color chosen for most of the Hopewell-related stone pipes found at the Mound City Site in Ohio (Mills 1922:402). Other archaeological evidence also indicates a special ceremonial affinity for things red. For example, an infant buried with many copper beads at a Hopewell-related site in Iowa (Cook Farm) was surrounded by a circle of small red stones, "arranged like the rays of the sun" (Farquharson 1875:120).

In Archaic times another red mineral substance, red ocher, figured very importantly in burial rituals. In fact, the Archaic Red Ocher peoples were so designated, because of the pervasive presence of that material in their burials. Red ocher continued to be of ceremonial importance in historic times. It was an essential element in the Ghost Dance ritual. The special substance used to paint participants in that ceremony was made of red ocher from the sacred mountain of the Paiute and was "endowed with most miraculous powers" (Mooney 1965:21).

Ethnological as well as visual evidence suggest that the red color of copper accounts in part, at least, for the frequent use of symbols associated with fire and the sun on copperwork. The relationship between copper and fire is likely not only on the basis of similarities in color. Fire was also essential to and very skillfully used in the manufacture of virtually all precontact copperwork. Evidence suggests that fire was also used in copper mining operations. Given these facts, it is interesting that the Potowatomi, who ranged through much of the copper producing area, have been traditionally known as the "people of the place of the fire." While it has been demonstrated that this is an incorrect translation of the word "potowatomi," the traditional tribal designation Potowatomi does seem to indicate special connections with fire (Clifton 1978:741–42). Furthermore, protohistoric burials associated with the Potowatomi (Dumaw Creek in Michigan, for example) are some of the richest, in terms of copperwork, from this period (Quimby 1963).

Copper is traditionally associated with both fire and the sun in the belief systems of the Tsimshian on the Northwest Coast.[2] Obviously, the Northwest Coast area is far from eastern North America. The inclusion of that area in this section of the discussion is justified by the importance of copper in the ceremonial life of its peoples. Moreover, similarities in that area in the traditions and taboos surrounding the use of copper are so reminiscent of traditions and taboos in the Northeast as to suggest that both traditions may have sprung from many of the same observations and perceptions regarding the metal itself. Copper is also closely associated with the salmon among the Tsimshian, Haida, and Kwakwakäwakwa peoples. The relationship is almost certainly based, in part at least, on the redness of both copper and the salmon's flesh (Mauss 1967:114).

Relationships between native copper and blood are even more frequent in the literature and are probably also based, in part, on color similarities between these two substances. In their studies of prehistoric ritual, both Hall (1977:28) and Maringer (1976:248) discuss the strong associations that were drawn between blood and red substances such as copper, cedar (a red wood), and sumac (a woody plant that turns a spectacular red in the fall) in the eastern United States. All were perceived to have the "ability to counter supernatural power." Maringer's study examines prehistoric blood ritual throughout the world and notes that red substances, especially red ocher, came to be perceived as the "symbolic equivalent of blood."

Strong linguistic ties also exist between copper and blood in some native North American languages—Ojibwa and Montagnais, for example. Often, words for copper and blood refer directly to the color red. That is, the word for red is incorporated into longer words meaning "copper" and "blood." In some languages (e.g., Ofo and Biloxi), although the words for copper and blood are clearly similar, no strong linguistic relationship to the color red appears, suggesting that the association between blood and copper may even go beyond mere similarity in color (Trevelyan 1976:8).

The most decisive evidence regarding the importance of color in the significance accorded native copper in precontact times was recorded by some of the earliest Europeans to arrive in North America. Observations by Verazzano (1841:47) indicate that the native peoples of eastern North America valued copper much more than gold, specifically because of its color. This preference even extended to "implements of steel or iron" at the outset and reinforces the point made earlier that metals were generally used for ceremonial rather than utilitarian purposes.

If criteria for value were based on practicality, iron and steel should have been in higher demand than copper since tools made from the former would have been far more efficient. Yet, copper was preferred, initially at least. Swanton (1946:491) quotes an early observer who said that Native Americans even felt that European copper was superior to their own because it was "redder," as opposed to the "pale" native variety. If copper was perceived to be a source of power (and it almost certainly was), then redder color presumably meant superior power. The relative potency of European weaponry, taken together with the very red color of the copper alloys they used, would have reinforced this early Native North American perception that the color of metal indicated the amount of power that was garnered through its possession.

Another interesting bit of evidence regarding the significance to Native Americans of things red in general (and, probably, of copper in particular) is recorded in an early account of Dutch explorations. On one of the Dutch ships was an unnamed individual who happened to be dressed all in red. The Native Americans who met the ship referred to him as the one in "red clothes which shown" [*sic*] and assumed, because he was so dressed, that he was the "great spirit himself"—although they found it puzzling that he had white skin (Miller 1841:72).

Several other characteristics of copper also have important power connotations. As the only metal available in any quantity to prehistoric North Americans, these characteristics were in many ways unique. The ability of copper to change form and appearance through forging (with the application of heat) or by friction (as in polishing) was probably a factor in copper's special status. Its fabrication into refined shapes from its rough raw state was probably the most dramatic. While most raw materials available to Native North Americans—stone, wood, shell, bone, etc.—were also transformed into complex objects, only copper could be returned to anything resembling its original state. Copper was capable of metamorphosis in a very real sense. Like shamans and various mythical beings, it could be formed and reformed without suffering any significant loss of substance.

There is also evidence that copperwork underwent other kinds of metamorphosis in conjunction with its ceremonial use during prehistoric times. In the Early Historic Periods, most copperwork, particularly those pieces used only occasionally in conjunction with annual rituals (like the Busk or Green Corn ceremonies), was probably polished in preparation for its use, a process of metamorphosis that was easily repeated. In one of the accounts of the Creek Tuchabachee plates, it is stated that they were annually exhumed, cleaned, and "rubbed" or polished for use in the Busk Ceremony (Swanton 1928a:510). Conversely, oxidation and exposure to certain chemicals can cause a dramatic color change in copper, from red to green. There is no clear evidence that copper was purposely altered in this way, but the native peoples that used copper and almost always buried it were certainly aware of this characteristic of the metal.

In his study of Ojibwa ontology, Hallowell (1975:163) notes that the capacity for metamorphosis was considered an "earmark of power," a capability that sets other-than-humans apart from humans. According to Hallowell's research, it is through relationships with these other-than-human beings, characterized by their potential for metamorphosis, that humans may acquire power.

In early contact times, copper was probably perceived in just these terms, and it seems plausible that prehistoric Native North Americans in the eastern area may have had views on metamorphosis similar to the Ojibwa, one of the largest native groups in the Northeast. If so, the conceptual analogue involved in the ability of copper to undergo such changes undoubtedly intrigued them and very likely was an important factor in its special status and importance in ceremonial traditions throughout the prehistory of the region.

Other obvious characteristics of copper and its procurement probably influenced the important role it played in prehistoric ritual. Both geological analysis and Early Historic documentation indicate that most copper was found in water or was extracted from subterranean mines. Float copper was usually found in streams, and many excavated mines probably flooded almost as soon as they were begun. In Early Historic tradition, designs applied to copper often involve subject matter associated with water or with other regions below ground level, in obvious reference to the locations in which copper was found.

In the multilayered universe, common in some form to most Native American cosmological systems, this association was undoubtedly significant. The Jesuit Allouez reported that Native Americans in the Lake Superior area regarded copper nuggets as gifts from underwater deities (Thwaites 1896, vol. 50:267). These nuggets were kept carefully wrapped and were cherished as "household gods." The close association between water and copper in northern regions may also help to account for beliefs among the Potowatomi that the powerful "underwater panther" had "brassy" metallic scales (Howard 1960:217). In many Native American languages few differences exist in words for brass and copper, especially in vocabularies collected more recently (Trevelyan 1976).

During early contact times in Virginia, shamans threw copper into the rough waters of rivers and the sea to pacify the "god" and thus calm the waters (Painter 1971:90). In the same region, Smith (1884:cv–cvi) observed that shamans also offered copper to the "deity" Quioquasacke in order to control rainfall. He went on to say that, on occasion, children were cast into the fire as offerings to this same "deity." Given the important connections established earlier between copper and fire, this practice not only indicates the importance accorded this particular being, but also may suggest links to the Hopewellian practice of burying infants and very young children with elaborate copper grave goods.

Given these important natural and historical links between copper and water in Native North American experience, it is interesting that Old Copper Culture copper implements are almost always found in gravel or sandy strata, and that the occasional finds of implement caches and human burials with copper are frequently in what appear to have been stream and/or lake beds (e.g. Griffin 1961:115).

In addition, burial traditions of the major prehistoric cultural entities that utilized copper usually involved sites that either overlooked waterways or were situated in areas subject to frequent flooding. The large Hopewell-related mound complexes of Ohio are typically situated on river flood plains, encircled by bluffs (*Michigan Archaeological Society News* 1953:4). In some cases, at least, these sites must have been subject to annual inundation.

Many Mississippian mounds were built in areas subject to the same conditions. In fact, Bullen (1951:11) suggests that the walkways built at the Terra Ceia Site in Florida were specifically constructed to provide "dry access" to the mounds in times of flooding. In addition, water-worn rocks from lakes and rivers were typically used for mound construction in Hopewell-related earthworks as well as in some Mississippian ones, even when they had to be transported some distance for this use (Kelly and Neitzel 1961:17).

Both historic and documentary evidence also indicate a strong connection between copper and certain parts of the anatomy, both human and otherwise—usually harder elements, such as nails/claws, teeth, and bones, but also hands and noses in the case of humans. Some evidence suggests that copperwork may have served as a sort of ceremonial equivalent of these parts. For example, a skeleton in an Oneota burial (proto-contact, in Iowa) included a copper awl in place of a missing tibia (Wedel 1959:18). Swanton (1946:502) quotes an early chronicler who indicated that certain shamans in Virginia might wear one of three items in their hair: an actual deer antler, an enemy's hand, or a copper crescent. That the commentator does not indicate any distinction between them may imply some degree of equivalency. Copper hands, crescents, and antlers are encountered among the remains of most peoples involved in the precontact copper complex. In many Copena burials, as well as in some from other cultures, copper (especially axes and adzes) was frequently buried in graves identical to those that were constructed to receive deceased members of the group, but with no trace of human remains.[3]

Additional shreds of evidence suggest part of the apparent connection between copper and bone may have arisen from the use of copper implements in the ceremonial preparation of corpses for their final disposition. Moorehead (1932:93) suggests the carefully cut human jaw bones frequently found in Hopewell-related burials were honed with tools of copper. Even more suggestive is the evidence offered by a burial at the Klunk Mounds in Illinois. In the central tomb of Mound 1 were two composite skeletons, made up of bones from a male, two females, and a child. The leftover bones of all four had been placed in a single tomb on the mound ramp, along with a copper adze (Perino 1968:37). It is tempting to surmise that the adze was utilized in the ceremonial removal of the flesh and disjointing of the decomposed bodies of all four individuals prior to the formation of the composite skeletons and then placed in the grave with the remaining bones. The flawless condition of most prehistoric copper implements would be more easily explained if they were mostly used for the fleshing of bodies in an advanced stage of decomposition (and/or spirit combat, as suggested above).

In both prehistoric and early contact times, copper was associated with (and applied to) the teeth, bones, claws, and antlers of deer, bear, beaver, puma, alligator, fox, lynx, otter, raccoon, and various raptors. Antler, dental material, and certain bones apparently held special significance for Native North Americans, one that was similar in part, at least, to the significance accorded copper. This similarity in significance is not only made apparent by their frequent combination within prehistoric burials, but by other facts as well. For example, in early contact times, elk and bear teeth were applied to Native American clothing in essentially the same ways as metallic decorations, but gradually the use of trade metal replaced other materials (Beauchamp 1903:10). Another indication of shared significance appears in prehistoric archaeological data developed by Winter (1968:182). He observed that at Late Archaic sites in Kentucky, artifacts made of local material were rarely included in burial contexts but appeared frequently in village middens. Burial goods were almost always items whose significance went beyond pragmatic utility and usually were made from exotic materials such as copper and imported shell. The only exceptions to this general rule were "perforated canine pendants," which were discovered primarily in burial contexts along with copper and other exotica.

Bear canine teeth and claws, more than those of any other species, appear in the prehistoric copper corpus. This special relationship may derive from the apparently very ancient and widespread practices of bear ceremonialism in the eastern United States, as described by Hallowell (1926:27–37). He points out that groups that practiced bear ceremonialism believed that the bear stayed alive throughout hibernation by sucking its paws. Apparently some life-sustaining substance was believed to be in the animal's claws and probably in his teeth as well. Thus, in some sense the bear's teeth and claws, like copper, were perceived to be endowed with special power.

Of the many aspects of the many facets of meaning discussed above, probably the most important is the fact that concepts associated with copper bear equally strong relationships to diametrically opposed elements in native models of cosmology and reality, in general: fire and water, blood and bone. An opposition of elements was inherent even in mining and forging methods for the raw metal. As noted above, in some cases at least, prehistoric miners heated the surrounding matrix with fire and then quenched it with cold water to release the copper. To fashion virtually all the metalwork it was also necessary to use both fire and water in combination, repeatedly heating and cooling the metal. Traditional myth suggests that Native American ritual was often aimed at achieving a balance of power between spiritual entities above and below the surface of the earth. It was probably the potent association of copper with similar opposites that made it crucial in so many important ceremonial traditions—a medium in every sense of the word.

Other aspects of bear ceremonialism provide further insights into the special significance of copper, as well as into practices associated with its use. One of the more interesting characteristics of the copper complex is the consistent importance of axe forms from Archaic times to early contact, despite considerable diversity in other respects. Also intriguing is the appearance of artificial copper noses (bear and human) in a few Hopewell-related burials. Both these facts correlate in interesting ways with aspects of bear ceremonialism in the eastern United States. Hallowell (1926:139–40) notes that virtually all Native American cultures who practiced bear ceremonialism prescribed specific methods and periods in which bears could properly be killed. Most groups believed bears should be despatched only by a blow to the head with an axe or war club, even long after guns were available for hunting. In addition, some groups insisted upon special treatment of the bear's nose after he was killed. The Ojibwa removed it, "carried it off into the woods and hung [it] up in some secret place." The Menominee reassembled the skull and jawbone and stuffed the nostrils with cedar twigs. (*N.B.* earlier discussion of the special significance of cedar, related to its redness.) While none of these practices can be persuasively linked with the forms apparently used in prehistoric ceremonial, they suggest belief structures that probably existed, in one form or another, throughout the history and prehistory of the area and clearly influenced the use of copper.

Native North American mortuary practices were such that precontact peoples must have been thoroughly familiar with the stages of decomposition through which corpses pass. It could not, therefore, have escaped their notice that bones and, especially, teeth remain almost unchanged long after the other parts have decomposed. They were probably aware, as well, that the nose and eyes are some of the first features of the body to disappear in decomposition. That these particular features were also important subject matter for coppersmiths is at least interesting. In mining native copper the surrounding matrix had to be stripped away to reach the vein of metallic copper. Perhaps this aspect of the mining process came to be understood as an analogue to the relationship between bone and flesh, establishing the conceptual relationship copper came to have with bony materials.[4]

The aura of mystery and magic that permeates Early Historic legends and comments about Isle Royale and other important Native American mining areas in the Lake Superior region is yet another indication of the significance accorded native copper as a material. While these data offer little insight into the reasons why copper was associated with certain sources of power, they strongly connect it with the realm of the sacred and/or supernatural. The Jesuit Dablon recorded a number of beliefs regarding the mining areas (Thwaites 1896, vol. 54:153–59). The waters around Isle Royale were said to be inhabited by underwater peoples, the goblin spirit of the water and "the thunder," possibly the underwater panther. On the island itself were said to be rabbits the size of dogs that ate canoes. Another island with copper was said to be a floating island, pushed by the wind. Still another island was called "thunder" because "it is said to thunder there all the time." In similar legends, Dablon indicates that a great deal of fear was associated with so much as setting foot on Isle Royale and particularly with the removal of copper from it. In one legend, four men who ventured there and attempted to take some copper away were driven off by the resident supernatural spirits and beings. Three died before reaching home, and the fourth died immediately after reporting what had happened. It is significant that traditions surrounding the ceremonial copper plates of the Tuchabachee Creeks predicted a similar fate to any stranger who looked upon the copper on any day but the day of the Busk Ceremony: they would surely die before reaching home (Swanton 1928a:510). Correspondences like these further demonstrate the underlying similarity in belief structures surrounding copper throughout the eastern area.

Evidence from the Lake Superior area in 1798 also indicates that some Native Americans were reluctant to enter the mining areas or at least professed such a reluctance. A group encountered by Europeans in the area admitted that they were near the place where their "grandfathers" came to procure copper, but when pressed, refused to proceed there, saying they dreaded coming near the place (Blue 1894:63). Of course, native spokesmen possibly told such tales simply to discourage the Jesuits and other Europeans from entering the mining areas. Given what is known about the use of copper prehistorically and in early contact times—the most logical explanation for such prevarication (if indeed it was prevarication) remains the suggestion that the mining precincts were, in fact, sacred areas.

If so, the mysterious disappearance of the Jesuit René Menard may have been the result of his own insistence upon establishing a Christian enclave within these very regions. He attempted to set up a mission on the Keweenaw Peninsula in the heart of the copper country, where more copperwork (finished and fragmentary) has been found than anywhere else in the region (Drier and Du Temple 1961:143–44). Menard remained in the area nine months and then disappeared without a trace while making a portage "between the west end of Portage Lake and Lake Superior" (Drier and Du Temple 1961:180). Perhaps the miners and manufacturers of copper took a dim view of Menard's kind of spiritual competition—or simply his cavalier trespass into a sacred area—and "arranged" his disappearance. In any case, very few if any other Jesuits met with so mysterious a fate in the Great Lakes area. It may not be coincidental that Menard met such a mysterious fate in the midst of a region so crucial to the procurement of important ritual material.

It also seems likely that historical accounts indicating that most local inhabitants avoided going to Isle Royale were not just a ruse to discourage European discovery of the mining areas; rather the accounts appear to reflect strong convictions about the island's supernatural inhabitants. (The treacherous fifteen- to forty-mile canoe trip across Lake Superior to that swampy, mosquito- and black-fly-infested place might have been incentive enough to stay away. The distance varies depending upon departure points. Poor drainage on the island has created many vast swamps that are ideal breeding places for mosquitoes.) Still, archaeological evidence indicates that proto-historic and historic peoples did spend time there (Griffin 1961:13, 133). If some Native Americans were afraid to approach the copper mining areas, others were not. Possibly only those whose special powers (acquired either through training or by birth) qualified them to deal with the potentially dangerous qualities of copper ventured with impunity into the areas from which it was taken.

Clearly the Jesuits were well aware of the special place of copper in Native American belief systems, since it was they who recorded most of the legends and traditions surrounding it. It is also likely that they recognized its ritual importance and took advantage of this knowledge. When they discovered the location of one of the mining areas, they immediately began their own mining operations and used the copper to make crucifixes for native converts.[5] Given the Jesuit record of detailed ethnographical observations, making crucifixes of native copper was not merely a matter of convenience. Rather, it was almost certainly a calculated amalgamation of Christian and native ritual traditions in furtherance of their evangelical work. The use of a material that was already central to native religious tradition would have transformed the crucifixes (in the eyes of most of their "flock") from trinkets of little or no intrinsic ceremonial significance (from a Native American point of view) to important religious paraphernalia. To Native Americans, this fusion undoubtedly made Christianity more attractive and probably raised the general estimation of the Jesuits' special powers as well. On the other hand, the Jesuits' usurpation of the right and power to manipulate and distribute so important and powerful a material as copper may also have heightened feelings of animosity toward them on the part of traditional spiritual leaders whose prerogatives included control of copper.

Considerable archaeological evidence of mining practices as well as ritual use of copper work also hint at the special properties traditionally accorded to the material. The earliest examples come from data gathered at the ancient mining works of the Lake Superior region. A number of anomalies and ostensibly contradictory practices are apparent at these sites. They are frequently mentioned in the archaeological literature, but rarely commented upon. First, it would seem the Native American miners were most interested in veins of copper 1/4" to 1/2" thick, since "refuse" piles around the mines reveal many larger nuggets, discarded in the mining process (Drier and Du Temple 1961:99–100). There are many mining sites where large amounts of copper were discovered but left behind by the miners. For example, one mine was "timbered" with pillars of the native copper vein (Drier and Du Temple 1961:85).

In still other mines, immense boulders of native copper, weighing many tons, were raised several feet on a "cribwork" of logs, worked smooth, and left in the mine shaft.[6] A thirty-eight-pound axe found in Ohio belies the suggestion that prehistoric coppersmiths were unable to work large masses of the material (Drier and Du Temple 1961:185); furthermore, smaller, more easily workable pieces of copper were also fairly often left behind in the mine pits.[7]

The idea that large nuggets were not exploited due to the difficulty of transporting them also seems unlikely, especially in view of the arduous nature of the mining enterprise in the first place. The fact that mining excavations were generally refilled after the prehistoric miners finished their work indicates more than simple economic exploitation of the works was going on as well (Griffin 1961:56). Instead, these anomalies indicate that decisions about exploitation were made on a ritualistic rather than an economic basis, and that the quantity and quality of material extracted was undoubtedly hedged about with spiritual sanctions.

Evidence from the early years of contact suggests a more specific reason why native miners may have left large masses of copper behind. Allouez (Thwaites 1896, vol. 50:267) reported that a huge boulder of pure copper which sat half submerged in a lake was regarded by the native peoples to be a "god." If the belief that sizeable masses of copper were spiritual beings was a conviction established in the Archaic Period, the practice of leaving large boulders of copper in the earth during prehistoric mining operations could be explained as a logical deference to those beings.

It may be that precontact mining practices were governed by rituals and traditions similar to those associated with the exploitation of important animals, such as the bear. The careful preservation and treatment of certain portions of killed bears was largely a strategy for assuring continued success in hunting as well as for appeasing the important spiritual entities associated with bears (Hallowell 1926). Perhaps the special treatment of exceptionally large masses of copper represents a similar strategy in the exploitation of another important ritual material.

Other evidence from the copper mining area also suggests that mining procedures were governed by spiritual rather than economic considerations. The largest and most productive lode in modern copper mining efforts in the Lake Superior area was covered by a mound. Native American miners had buried over twenty tons of native copper there (Drier and Du Temple 1961:123–26). The pit was fifty feet in diameter and covered with a layer of earth four feet thick, "well laid and free from stone or rock." A similar cache was discovered above another rich vein that has been subsequently exploited in modern copper mining operations. It has been suggested that these huge caches of native copper were "storage pits." However, it seems unlikely that the native miners would have expended so much effort when it would have been far easier to store the copper in the mines themselves. Furthermore, these examples of the burial of copper in carefully constructed mounds mimic the structures built over humans buried with finished copperwork farther south. The relationships between these two approaches to the treatment of copper—whether in its raw state or in the form of refined ceremonial gear—are obvious and seem to be based in large part on the perceived nature of the material itself.

The distribution of copperwork in burials and the ways in which it was used also indicate that the material was believed to have special properties. This is true for the Old Copper Culture as well as for later participants in the copper complex, even though the predominance of implement forms in the Archaic Periods suggests interest in copper at that time was purely utilitarian. Although there has been a large number of isolated finds of archaic copper implements, whenever Old Copper Culture burials have been discovered, possession of copperwork is always limited to very few individuals (e.g., Baerreis et al 1957). If copper was freely in use among all participants in the Old Copper Culture and the process of copper mining and its manufacture were common knowledge and practice, copperwork would have likely been included in most burials, and not restricted to a small minority.

Farther south, from Late Archaic times on, burial placement as well as the kinds of items produced in copper point unmistakably to copper's role as a material used only in ceremonial contexts, despite the continued manufacture of some apparently utilitarian items. Winter's (1968:182) thorough study of the Archaic Indian Knoll Culture of Kentucky shows that 75 percent of all items of ritual importance, regardless of material, were found in burial contexts—as opposed to living areas. One hundred percent of the artifacts made from copper were found exclusively in burials, even ostensibly utilitarian pieces like awls (Winter 1968:181).

The same distinction obtained between beads made from local materials and beads made from imported materials such as shell and copper. Those of local material "tend to be disposed of rather casually," while copper beads always "tend to occur in special contexts" (Winter 1968:182). Thus, Winter concludes that the "important variable here is the raw material involved not the basic function of the artifact." If this is true, to define these pieces in exclusively utilitarian terms is to ignore a crucial factor in their significance, the material from which they are made.

McPherron (1967:170) also emphasized the central importance of certain raw materials in the manufacture of ostensibly utilitarian pieces in the

Woodland Periods. He notes, for example, that not only do Late Woodland copper awls show no evidence of having been used, they also are sometimes excavated in what appears to have been a kind of "medicine bag"—obviously made for ritual purposes. Middle Woodland "tools" frequently occur in such contexts. A good example was excavated from the Tunacunnhee Site in Georgia. An antler-handled copper awl had been placed in a leather bag with two human mandibles, one copper breastplate, two copper ear spools, fragments of mica, two drilled shark teeth, and two drilled shark vertebrae (Jefferies 1976:24). Another awl, from the Dickison Mound in Illinois, was buried with a number of bone awls, flake knives, bear teeth, and a mussel shell (Bluhm 1960:8). Still another, from the E.R. Wilson Site, also in Illinois, was buried in a cache with a copper adze, a flint flake knife, six antler punches, two antler tines, some cannel coal, a sandstone abrader, part of a raccoon penis bone, and eleven beaver incisors (Newman and Fowler 1952:206).

Archaeologists most often define such groupings in utilitarian terms, such as the tool kit of an important "artisan" (Newman and Fowler 1952:206). Like the copper awls, many of these items do seem to be utilitarian ones. However, the inclusion of objects such as bear teeth, human jaws, shark vertebrae, and raccoon penis bones seems to indicate that these bundles and the items in them had a significance beyond the merely utilitarian. McPherron (1967:223) also suggests that copper "gorges" probably were not used for fishing, unlike wood and bone ones, given the time and difficulty involved in their manufacture. The same was probably true of copper hooks and plummets. McPherron's statements imply that he felt the significance of this copper material was more ceremonial than utilitarian. For all such pieces, if the form did not determine the function, it must have been the material that did.

Another aspect of the burial placement of copper in prehistoric times indicates the significance of the material was paramount. Unworked and partly worked nuggets of copper were often included in elaborate mound burials. In the Ohio area, most of the copper in this category was discovered among finished and/or fragmentary artifacts in crematory basins at the Seip, Turner, and Hopewell sites.[8] Willoughby and Hooton (1922:473) suggest that in Hopewell-related burials, these pieces "contained impurities which rendered their further working impossible or unprofitable." If they were correct, the fact that those chunks of copper were buried in the same mounds and with the same care and ritual as finished pieces suggests once again that the importance of copper ritual gear was based primarily upon its material properties, not its form. If the main significance of copper was as a raw material for the manufacture of utilitarian items, useless pieces would have been discarded with potsherds and other trash and not placed in elaborate burial mounds.

Throughout the eastern area, burials containing copper often tend to be as elaborate in construction as they are in grave goods. The meticulous care taken in the preparation and burial of most copperwork and those buried with it, suggests that the material was believed to have properties that required special precautions in its handling and disposition. For example, a Late Archaic burial mound at the Etley Farm in Illinois covered a ring of skeletons with their heads oriented toward a central cache of artifacts, including a copper awl, three copper axes, and a large amount of red ocher. Stone slabs were placed over all the artifacts, as well as over the heads and upper torsos of the skeletons (Perino 1962:86). Early Woodland Adena copper burials and later Hopewell-related ones were frequently covered with multiple layers of bark and wood. A bundle burial in the Adena Mound (the Adena type-site in Ross County, Ohio) was covered with three layers of bark—oak, elm, and cherry or birch (Mills 1902:464). The body of a child in the same mound was wrapped in cloth and then enveloped in successive layers of birchbark, strips of wood, and basswood bark (Mills 1902:466). The burials at still another site near Charleston, West Virginia, were encased entirely in black walnut bark (Thomas 1890:425–27).

A cremation in Mound 20 of the Hopewell Group in Ohio (containing a copper panpipe and a pair of copper earpieces) was entirely covered by a corbelled dome of stones (Shetrone 1926:52–53). In the Hopewell-related North Benton Mound, also in Ohio, the two burials with copper (a child four to five years old and an elderly man) also had very elaborate burial coverings (Magrath 1945:40–45). The child was wrapped in layers of matting, cloth, and fine buckskin, and the man was placed within a corbelled sandstone vault. Another Hopewell-related mound at Ladd Mountain, Georgia contained only one burial. The body, a copper breastplate, a piece of sheet copper, and some sheets of mica were placed on the surface of the ground in a stone enclosure. All were covered with a circular pile of rock six feet deep. A copper axe was buried in the rock above the burial (Waring 1945:120). Most Copena copper burials were encased in envelopes of puddled clay. As noted above, in some cases similar graves held only copper work, no human remains.

Mississippian copper burials are often as elaborate as any from the Woodland Periods. At the Norman Site in Oklahoma, for example, burial #40 had been placed on a "bark carpet" before being buried within a mound (Finkelstein 1940:2). According to Moorehead (1932:73), at Etowah in Georgia, all of the copperwork was taken from "specially constructed graves" that exhibited "meticulous care in construction." Often, Mississippian burials with copper were also spatially segregated from others within the mound. Peebles (1971:87) took special note of this fact in his exhaustive study of the burial complex at Moundville, Alabama; and it seems to be the case elsewhere as well.

The examples of wrapping and covering procedures cited above are not isolated cases but are typical of the elaborate care taken in the disposition of copper burials. Specific aspects of burial practice varied widely throughout the eastern area and were determined in large part by the distinct characteristics of each culture and the degree to which the religious concepts associated with the copper complex affected them. Nevertheless, the elaboration of tombs with stone, wood, bark, sand, gravel, and clay are the norm—as are the large mounds and earthworks that cover most of them.

The copperwork itself was frequently as elaborately encased and wrapped as were the burials. A cremation in the Seip central mound in Ohio, for example, was placed atop six copper breastplates, two of which were wrapped (one in several layers of fabric, and the other in leather). Copper earpieces were on either side and the whole group was encircled by bear teeth and then encased in bark (Mills 1909:117). The large deposit of copperwork (120 finished pieces) in Mound 25 of the Hopewell Group had also been encased in bark (Moorehead 1922:109). Many Hopewell-related copper adzes and axes still bear evidence of careful wrapping in textile, and several were also wrapped in layers of bark (e.g., Shetrone 1930:50). Even awls and beads of copper were often placed in some kind of covering—primarily wood and bark (e.g., Adams 1880:561).

Mississippian burial practices also included this special and often elaborate treatment of copperwork, even of those pieces apparently worn by the deceased.[9] The copper axes and repoussé work found in the Hollywood Mound in Georgia, for example, were wrapped, first in cloth, then matting, and finally encased in bark before being placed within the burial (Thomas 1890:385). This kind of extra care does not seem to have been accorded burial goods made from other materials, but is quite consistently associated with copperwork.

The careful treatment of so much copperwork buried in precontact times is very similar to the care with which extremely powerful materials were treated in the Early Historic Period. Among Historic Period groups the burial of powerful ritual materials was a common practice. Apparently it was extremely dangerous for individuals without proper training or sufficient spiritual power to come into contact with such materials, as dangerous as they were powerful. The "bear-walker bundle" of the Potowatomi is a good example. The climax of the complex rituals involved in becoming a "bear-walker" (a powerful shaman) was the acceptance of the medicine bundle, a pouch filled with various supernaturally potent items. The pouch was usually made of bearskin and was buried except when in use, as a precautionary measure to assure that its potentially malevolent powers did not harm the innocent by mistake (Salzer 1974:135).

The two most powerful "medicines" of the modern Seminole, passed down within a certain clan from "shaman to shaman," consisted of two bags containing powdery substances, one silver and the other clay-colored or red (Greenlee 1944:317). These substances were considered to be so powerful that they were kept hidden at the ceremonial dance ground (probably buried) and were brought out only once a year for the Green Corn Ceremony. This "medicine's" properties were such that, if spilled, it had to be scraped together and replaced in the bag with a buzzard feather, since the contents could not be touched without the direst results.

Traditions surrounding the Creek Tuchabachee plates involved similar precautionary practices (Pickett 1851:86–87). The plates, a collection of copper circles and implement forms, were kept buried at the "square ground" and were removed only during preparations for the first day of the annual Busk Ceremony. It is clear from most accounts that only certain, very special persons could handle the plates, and only after considerable rites and rituals had been performed. When the Creeks were relocated in 1836, the plates were carried to their new home. No one could carry more than one at a time and everyone assigned to carry a plate had to carry special medicine in order to protect himself from the powerful metal.

Other information about these plates involves burial traditions that also suggest parallels with precontact use of copper. In the early twentieth century, tribe members stated that the Tuchabachee copper plates had not been exhumed and carried in the Busk Ceremony for many years (Swanton 1928a:509–10). The reason given was that the "old medicine men who by their powers of magic could handle them without detrimental consequence had all passed away." The informant also indicated that if lesser persons were allowed to handle them, the horrible consequences might include an onslaught of disease and death for the town, or violent wind storms, and other detrimental, weather-related calamities (Swanton 1928a:509–10).

The distribution of mound burials and of the copper within them also provides evidence of the special nature of copper as it was perceived by prehistoric Native North Americans. Archaeologists agree that, as a whole, individuals interred at sites where copper artifacts have been discovered (whether or not they were actually buried with copperwork) usually represent only a fraction of the populations of the prehistoric societies involved in the copper complex. The individuals actually buried with copperwork almost always represent an even smaller proportion of the groups involved. Typically, members of these cultures were buried with relatively few, fairly mundane grave goods (if any), and most were interred in large burial grounds or beneath the floors of their houses—not in the elaborate mound complexes.[10] The only partial exception to this pattern occurs in Hopewell-related burials at a site in Wisconsin (Trempealeau County) where most of the individuals buried at the site were buried with copper beads (McKern 1931:215).

It may be that the use and significance of copper beads was different than the use and significance of some other types of copper paraphernalia. Perhaps beads and other smaller copper items were available to members of a kinship group who, by virtue of their ancestry, were deemed powerful enough to possess copper, but were not full-fledged participants in copper-related ritual—children, for example. Larger and more elaborate examples of copperwork at the Wisconsin site were buried with and probably worn and/or handled by only a few powerful individuals. A similar kind of classification for important ritual material, according to context and function, was also apparent in Peyote rituals on the Plains (La Barre 1938:23–29).

Whatever the precise facts of the situation, individuals accorded the special burial treatments typical in the copper complex may be safely assumed to represent some kind of cultural elite. In death, at least, the possession of copper was limited to members of this elite and, in most cases, was the province of an even smaller enclave within that group. The members of the "elite" (whether or not they were buried with copperwork) almost always include individuals of both sexes and range in age from infants to the very elderly. The preponderance of males seems to be large, but it should be remembered that, according to Weiss (1972:239), the degree of imbalance may be due in part to problems in the identification of sexual characteristics in bone for "preindustrial societies."

Another less technical problem was the early tendency among archaeologists and amateurs to assume that all individuals of suitable size that were interred with considerable burial goods were males. Variations from site to site in the age and sex of those interred with copper were undoubtedly determined in large part by the individual traditions of particular groups, since participation in the rituals associated with copper may have been the only element of cultural unity shared among groups in the complex.

Because this elite is identified primarily through burial traditions involving copper, analysis of these elites and similar groups in the Historic Periods also provides insight into the significance of copper as a ritual medium. The answers to three essential questions are crucial to developing a clearer perception of the nature of this elite and its relationship to copper:

1. How was membership in this elite determined?
2. How did the elite use copper, particularly in terms of their relative position and function within the larger cultural group?
3. Why was possession of copper limited to members of this elite?

The answers are difficult (if not impossible) to discover on the basis of archaeological data alone. However, limited information regarding the use and significance of copper in early contact times offers broad hints and suggests conclusions that coincide very favorably with the archaeological record.

The validity of drawing broadly conceived relationships across so many centuries is supported by the evidence offered above that copper continued to be used in much the same way and within most of the same contexts throughout the thousands of years spanned by the copper complex. There is no apparent reason why that tradition would not have survived at least the first years of contact with Europeans. The study by Winter (1968:186), cited above, also supports this contention. He examined material in the burials of the proto-historic Shawnee at the Hardin Village Site in Kentucky (A.D. 1500–1675) as well as in the burials of the Late Archaic Indian Knoll cultures in the same region. His analysis shows that the cultural values indicated by the contextual arrangement of artifacts (according to function and raw material) in burials and village middens were essentially the same despite the wide chronological differences between the two groups. That is not to say that the ways individuals might have interpreted the significance of those materials were identical. The kinds of materials used and the ways in which they were utilized and distributed were, nevertheless, the same.

In his discussion of many early contact peoples in the Great Lakes area, Hickerson (1970:122) states that the "socio-political systems of tribes were universally founded in kinship." This was very likely the case among the groups utilizing copper in early contact times. In fact, the bulk of available evidence suggests that membership in the "copper elite" was based on traditional kinship structures. Many burials include young couples, children, and elderly individuals, as though in family groupings.[11] Some concrete data even indicate an emphasis on the perpetuation of a particular line of ancestral progression at some Adena- and Hopewell-related sites. Skeletal evidence shows that a certain amount of inbreeding took place within the copper elite in those groups (Griffin 1949:82).

Most references to copper at the time of European contact also indicate that its use was limited to a kinship-based elite of some kind whose demographics are roughly similar to those of prehistoric users of copper. No particular restriction with regard to the sex and/or age of those who possessed it seems to have been in place. Information from several European observers indicates that only certain "Indians of the better sorte" [*sic*] among native groups along the East Coast actually used copper. These individuals wore copper headdresses, beads, and gorgets on specific extraordinary and solemn occasions.[12] Apparently, most members of this "copper elite" wore copper beads or carried large copper plates[13] or were buried in their copperwork (Strachey 1849:89).

These facts also coincide with what is known of the precontact copper elite. A few Early Historic accounts also indicate that the individuals who actually used the material (beyond the wearing or display of it) were religious specialists or at least appear to have had special powers of some sort.[14] The distinction between those who merely displayed copper and those who invoked and utilized its supernatural properties in Historic times may also have been important prehistorically. If so, the distinction would help to explain the considerable variation in distribution patterns for copper within the burials of individual prehistoric sites.

The observations of many Early Historic Period writers offer clues to the ways in which copper was used by native peoples at the time of European contact. Most of these observations also coincide with the archaeological record, suggesting that the copper elite in Early Historic times were probably established and functioned in much the same way as they did in precontact times. For example, Rickard (1934:3, 223) states that early European explorers saw copper being worn as earpieces in Newfoundland and being made into bracelets and spoon-shaped pieces farther inland. Copper bracelets were also worn by Chitimacha men and women in the Southeast (Swanton 1946:522) and copper headdress elements were observed in Virginia as well as in the Carolinas (Swanton 1946:501–3).

There are also clear references to the use of copper in connection with Historic Period smoking practices. Apparently pipes were often elaborated with bits of copper, just as they had been in the precontact periods. For example, Percy (1969:136) noted that Native Americans in Virginia smoked tobacco in a large clay pipe, the bowl of which was "fashioned together with a piece of fine copper." In the journal of the voyages of the *Half Moon,* a Dutch explorer also mentions several times that the natives used copper pipes in smoking tobacco (Juet 1841). As noted above, copper was an important added element on many of the stone pipes of Hopewell-related peoples. It was also used to repair broken pipes in prehistoric times (Squier and Davis 1848:207, 273). Copper elements were also found on two Mississippian pipes.

Even European trade copper was used in essentially the same ways that the native material had been, hundreds of years earlier. A body interred in an Early Historic mound burial on the Kent place in Arkansas wore a rectangular gorget made of European copper (Moore 1911:409). It was 3 1/4" by 5" and had two centrally spaced perforations—remarkably reminiscent of Hopewell breastplate forms, as well as of some Mississippian ones in this region. Of the few copper kettles found intact in Historic burials, several were placed over the heads of select individuals among the Wampanoag (Bushnell 1920:15)—a historic version of the copper headdresses and headplates so common at prehistoric sites where copperwork has been discovered.

Flutes and whistles were important burial artifacts in Archaic times in

New York (Ford and Willey 1941:333). They continued to be important in various eastern locations throughout Middle Woodland times when they were elaborated with copper and became a diagnostic element at Hopewell-related ceremonial sites. Quimby's (1966:10) report that "courting flutes" were made from gun barrels in the Lake Superior region during Historic times is especially interesting in view of the central importance of metal-clad flutes and whistles in these earlier Native American traditions. The continued association of flutes and copper or other metal is also hinted at in Percy's (1969:137) description of the Werowance of Rapahanna, who not only wore a copper headdress and copper-covered bird claws through each ear, but also played a flute—apparently integral aspects of his chiefly and religious office.

Early accounts that mention copper indicate that its use was primarily ceremonial and often give specific details regarding these rituals. Again, in every case, ceremonial uses of copper recorded in Historic times either parallel prehistoric uses (in terms of the kinds of ritual items made or described) or were important in rituals that could have been a part of prehistoric ceremony involving copper. Practices and beliefs recorded by the Jesuits (Thwaites 1896, vol. 50:267) in the Great Lakes area provide a good example. The Jesuits were of the opinion that Native Americans in this region made no practical use of native copper, that they simply regarded large nuggets of it as "deities," whether in the form of large boulders or the smaller nuggets treasured by certain families "from time immemorial."

The elaborate treatment of nuggets of raw copper found at some prehistoric sites, as well as some prehistoric mining practices, suggest a similar reverence for the material. That only "certain families" had these nuggets is also significant and suggests that a specific kin group was the traditional guardian of copper, even among the hunting and gathering peoples of the upper Great Lakes. Along the East Coast, the images of certain supernatural beings were hung with copper and the bodies of important individuals were buried wearing and even stuffed with copperwork.[15]

The clearest parallel between Historic Period use of copper in a ceremonial context and similar use prehistorically is apparent in the descriptions of the Creek Tuchabachee plates discussed earlier.[16] Occasionally, although no account provides a detailed explanation as to why, individual plates were interred with various members of the community and thereby permanently removed from the ritual cache available for ceremony.

Historic Period data also suggest that at least some native peoples knew the locations of the mining areas and even of some copper-rich burial sites. A group of Native Americans gave a Spaniard named Dorantes a copper rattle with a human face on it and told him that it came from a place to the north, "where there were a great many sheets of the same metal buried in the ground" (Nuñez Cabeza de Vaca 1971:84). These Southeastern native peoples may have been aware of the mining areas hundreds of miles to the north. If not, they may have been referring to prehistoric sites at either Spiro in Oklahoma or Etowah in Georgia. Copper rattles with human faces as well as "a great many sheets of copper" have been found "buried in the ground" at both of these sites in modern times.

Documents from early contact times suggest that copper occasionally functioned in political contexts as well as ceremonial ones. As noted above, according to most observers, the leaders of certain kin groups were the ones who wore and used copper at the time of European contact. These individuals were almost always identified as kings in the early documents. Other members of the copper elite were described as nobility. "Such as weare [*sic*] red pieces of copper on their heads" mark the "difference betweene [*sic*] the noblemen and governors of countreys [*sic*] and the meaner sort," according to a sixteenth-century chronicler in Virginia (Amadas n.d.:125–26). He added that "no people in the worlde cary more respect to their King, Noblitie and Governours than these doe" [*sic*].

Apparently the display of copper was believed to signify similar "class" distinctions among the Tuscarora and other groups farther south, including those that lived along the North Carolina coast (Swanton 1946:510). Even as far west as the Arkansas River, European explorers indicated that the "lords" and "kings" of native groups wore copper headdresses (Castaneda 1907:337). The visitors occasionally even recorded meeting a native "queen" or "chieftainess," distinguished, again, by the wearing of copperwork (Newport 1969:92).

Clearly these descriptions of Native American political structure and activity were very thoroughly colored by European preconceptions about the nature of political organization. Europeans described native cultures as though they were primitive versions of Old World monarchies—highly stratified societies, composed primarily of peasants and ruled by a hereditary king and lesser nobility. Many early descriptions of native social and political structures also suggest that the power of the ruling class was derived from its control of subsistence resources, a control achieved partly through the monopolization of a monetary system in which copper was the most important medium of exchange. These early accounts conform too well to what is known about sixteenth- and seventeenth-century European social, political, and economic structures to be considered accurate descriptions of the traditions and institutions of Native North American peoples, whose values and lifestyles were so obviously different from those of their contemporaries.

References to Early Historic Period use of copper in these documents also indicate that many of the writers made faulty assumptions about the nature of native social and political structures. For example, according to early sources, the only real difference (other than the possession of copper) between members of the "nobility" and other tribesmen and women involved special privileges in trading negotiations with Europeans, and only a few who wore copper were accorded that privilege (e.g., Amadas n.d.:126). The lack of further substantial distinctions between "classes" in the native societies encountered suggests that the designation of individuals who wore copper as members of the "upper class" represented a less-than-informed judgement on the part of the early explorers. Given this tendency to impute European values and structures to native traditions, it is hardly surprising that Europeans frequently found native behavior and demeanor strange and illogical. For example, one early observer noted (to his great surprise) that no one seemed to be in any way envious of this "nobel [*sic*] class," the copper elite (Adair 1930:232).

Comments like this also indicate that European explorers misunderstood the nature of native social and political structures, in part because they did not recognize the importance of spiritual potency as opposed to economic and political power. Ignorance of the crucial importance of the spiritual dimension in other aspects of Native American life has also obscured an understanding of the primary significance of copper and its use today.

Early descriptions of the Powhatan in Virginia highlight many of the misconceptions found in this early data. Powhatan, leader of the Virginia Algonkian group of the same name, controlled more copper than any other leader in the area and, perhaps, in the entire eastern United States at the time of contact. Early documents indicate that other groups over which he held sway (many of whom spoke different languages) were required to pay him "tribute" in the form of copper beads or "vitall" whenever he visited (Smith 1907:114). In fact, it was this aspect alone of Powhatan's position that set him noticeably apart from other headmen in the area.

Several accounts describe the care Powhatan took to monopolize the copper trade with the Europeans (e.g., Strachey 1849:103). Considerable comment also exists on how Powhatan was prone to increase the amount of copper required to obtain corn and other supplies in barter with Europeans.[17] Clearly copper was of tremendous importance to the Powhatan. In all trading with the Europeans, at least, they were interested first and foremost in procuring copper (Strachey 1849:113). From the documents, it is difficult to establish why copper was so important. The obvious economic interpretation, that copper was a medium of exchange and that the Powhatan and others were operating on a money economy, seems unlikely. For one thing, if possession was limited to a single kin group within each tribal unit, copper would be an inefficient medium of exchange at best. Other aspects of its use and of the position of those who used it also belie this explanation.

A close look at Powhatan and his position as head of the Powhatan Confederacy suggests his power was based primarily on his role as a ceremonial leader rather than a political one. Chief Powhatan was so named because "Powhatan" was the name of his "principal place of dwelling" (Smith 1907:114). His proper name was entirely different. The name Powhatan was also associated with a sacred area near this "principal place of dwelling" and only a few individuals, priests and Powhatan himself, were allowed to enter there (Swanton 1946:643). This fact indicates that Powhatan's power may have been as much spiritually as politically or economically based. Furthermore, the nature of Powhatan's power and authority puzzled Smith (1907:114–16), who indicated that the chief seemed to command more awe and reverence than his political position (as Smith perceived it) should have dictated. Powhatan, he said, was esteemed not only as king, but as "halfe a god . . . at the least frowne of his browe, their greatest spirits will tremble with feare" [*sic*]. Again, such an evaluation suggests that the power base for Powhatan may have rested on supernatural abilities as much as on political or military ones.

Other details surrounding the use of copper at the time of contact with Europeans also indicate that its importance was not primarily economic. Some of the ways in which the Powhatan and other groups used copper suggest that although its use was generally limited to certain kin groups, copper and whatever it represented belonged to the community as a whole. This was certainly the case regarding the Tuchabachee plates discussed above. The "health and prosperity" of the entire town were believed to depend on the proper performance of rites associated with the copperwork, although those rites were performed by only a few special members of the community (Howard 1968:69). Details regarding the use of copper along the eastern seaboard suggest that the communal use and significance of copper at Tuchabachee was typical of much of the region.

For example, if one was not born into the "copper elite" of the Powhatan, the only way to obtain copper was through great deeds and/or exploits that were of benefit to the community as a whole, especially in war (Strachey 1849:111). Individuals who performed such feats were honored with a ceremony in which they were given a new name by the "king," along with a small amount of copper. In addition, among the Powhatan and other Algonkians in Virginia, the only capital offenses were the stealing of copper or corn (Smith 1884:cx–cxi). The latter was generally the property of the entire tribe, kept in communal storehouses and distributed by tribal leaders. The implication is that copper was community property as well. The gravity of the punishment for stealing copper suggests that copper was believed to be as vital in importance to the survival of the community as was their food supply.

Allouez (Thwaites 1896, vol. 50:265) recorded allied sentiments among Native Americans in the Great Lakes area. These peoples were convinced that the nuggets of copper certain families stored and treasured were gifts from "gods dwelling beneath the water . . . upon which their welfare is to depend." An incident described by Cartier (1924:233) also suggests that the possession of copper may have represented a kind of stewardship rather than ownership. At one point Cartier's men kidnapped a tribal "chief." After they convinced other members of the group that the "chief" would be returned to the tribe in due time—and only after this assurance—the others left and returned with a large copper knife which they presented to their kidnapped "chief." This sequence of events is not difficult to understand if the copper is assumed to be community property under the stewardship of the current chief. The chief's fellow tribesmen were perhaps convinced that the copper was properly maintained in the kidnapped chief's possession (as it had been traditionally), only as long as they were assured of the knife's return to the community. The logic is less clear if the copper involved is assumed to represent personal wealth. Communal ownership of copper helps to explain other aspects of native behavior as well. If all copperwork belonged to the community as a whole (although rights of stewardship were limited to a single kin group), that might explain why early chroniclers found that other members of the community were not envious of the copper elite.

The attribution of spiritual significance to copper also clarifies some of its political uses. Other traditions surrounding the copper plates of the Tuchabachee Creek are an excellent example. This communally-owned copperwork was important politically as well as spiritually (Swanton 1928a:507–10). The individuals who originally brought the plates to the Creeks indicated that the Shawnee had received similar examples of copperwork and that this material, along with related rituals and philosophies, would form the basis for an alliance between the two groups. It did, in fact, form the basis for such an alliance, although the Shawnee later moved north and took their copperwork with them. The tradition suggests that the possession and presentation of copperwork validated the messengers' claim to have been sent by the "Great Spirit." Thus, it was a supernatural authority (not the authority of any earthly political figure), proceeding from and symbolized by copperwork, that forged the alliance between the Creek and the Shawnee.

The plates presented to the latter were supposed to have been with the Shawnee Prophet on the battlefield at Tippecanoe (Swanton 1928a:508). It is tempting to wonder whether Tecumseh had used them in his attempts to unite his fellow Native Americans during his efforts to stem the tide of European hegemony. It may also be that they were carried into the battle in the hope that their special power might bring victory. Copper appears to have played a similar role in Virginia as a crucial vehicle in the formation of an alliance of several native groups against the English. Both Strachey (1849:104) and Lane (1965:745) refer to the incident.

Apparently one Native American leader in the area convinced several others to move against the English through either an impressive display or distribution of copperwork. The documents make the assumption that the copper used to foment the uprising was simply a bribe. If traditions and beliefs associated with copper in early contact times were as generally uniform as they seem to have been in the prehistoric periods, it seems more likely that the Virginia natives were trying to set up an alliance along the lines of the Tuchabachee-Shawnee model. The native leader apparently hoped to counter the threat of an increasing English presence by using the spiritual power and influence associated with copper to unify otherwise diverse groups. Similarities in ritual, design, and material represented by the copper complex throughout the eastern area suggest that copper may have acted as a similar kind of religio-political unifier in prehistoric times as well.

Even references to the ostensibly economic use of copper in early contact times hint at the spiritual importance of the material. For example, some mention is made of copper being used for trading purposes, although most observers agree that the possession and display of copper was limited to a small elite.[18] This suggests that there must have been something about copper as an item of trade that set transactions in which it was involved apart from the more mundane barter of everyday life. In fact, the one distinct privilege of the copper elite (beyond the possession of copper) noted in the documents involved a dominant trading position (Amadas n.d.:126). When individuals wearing large copper plates appeared at trading sessions between Native Americans and Europeans, the Native Americans withdrew until the members of the copper elite had completed their transactions and departed. Other sources mention gambling and obtaining wives as activities in which the exchange of copper was involved (Strachey 1849:105).

However, only those kinship groups to whom possession of copper was limited could have participated in these activities, which suggests that more was involved than mere games or economic transactions. The unique aspects of trade among so-called primitive groups have been examined at length in anthropological literature, providing support for this interpretation. For example, Wright (1967:194) writes of the native peoples of the western Great Lakes: "If avarice and hand-to-mouth economics were the only motives behind trade, then intertribal ceremonial gift giving to the point of poverty would not have occurred in rites like the Feast of the Dead. Further, valuable goods would not have found their final resting places with the dead." According to Anderson (1979:33), the economic significance of trade among traditional societies is often superseded by other aspects of the relationship. This may be true to the point that non-utilitarian objects, especially artwork, can be the foundation of a relationship that is ostensibly based upon trade although no economic basis exists for it. The corollary is that the basis for trade in these cases rests elsewhere. Where copper is involved, that other basis was almost certainly ceremonial.

A number of details about copper and its use, recorded just after the arrival of Europeans, seem highly implausible if the importance of copper is regarded as primarily economic. On the other hand, if copper is defined in the terms outlined above (as a communal repository for power entrusted to a single kin group in general and, in its most powerful forms, to specific members of that group), historical data on copper fit together in very logical ways. For example, the English referred to the copper and other goods Powhatan received from area tribal headmen as "tribute," implying that the goods were a forced payment based upon Powhatan's social and political power—a kind of primitive taxation. However, the Powhatan "Confederacy" included so many diverse groups and covered such a vast territory that it would have been virtually impossible to have formed and maintained that political entity by force, given native military technology and organization. (Had Powhatan and the other Virginia Algonkians been so organized in their futile uprising, they would have had little trouble defeating the English.)

If the rule of the copper elite is seen to be a matter of stewardship over a powerful, essentially beneficial substance by those best qualified to keep it, the nature of the "Confederacy" and the power of Powhatan take on more believable proportions. If Powhatan's position was based on his role as head of the kin group traditionally responsible for the maintenance and manipulation of copper, it follows that the copper "tribute" he received was not necessarily extracted by force. The copper may well have been given willingly to that group and/or individual perceived to be most capable of utilizing it beneficially on everyone's behalf. The other goods (primarily foodstuffs) that early chroniclers describe as part of this "tribute" could well have been a form of assistance to these traditional guardians of power, whose ceremonial responsibilities prevented their full participation in subsistence activities. The idea of a hereditary religious elite, responsible (among other duties) for carrying out important ceremonial functions and given the full and willing support of the rest of the culture group, is not at all farfetched. Willey and Shimkin (1973:477–78) posit a very similar cultural arrangement in the "small central Asian states of the first millennium A.D."

Admittedly, the documents suggest that the inclusion of individual tribes in this religio-political system in which copper played such an important role may not always have been a matter of choice. Some may have been forced to join the confederacy, but it would hardly have been the first time that a grand plan with a religious basis was forced by the majority upon a few unwilling "converts." A model for the confederacy that posits the political and military coercion of only a few "members," supported by the cooperation of the majority, provides a more credible estimate of the military capacity and personal power of Powhatan. The accuracy of this assessment of the situation among the Powhatan is supported by the logic it lends to virtually every account of Powhatan tradition as recorded by early explorers. More conventional politico-economic explanations of Powhatan history and the role of copper within that group often do not.

Many of the rather curious practices of the Powhatan are also easier to understand when the function of copper is described in primarily ceremonial terms. According to Smith (1884:cvii–cviii), the many women who bore children to Chief Powhatan left the chief's household after giving birth. Thereafter, he says, mother and child were "provided for" with copper and beads until the child was weaned and returned to Powhatan. It seems unlikely that the copper was used as currency to buy foodstuffs and other items, since its use was strictly limited to Powhatan and his family. The new mother would have been able to trade only with other members of the elite, who may or may not have been represented in her own village. Instead, the copper more likely served as a validation of the mother's new social and ceremonial status, established through having borne Powhatan's child. As such, her possession of copper perhaps assured that her needs and those of the child should and would be met by other members of the community.

Another well-known but curious set of circumstances involving the English and the Powhatan also seems far more logical when seen in this context and offers new insight into the Native American perception of Europeans. The actions and customs of Europeans probably seemed as illogical and "uncivilized" to Native Americans as vice versa. If native people saw copper to be a source of power, it was probably difficult for them to understand why, despite the possession of large amounts of copper, the English seemed quite incapable of manipulating it to their advantage in early attempts to survive in the New World. On the other hand, the extraordinary abilities of European weaponry (from the Native American point of view) would probably have been perceived as special control of powers in other areas. Lurie (1959:42) has pointed out that Chief Powhatan's primary motivation for promoting the marriage of his daughter Pocahontas to John Rolfe was his interest in English copper and firearms.

Perceived in accord with the above interpretation of the function and significance of copper, this combination of interests is hardly coincidental. If copper were perceived to be a repository of power entrusted by tradition to a specific kin group, this entire episode makes good logical sense. Since the control and possession of copper were fundamental to his own power base, Chief Powhatan may well have been convinced that the extraordinary powers of English weaponry lay in the large supply of copper they maintained. Smith, Rolfe, and others were perhaps believed to be members of a kin group among whites with a ceremonial role that paralleled his own; one that was based on their possession of great amounts of copper. Thus, the marriage of Rolfe and Pocahontas would have represented a very natural union of equals in the eyes of the Powhatan, an extension of the traditional kinship arrangement that would (theoretically) have greatly multiplied the store of power available to the community. Of course, the English perception of those arrangements was considerably different, and the results of the marriage/alliance varied accordingly. The fact that the Powhatan did not teach the English how to grow tobacco (another important element in the ceremonial life of the native peoples of Virginia) until this marital alliance was solemnized (Brandon 1965:16) adds weight to this interpretation of the account.

It is interesting that an important ceremonial connection between copper and tobacco is also to be found in traditions surrounding the Tuchabachee copper plates. Only one member of the original "messenger" group that brought the copper to Tuchabachee remained in the town; the others returned from whence they came. Eventually, the messenger "took the wrong medicine" and died. Tradition says that at the place he was buried, wild tobacco grew up. In recognition of this fact, a bit of tobacco was always buried with the plates after their use in the Busk rituals (Swanton 1928a:510).

Still another curious phenomenon regarding the attitudes of Native Americans toward copper in contact times makes more logical sense if copper is understood to have had special power associations. Smith (1907a:307) indicates that the native peoples of Virginia would do almost anything for a copper kettle. This was apparently true to some extent elsewhere, since fragments of European copper and brass kettles are frequent finds in most Early Historic sites (Quimby 1966:72).[19] A list of trade articles taken into the Illinois country in 1688 included "65 livres of copper kettles" (Quimby 1966:65). Copper and brass kettles are almost never discovered whole.

In addition, while the fragments of copper kettles are common in Early Historic sites in the Great Lakes region, iron ones are very rarely found. In fact, iron kettles were not generally in great demand among Native Americans, and some upper Mississippi valley groups actually refused to accept them in trade (Quimby 1966:64). The clear preference for copper (or brass) kettles alludes again to the special powers associated with these metals. From a practical standpoint, copper and iron kettles would have been equally as useful for activities such as cooking and carrying water. Utilitarian considerations were not a factor, however. The fact is that for a long time Native American groups had little interest in the utilitarian advantages of metal containers over traditional ceramic ones. Rather, metal containers were usually cut to pieces to make items that had traditionally been made from native copper (Lewis 1946:14). Copper (and eventually brass) kettles were valuable "raw" material because of the special powers associated with the metals from which they were made. Iron kettles were apparently useless for such purposes.[20]

The linguistic status of the word "kettle" in Algonkian languages is intriguing, examined in the light of the above facts. A formal distinction is made between nouns which are considered to be animate and those which are inanimate (Hallowell 1975:146–48). Animate nouns include all animals and persons as well as certain objects and natural phenomena, including pipes, kettles, the sun and moon, thunder, and stones. According to Hallowell, these objects and phenomena appear to have the same "ontological status" as persons or animals, but with an important distinction: these objects have a *potential* for animation, identified through experience. It is interesting, in this context, that tradition surrounding copper itself (not just kettles) among the Haida and Kwakwakäwakwa also avers that "copper is alive" and that its "mine and mountain are magical" (Mauss 1967:114). Pipes, the sun and moon, thunder, and stones are all items and entities that have important ritual and cosmological connections, as well as the apparent potential for animation. It is highly unlikely that kettles were included within this group of special entities as mere cooking utensils. No other such items are on the list presented by Hallowell, and in Early Historic times kettles were rarely used for cooking, in any case. Whatever the specifics of the association between kettles and other potentially animate entities in the Algonkian languages, the material from which brass and copper kettles were made almost certainly accounts for their special inclusion.

If the possession of copper was limited to an elite, its mining and manipulation must have been an exclusive right as well. Winter (1968:209) draws similar conclusions regarding the working of imported marine shell in Archaic sites in Kentucky. This exclusivity, in turn, suggests that the manufacture of copperwork and, probably, the mining of copper and other exotica were also of considerable ritual significance. The manufacture of sacred materials among traditional societies is frequently believed to be an essential aspect of the ritual for which the piece is constructed (Levine 1957:961). This was probably true for the working of copper. On the Northwest Coast, the "privilege" of working copper forms the basis for an important cycle of Tsimshian legends (Mauss 1967:114). Elsewhere in the world, the mining and working of copper among traditional societies is the object of considerable ritual, and participation in such activities is restricted on that basis (e.g., Bradley 1952:33–38).

The existence of similar traditions surrounding the manipulation of copper in the prehistoric eastern United States may explain why a number of individuals given elaborate burial treatment appear to have been artisans, buried with specialized tools and raw materials. Additional evidence that such beliefs may have been current in the region during precontact times is the frequent appearance beneath mound complexes of workshop areas and tools for the manufacture of ceremonial goods.[21] If ceremonial manipulation of the raw material was an integral part of the belief systems associated with the copper complex, the death of an individual deemed ceremonially qualified to work with such exotica might render his supply of raw materials useless to his successor. This rationale could explain why large quantities of unworked copper are occasionally included in burials.

A ceremonial emphasis in the manipulation of copper may also explain some very unusual constructions at the Hopewell-related Turner Mounds in Ohio. The base of one of seven connected mounds within a large earth enclosure was "concrete" (probably fire-hardened earth) with a network of pits and tunnels beneath it (Willoughby and Hooton 1922:35–44). Above this network of tunnels and pits was a large hearth. The tunnels were 12" wide, 11" high and 8'7" long. Two of the thirty pits in the complex ended in chimneys, and the entire network contained a fine layer of ash. The excavators noted that Historic Period Hopi cooked corn in constructions similar to the Turner pits, but doubted whether the Turner pits had the same purpose because they were so numerous.

Construction reminiscent of oven forms was also discovered in Mound C at Etowah (Moorehead 1932:81). These structures could have been used as "furnaces" to heat native copper in preparation for its manufacture into ceremonial paraphernalia. If so, their inclusion in ceremonial enclosures and mounds implies the ritual significance of the processes for which they were constructed.

The remarkable skill and expertise exhibited by prehistoric miners also suggest that the basic significance of copper was ceremonial. A longstanding, carefully preserved ritual specialization in copper mining techniques would be more likely to produce the precise skills apparent at the mining sites than would a simply mercenary and essentially random interest in the copper deposits; this would also explain how the complex sprang repeatedly into full blown expression of sophisticated technological design after centuries of almost no apparent activity.

The most convincing argument against a primarily economic basis for the significance of copper, however, is the fact that virtually all of the copper was ultimately returned to the ground in the form of burial goods. Although the burial of the wealth of the community with the dead may appear to be systematic self-impoverishment to modern eyes, it is unlikely that such practices were so perceived by precontact Americans. Thus, we must assume that economic motivations and perceptions, in the modern sense, either did not exist within these societies or were defined in entirely different terms. The validity of this contention is supported by the fact that, although later groups were apparently aware that copper was buried in the mounds, I have found no evidence that *any* prehistoric grave sites were ever plundered for their copper by anyone but Europeans—even when the native groups inhabiting a given area seemed to have had no ancestral connections with the peoples interred in the mounds (e.g., Gibson 1954:22). Some native groups seem to have purposefully intruded the burials of their own members into earlier burials at some sites, but there is no evidence of grave robbery, even in these instances (e.g., Webb and Wilder 1951:127).

Even the wholesale reburial of grave goods from earlier burials in the Great Mortuary at Spiro is clearly more a matter of recycling than plunder. Furthermore, in at least one case, later peoples inhabiting a site (Etowah) made frequent use of domiciliary mounds built by earlier inhabitants, but avoided all contact with Mound C where the copper burials were located (Kelly and Larson 1957:45). Surely, if the importance of copper were primarily economic, ambitious groups and individuals would have looted some of these graves, especially considering the lengths to which they went to obtain copper elsewhere.

Thus far we have established that membership in the "copper elite" probably depended on certain kinship affiliations. Its use by the elite was determined, in part, by the nature of that group's collective and individual "stewardship" of copper and its meaning for the larger community. The need to restrict the use of copper to this elite follows naturally from these data and the nature of the objects and designs made. If the significance of copper in these societies was not economic and copper was perceived as a repository for power, the supernatural elements and beings depicted on the copperwork were probably conceptualizations of that power. In most cases, those entities and powers were believed to be as capable of causing disaster as they were of promoting great good. The powers embodied in copper were probably perceived in the same terms. If so, prudence would dictate limiting the possession of copper to those whose ancestry and/or training would enable them to control its power and to channel it in directions that would benefit the community, while avoiding harm to themselves or others. In addition, Native American tradition frequently defines death as a transition from one part of the universe to another rather than as the termination of life.

Given such beliefs, if copper represented a repository for spiritual power which certain individuals could control in ways that were beneficial to the community, the most reasonable thing to do with copperwork following the death of those who used it well would be to bury it with them. It could logically be assumed that in the afterlife, the individual would continue to manipulate the power embodied in copper to the advantage of those left behind (or, perhaps, to the advantage of members of the community already residing in the land of the dead). Thus, the community would be assured of continuing benefits from the copper and, at the very least, could effectively prevent its falling into the wrong hands and bringing harm of some kind to the group.

The analysis and comparison of archaeological and early ethnological evidence cited above indicate that many of the same designs and related concepts were associated with copper throughout its centuries of importance in Native North American societies. These same sources show little change in methods of use and disposition of copperwork through the prehistoric periods, as well as in Historic times. Copper was displayed and used by a small, probably hereditary, elite, and its significance was primarily ceremonial, although it clearly had economic and political roles as well. This remarkable consistency over space and time suggests that very ancient traditional ideas regarding the material itself probably formed the basis for the ceremonial practices that involved its use.[22]

The remarkable consistency apparent throughout the copper complex would be virtually impossible to explain were it not for the continuity provided by the characteristics of the metal itself. The significance of the color and other physical properties of copper in Early Historic Period use indicate that those same characteristics formed the basis for traditional beliefs about copper from earliest times. Ideas based upon the essentially static physical properties of the metal itself could account for the extraordinary longevity of those beliefs. The primary uses of copper through the years indicate that those beliefs were associated with aspects of the supernatural. As such, the religious significance of copper went far beyond any economic or political importance it may have had. In fact, those economic and political functions were almost certainly an outgrowth of the special powers associated with copper.

The closest analogy in our own society would be the status of certain radioactive elements like plutonium—of great potential benefit to the community by virtue of the power contained therein. Obviously, it is the power resident in these materials and their ability to do great harm and/or good that renders them economically and politically important. Furthermore, the average citizen, without proper training and/or protection, has no desire to possess these materials and, in fact, generally avoids any contact with them whatsoever. Society, in general, is happy to leave the manipulation of these materials to those who know how to put them to use for the benefit of the community as a whole, as long as proper precautions are taken to prevent disaster that might result from the material's falling into the wrong hands, or through careless use on the part of the "experts." Clearly a similar logic and practicality must have formed the basis of Native North American attitudes and beliefs regarding native copper, whatever they may have been.

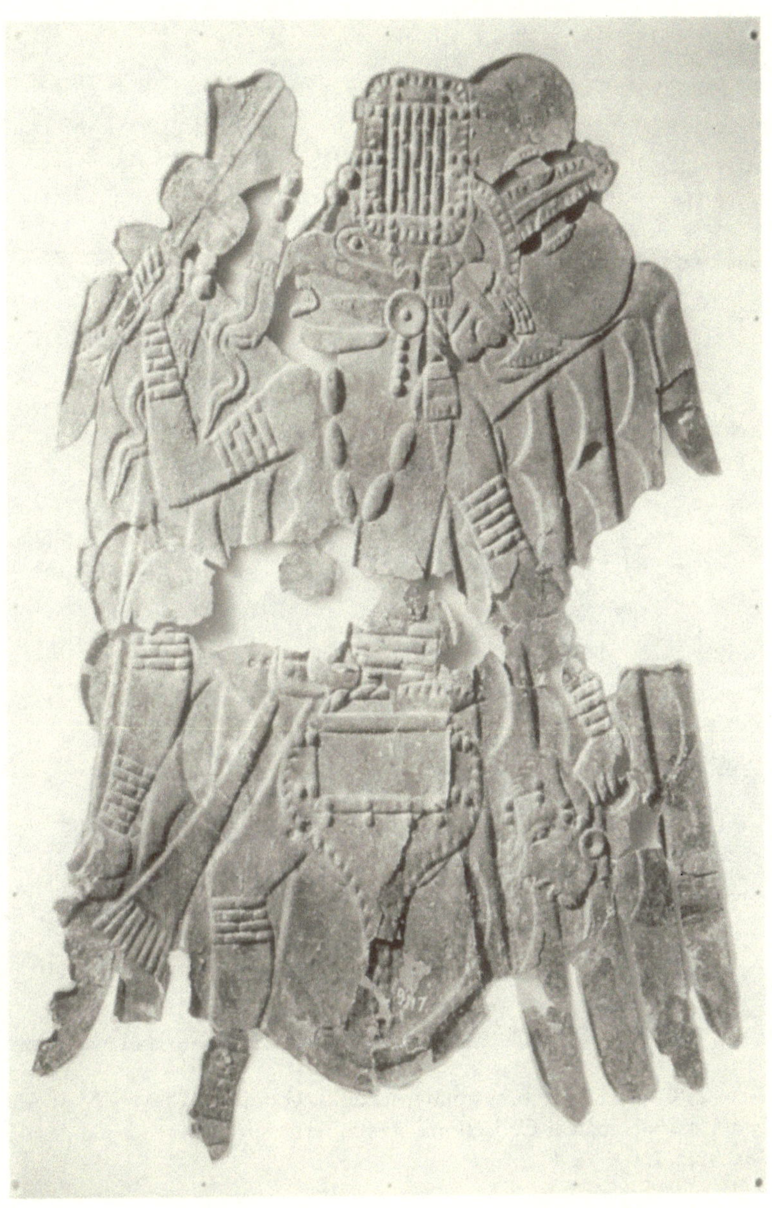

Plate 1. Repoussé Headpiece with Dancing Figure, Mississippian. Catalogue No. #91113, Department of Anthropology, Smithsonian Institution, Washington, D.C. Etowah Mounds, Bartow Co., Georgia. 15½" x 8".

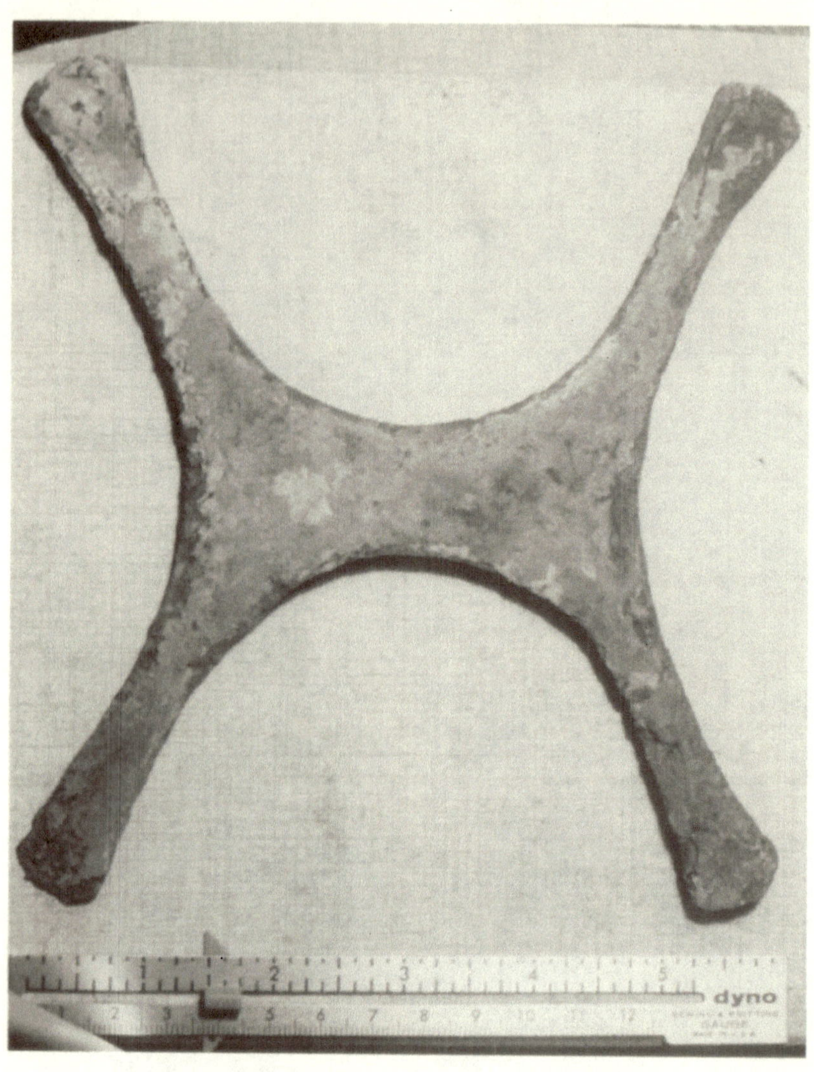

Plate 2. Copena Style Breastplate, Middle Woodland. University of Alabama Archaeological Collections, #a40. Terry Site, Lawrence Co., La43, Alabama. Ca. 4" x 4".

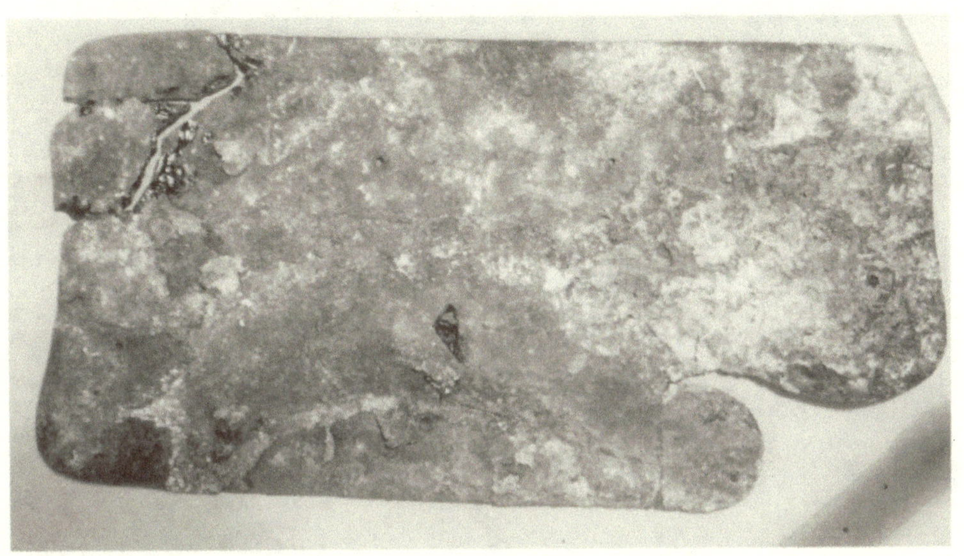

Plate 3. Large Hopewell Style Breastplate with Scroll Design, Middle Woodland. Ohio Historical Society, Columbus, #957/313. Seip Mound, Ross Co., Ohio. Ca. 9" long.

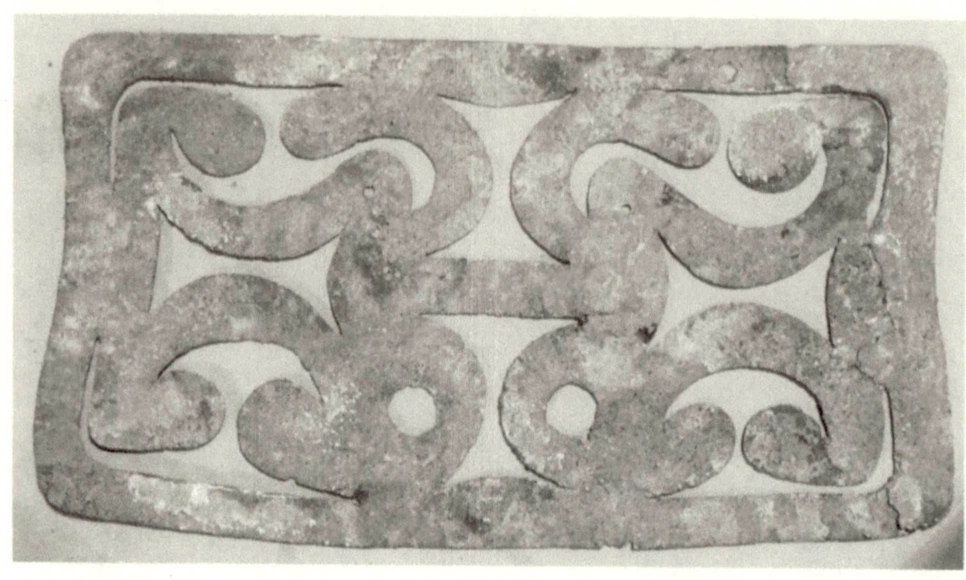

Plate 4. Openwork Breastplate with Raptor Design, Middle Woodland. Ohio Historical Society, Columbus, #260/123. Mound City Mounds, Mound 7, bu. 9, Ross Co., Ohio. Ca. 8" long.

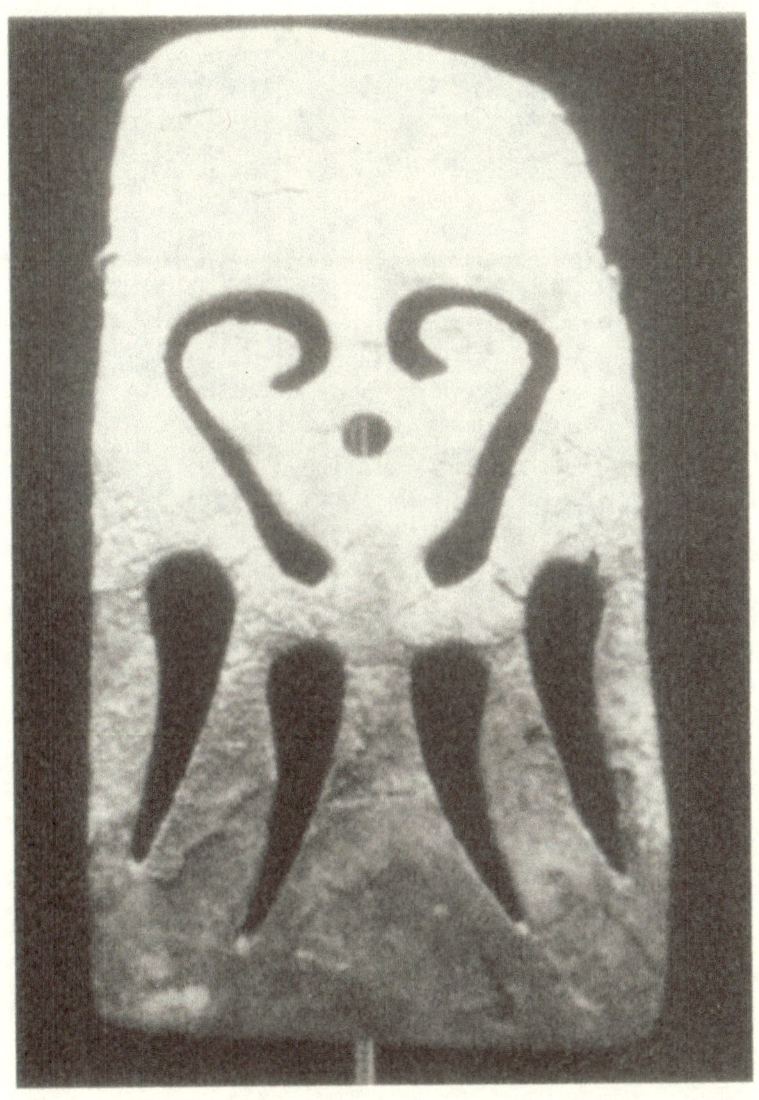

Plate 5. Openwork Hopewell Style Headplate, Middle Woodland. Ohio Historical Society, Columbus, #283/109. Hopewell Mounds, Ross Co., Ohio. Ca. 10" across.

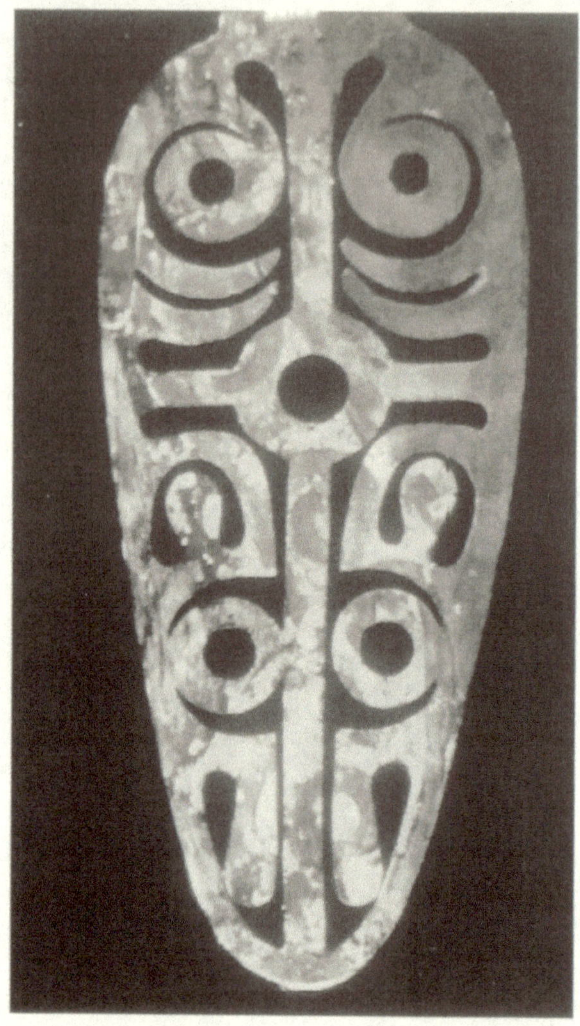

Plate 6. Large Openwork Composite Bird/Bear Figure, Middle Woodland. The Field Museum, Chicago. #56165. Courtesy, Pictures of Record, Inc., Hopewell Mounds, Ross Co., Ohio. 12 1/2" x 5 1/2".

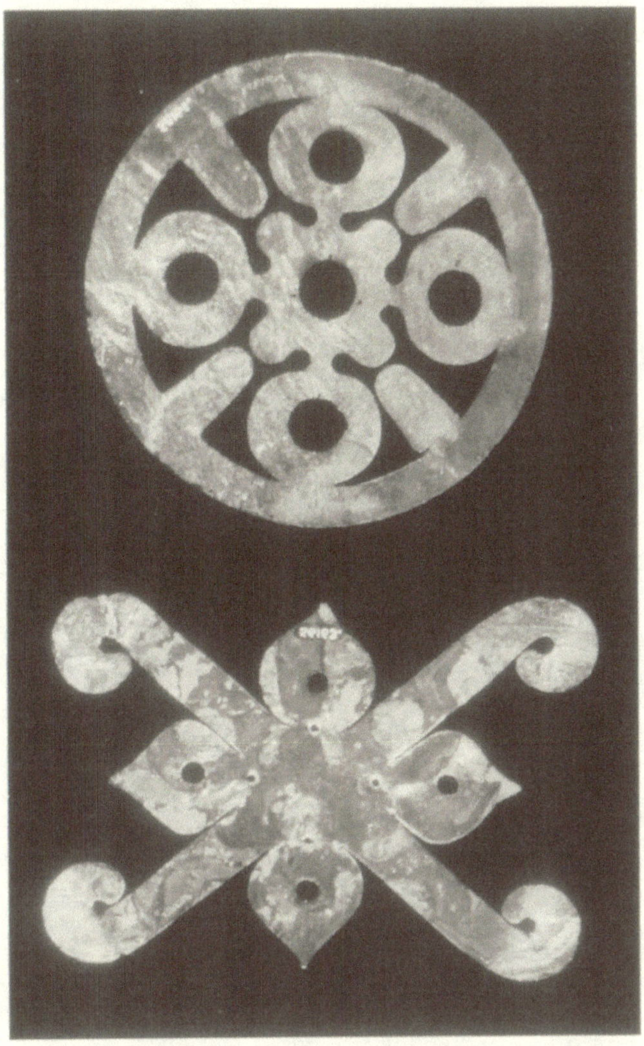

Plates 7a & 7b. Large Openwork Designs (part of a cache of over 250 similar pieces), Middle Woodland. The Field Museum, Chicago, #56163 and #56164. Hopewell Mounds, Ross Co., Ohio. Ca. 10" and 8".

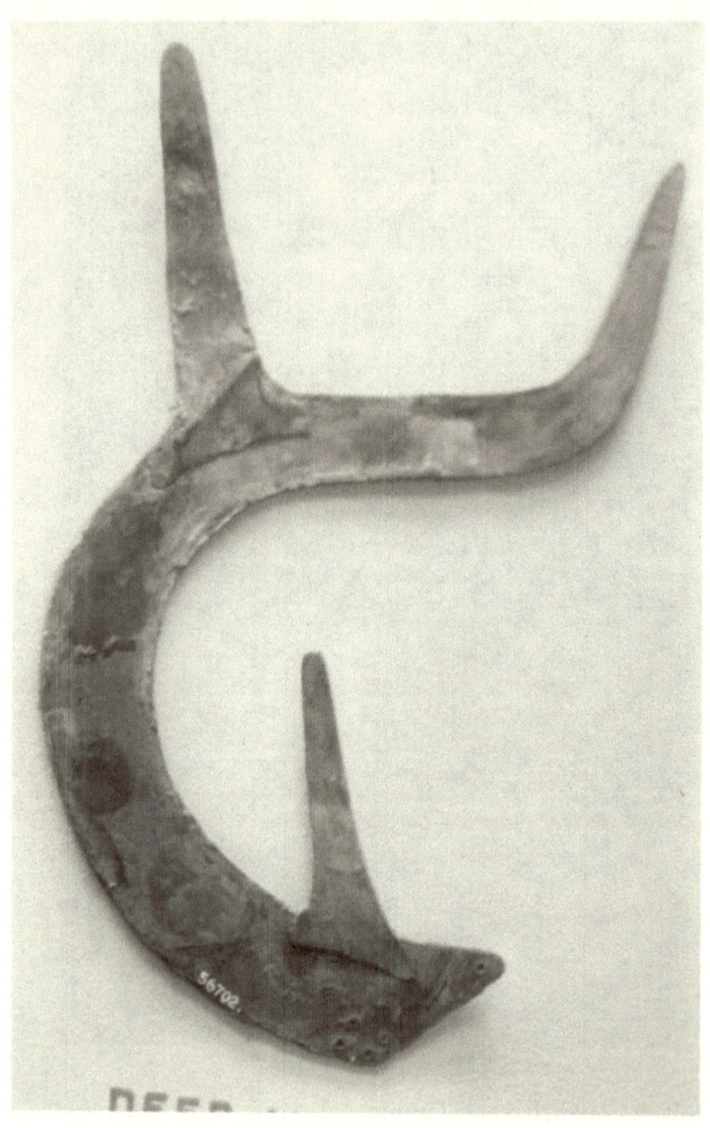

Plate 8. Copper Antler, Middle Woodland. The Field Museum, Chicago, #56702. Hopewell Mounds, Crematory Basin, Ross Co., Ohio. Ca. 13" tall.

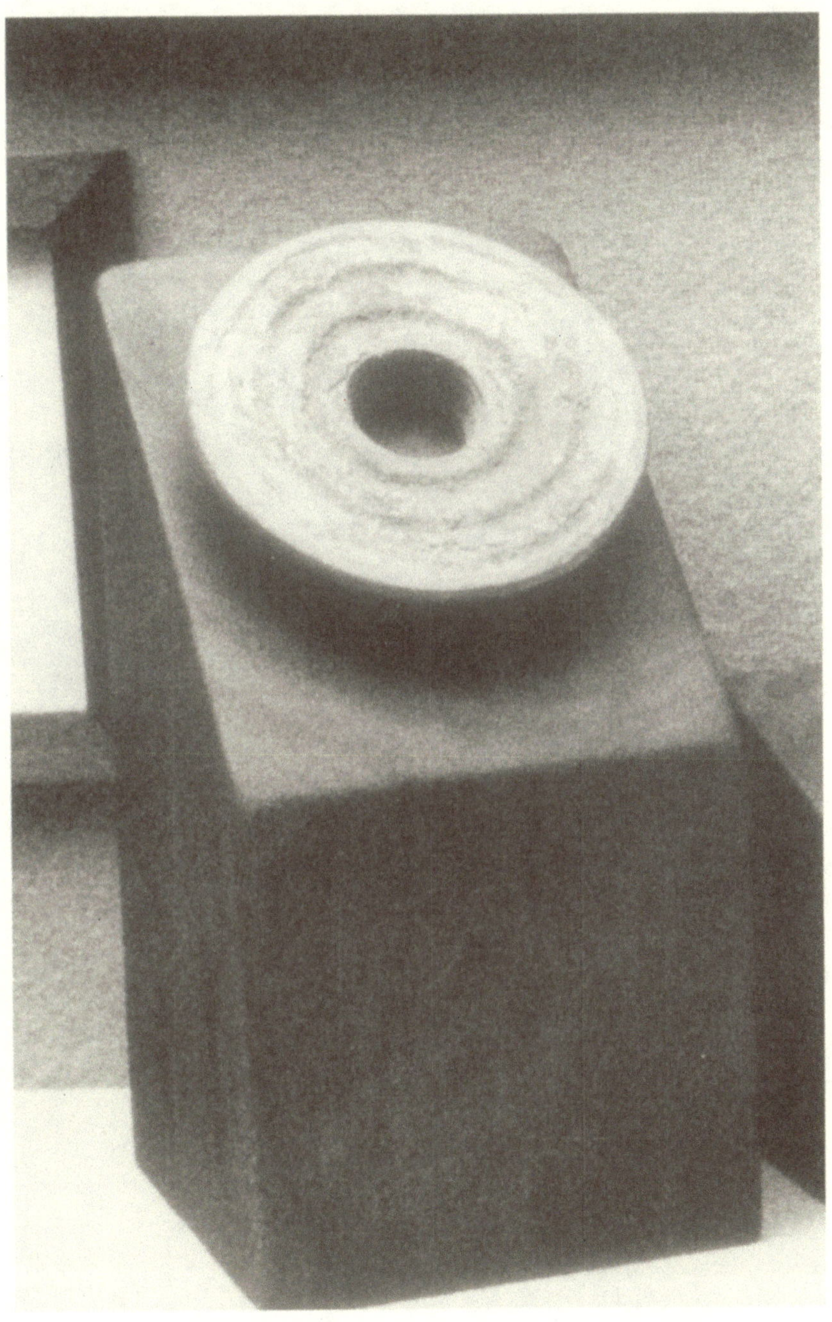

Plate 9. Mississippian Style Stone/Copper Earpiece. Woolaroc Museum, Bartlesville, Oklahoma. Spiro Site, LeFlore Co., Oklahoma. Ca. 3" dia.

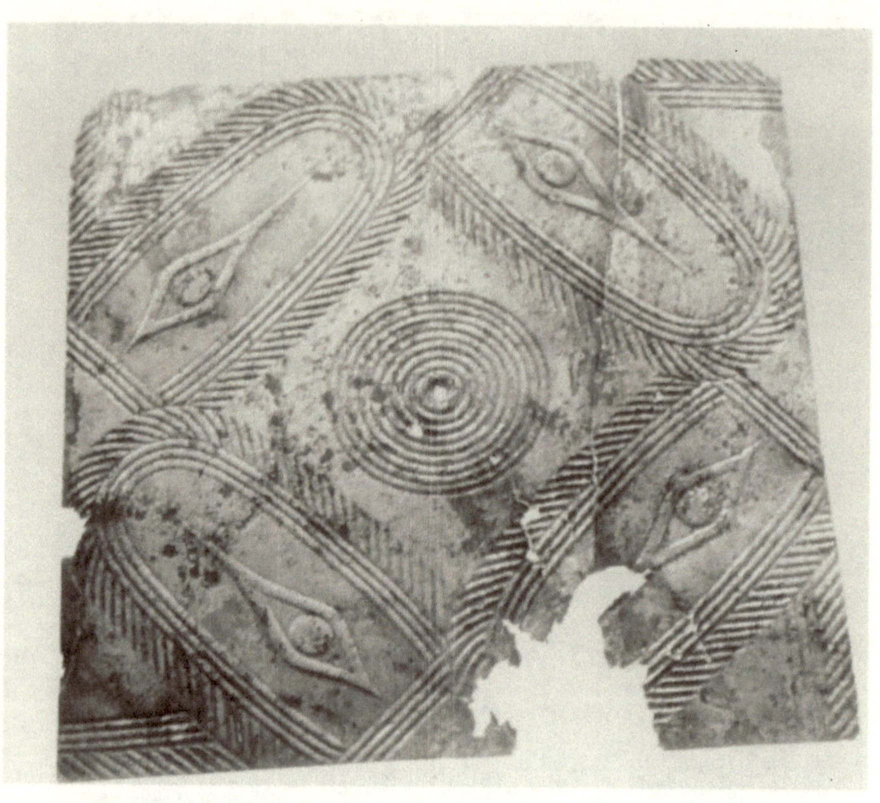

Plate 10. Large Repoussé Plate, Mississippian. Ohio Historical Society, Columbus. Spiro Site, LeFlore Co., Oklahoma. Ca. 1' square.

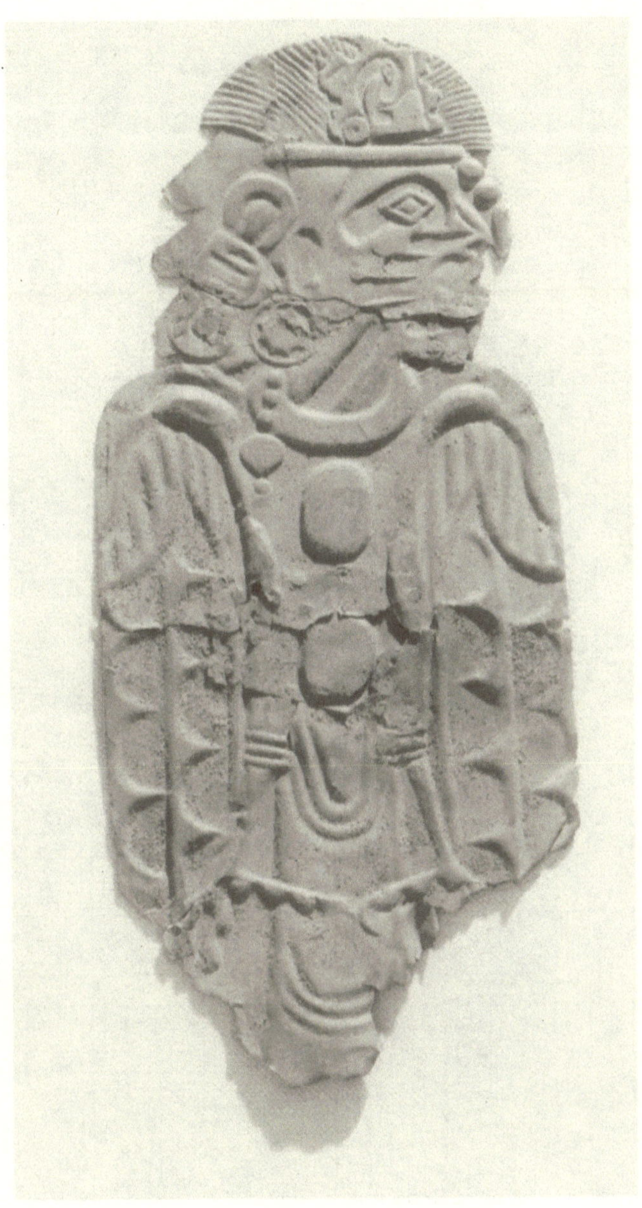

Plate 11. Copper Repoussé Plaque, Mississippian. Washington University Gallery of Art, St. Louis, #3679. Gift of J. Max Wulfing, 1937. Malden, Dunklin Co., Missouri. $11^3/_4$" x $5^1/_4$".

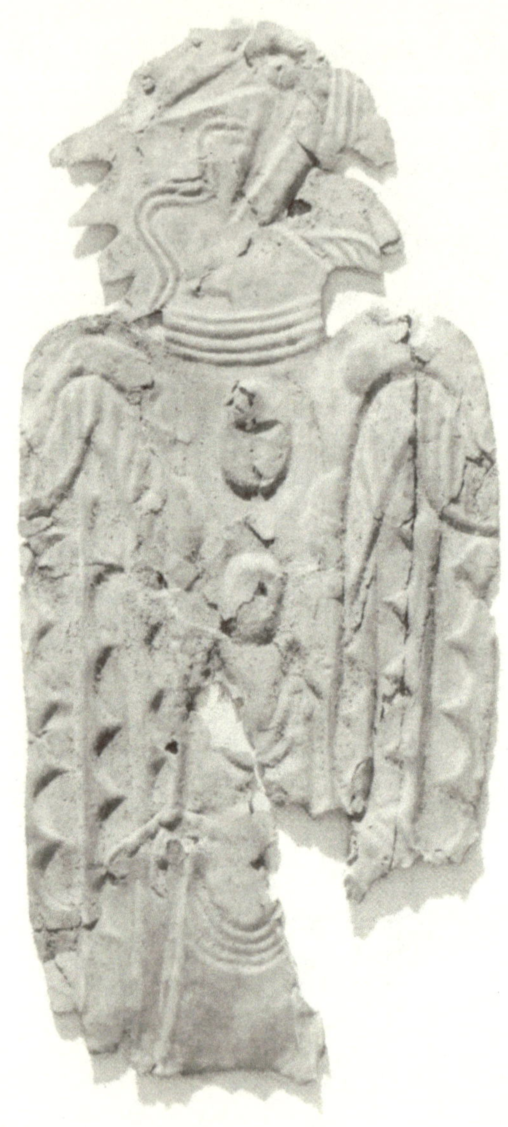

Plate 12. Copper Repoussé Plaque. Mississippian. Washington University Gallery of Art, St. Louis, #3681. Gift of J. Max Wulfing, 1937. Malden, Dunklin Co., Missouri. 13" x 5 3/4". Copper Plate. Washington University Gallery of Art, St. Louis, #3681. Wulfing Plate, Malden, Dunklin Co., Missouri. Ca. 15 1/2" x 7".

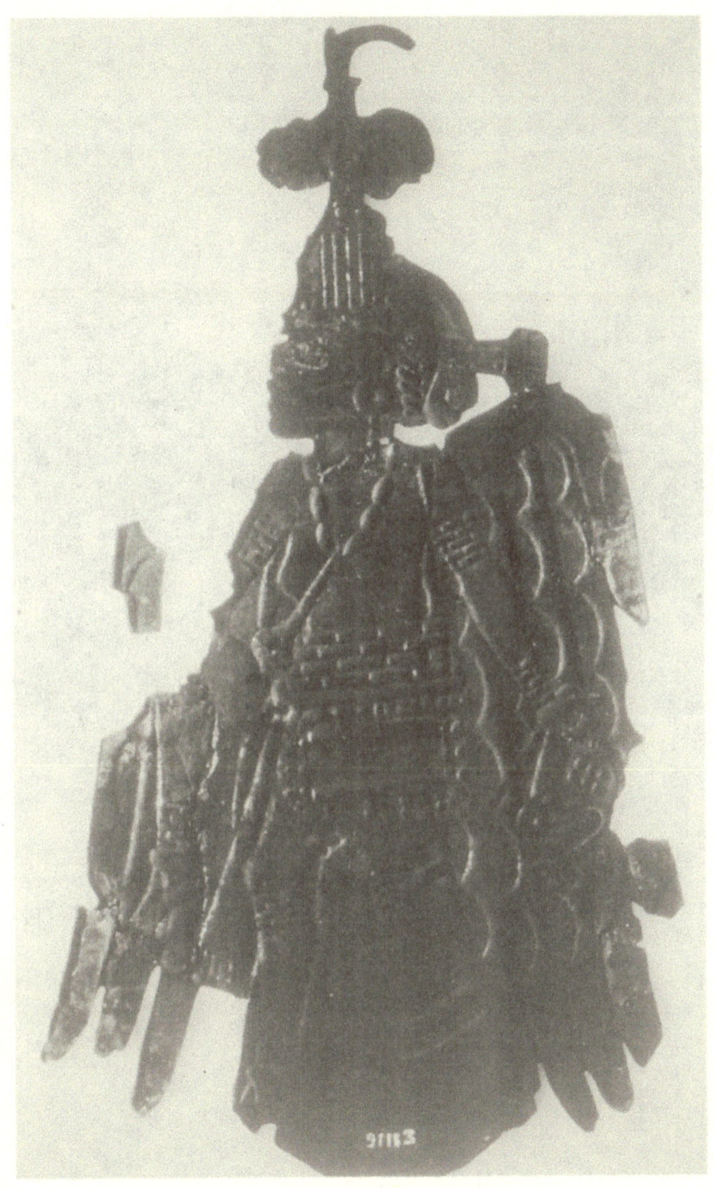

Plate 13. Repoussé Headpiece with Dancing Figure, Mississippian. Catalogue No. #91117, Department of Anthropology, Smithsonian Institution, Washington, D.C. Etowah Mounds, Bartow Co., Georgia. 15½" x 8".

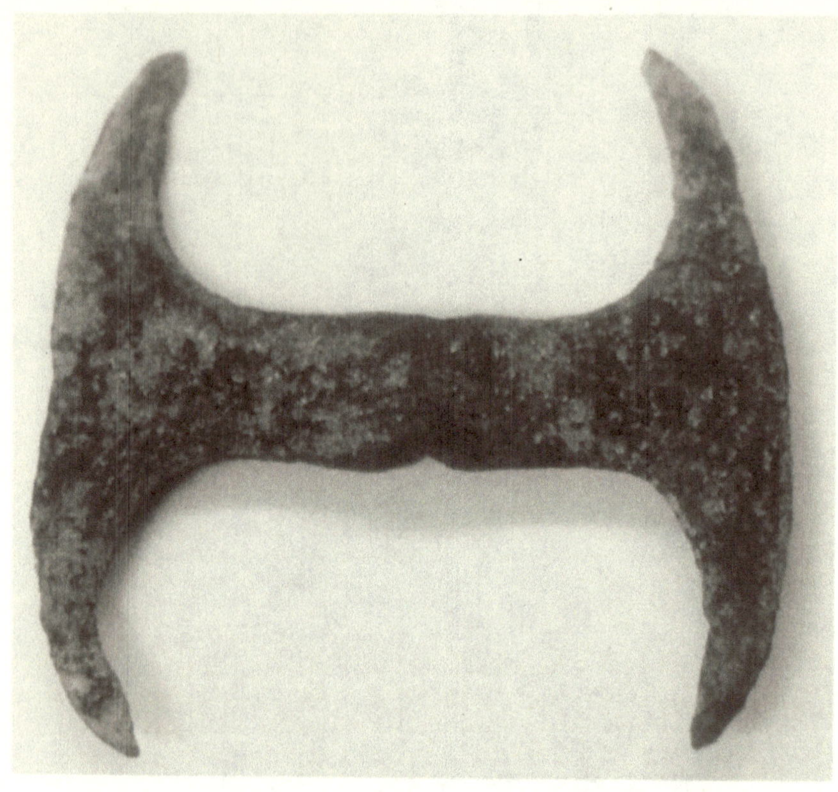

Plate 14. Large Double Axe (with vertical hole for haft), "Old Copper Culture." Milwaukee Public Museum, #43402/11996. Found near Scott, Fond du Lac Co., Wisconsin. 5" across.

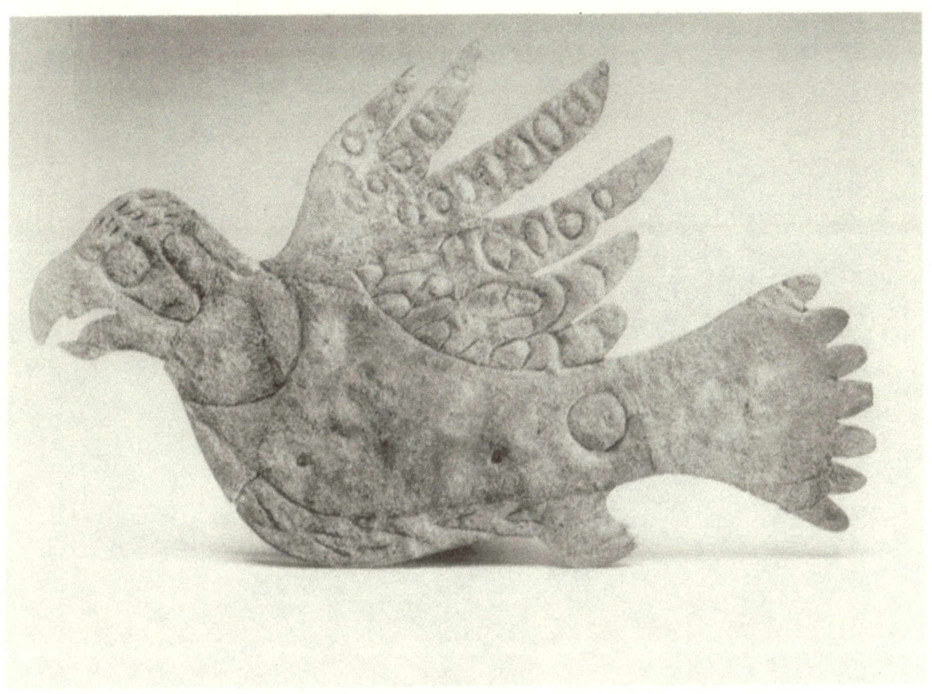

Plate 15. Repoussé Peregrine Falcon, Middle Woodland. Ohio Historical Society, Columbus, #260/125. Mound City Site, Ross Co., Ohio. 12 1/4".

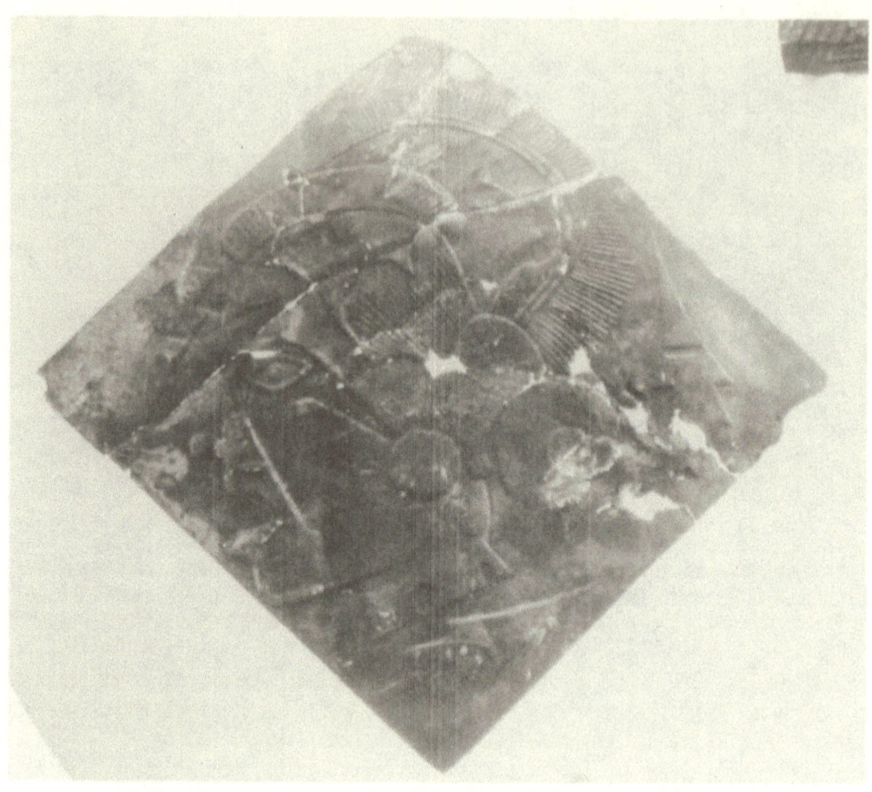

Plate 16. Large Repoussé Headpiece with Human Head, Mississippian. Ohio Historical Society, Newark Mounds. Spiro Site, LeFlore Co., Oklahoma. Ca. 1' square.

4

Copper: Its Ceremonial Role

Clearly copper played a central role in the ceremonial life of many prehistoric Native Americans. Their material remains suggest that culture and lifestyle in prehistoric times were not greatly different from the lifeways observed by early European visitors in North America (although the Europeans rarely understood much of it). This evidence suggests that prehistoric ceremonies and rituals probably developed and changed in much the same way that Early Historic religious practices did. Ecological factors and longstanding patterns of behavior were crucial elements in these processes, both before and after contact, and certainly influenced the long tradition in which copper was so crucial. The bulk of this chapter will be devoted to discussion of cultural patterns and ecological conditions that obtained in the eastern United States during prehistoric and Early Historic times.

Problems with Certain Traditional Approaches

Traditional approaches to the examination of Native American and other so-called primitive societies often have built-in prejudices and misconceptions. These problems originate in the tendency to apply modern Euro–North American values to groups for whom such values have no relevancy. The most basic motives, values, and assumptions governing Native American cultures could not have been at all similar to modern Western ones, or those cultures would not have developed in the very diverse ways in which each has. Many will disagree with this assertion, some with valid and defensible points of view. The fact remains, however, that a clear picture of the prehistoric copper complex (how it functioned and why it ceased to be of importance after the arrival of Europeans) simply does not emerge from the data without careful avoidance of certain assumptions and modes of thinking. These traditional and not altogether uncommon patterns of reasoning are defined here as impediments to accurate interpretation and as thought patterns that have been consciously avoided in this study. Three of these traditional assumptions are particularly problematic in the analysis of the prehistoric copper complex. They are:

1. the suggestion that culture evolves in much the same way as man himself is believed to have evolved—from certain lower life forms to the current state of foremost advancement as represented by modern Euro–North American culture and technology;
2. the assumption that the significance of artistic production and the procurement of appropriate raw materials by Native North American cultures can be explained accurately in purely economic terms;
3. the conviction that development of a viable art tradition depends upon and is determined by the amount of leisure time available within the subject culture.

The first proposition, that culture evolves in essentially the same way as organisms, is problematic in at least two ways. First, such a theory indicates that so-called primitive hunting and gathering or agricultural societies are somehow less evolved than are modern, industrial ones. The implication that the human beings involved are also at different evolutionary levels is a proposition that most would agree is not viable. Modes of subsistence and evolutionary stages simply do not directly correlate.

Second, the idea that culture evolves suggests that later states and stages are somehow better or more progressive than earlier ones, that a move toward a more complex social organization or mode of subsistence represents a positive step while developments in the other direction are somehow regressive, and that the relative speed with which a culture proceeds in one direction or the other has some kind of qualitative significance. Moreover, such a line of thought implies that this evolutionary trend should be recognized and consciously advanced by the peoples involved, to achieve higher and higher levels of culture or to avoid falling into lower ones. This thinking inevitably includes concepts such as "progress," "advancement," and movement toward "civilization" as well as the possibility of cultural success or failure. These concepts are basic to traditional Euro–North American modes of thought but are almost certainly alien to Native American value systems and approaches to culture. If such ideas had been a part of those systems, it does not seem likely that the history and prehistory of precontact North America would have proceeded as it did.

The claim that culture evolves in an irreversible march toward industrialized society is also belied by the fact that agriculturally based subsistence systems and sedentary lifestyles in eastern North America were abandoned "overnight" for a lurch "backward" into the nomadic hunting and gathering subsistence methods of Plains groups. Such a step would have been unthinkable if the achievement of a higher and more complex expression of "civilization" motivated subsistence-related decisions of Native North Americans in any way.

In fact, an evolutionary theory of culture leaves a number of well-known aspects of prehistoric Native North American societies without any reasonable explanation. It suggests no reason why certain prehistoric eastern groups should maintain a simple Early Woodland kind of lifestyle despite their inevitable exposure to the "higher civilization" possessed by close neighbors who participated in the cultural complexities of the Hopewellian ceremonial fluorescence. Nor can an evolutionary theory of culture explain why those same neighbors eventually abandoned that more "civilized" way of life for simpler lifeways and subsistence modes, as had so many other pre-Columbian American civilizations farther south.

The fact that Native Americans were a metal-using culture for thousands of years that never bothered to develop smelting or alloying technologies also renders evolutionary theories regarding the development of culture and technology less than credible. Even if an evolutionary interpretation of culture could be proved valid, reasoning from that standpoint can offer no assistance in the attempt to understand the thought processes and motivations of Native North Americans, if accurate results are to be achieved.

Most evidence examined in connection with this study suggests that Native North American groups, in whatever time period (to be discussed in detail below), chose to live in the simplest, least complex way possible, given the climatic, topographical, geographical, and demographic circumstances. As those circumstances varied from place to place, so did the responses of the inhabitant groups. If situations arose that required more complex social and political responses, Native Americans were certainly capable of making appropriate ones and apparently did. Yet, repeated indications are that as soon as maintenance of the basic needs of the community no longer required such complexity, that complexity very quickly disappeared. Copper and other exotica likely played an important role in helping to bring about these relatively rapid alterations in cultural complexity. (This issue will also be explored in more detail below.)

Regarding the second assumption, for decades scholars have made detailed studies of prehistoric trade patterns. They have traced the movement of various items throughout the eastern United States.[1] Such interests continue to be a focus of study for many archaeologists. Most of such analyses have gathered and interpreted important data and have contributed much to an understanding of the prehistoric peoples living in the eastern United States.

However, the economic focus of these studies consistently ignores crucial aspects of the copper complex and related aspects of prehistoric life. Because the use of copper in prehistoric societies was almost exclusively ceremonial (as the bulk of the archaeological evidence indicates), to be perceived accurately the complex must be analyzed in ceremonial terms, as an outgrowth of ritual. Studies that focus only on the economic implications of the complex imply that the Hopewell "Interaction Sphere" and the Southeastern Ceremonial Complex were structures developed primarily to promote an efficient trade system for various exotic and more mundane goods. Such an approach tends to obscure the real significance of the objects and artifacts under examination, as well as other material remains of prehistoric peoples. Major sites are often defined as centers for trade, for example, rather than ceremonial centers, first and foremost.

Economic interpretations also ignore the most significant element in the development of the copper complex as a whole; its initial and sustaining motivation. Ignorance of these crucial issues prevents any real understanding of the peoples who built, maintained, and ultimately deserted those important prehistoric centers of religious activity.

Evidence is ample of some kind of trade occurring in connection with the copper complex. Obviously the copper, whether in raw or finished form, was somehow transported from source areas to widespread locations throughout the eastern region. The most likely means for this distribution was certainly some kind of trade network. The problem lies in insisting upon an economic interpretation of these phenomena, a misunderstanding in approach that has plagued relationships between Native Americans and Europeans since their earliest meeting.

Ethnographic data for all major Native American religious movements after contact suggest that "trade" in exotica that was central to important rituals was not "trade" at all; instead it amounted to the sharing of ritual paraphernalia among religious specialists or even one-sided bestowals from "prophets" and "disciples" to their new converts, rather than exchange in any economic sense. There is little reason to assume items of major ceremonial and ritual importance changed hands in any other way prehistorically. (This situation will also be discussed in more detail below.) Considerable evidence also suggests that these exchanges involved much more than mere religious proselytizing. Group survival was likely a major factor in the founding of these religious movements, as well as in the interest generated among "converts."

Regarding the third assumption, for many years scholars assumed that significant artistic endeavor in traditional societies was possible only with the achievement of a standard of living that allowed a certain amount of leisure time. The suggestion was that Paleolithic man created relatively little art because he was much too busy trying to survive to bother with something so superficial and unnecessary as art. According to this rationale, art was produced only after man was able to make more efficient use of resources and thus had more time to amuse himself with artistic expression. In other words, when life became good enough, man could relax and create art. Thus it was implied that primitive art was a luxury, a way to "while away the hours" and to utilize blocks of time previously devoted to crucial subsistence activities.

If this is true, if art production is indeed a function of relative leisure, it should follow that increased leisure time should result in more and better art production. Increased quantity and quality should go hand in hand with an easier lifestyle. The most superficial examination of relative art production through history and throughout the world proves this to be faulty logic. Even Boas (1928:300) was guilty of suggesting leisure as a determinant in the nature of art production, although the introduction to this same work contains a more accurate statement of the facts. There Boas points out that all societies, regardless of the barrenness of their existence in terms of the struggle to survive, are involved in art production (Boas 1928:9).

It follows that art production is probably not the superficial activity that it may seem to be, especially for traditional peoples. Anderson (1979:31–32) is more specific than Boas in his evaluation of the function of art in traditional societies. He states that art is, in fact, a need for all peoples and often serves as a reservoir of energies to draw upon in times of unprecedented or unpredictable trouble. Geertz (1973:140) goes a step further. He indicates that art production can be a very real need, stemming from the "drive to make sense out of experience, to give it form and order," and suggests that this artistic need is "as real and as pressing as the more familiar biological" ones.

The most prevalent designs and themes found on precontact copperwork certainly suggest that "real and pressing" needs and interests motivated prehistoric coppersmiths. For example, the consistent interest in circular forms and their association with cosmological concepts clearly alludes to the conceptual expression of order. Continual reference to and balancing of potentially evil and good forces or beings in the motifs found on copperwork also correspond to Geertz's interpretation of the function and significance of art.

Surely the arduous nature of prehistoric mining practices and methods of manufacture indicates that what Geertz says about artistic motivation is a more accurate statement of the facts regarding native art in copper than is a theory that suggests that art was just a way to "while away the hours." Furthermore, archaeological and ethnological evidence, much of which is cited below, indicates that increased art production and related ritual developed is in response to bad times and to cultural crises, not as the result of a general sense of prosperity and well being—conditions one would expect to find in a society enjoying a significant increase in available leisure time.

Review of Characteristics of the Copper Complex

The preceding chapters have established and discussed a number of important facts regarding the copper complex:

1. the designs applied to native copper,
2. the characteristics of those who used it, and
3. the likely significance of the metal itself.

In each of these areas, the evidence indicates a remarkably unified tradition. The gradual yet distinct evolution in the types of objects made from copper as well as the kinds of designs used throughout the copper complex all point to a long and essentially unitary development. Basic uses of copper as well as the kinds of motifs employed in the latest periods do not seem to be radically different from those apparent in earliest times—phenomena that are especially remarkable in view of the millennia spanned by the complex.

It seems likely that the rituals in which copperwork was so important were associated with subsistence activities, probably their successful maintenance. A number of factors point to this conclusion. For example, the two most radical shifts in general subject matter on copperwork occur between the Archaic and Woodland Periods and the Woodland and Mississippian Periods; both shifts are marked by important changes in modes of subsistence and related shifts in social structures and demographic patterns. As native peoples turned from Archaic hunting and gathering economies to the cultivation of local plants, the use of pottery, and other Woodland characteristics, the emphasis on implement forms in copperwork gave way to the esoterica and paraphernalia of the Middle Woodland and Hopewell-related fluorescences (although the copperwork from the Woodland Periods maintains a strong interest in implement forms and references to important game animals).

In turn, as eastern area groups came to rely more and more on maize agriculture for subsistence and became comparatively sedentary, Woodland interest in potentially functional implements and economically important animal forms in copperwork faded. Instead, the native peoples made Mississippian-type implements, most of which could only have functioned ceremonially. Designs on copperwork indicate primary interest in the human form and birds of ceremonial significance but little or no economic importance. Waring (1968:65) noted the latter style shift and linked it primarily to changes in subsistence concerns, although he mentions other possible causal factors.

These shifts in subject matter and basic form are paralleled by general changes in ritual and ceremony, also indicated in the kinds of paraphernalia fashioned out of copper. Once again, the changes that occur with regard to ritual practice suggest increases in social and political complexity, identical to those that would accompany a shift from simple hunting based economies to more complex ones: first, the combination of hunting and the cultivation of local plants; and, finally, the highly organized social and political structures of societies that practice intensive maize agriculture.

Evidence is scarce from the Archaic Periods, but generally the kinds of ritual paraphernalia made from copper vary widely from site to site. Many pieces are truly unique. Except for spear and arrow points, copperwork from this period shows little or no formal consistency, although it frequently appears in burial contexts. This lack of uniformity extends to the quality of the work (excepting, of course, the implement forms that show consistently fine craftsmanship) as well as to the kinds of paraphernalia produced and the ways it was worn or placed in burials. In Hopewell times there are more standard pieces of regalia—earpieces, breastplates, panpipes, headplates—found throughout. However, each site and important burial is highly individualized, reminiscent of earlier periods. As before, the technical quality of standard regalia found with the remains of most participant groups is uniformly high, while the quality of unique items varies greatly. Still, despite the existence of standardized items of paraphernalia that suggest the possibility of semi-institutionalized religious positions or offices, there is little clear evidence of such organization.

In the Mississippian Periods the kinds of copper paraphernalia in use still vary considerably from site to site. However, clear categories of earpieces, headdress elements, breastplates, etc., have relatively standardized design types and sizes and even show customary burial treatment and placement (Larson 1954:21), although they also vary considerably from region to region. Larson (1971:76) even went so far as to state that the same kinds of regalia appeared in Mound C burials at Etowah with "a monotonous regularity." Although something of an overstatement, his observation certainly indicates that the excavation of Mississippian sites did not offer the surprises typical of so many burials at major Hopewell sites. This evidence suggests a more highly organized and standardized religious structure with established ceremonial positions and functionaries within the various regions associated with each major center.

The persistent interest in implement forms throughout the complex from the Archaic Periods on, as well as continual references to animals that were of some importance as game, imply that early ideas and traditions surrounding copper—ideas that linked it to hunting-related subsistence patterns—were not entirely supplanted by later, more horticulturally-oriented concerns, although the emphasis clearly shifts through the centuries. Apparently, the original connections remained and later ones were simply grafted onto the existing tradition. Witthoft (1949:79–81) quotes a Cherokee myth in which a similar grafting of new traditions onto old had obviously taken place. In fact, a tendency to readily accept new religiously oriented concepts and ideas through their incorporation into existing traditions, is a quite common phenomenon in many Native American groups. The same process was almost certainly important in the growth of concepts that surrounded the use of copper in prehistoric times.

In every period of use, copperwork was used almost exclusively in death ritual. Furthermore, burial evidence indicates that from earliest times the wearing and display of copper was virtually always limited, in some degree at least, to an elite group. This fact also indicates that copper mining and manufacture were probably carried out by a select segment of each society involved. These elements of consistency in practice also point to a long and unified ceremonial tradition. Considered together, this longstanding consistency in both form and practice suggests that the general significance of the copperwork as it was utilized in ritual also remained essentially the same. This is particularly interesting since, as Boas (1928:353) noted long ago, the tendency of the art of traditional societies has generally been to "keep intact the form, but to endow it with new meaning according to the chief cultural interests of the people."

The evolution of subject matter over the centuries indicates that Boas's assertion was undoubtedly true to some extent with regard to the copperwork produced in the prehistoric eastern United States. The kinds of imagery used shift as times and lifestyles change. However, most evidence points to a longstanding and probably ancient body of belief regarding copper that changed very little. The apparent contradiction here (changing subject matter without changing significance) is not difficult to reconcile. Although circumstances changed relatively frequently, along with the specific interpretation of symbolism, the reasons for using copper under those circumstances apparently did not change, nor did the ways in which the use of copper was believed to affect those circumstances. Because the basic concepts and modus operandi associated with copper seem to have undergone very little alteration in the thousands of years of its use in eastern North America, most of the significance accorded native copper was likely tied to certain qualities of the metal itself, both natural and traditional.

Outline of Native North American Religious Movements in Historic Times

Levine (1957:196) states categorically, and most would agree, that art production is generally a ritual activity for "traditional societies" such as those in eastern North America during the prehistoric periods. Both the subject matter and general use and distribution of copperwork indicate this was certainly the case within the copper complex. Many would also agree that, in general, religious developments among the prehistoric peoples that produced most of the copperwork were probably similar to major Native North American ceremonial movements that were important in proto-historic and Historic times.[2] As far as can be determined, all these later religious developments grew up in response to some kind of cultural crisis.

In the eastern area, religion maintained close ties to early shamanically based traditions, even in historic times. That is, individual religious specialists, whose positions were usually based on hereditary factors and/or aspects of their personal mental makeup, carried out (or at least directed) most important religious ceremonies. These ceremonies and rituals were based on long-held traditions. The nature of this religious approach, based so thoroughly upon the individual experiences and interpretations of religious specialists within each community, probably accounts in part for the tremendous cultural diversity apparent in the eastern United States, despite an environment that is (or was) fairly uniform in many ways.

Generally speaking, the two main vehicles for the implementation of change in these religious traditions were:

1. important visions or trances in which an individual member of the group (usually a religious specialist or other specially endowed person) received instructions for changes or, more likely, for additions to normal ritual activity in order to meet special problems The original structures themselves were likely based on this kind of activity.;[3]
2. the borrowing of rituals and/or ceremonies (usually developed in much the same way) from other groups.

The adoption of new ritual through either of the means described occurred only if the ritual fit well into the traditional round of ceremonies in the adopting group.[4] Mooney (1965:x) indicates that even when a new ceremony addressed problems acutely felt by potential adopters, it was not adopted if the basic premises did not coincide with traditional beliefs. If the ceremony was accepted, the newly adopted tradition was inevitably given a highly personalized interpretation by its new devotees that not only determined how the new ceremony was performed initially, but also how long it lasted and how it subsequently evolved.

One of the most basic facts regarding the copper complex in each prehistoric period is the great diversity in culture and practice among the groups that participated in the complex (e.g., Quimby 1960:81, 82), as well as among their neighbors, who apparently had no interest in participation. Within each major period of copper usage is widespread similarity in the use and appearance of copperwork, but very wide diversity with regard to other cultural traits. The typical state of affairs in certain historic religious developments, as outlined above according to Mooney (the continual emphasis upon individualized initiative and experience as a determinant in ritual), could more than account for this diversity. A universal reluctance to adopt religious strategies that do not coincide with traditional beliefs helps to explain why many groups apparently had no interest in copper, although they shared geographic and chronological proximity with those who used copper profusely. Despite the considerable diversity in distribution patterns for individual items and designs on copperwork from site to site, the broadly uniform character of each major prehistoric religious movement that utilized copper is also clear.[5] Once again, these phenomena are more easily understood if the impetus and criteria for the spread of those movements is perceived in terms of historic religious developments, although it seems likely that the extraordinary circumstances of post-contact times may have caused such developments to occur more abruptly than they would have prehistorically.

The phenomena associated with the copper complex are considerably more difficult, if not impossible, to explain if the interest in copper is perceived in economic or mundane utilitarian terms. A rejection of strictly economic explanations is implied in Seeman's (1979:305) work when he notes that in Hopewell trade patterns "it does not appear that the availability of particular resources figured significantly in the demand" for copper and other exotica. Nor did he find that economic concerns determined the methods surrounding procurement of exotica that seemed to have been based instead on the "demands of the ideological system." It was this ideological system that, in fact, formed the basis for the copper complex, a system rooted in anciently conceived religious ritual and tradition.

Over forty years ago, major Native North American ceremonial developments such as those that probably gave rise to the copper complex in its various manifestations were dubbed "revitalization movements" by A.F.C. Wallace (1956).[6] More recently, scholars have tended to discount his comprehensive research on the nature of these Native American religious movements. This skepticism is based primarily on the assumption that the structures he proposes must be seen as nearly universalist in scope, vast and essentially unitary religious movements akin to Christianity.

This is an unfortunate misreading, for many reasons. In the earliest stages, it is possible to see some relationships between the structure and process of Christianity and the rituals that developed in connection with the prehistoric copper complex. However, a number of factors account for important differences that arose almost immediately. Perhaps the most important difference is seen in the fact that, despite its focus on the supernatural connections and abilities of individuals, much of Christian tradition was based upon the relationship between the prophet and a large body of religious literature.

Ritual associated with the copper complex in North America developed among wholly non-literate peoples. This fact explains the important differences between the practices and structures that eventually developed. This hardly negates the value of Wallace's model, however. Understood in microcosmic terms, his model still accounts most plausibly for the full range of social and ceremonial developments surrounding the copper complex. For example, rather than interpreting the Southeastern Ceremonial Complex as a vast region-wide phenomenon that swept the whole area, the model, to be accurately applied, must be seen as a way of understanding developments within the many smaller polities that participated in the copper complex during Mississippian times. These organizations shared common characteristics, including the use of copper in elaborate burial ritual. The differences among them are important and were probably influenced by individualized leadership within each group. The crises faced and the responses to them were similar, but the details of the latter differ widely because of the centrality of local religious specialists and the absence of written texts in whatever aspects of ritual may have been shared.

Wallace's study of such phenomena indicates that in every case these developments seem to evolve through predictable stages. Aspects of the archaeological remains of many groups actively involved in the copper complex appear to reflect similar developmental patterns despite important variations in detail. Wallace has identified five specific stages through which all revitalization type ceremonial movements pass (Wallace 1956:268). They are:

1. steady state;
2. period of individual stress;
3. period of cultural distortion;
4. period of revitalization; and
5. new steady state.

In many ways the most significant aspect of this model lies in Wallace's complete avoidance of any implication that "progress toward civilization" is inherent in these developments. Instead, the process is defined as a cyclical one. Societies involved in revitalization movements are pushed reluctantly from one "steady state" to another by intolerable circumstances—only because maintenance of the status quo is an impossibility and not because of any culturally based drive for "progress." When circumstances bring an end to the revitalization process, societies return to another "steady state" that is essentially the same state ritually, although with some rearrangement of ceremonial detail. The evidence Wallace cites indicates that this is the most accurate way to describe major determinants in the gradual development and alteration of ceremonial ritual apparent in many Native North American societies. His model also offers a very credible explanation for the remarkable longevity of certain social and economic traditions and the values observable within those groups.

Two other defining criteria for revitalization movements provide decisive links between historic ceremonial developments and prehistoric phenomena:

1. Revitalization generally represents the coordinated action of a society taken to preserve its own integrity (Wallace 1956:256).
2. Revitalization movements were not a matter of gradual evolution but involved an abrupt and simultaneous shift of cultural elements that often blossomed within a single generation (Wallace 1956:265). (It seems likely that the extraordinary circumstances of post-contact times may have caused such developments to occur more abruptly that they would have prehistorically.)

In Historic times, the arrival of Europeans and the resulting pressures constituted a major threat to the integrity of virtually every Native American society with whom the new arrivals came into contact. Major Historic revitalization movements were clearly a response to those pressures. In a prehistoric context, the ways in which that kind of cultural pressure could have been brought to bear were relatively few. Intertribal warfare might have been the cause in isolated cases. Extensive migrations or widespread disease might also have presented a challenge to cultural integrity in some areas. However, all these conditions may be said to be symptomatic of larger, more universal problems, especially among traditional peoples. Drastic changes in climate and ecological conditions that resulted in significant demographic shifts are about the only factors likely to cause these kinds of upheavals on a large scale among prehistoric groups. Evidence gathered for this study indicates that climate was, in fact, a major factor in the ceremonial developments associated with the copper complex. (Those climatic changes will be examined in detail below.) Obviously, aspects of human agency and random economic, political, and religious shifts within individual societies are important determinants in the history of all human populations. Still, the widespread nature of ritual developments associated with copper and important coincidences in the temporal and subsistence sequences suggest that larger agents of change must have been at work.

One of the constants of the copper complex is the rather sudden appearance of full-blown artistic and ceremonial traditions in areas and among groups that exhibited far less complex traits in earlier as well as later periods. These phenomena coincide precisely with Wallace's description of the speed with which revitalization movements grow up and become a major factor in the lives of participant societies. Archaeological evidence suggests repeatedly that the more elaborate aspects of ceremony and ritual involving copper were grafted on to related, but simpler cultural traditions.[7] These phenomena, in addition to other factors, suggest a Wallace-type revitalization movement was probably the basis for the relatively sudden introduction of large amounts of copper and related ritual at some sites.

Wallace (1956:268) also postulates that human responses to the developments which bring on revitalization movements have "genotypical structures independent of local cultural differences," that the sequence of responses to given situations, although experienced by very different societies, "will display a uniform pattern, colored but not obscured by local differences in culture." In fact, copper-working traditions and associated cultural developments from Archaic to post-contact times show just such patterns.

In most cases the "prophet" or individual who has the vision that forms the impetus for the cultural response, termed "revitalization," also receives special instructions regarding new rules and ceremonies (Wallace 1956:270). Usually the problem that has caused the cultural crisis resulting in revitalization (whatever its specifics) is conceived to be the result of having neglected certain rules and taboos, and new ones are designed to correct the situation. Disaster is generally the prediction if the instructions given in the vision are ignored.

This description of motivation and activity in the development of ritual coincides very closely with traditions surrounding the Creek Tuchabachee plates discussed earlier. Many statements regarding the care and use of the plates also suggest very strongly that the ceremonies connected with them probably represent remnants of those connected with the copperwork of the Southeastern Ceremonial Complex as practiced within the same region. This, in turn, implies that the Complex itself may have begun as a revitalization movement that conformed to patterns outlined by Wallace.

For the purposes of this study, the most significant step in the process of revitalization that Wallace (1956:268) describes is step number four, the "period of revitalization." During this stage the six important functions of revitalization are initiated and carried out:

1. mazeway reformulation,
2. communication,
3. organization,
4. adaptation,
5. cultural transformation, and
6. routinization.

During the first stage, "mazeway reformulation," old traditions and rituals are restructured and recombined to form new ones. In North America this usually amounts to a "revival of the old culture by ritual and moral purification" (Wallace 1956:276). A tendency to rely on the ceremonial past in this process is obvious in Spier's analysis of the Sun Dance on the Plains. Even when "requisite objects and principles for action were lacking, they drew on their fund of ceremonies, not their imaginations for substitutes" (Spier 1921:516).

Another highly feasible explanation for the unique character of each site involved in the major copper-related ceremonial fluorescences is one that proceeds along these same lines. That is, the ways in which copper was grafted onto less elaborate traditions was determined by the nature of those original and less complex ritual practices and paraphernalia. Preferred subject matter, design, and even object types produced apparently depended to a large degree on previous traditions within each participant group. The concentration of particular types of items at individual sites yet distributed widely (like panpipes, breastplates, earpieces, and pipes in Middle Woodland times) probably reflect such patterns. Viewed in this context, it also seems likely that the long tradition of copper as an important material for ritual paraphernalia in the eastern United States was in itself crucial to copper's central role in all major prehistoric ceremonial developments for which we have significant archaeological data.

The second aspect of the revitalization stage described by Wallace (1956:273) is "communication." The original dreamer of the vision becomes a "prophet," preaching that:

1. individuals who espouse his teachings will be protected by the supernatural beings he has consulted with in his vision and
2. both the individual and the society will benefit from the new "cultural system"—whether the revival originates within the prophet's culture group or through inspiration borrowed from outsiders.

Communication of the prophet's ideas is an essential element of revitalization and remains so even in later phases. The importance of communication in Native North American religious movements was a crucial factor in the significance of copper in prehistoric ceremonial developments—at least in the degree to which those developments spread from region to region. There is ample evidence of interaction among contemporary groups within the copper complex, regardless of the degree to which the associated religious movements were local developments or part of a larger ceremonial manifestation. To postulate whether developments were exclusively local or panregional is unnecessary. Some mixture of the two is most likely.

Spreading of the prophet's message was a focus of activity in all the major Native North American revitalization movements of Historic times. The prophet as well as his disciples traveled about, teaching and explaining the new ceremonial ideals and rituals.[8] Apparently it was almost as common for other groups to travel to the prophet's home, seeking information about the new ritual. When the Ghost Dance was instituted, for example, many traveled long distances to learn of it; the same was true regarding interest in the rites associated with peyote. Disciples of the various movements might also be asked to visit villages and teach.

Myer (1924:736–46) indicates that avid interest in new ceremonial rituals and the desire to learn their proper performance is typical among Native North American groups. In this context, he mentions "well-authenticated cases of Indians . . . covering 1000 to 2000 miles," simply for social visits. He says that "in times of war or when on special missions, they went much further."

According to Wallace's model, revitalization movements always involve important alteration of current ceremonial patterns as well as of lifeways. Moving conservative traditional societies to accept and implement such changes was probably difficult, even within groups facing the massive pressures brought on by European contact. In precontact times, few (if any) difficulties could have wreaked a similar degree of social and cultural havoc. Under precontact conditions, then, the leaders of revitalization-type movements would probably have had to be even more convincing and charismatic than would those of Historic times. Their success in presenting and implementing a revitalization program probably depended in large part upon whether the prophet could present sufficiently convincing evidence of support from the supernatural powers that had contacted him. This kind of evidence was crucial to the success of such movements, even in Historic times.

The early and precipitous demise of the Ghost Dance is a case in point. Several factors were important in that demise, but a crucial one involved growing skepticism regarding the validity of Wodziwob's (the Paiute prophet) powers after it was discovered he used dynamite in one demonstration of his spiritual prowess (Hittman 1973:251). This need, to present convincing evidence of support from the supernatural "powers that be," may lie at the root of the obvious interest in accumulating as much copper as possible (within prescribed, traditional, and religious restrictions) that is apparent both before and after contact among copper-using groups.

Artwork, especially in copper, undoubtedly played another, even more basic role in prehistoric Native American revitalization movements. The crucial nature of that role is clarified in Anderson's (1979) study of art and its functions within so-called primitive societies. He indicates that because most primitive societies are non-literate, artistic modes are essentially the only ways to give concrete form to ideas and information. This was certainly true among precontact Native North Americans in the eastern United States. For them, artistic media would also have provided an effective way for peoples of differing languages to communicate. The virtually universal use of certain symbols and motifs found on copperwork throughout the eastern area suggests that some ontological and cosmological concepts were very similar among most groups in that region despite cultural and linguistic differences. The combination of such symbols with the copper medium would have been a very efficient means for the communication of new religious concepts and ideals, particularly among groups without a common language.

The likelihood that copper held a central position as a vehicle for spreading concepts associated with prehistoric religious movements is also supported by the fact that all the important motifs associated with the Southeastern Ceremonial Complex are found in copperwork. Locally distinctive variations of certain symbols (the bird/human combinations, for example) appear in other media, but the symbolic content of copper versions found universally are consistent despite stylistic variation (Waring 1968:43; Howard 1968:11–12). The capacity for flexibility of such a medium of communication for the expression of religious doctrine among groups with distinctly different linguistic and cultural traditions (as opposed to the discourses of a St. Paul or an Erasmus, for example) is obvious.

First of all, the visual content as well as the choice of copper as a medium was part of a ceremonial tradition that was probably already familiar to potential converts. In the absence of any possibility of presenting detailed explanations of doctrine, the generalized concepts delineated on copper, whatever their combination, could easily be interpreted and adapted according to the specific needs and interests of each cultural unit approached. Whether or not verbal communication was possible, this was a very effective vehicle for the expression of religious concepts, indeed.

In Historic times, whenever the "disciples" or "priests" of these religious movements traveled to communicate the basics of their new ceremony, they carried important items of paraphernalia with them, such as badges of priestly office, sacred paint and ceremonial fans and rattles, as well as instructions regarding how various items of ritual gear were to be decorated and worn. Virtually all accounts indicate that it was religious zeal that motivated them and suggest that the only payment received amounted to no more than room and board (e.g., Mooney 1965:21).

Obviously, certain kinds of paraphernalia were left behind when the disciples returned home, especially items such as badges of priestly office and whatever else was essential to the communication and proper performance of the ritual. For the initiates, obtaining these items was probably not a matter of purchase or economic exchange (e.g., La Barre 1938:113). In fact, to describe the ritual acceptance of religious paraphernalia as "trade" would be to misrepresent the nature of the process. The situation was probably not very different in prehistoric times. Dissemination of ceremonial materials was probably a crucial aspect in the communication of ritual ideas then also and was probably a matter of bestowing such goods on new and/or prospective converts, not a matter of economic exchange. Evidence of "uneven" or one-sided trade relationships involving copper and other ceremonial materials among prehistoric groups is fairly often noted in the archaeological literature,[9] but explanations for it are generally vague.

The archaeological remains of the centers of such religious activity—the home of the prophet and his principal disciples and the area where sacred materials were produced for dissemination—would likely have a distinctly different flavor and a different artifactual distribution than would sites where the ideas and paraphernalia were imported. Variations in archaeological data that might be explained in this way are described by Peebles in his analysis of some Mississippian sites in the Southeast. Ceremonial differences could account very easily for differences in the amounts of ritual material found at Moundville and Bessemer, two Alabama sites (1971:87–88).

Instead, based on the greater availability of some materials to Moundville and not to Bessemer, Peebles speculates that the differences stem from Moundville's political domination the latter group. The problem here is one of misplaced emphasis. Seeman (1979:305) has demonstrated that availability of certain raw materials was not a factor in their use and importance farther north. As an apparent continuation of earlier copper-related tradition, the ways copper functioned in the Southeast were probably not greatly different from the ways it was utilized earlier among Hopewellian groups. There is little reason to assume that relative availability of raw materials used for ritual paraphernalia in the Southeast was an important factor in their use or significance either. Furthermore, political domination may have existed, but the importance of copper in defining the relationship between the two sites implies that this relationship was primarily ceremonial, not political and not economic.

Evidence gathered for the present study indicates that Moundville was an important ceremonial center *first*. The accumulation of copper and political and/or economic power followed as a result of that spiritual prowess, and not the other way around. This was almost certainly the case at other important sites where copperwork has been found, as well. Unless this order of priorities for the function and significance of copper is recognized, the real importance and nature of its role in native culture is obscured.

The extraordinary numbers of complex and important sites (in terms of the amount of ceremonial material found there) discovered in both Middle Woodland and Mississippian Periods pose no problem in this interpretation of the religious phenomena of those times. If the major ceremonial movements in prehistoric times were in fact revitalization movements, several factors suggest that the crises precipitating those developments must have been severe and widespread. The complexity of resultant ritual manifestations and their widespread espousal (seen in terms of the ceremonial goods involved, especially copper) would support this idea. Under such circumstances, it is reasonable to assume that more than one visionary might come forward and that, therefore, more than one center for the emanation of new religious ideals and rituals might develop. In addition, it is likely that variations in the severity of the crisis, whatever it may have been, would have produced some areas of fervent and highly organized practice and proselytizing efforts, and others of relatively little similar activity.

All these differences would, naturally, produce like differences in the amounts of ritual paraphernalia needed and/or produced. Again, this would be especially true in regard to proselytizing; those centers of religious activity engaged in large conversion efforts would need large amounts of appropriate items and vice versa. These kinds of important differences could easily account for artifact variations between major sites. Given the ritual focus of these centers and the kinds of exchange that would have occurred within them, references to sites where important ceremonial materials were manufactured and stored as "focal trading centers" or as important points of distribution in an "evolving trade sphere" or "regional system of exchange"[10] clearly misrepresent the realities of the situation.

The third aspect of the "revitalization stage" in the development of major native North American religious movements involves "organization" according to Wallace's model. The social structure of the movement is composed of its originator (the "prophet") and his disciples and followers. Often it also includes individuals who wielded considerable influence within the cultural unit before the new developments. What is most significant for analysis of the situation prehistorically is Wallace's (1956:273) indication that the new religio-cultural program is frequently "administered in large part by a political rather than a religious leadership." This likelihood may account for the repeated evidence of political organization and dominance found in careful study of prehistoric ceremonial burial complexes and remains, as in Peebles's work (1971:85). What is consistently ignored in such studies is the ceremonial basis for this evidence. Again, political ascendancy was apparently legitimized and based upon spiritual and religious factors. This weighing of political and economic significance, as opposed to religious, may seem to be a rehashing of Old World arguments about the historic position of the papacy and its power. Such questions revolve around whether the power of the Pope rested in his spiritual prowess or his control of huge amounts of land and other assets throughout Europe and the world. However, in this instance, those traditional arguments almost certainly do not apply. The fundamental differences between Native American societies and their Old World counterparts indicate that basic thought patterns and motivations must have been as fully antithetical. Thus, an understanding of the revitalization process, especially of the religious and/or supernatural nature of its raison d'être, is essential to a clear understanding of Native American cultural and political developments and their artistic expression.

Wallace (1956:277) indicates that not only were the cultural programs of revitalization movements often administered by a political rather than a religious leadership, but also that the individual movements themselves tended to become more and more "political" in emphasis. This is hardly surprising. The sudden intrusion of a figure with a generally acknowledged (though basically supernatural or spiritual) power base into an essentially egalitarian group, coupled with the cultural changes instituted by that individual and his followers, would certainly result in administrative changes within the society, including the development of a formal religio-political structure.

The development of such structures would facilitate whatever social changes might be necessary to deal with the crises that gave rise to the movement in the first place. Success in this arena would tend to solidify those changes and the political structure that developed along the way. Of course, the functions of the individuals involved would be religiously based, but the material remains of that organization would appear to be political, especially to the members of present-day societies.

In fact, all the most politically complex native North American groups extant in early contact times—the Iroquois, Creek, and Powhatan Confederacies as well as the Natchez—appear to have grown up as a result of regionally based revitalization type movements many years before. Analysis on this basis suggests that among Native American groups in the eastern United States, political power was garnered, initially at least, through successful communication and cooperation with the supernatural. This was a religious process, over which individuals and communities seem to have had relatively meager control. Nevertheless, it was a process that native North American societies apparently were convinced was both viable and effective. This conviction no doubt was firmly grounded in basic ontological perceptions. The spiritual nature of those perceptions also accounts very likely for the precipitous demise of those political structures.

During the organizational stage of development in the revitalization process, the "prophet's followers" develop a relationship to him that is similar to one the prophet was believed to have had with the supernatural beings responsible for the initial vision. This, in turn, begins to endow the "prophet" himself with a "power higher than human" (Wallace 1956:274). Eventually, Wallace (1956:258) suggests, the prophet and the supernatural being who was believed to have imparted the new religio-social movement to him tended to merge in tradition. The resulting composites are the various "culture heroes" of Native American myth and legend.

In fact, this is almost precisely the scenario proposed by Waring (1968:50) in his discussion of the copperwork from the Southeastern Ceremonial Complex and of the human/bird motifs found on some of it.[11] He bases these conclusions on early accounts of Natchez political structure. Many feel that the social and political organization of the Natchez at contact probably reflected the way many earlier groups in the Southeastern Ceremonial Complex functioned, even though that way was intensified by the intrusion of European cultures. Waring points out that the so-called "Great Sun," the central political figure of Natchez society, held his position by virtue of his descent from the "cult bringer and his wife" who were themselves supposed to be descended from the sun (Waring 1968:48). Other parallels with what would seem to be Southeastern Ceremonial Complex practices, although perhaps distorted in legend, included the Natchez tradition that the original cult bringer turned to stone and was kept in a box in the temple (Waring 1968:48). Large stone sculptures of a man and a woman were found in one of the mounds at Etowah and at several other sites in the Southeast.[12]

Many details regarding the organization and activity of the so-called "Powhatan Confederacy" under Chief Powhatan suggest that his position and its legitimacy may have been based upon the same kinds of developments and traditions Wallace and Waring describe. That is, a hereditary political hierarchy was based directly upon the reception and retention of supernatural religious powers that were bequeathed to the ruling kinship group through an ancient forebear, for the benefit of the community as a whole.

This all sounds suspiciously like the "divine right of kings," so basic in medieval European political organization, suggesting that the Powhatan tradition may indeed have originated in essentially the same way. However, the nature of Native American non-literate societies and their belief systems developed in such completely different directions from those in the Old World that this political theory must have been perceived and probably functioned in very different and much more pragmatic terms in prehistoric North America.

What is interesting for the purposes of this study is the central role copper seemed to play in the Powhatan example. The role of copper in Powhatan society, as well as prehistorically, is accorded heightened significance in the light of another aspect of the "organizational" phase of revitalization described by Wallace (1956:274). He points out that, unless there is a vehicle for the transfer of the supernatural power eventually associated with the prophet to others, "in a stable institutional structure, the movement itself is liable to die with the death or failure of the individual prophet." The long traditional use of copper for important ceremonial material in precontact times, as well as the bulk of the designs applied to copperwork, suggest that copper would have been an ideal vehicle for the transference of supernatural power. This potential, as a vehicle for the transference of power, may well be the main reason why copper appears to have been so important in so many prehistoric religious developments.

The fourth stage of the revitalization process delineated in Wallace's (1956:275) model is "adaptation," a phase in which resistance to the revolutionary nature of the movement is met. Resistance, he says, is inevitable and is dealt with through "doctrinal modification; political and diplomatic maneuver; and force." The introduction of unique items of copperwork paraphernalia within each major Hopewell-related mound site suggests that Hopewell ceremonies were indeed adapted to the local traditions of participant groups. The obvious preference for certain styles and motifs at different Southeastern Ceremonial Complex sites as well as differences in details of paraphernalia suggest similar adaptive strategies were also important later.

In obvious accord with Wallace's model, virtually all known Native North American religious movements include aspects of alliance and reconciliation, as well as specific moral and ethical tenets, e.g., the Creek Busk Ceremonies,[13] various versions of the Peyote ritual,[14] Hiawatha and the formation of the Iroquois Confederacy (Wallace 1958:121), and the Feast of the Dead Ceremony (Hickerson 1970:39).

Evidence cited earlier that suggests a degree of political domination at prehistoric sites, as well as the significance of the Tuchabachee copper plates in treaty arrangements between the Creek and the Shawnee, coincide with Wallace's description of this aspect of the revitalization process.

Howard (1960:218; 1968:52) discusses an aspect of the cosmological beliefs of the Prairie Potowatomi that suggests at least one reason why this concept of alliance and reconciliation was such an important element in these movements. He indicates that the Potowatomi believe storms and other natural violence are the result of battles between animals and beasts that control the various realms of the cosmos (especially hawks or eagles and rattlesnakes). Such storms, they are convinced, represent an imbalance in nature and result ultimately in "bloody wars between various tribes of Indians." If the supernatural "powers that be" were believed to be the source of all conflict and destruction (whether in nature or between human groups), then logically the only solution to such problems must lie in an appeal to and/or the control of those supernatural powers—the very powers referred to most often in symbolism applied to copperwork. Peaceful alliance and prosperity would not be possible without the participation of those powers and would occur on the human scene only after being achieved in those higher realms.

Revitalization movements have usually grown up in response to major conflicts and crises such as those mentioned by Howard, and are a collection of new attitudes and rituals essential to the resolution of those difficulties. If participation in the new ceremonies was seen to be essential to solving the problem, it would be crucial to include everyone in the area affected by the crisis in the revitalization process. Appropriate designs on impressive amounts of an important ceremonial material like copper would be an effective means to convince other groups to participate. Furthermore, if participation in the revitalization movement was believed to be the only solution to the crisis situation, the need to achieve harmony in the spiritual realm might very well require military conquest of those who refused to join—even if the ritual itself was introduced as a means to quell widespread intertribal bloodshed.

Disagreements among scholars regarding the interpretation of symbolism applied to ritual objects associated with these movements may well arise from this apparent dichotomy—a push to establish regional peace, although peace was effected through conflict. Very little evidence exists of enforced participation in ceremonial developments prehistorically. However, the suggestion of coercion suggests the Powhatan situation once again. Apparently some members of the Confederacy were willing participants and others were quite forcefully coerced into joining (Swanton 1946:644).

Following successful "adaptation," the fourth stage in Wallace's model (1956:275), Wallace indicates that a degree of "cultural transformation" takes place and is signaled by cultural changes and "enthusiastic embarkation on some organized program of group action." The most spectacular and obvious remains of the groups involved in the later phases of the copper complex are the large mounds and elaborate ceremonial earthworks they built. If the major prehistoric cultural fluorescences that utilized copper are perceived as various revitalization movements, it seems clear that the elaborate mound complex/ceremonial centers that grew up in connection with them may represent this kind of group response. In Archaic times this group activity may have consisted of ritual hunts in which copper spears and arrow points were used exclusively. Many of these beautiful implements have been found scattered, as though lost in the hunt, although their burial with so few individuals suggests that they were probably not available to everyone. A series of ritual hunts that were organized by religious specialists who temporarily endowed all participants with sufficient power to use copper implements would explain this apparent anomaly.

The sixth and final step of the revitalization process in Wallace's (1965:275) model is referred to as "routinization." Organizational and communication structures are developed for transmittal of the new religious traditions during "cultural transformation" contract; the new concepts and rituals associated with the movement become the norm; and the activities of the religious specialists are reduced to a "religion," maintaining "doctrine" and the "performance of ritual" but no longer affecting the total culture as thoroughly as before. In the case of the copper complex, it appears that the most spectacular objects created at the height of such developments were curated for a few generations and gradually passed out of use. New ones were less likely to be created and the others disappeared, apparently buried with the most prominent members of the religio-political elite.

Reference to the important stages in the revitalization process described by Wallace, coupled with what is known about the copper complex, suggests that the following very generalized scenario might have occurred in the prehistoric eastern United States:

> When times were good, there was no need to utilize the powers available in copper, which always involved risks. Individuals with particularly strong spiritual powers might still possess copper items for use in important ceremonies, and maintain and pass along the knowledge necessary to forge them, but the objects were probably never seen and certainly not ever used by the community at large. (In fact, there are many sites, dated in between the major copper-producing eras as well as during them, where only one or two pieces of copper have been discovered.) Ceremonial tradition could easily have preserved the knowledge of where to procure the material as well as how to work and use it, even if that knowledge was limited to just one or two individuals within each generation.
>
> When human or animal migrations, changes in climate, improved methods of food production, population growth, or other influences caused problems so challenging that less dangerous solutions were ineffective, the considerable powers resident in copper could be called upon to resolve the situation. The sequence of events was probably not very different from that apparent in Historic times. The major problems of the precontact periods almost certainly precipitated similar nativistic movements that were led by religious specialists or prophets. The conditions brought on by those problems would have provided sufficient motivation to implement any changes the prophet might propose.
>
> The function of copper in these developments, at the outset, would probably have been to legitimize the leadership role of the prophet, especially for cultural units beyond the tribal or territorial limits of the originating group. (It must be remembered that, according to ethnographic data as well as archaeological evidence, the special properties associated with copper as well as traditional taboos would have precluded copper's use by any but those endowed with considerable spiritual powers.) The power and position of the prophet could be introduced to other cultural units very easily through the display and manipulation of copper.
>
> The major concepts associated with the movement could also be communicated to other spiritual leaders through this familiar ritual medium, even if the new "converts" spoke a different language from the originating group. Even if

those exposed to these new ideas were fellow "prophets" from other regions, copper paraphernalia would be an effective way for these specialists to share ideas. Finally, when necessary, copperwork could serve as an effective vehicle for the transfer of each prophet's power.

If the special properties of copper were universally appreciated (and it appears that they were), possession and manipulation of the metal would offer a focus for united effort in a way that would not require much alteration in the economic or social organization of most participant groups. Since the movement itself probably developed in response to necessary, if grudging, change, the only additional changes in lifestyle and culture would probably take place in the immediate social group of the prophet and his primary followers. In order for those individuals to pursue their religious activities, other members of the communities involved would have to support them. This support would probably have been primarily in the form of perishable goods. The groups providing that support would not be required to materially alter their own lifestyle and organization to provide that kind of support. The required portion of subsistence goods gathered and/or produced by the others would simply be assigned to the religious specialists. Since this kind of support would be provided to alleviate a major crisis faced by the whole community, it would certainly not have been given grudgingly. When, for whatever reasons, the increased level of social complexity was no longer essential, everything could return to its previously decentralized and comparatively simple status very quickly.

The remains of most prehistoric and early contact groups that utilized copper suggest that such a series of circumstances could have occurred. The consistent, unitary evolution in design and use of copperwork in all precontact periods suggests that the power and significance of copper was universally appreciated and understood throughout the eastern United States. Hall (1977:515) suggests that just such a set of universally understood concepts and motifs must have been a crucial element in the Hopewellian fluorescence. He says: "It worked because there was a broad base of shared symbolism validated by a long tradition which could be mobilized to serve the needs or opportunities of the day." Most characteristics of prehistoric copperwork indicate that copper and its associated beliefs constituted such a tradition. Because the traditions involved lasted so long and touched virtually every area of the Eastern Woodlands at some point in its long history, it seems inconceivable that the fundamental significance of copper as a special material was not universally appreciated throughout region.

Archaeologically, societies involved in the copper complex usually appeared as pockets of cultural complexity amid contemporaries that seem largely unaffected. Each society seemed to blossom fairly quickly and then disappear with like speed, although the increased ceremonial activity lasted longer in some locations than others. All this evidence fits well into the proposed scenario.

It is not difficult to see how effectively copperwork could have functioned in the spread of major prehistoric Native North American religious movements in the eastern area. However, the problem remains of identifying the conditions that caused revitalization-type movements and associated artistic developments to spring up in the first place during precontact times. Clearly the spectacular artistic developments that included the production of thousands of pieces of metalwork must have resulted from some change in the cultural status quo of those societies that participated in the copper complex. Few would disagree. Opinions regarding the kinds of changes that took place vary, however. If these phenomena are regarded as primarily economic or political in importance, the logical conclusion is to assume that the copper complex and related artwork mark a high point of development: increased trade and greater prosperity, resulting in higher levels of social and political complexity as well as artistic activity—the best of times. Similarly, the old argument that sufficient leisure results in more and better art, implies that the blossoming of the copper complex was the result, once again, of unusually good times.

The bulk of the evidence, however, indicates that the developments associated with the copper complex were essentially ceremonial, as noted above. If so, the conditions that precipitated those developments were probably disastrous—periods of crisis not sweet prosperity—just as they were in Early Historic times. As a crucial concomitant of native religious tradition, it can be assumed that the copperwork came to be produced under the same conditions and for many of the same reasons that gave rise to the rituals and ceremonies in which it was used.

Some of the world's most respected anthropologists are of the opinion that religious traditions within societies such as the prehistoric ones in eastern North America develop in response to crisis situations. For example, Malinowski (1936) has suggested that most ritual in traditional societies is an outgrowth of anxiety or mental stress. Wallace (1956:257) also indicates that the rituals of revitalization movements result from intolerable cultural stress. Hickerson (1970:52) is of essentially the same opinion about the development of nativistic religious movements in North America in general, as are Barber (1941:673), Hittman (1973:256), and Bittle (1954:69) in their discussions of the Ghost Dance on the Plains. The research of Kavolis (1972:163) indicates that important art work, whether or not it is associated with religious developments, tends to "spring from various states of tension." This would also seem to belie the old insistence that art production depends upon the amount of leisure time available to members of a given culture.

In fact, Kavolis (1972:26–27) asserts that "artistic activity is not proportional to the amount of a society's wealth, nor is it impossible in the absence of a large economic surplus. Art creation is not primarily a symbolic projection of material prosperity." Instead, he suggests that *changes* in economic prosperity rather than specific degrees of prosperity tend to affect levels of artistic activity. Thus, a downturn in the economic picture might be as likely to produce an increased level of artistic production as would more prosperous times. Social changes initiated by any number of factors would likely have a similar effect, regardless of the details associated with those developments. This twofold possibility is a crucial point in understanding the conditions that were probably responsible for the rise of the copper complex.

In order to identify the kinds of crises that gave rise to the phenomena of the copper complex, other criteria for high and low levels of art production among Native North American societies must also be defined. Kavolis and others have offered some explanation for changes in levels of artistic activity. However, to really begin to understand the relationship of art levels to social and economic conditions in Native North American societies, one must also account for consistently high levels of artistic activity, as opposed to consistently low levels. The Northwest Coast of the United States and Canada is undoubtedly one of the two richest areas in production of Native North American art. The Southwestern United States is the other. In both regions, relatively large populations lived together in relatively small areas. This situation was possible only because of the particular means of subsistence in both areas.

Northwest Coast groups lived in an area so rich in food resources that the development of agriculture was unnecessary. The richness of Northwest Coast subsistence resources supported relatively large populations, although the functional living and foraging areas were severely restricted to a narrow strip of land along the coast. Settlement in the Southwest was also more or less limited geographically to areas that were capable of producing the particular variety of corn agriculture practiced by Native Americans in that area. As was the case on the Northwest Coast, the limited area suited to the Southwestern Native Americans' subsistence methods was, nonetheless, capable of supporting relatively large populations.

By contrast, in the Great Basin, art production by native groups has been consistently meager. Unlike the Northwest Coast and the Southwest, the areas in the Great Basin that have been exploited for resources are vast and the potential food sources are fairly evenly, if skimpily, available throughout. The situation is such that a very great expanse of land is required to support only a few individuals. The contrast between the amount of art produced by these peoples and the amount of area required for subsistence activities (as opposed to the level of art production of the peoples of the Northwest Coast and the Southwest and the limited areas these groups exploited in their subsistence activities) is instructive. The correlation is clear between the size of each population in relation to the expanse of land required to support it and the level and quality of art production within that population.

It is possible to deduce at least two ways in which levels of artistic activity would increase under crowded but tenable conditions. While one is theoretical and the other is apparent, both are important. First, crowding, regardless of extent, is bound to produce more tension and stress than is adequate space. Problems, particularly those affecting subsistence, would certainly be felt more quickly and more severely where many people share restricted space for subsistence activities. Again, such situations tend to increase levels of stress, tension, and anxiety, and provide conditions that many agree give rise to increased artistic production (as noted above).

In addition, it is obvious that greater social and political complexity would be a necessity for large populations sharing severely restricted subsistence resources, agricultural or otherwise, simply to organize production and distribution. As suggested above, in Native North American societies those social and political structures tended to be based on and developed according to ceremonial tradition. In the absence of written communication, this ritually based system of resource distribution with associated badges of bureaucratic office for those who implemented it would have to be expressed through symbolic imagery rather that the written word, and would require increased "art" production. The ceremonial basis for such structures and the spiritual orientation of associated artwork, as well as the way these systems seem to have developed in the history and prehistory of the Americas, suggest that distributive systems were not perceived by their participants in any but ceremonial terms. All these factors are important in developing an understanding of the significance of the copper complex.

Still, unless some or all of the conditions likely to produce cultural crises (mentioned above) can be demonstrated to have actually existed among groups participant in the copper complex—particularly to have produced crises severe enough to precipitate a revitalization-type response, and universal enough to affect the entire region—the explanations detailed above do not prove that revitalization processes were central to the development of the copper complex. It is necessary to examine the periods during which the complex flourished, as well as the specific geographical areas involved, to determine whether such conditions did exist and were likely to have affected the eastern region. Further, if those crisis-causing conditions can be identified, in order to cement the relationship between them and the copper complex, it should be possible to show that the designs used on the copperwork correspond in a meaningful way to the nature of those conditions.

According to Wallace (1956:269), the kinds of stressful conditions likely to precipitate religious revitalization movements in native North America are: changes in "climate; floral and faunal change; military defeat; political subordination; extreme pressure toward acculturation, resulting in internal cultural conflict; economic distress; epidemics." Most of these situations would bring about changes in economic conditions (both improved and otherwise) and, thus, probable changes in the level of art production, according to Kavolis. Many situations might also serve to restrict areas available for subsistence activities or to increase the number of individuals supported by a given area of subsistence exploitation and would thus create conditions favorable to increased levels of artistic activity.

Three factors indicate that the tensions that gave rise to the major fluorescences of the copper complex must have resulted from conditions that affected societies throughout the area:

1. the large geographical areas embraced by the major ceremonial fluorescences, the Hopewellian and Mississippian manifestations;
2. evolution throughout the copper complex that seems to coincide with important changes in social structure and demographics associated with shifts in subsistence modes; and
3. the continual emphasis on subject matter relating to subsistence and the maintenance of order in the cosmos.

Many of the conditions discussed by Wallace would have been unlikely to have region-wide effects in prehistoric times. Before contact with Europeans and their Old World traditions and approaches to warfare, military operations among Native Americans in the eastern United States occurred on a relatively small scale. Even full-scale "war" in Historic times consisted of little more than successive skirmishes between war parties (e.g., Edmunds 1983:10–11).

Without the pressure of European encroachments, it seems highly unlikely that military conflict between precontact groups would have affected lifestyles over a large enough area to give rise to pan-regional cultural developments like those associated with the copper complex. Thus, military defeat was probably not instrumental in the development of the religious traditions associated with the copper complex. Nor was political subordination a likely reason for the phenomena of the precontact copper-working tradition. When evidence exists of political subjugation at archaeological sites, copperwork is almost always associated with the remains of groups that appear to be politically dominant. When revitalization occurs as the result of such subjugation, the stress is felt by those dominated (the rise of the Ghost Dance on the Plains, for example) and the new religious and artistic traditions are established by that group, not the dominant one.

Other conditions mentioned by Wallace simply were not a factor in precontact times. Extreme pressures of acculturation for Native American societies are really a post-contact phenomenon and were unlikely to have been very acute prehistorically. Nor is there any archaeological evidence of widespread epidemics during prehistoric times.

Changes in climate, flora, and fauna, then, are the most likely conditions to have given rise to the cultural developments associated with the copper complex. In Wallace's study these two factors are separated. He deals in large part with situations such as changes in fauna and post-contact responses to the killing off of the buffalo and the depletion of the beaver, etc. All these situations were effected directly or indirectly by the European presence. In precontact times, major changes in flora and fauna would more likely have been linked to changes in climate. In fact, data cited below indicate that the sequence of events resulting in the ceremonial and artistic developments of the copper complex proceeded in essentially this order:

1. major shifts in climate,
2. changes in flora and fauna,
3. population growth or demographic shifts,
4. increased social tension, and
5. revitalization process initiated.

The central importance of change in climate and population in the inception and growth of the copper complex was itself a major unifying factor in the long tradition upon which the copper complex was based. The continuity of the copper tradition and the conditions that affected it are best discussed together in order to illustrate the strong connections between climatic developments and cultural ones.

The intent is not to draw precise parallels between the climatic situation and increases in artistic and ceremonial levels, however. Nor shall any attempt be made to determine whether related economic conditions improved or deteriorated. (As was noted above, a *change* in economic fortunes seems to encourage artistic activity, not a particular kind of change.) The specifics of the situation remain to be analyzed in subsequent studies.

My hope is simply to demonstrate that significant shifts in climate, subsistence possibilities, social organization, and/or population density coincide with every major manifestation of the copper complex, from Archaic times to the post-contact periods. We shall proceed now with a chronological review of the major fluorescences of the copper complex, the climatic conditions that coincided with its appearance in those periods and other data that help to define and explain the nature of that phenomenon of prehistory in the eastern United States.

In the archaeological literature, Old Copper Culture manifestations are frequently ignored in discussions of phenomena that may have influenced later cultural developments involving copper. Archaeologists often acknowledge a degree of ceremonial continuity extant from Archaic through Woodland times, but rarely (if ever) deal with likely reasons for it, or details regarding its significance (e.g., Griffin 1960:98). Most agree that alterations in Native North American ceremonial tradition were always based upon "ancient usages" and "ritual practices,"[15] and it is fairly common to suggest the importance of considering Hopewell traditions in the analysis of later Mississippian ones.[16]

Still, few scholars recognize the likelihood of similar influence from the Archaic Old Copper Culture. There are several reasons for this. Most Old Copper Culture copperwork was weaponry, not obviously ceremonial paraphernalia. The vast majority of known examples were isolated finds, picked up in sand and gravel pits and on the banks of lakes and rivers (Wittry 1957:205). Hopewell and Mississippian finds are usually part of an extensive corpus of ritual gear, carefully buried in large ceremonial complexes.

Since, by contrast, most Old Copper Culture copperwork appears to have been scattered at random, scholars have generally assumed that Old Copper Culture implements were manufactured for utilitarian purposes and that little relationship existed between this metallurgical tradition and later ones. Nevertheless, as noted above, considerable evidence suggests that the conditions that gave rise to the importance of copper within the Old Copper Culture were very similar to conditions that influenced decisions to utilize copper ceremonially among later cultures. Furthermore, indications are that the traditional associations and significance accorded copper were first established in Archaic times by Old Copper Culture peoples and formed the basis for later copper-working traditions.

Many facts regarding Old Copper Culture copper-working tradition are nearly identical to aspects of the copper complex among later groups. Once again, whenever Old Copper Culture copperwork is found in burial contexts, distribution patterns suggest the same hierarchical traditions regarding possession that obtained later (e.g., Ritzenthaler et al 1957:279). Furthermore, the degree of technical expertise most Old Copper Culture implements exhibit and the quite remarkable similarity of pieces within each type of classification indicate well-defined "cultural standards" regarding their manufacture (Wittry and Ritzenthaler 1957:208). The apparent skill applied to their forging and the obvious standardization of the copperwork, as well as aspects of prehistoric metallurgy worldwide, suggest a special class of miner-forgers were responsible for their manufacture (Bradley 1952:33–35). As suggested above, these miner-forgers were probably religious specialists.

The longevity, alone, of the Old Copper Culture as a cultural entity offers a good reason why its traditions regarding the significance of copper were likely to have formed the basis for later ones. The degree of conformity to certain concepts and motifs in the ceremonial developments surrounding the use of copper throughout the prehistory of the entire eastern United States suggests that the tradition was established very early. Early radiocarbon dates also indicate the longevity of the tradition. Old Copper Culture-type items have been found in New York, Illinois, and Kentucky—far from their original source—with material dated at 3000 B.C. and earlier (Quimby 1960:58). A number of other facts also indicate that the Old Copper Culture persisted through many hundreds of years. Most convincing is the large number of pieces of copperwork found from Old Copper Culture times (some twenty thousand).[17]

Moreover, the remarkably large number of distinct point types also indicates the Old Copper Culture "existed over a considerable length of time."[18] "Presumably each type occupied its own time level and was shared by all contemporary human groups on a regional or areal basis" (Funk 1978:23). Differences in hafting methods on the stone mauls used in mining operations also point to a lengthy tradition in mining activities.[19] That copper held a central position in the Old Copper Culture and that its influence was widespread throughout the region (implied by patterns of distribution of Old Copper Culture-type implements) would also indicate that copper had a strong influence on the ideological basis of pan-regional ceremonial tradition. Examples of implements found are: a copper harpoon near Fannin, Georgia (Moore 1903); a large spear point in Custer County, Oklahoma (Bell and Block 1972); three Old Copper Culture-type artifacts on the Georgia coast; and a fourth near the Crystal River in Florida (Goad 1978). Other convincing physical evidence of ceremonial continuity—between Archaic and Woodland manifestations, at least—is the existence of Archaic remains in mounds below those with obvious Hopewell-related ceremonial influence.[20] The fact that coppersmiths from both Woodland and Archaic cultures exploited the same massive deposits of copper in the Lake Superior area also implies that there was very likely some continuity between the two traditions.

The idea that copper-working and its ceremonial associations that were important in Woodland, Mississippian, and even early post-contact times began with the Old Copper Culture—despite obvious differences in focus—is also reinforced by Ritzenthaler's (et al 1957:278–79) suggestion that Glacial Kame traditions may well represent a "continuation" of the Old Copper Culture. Ritzenthaler bases this conclusion on the "identical burial practices" of both groups, even though there are differences in the details of the copper artifact assemblages of the two cultures. The formal qualities and object types in the Glacial Kame material examined in conjunction with this study showed fully as much in common with Adena copperwork as with Old Copper Culture material. The continuity between Adena and Hopewell manifestations is obvious and generally agreed upon. With Glacial Kame peoples providing the missing link, this ceremonial continuity with associated use of copper is easily extended back into Old Copper Culture times and traditions.

A few archaeologists have also observed that Middle and Late Woodland copper traditions close to the copper-producing areas may actually represent a continuous tradition in copperwork, beginning with the Old Copper Culture.[21] Indeed, certain copper implement types found in these areas, although discovered at sites with widely divergent temporal designations, are almost identical. The obsidian chips discovered at the Riverside Site (a site in the copper mining area, said to have been occupied originally in Old Copper Culture times) indicate that Middle Woodland Hopewell-related peoples also occupied the site (Griffin 1965:138).

Certain unique pieces of copperwork—from Hopewell-related sites in Wisconsin that were described earlier—represent an intriguing meld of traditional Old Copper Culture surface decoration (simple rows of punctate dots found nowhere else in the complex) and more common Hopewellian forms. These finds offer yet another link between these two copper-working traditions. All this evidence suggests very strongly that the earliest concepts regarding the significance of copper could have been and apparently were, transmitted from Old Copper Culture groups to later peoples.

Having established the likelihood that ritual ideas associated with copper were passed down from Old Copper Culture peoples to later groups, the next step is to determine, if possible, how this transmission could have taken place. Some finds of copperwork exist from virtually every period between the Old Copper Culture and post-contact times in eastern North America, even when copper ceased to be of widespread importance ceremonially. This fact alone might account for continued application of certain associations and symbols to ritually important copper, from earliest times into the Historic Periods. Aspects of early Archaic culture in the eastern United States indicate even more clearly, both the likelihood that the basic traditions of the copper complex were well-established by the end of that period, and that the means by which they continued were basically unaltered through so many centuries.

In their interpretation of the prehistory of the eastern United States, Ford and Willey (1941:267, 332) state that the Archaic Period in that region "appears to provide a sort of foundation cultural pattern" for the entire area. They also note a remarkable cultural homogeneity during this period and suggest that it indicates a single language was in use throughout the region. As time went on, cultural traits among the native peoples in the northeastern sections began to diverge.

Eventually, the only elements of culture that continued to reflect this early homogeneity were ritual in nature, "consistently recurring and ever elaborating elements of mortuary ritualism," according to Tuck (1978:43). The same could probably be said of the Southeast. Of course, it was mortuary ritual in which copper figured most importantly, and concepts regarding its proper use and significance appear to be important elements in that ongoing ceremonial tradition, shared by the entire region.

A strong possibility exists that the symbolic associations of copper were transmitted across the centuries linguistically, as well as by continual ritual use in some areas. If there was a single cultural tradition (including a common language) throughout the area, and copper implements were possessed by some individuals throughout as well, words and concepts associated with the material must have been essentially universal during those early times. Continued use of copper in important ceremonies from that point on (however meager the use may have been during some periods) apparently perpetuated those important ritual associations—especially linguistically—even after distinct cultural differences developed.

As noted above, words for copper in a number of Native North American languages show no relationship whatsoever to words for metals received after contact. Words for all metals acquired as the result of contact with European cultures show obvious similarities to each other in all of the Native North American languages examined. It may be that words for copper in the languages of the peoples of the eastern United States contained elements that signalled appropriate ritual and artistic associations automatically, due to that early linguistic uniformity and the ceremonial importance of copper during Archaic times.

A key factor in this proposal is the fact that copper was important *ritually* among groups with extremely conservative religious traditions. Words used in exclusively ceremonial contexts would not have evolved as quickly as other aspects of language. Ethnological literature contains numerous references that indicate that the language used by Native American religious specialists in ceremonial ritual was distinct from common usage and that those language forms were ancient ones.[22]

Magico-religious practices in Old World medieval society reflect similar characteristics. The magical power believed to reside in the writing or repetition of runes, remnants of ancient language, is a perfect example. A similar kind of religious conservatism obtains in the present-day Catholic Church. That many important ceremonies (including the mass until a few decades ago) are performed entirely in Latin, even though few in attendance can understand the language, is a tradition stemming from the earliest centuries of the religion.

Hall (1977:505) suggests that in the ceremonial practices of Native American societies, "culturally transmitted beliefs and understandings which manifest themselves in many different but recognizably related ways" may exist. Underlying linguistic significances no doubt exemplify some of those ways. A related explanation of widely shared symbols of ceremonial importance among native North Americans is suggested by Rands (1957:256). He says that the hand/eye configuration seen in Northwest Coast, Meso-American, and Southeastern American native arts may represent "religious concepts which were widespread on an early horizon and which, perhaps, may have crystallized out under certain conditions of artistic climax." Again, the state of affairs postulated by Ford and Willey and described above suggests that ritual as well as language and other important elements of culture were, in fact, "widespread on an early horizon" in eastern North America. Words and concepts associated with copper were almost certainly a part of that shared culture and apparently reappeared again and again throughout the prehistory of the region.[23]

Whorf's ideas (1941:75–77) also support the feasibility of linguistic explanations for the uniformity in design and usage apparent in the copper complex, since he states that the linguistic designation of certain items may, indeed, occasion specific kinds of behavior. He goes on to explain the close relationship between language and culture and their effect upon one another. Language, he says, is the "factor" (as opposed to culture) which "rigidifies channels of development" in the most autocratic way (Whorf 1941:91). Given this affective status on the part of language, it is certainly possible that linguistic factors, based in early Archaic times and Old Copper Culture practices, were important in the consistent transmission of concepts and symbols associated with copper up until contact times.

Extremely complex symbolic and design systems are common in the arts of many Native American groups. These systems have proved so complex that very few have ever been successfully analyzed in modern art historical terms. Yet, they have been transmitted precisely between native artists and religious specialists across hundreds (perhaps even thousands) of miles and as many years—and without any clear formal structure for such transmittal. The art of the Northwest Coast is a clear case in point.

Another example of this almost mysterious transmission of ancient symbolic tradition is apparent in an illustration in Howard (1968:79) (Fig. 46). It shows a ceremonial drum made in the early twentieth century "by an illiterate member of the Louisiana Koasati community." Symbolic decoration on the drum was composed of a repeated design motif that was common on ceremonial paraphernalia from the prehistoric Southeastern Ceremonial complex (compare with Figs. 70 and 74). Howard states that the artist had no knowledge of the ancient art tradition, per se, yet apparently felt the design appropriate for ceremonial gear. If it could be demonstrated that the very words that are used to describe these artistic processes, the materials used and the ceremonial functions of the finished products,

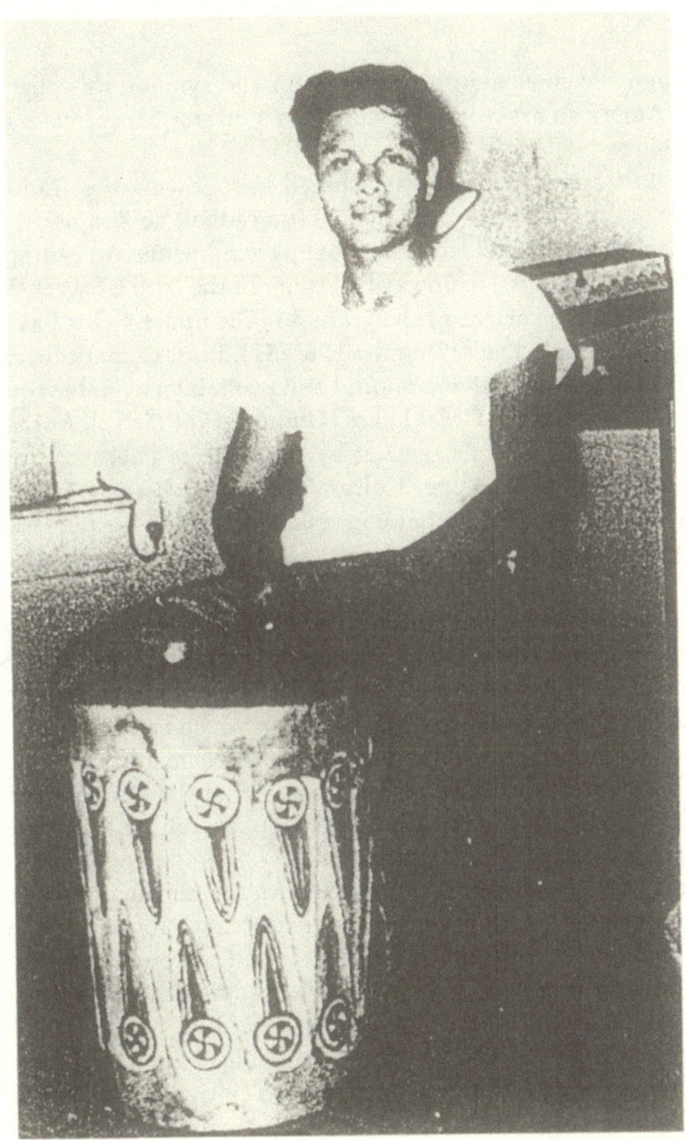

Figure 46. Jack Battise, Koasati tribe, with Ceremonial Drum. Courtesy, Missouri Archaeological Society, from "The Southeastern Ceremonial Complex and Its Meaning," James H. Howard, *Missouri Archaeological Society Memoir* no. 6, 1968, p. 79.

contain linguistic clues to appropriate form and symbol, this phenomenon of Native American art would be much less a mystery. It seems to be a very real possibility.

The Old Copper Culture was ushered in following the gradual recession of the glaciers and the quite radical (if gradual) geographical and ecological changes that coincided with those developments. An example of the latter would be the massive upward warping of the land between 3000 and 1500 B.C., when the surface of the ground in the upper Great Lakes region rose up to five hundred feet (Quimby 1960:52). Prior to that time, land and lake levels had been such that a natural and probably navigable route to the sea was possible from the Great Lakes (Quimby 1960:5, 52). As the glaciers receded, flora and fauna frozen out by the glaciers migrated northward, and man followed. Old Copper Culture peoples were a part of this migration, and indications are that they continued to move in northerly and westerly directions until they disappeared as a distinct cultural manifestation (Quimby 1960:61–62).

At the time of the earliest appearance of Old Copper Culture peoples, the climate in the upper Great Lakes area became the hottest and driest it had been in the preceding twenty thousand years. These climatic conditions coincided with the total extinction of the mastodon which had been present in the area[24] and, no doubt, resulted in a massive northerly migration of most of the large animals upon which the earliest members of the Old Copper Culture relied for food. (The large size of most Old Copper Culture and related points suggests large game was their primary quarry.) Old Copper Culture copper implements have reportedly been located with the remains of the mastodon and the early horse, both of which were extinct by 3500 B.C.[25] A hide bag, preserved by contact with copper salts and found at a prehistoric mining site, has been identified as walrus hide—another animal that disappeared from that area very early (Drier and Du Temple 1961:30).

The warm conditions undoubtedly made life easier in some ways, especially for those groups who were beginning to cultivate local plants. Yarnell (1964:269) states that the domestication of local plant foods in the area began by the second or third millennium B.C. Birthrates probably increased accordingly. In fact, Funk (1978:27) indicates that quick increases in "population" and/or intensity of occupation throughout the Northeast resulted from all these changes in climate and environment. Growth in population was apparently a crucial factor in the development of the entire copper complex. Increases in population, or developments that imply such increases, are associated with the introduction of copper ceremonial paraphernalia into every major group—and into several minor groups[26]—utilizing copper in prehistoric northeastern North America. It is interesting in this context that the growth of Classic Mayan ceremonial centers also coincides with rapid population increases (Willey and Shimkin 1973:460).

For the Old Copper Culture peoples whose traditional source of food was large game animals, the migration and disappearance of so many must have posed a challenge at first. Not only were they forced to alter traditional subsistence patterns, but a certain amount of social tension may also have arisen. If traditional ideas regarding the division of labor in hunting and gathering societies obtained among Old Copper Culture peoples, the primacy of hunting in the subsistence activities of Early Archaic times indicates that men, being the chief providers, held the most economically significant position in these groups. As smaller game—and, more important, the cultivation of local plants—increased in importance, this position as primary provider would have to be shared more and more with women, forcing even greater social and cultural adjustment. These kinds of problems, all stemming ultimately from climatic factors, could have been the impetus needed to begin the arduous exploitation of the copper in the area.

One to two thousand years later, between 2000 and 1000 B.C., the Old Copper Culture "reached its height" (in terms of the amount of cultural remains discovered). This timing coincides with the beginning of an "abnormally cold period" from approximately 1500 to 1000 B.C. (Quimby 1960:26). Such conditions would have increased competition for prime subsistence areas among these groups that had earlier experienced extensive population growth. That copper-working activity should increase under these conditions reinforces the suggestion that copper mining and manufacturing initially arose in response to population and/or subsistence pressures.

This cold spell also coincides with the so-called "peak or climax of the whole Boreal Archaic culture" (between 1500 and 500 B.C.) that was marked by a greater differentiation of local groups and the introduction of more elaborate burial practices—especially in terms of caches of burial goods and the use of red ocher (Quimby 1960:49). That is, during a major shift in climate, an increase in the use of copper among Old Copper Culture peoples parallels an increase in the levels of religious and artistic activity among many peoples in the region at this time.

If other groups in the Northeast responded to these conditions with increased levels of ritual activity involving a red mineral substance, there is no reason why the very similar response of the Old Copper Culture peoples should not be considered to have been primarily ceremonial as well. Note carefully that all these phenomena occur in conjunction with a change in weather conditions. The results of such weather conditions would probably have been increased subsistence and population pressures, factors that would have ultimately brought about important changes in cultural patterns. This dynamic is characteristic of the copper complex in every period of prehistory in the eastern United States.

The problems Old Copper Culture peoples faced during this second major shift in climate were probably not greatly different from those faced earlier when copper weaponry was introduced. Thus, it might be expected that copper would once again be central in ritual responses to those problems (although that did not happen until one or two thousand years later)—especially since there was no complete cessation in the use of copper during the intervening centuries; the numbers of pieces produced during those periods was just smaller.

Other explanations for the emergence of the Old Copper Culture, explanations that ignore the possibility of a ceremonial impetus in the extensive exploitation of copper during Archaic times, are far less convincing. Suggestions that the native miners were economically motivated do not seem valid. Once again, archaeological evidence gathered from the ancient mines demonstrates that interest in mining copper was not prompted by economic concerns. Aspects of mining practices cited in the last chapter also suggest that those activities involved methods that went well beyond the pragmatic. Clearly initial motivation was not merely based upon the presence of deposits of native copper in the area. Many deposits ceased to be intensively exploited by area groups with the disappearance of the Old Copper Culture and were never again of much significance as a source for raw material, although native peoples continued to live in close proximity to the deposits.

If the use of copper was based on a perceived technical superiority in the manufacture of implements, it seems unlikely that copper exploitation would have all but ceased in some areas. Nor is it likely that the technical superiority, if it existed, would have escaped the notice of Hopewell-related Middle Woodland peoples, who virtually never used copper to make points, although they obviously had prodigious amounts of the metal available to them and the expertise to manufacture such implements. Again, the frequent discovery of unused Old Copper Culture implements also suggests that their function was more than just utilitarian (Griffin 1961:67).

Occasionally bone implements have been found that were the obvious prototypes for Old Copper Culture copper ones.[27] In the early metal traditions of the Old World, this similarity between early metal tools and their prototypes in less exotic material is also apparent (Aitchison 1960:22). The Old Copper Culture bone points were apparently utilized at the same time that the copper ones were being produced. The bone points were probably in widespread use in the area, although just a few have been found. (Old Copper Culture material is so old that it is remarkable any examples of bone weaponry have survived.)

In addition, Quimby (1960:45) states that copper was utilized only occasionally for implements used in fishing—hooks, gorges, and harpoons—and that the majority of these implements were also made of bone. Even if copper implements were used in purely utilitarian contexts, clearly they never wholly replaced those of less exotic material, even in the copper mining areas (Drier and Du Temple 1961:157).

Thus, there was a strong tradition of implements made from mundane materials that paralleled the copper-working tradition of the Old Copper Culture. This tradition is also characteristic of all other important copper-working periods. The weight of the evidence indicates then that the use of copper, even for these early implements, probably had an important ritual significance, one that almost certainly formed the basis for subsequent ceremonial tradition in the eastern region.

A review of climatic and other subsistence-related factors during later periods of extensive copper usage in the eastern United States indicates that, once again, such factors were probably central to the growth of tensions that resulted in increased ceremonial activity involving copper. Again, it should be stressed that my purpose here is to identify factors that would account for the widespread adoption of copper-related burial ritual throughout the region, hence, this focus upon developments that might have such wide-ranging and relatively simultaneous effects. Other localized factors were no less crucial, but they are less important in analysis of the phenomenon as a whole.

Griffin (1960:29) discusses the effects of climate on developments in Hopewell-related groups quite thoroughly, noting that they reached their "height" during a warm period between 200 B.C. and A.D. 200. He says they began to "decline" during the cold period that followed, between A.D. 200–700. His terminology implies that the height of Hopewellian ceremonial activity coincided with a period of "good times," general prosperity and economic success. In fact, as noted above, general developments in Native North American religion indicate that increased ceremonial activity tends to be a result of increasing tension and stress.

So, in the Hopewell experience it could be assumed that initial economic prosperity based upon a warming of the climate probably also produced intolerable social problems and pressures—that the times were relatively bad, not good. These pressures may have included competition for suitable agricultural lands necessary to support burgeoning populations. Archaeological analysis has indicated that varying levels of intensity in this kind of competition may account for differences in Hopewellian ceremonial manifestations, particularly for those in Illinois as opposed to those in Ohio (Seeman 1979:406–7).

Related variations in social structure and change in the two regions were undoubtedly important, as well. Similar differences that were related to the nature of and competition for subsistence resources may also account for the blossoming of isolated pockets of agricultural and ceremonial complexity at sites far to the north of the Hopewell core areas. Yarnell's (1964:150) assertion that locations for these sites seem to have been chosen on the "basis of duration of a frostless" growing season adds weight to this argument.

Tensions that arose during the "peak" years for these Middle Woodland groups may have been based on twofold developments, since subsistence at the time depended increasingly upon successful domestication of plant foods (including some maize by approximately 100 B.C.) as well as upon hunting. That the cultivation of maize was only added to already successful agriculturally-based subsistence modes has been indicated by both Yarnell (1976:266) and Witthoft (1949:4) among others. The agricultural sophistication that supported the introduction and eventual success of maize agriculture (as well as its growing importance as a food source) was undoubtedly an important factor in the changes in settlement patterns and population size that occurred even before those developments.[28]

Once again, according to traditional beliefs regarding the division of labor in hunting and gathering societies, another important element in the resulting cultural tensions may well have been a gradual growth in the economic position and importance of women (the traditional agriculturalists) at the expense of men, the hunters.

This gender-based shift in social as well as economic positions may be reflected in the obvious emphasis in Hopewell copper ceremonial paraphernalia upon motifs associated with hunting—despite the ever-growing importance of horticulture in the development of Middle Woodland societies. This anomaly may have resulted from increased interest in hunting ritual on the part of the male half of the population to compensate for a decline in the importance of actual hunting activities in economic terms. Again, similar conditions may also have been a factor in the increased number of copper points manufactured by Old Copper Culture coppersmiths as climatic conditions improved during Archaic times.

In the early centuries of the copper complex, relatively little variation existed in the types of copperwork produced. Most of the copper was made into implements, primarily points. By Middle Woodland times, however, there were many distinct variations on the theme. Even in Late Archaic times, with the appearance of Adena manifestations, the complex showed more variety in terms of the kinds of pieces made and the ways in which they were used.

Various theories have been proposed to explain this variety, as well as the more general shifts in subject matter and object type throughout the history of the complex. It has been suggested that the gradual shift from implements to more and more delicate items of paraphernalia may represent an evolution in the ability to work the material successfully (Goad 1978:91). However, most Old Copper Culture copperwork examined in conjunction with this analysis exhibited extremely fine craftsmanship. I am convinced that these early metallurgists could have manufactured any type of object they cared to produce.

Fogel (1963:129) suggests that the various versions of the copper complex reflect differing social organizations among participant groups. They probably do, but evidence collected for this study suggests that both ritual traditions and social organization depended in large part upon subsistence methods and restrictions. Variety within the copper complex most likely reflects differences in these areas which, in turn, affected relative levels of social and political complexity within each participant group.

As suggested above, basic differences in Hopewell ceremony and social complexity between groups in Illinois and Ohio can be explained, at least in part, on the basis of subsistence-related factors. According to Seeman (1979:406–7), the "environmental circumscription" of the Ohio area required considerable social reorganization as populations increased. The result was the artistic and ceremonial complexity apparent in archaeological remains in that region.

On the other hand, in the Illinois area, the broad valleys of the Mississippi and its tributaries allowed for easy population growth that spread gradually into less favorable "ecological contexts." Such a development pattern would have demanded little, if any, reorganization and is reflected in the ceremonial remains in Illinois that reveal proportionately less richness and complexity. Apparently, where subsistence resources were fairly generally available and no real need existed for social or political reorganization (either between groups or among the individuals in a single cultural unit) to exploit them, the pressures that tended to trigger heightened ritual activity were less likely to occur. Little social or political complexity was required and increase in the production of copperwork was insignificant.

The ongoing problem archaeologists seem to have in attempts to define the Adena people[29] may be due to this characteristic of ceremonial development in precontact eastern Native North American societies. In Early Woodland times, the essentially universal ritual traditions established in the Archaic Periods were probably still generally practiced. Copper was in use but, in the absence of any major crises, on a relatively small scale. Occasionally some group possessed and used copper more than most others, but that blossoming of the complex may well reflect the attempts of locally powerful individuals to solve problems within their own groups. Gradually increasing expertise in agricultural production and differing ecological situations on a local basis, may also have played a part in these occasional pockets of increased ritual activity and related production of copperwork. However, only conditions that forced pan-regional cultural adjustment could have produced the kind of full-fledged expression of the copper complex that was represented by Old Copper Culture, Hopewellian or Mississippian developments.

Subsistence factors also appear to have been important in the development of Copena culture in the Southeast. Goad (1978:125) describes the regions inhabited by these peoples as "small and sharply defined," winding along a 240–kilometer stretch of the Tennessee River in Alabama and Tennessee and ending where the "river narrows and the flood plain is constricted." Walthall (1972:146) suggests that the beginnings of Copena coincide with the introduction of corn agriculture into the area in approximately A.D. 150. Considerable increases in population and shifts in settlement patterns are apparent at about the same time. The resulting situation probably produced conditions much like those Seeman describes in Ohio at the height of Hopewellian developments: a growing population that is supported by a decidedly limited, if sufficient, area for subsistence exploitation.

The tensions associated with a gradual shift from the patrilineal social organization characteristic of hunter/gather societies to the matrilineal traditions that characterize most Southeastern groups in Early Historic times was undoubtedly a factor in these developments as well. Again, increases in levels of stress and social tension that these conditions tend to produce in Native American societies are those most likely to trigger revitalization-type movements. The results are always increased levels of ritual activity accompanied by increased social and political complexity.

Goad (1978) has demonstrated that Southeastern sources for copper were gradually exploited from Copena times on. However, connections with earlier copper mining and working traditions appear to have been maintained to some degree, since copper from Lake Superior area sources was also utilized in the making of Mississippian copperwork.[30] Once again, this evidence suggests that similarities between copper-working traditions from different periods in prehistory can be traced to shared aspects of culture, established very early in the region. Important differences between those earlier traditions and later ones arose as the result of the passage of time (often thousands of years) and as the result of changes in subsistence modes and social structure (which affected the kinds of problems those rituals were called upon to solve).

Still, the continuity of ceremonial traditions stretching from Archaic to Mississippian times is apparent in the evidence gathered from many Southeastern sites. Superimposed levels of occupation attest to this continuity, just as do similar phenomena in sites farther north.[31] A clear progression of local ritual traditions exists that precedes the flowering of the so-called Southeastern Ceremonial Complex in Mississippian times (e.g., Kelly 1954). Copper is often found in conjunction with these earlier horizons, but appears in the largest quantities at sites associated with the Southeastern Ceremonial Complex.

Factors of climate were also important in the development of this important Mississippian ceremonial manifestation. Many of the conditions that seem to have precipitated the flowering of the copper complex in other areas and in earlier times obtained in the Southeast during the Mississippian Periods. In fact, much the same scenario (described above) for the development of Copena culture can be applied to events leading up to the Southeastern Ceremonial Complex. Fairbanks (1956:293) states that "population pressures" may be the "key" to an understanding of that cultural phenomenon. Waring (1968:65) points out that the changes that preceded the inception of the Southeastern Ceremonial Complex included new agricultural technologies, "enabling a smaller area to support a larger population." The validity of suggestions that climatic factors triggered the cultural complexity of the Southeastern Ceremonial Complex is also reinforced by associated developments farther north. A general warming trend apparently resulted in increased ceremonial activity in those regions, as well as in increased intensity in agricultural pursuits (Quimby 1960:85–100). Considerable archaeological evidence indicates that the primary impetus for Mississippian ceremonial developments was agricultural, the result of this favorable shift in climate. Mound D at Ocmulgee in Georgia, a very early and primitive Mississippian site, was built over an ancient cornfield (Stirling 1934:391). According to Waring (1968:64), most evidence indicates that the emphasis in Southeastern Ceremonial Complex ritual was agricultural in orientation. Howard (1968:87) discusses a number of other factors that point to the same kinds of conclusions regarding the initial impetus for the development of the Complex.

Waring (1968:65) cites an anomaly in the history of the Southeastern Ceremonial Complex that offers further insight into the way these religious phenomena developed. Although the full-blown Complex did not appear until after apparent Muskogean migrations into areas of Georgia, Creek oral tradition maintains that important rituals (associated occasionally with copper) were received prior to this migration. Thus, the ritual tradition itself would seem to have preceded its elaborate expression in ceremony and artwork known as the Southeastern Ceremonial Complex. Probably no anomaly exists here, for the tensions that precipitated the migration represent only the first stage of developments. The ideas were not likely pushed into full ceremonial and artistic expression until the Muskhogean peoples began to intrude into the Macon area. Once again, a sudden explosion of population (perhaps an intrusive one this time) appears to have triggered considerable social and demographic adjustment. Competition for available resources (agriculturally rich land) may also have increased, either between themselves and the people already there, or within Muskhogean groups whose new, more fertile location resulted in a population explosion.

Peebles's (1971:88) discovery that Moundville is located on the "boundary of an ecozone-transition area" in Alabama (an ideal location for the exploitation of food resources from both the ecozones it straddled) suggests that population growth and a quest for prime subsistence areas may also have determined its location as a major ceremonial center. More recent ceremonial developments add weight to this line of reasoning.

According to Witthoft (1949:6), Green Corn ceremonies (closely related to aspects of Mississippian ceremony) are not found in areas with marginal cultivation. That is, complex agricultural rituals grow up and persist only in areas of intense cultivation where a relatively large population is supported by relatively limited areas of subsistence exploitation. Where marginal cultivation is the norm and populations are small and/or dispersed, the cultural pressures that bring about increased ceremonial activity and artistic production apparently never materialize, nor do more complex social and economic systems to control production and distribution.

Conclusions along these lines parallel Seeman's with regard to Hopewellian developments. In his analysis of the Southeastern Ceremonial Complex, Waring (1968:64) states that it was "a highly involved affair and is best regarded as the culmination of a complicated developmental process" which also manifests the effects of "sweeping religious activity." While this statement clearly identifies two important aspects of Mississippian ceremonial development, it may be more accurate to describe the entire phenomenon as part of an ongoing religious tradition that blossomed into increased complexity as a result of conditions that had a widespread and similar effect upon many societies in the region.

There were two distinct climatic trends during Mississippian times, a warm period between A.D. 700 and 1200, and a cold period between A.D. 1200 and 1500. Baerreis and Bryson (1965:215) suggest that the warm period begins approximately A.D. 900 and they cite a sharp shift to a colder climate approximately A.D. 1250. Griffin (1960:29) associates the first trend with the rise of Mississippian culture and, once again, links evidence of complex ceremonial practices with the "highest . . . level of accomplishment" of Mississippian cultures (Griffin 1944:300), the "good times." Again, this terminology obscures the fact that those artistic and ceremonial developments almost certainly represent a reluctant response to extreme social and cultural pressures and were hardly "good times." Just as two distinct climatic trends existed during Mississippian times, two distinct and chronologically separate trends in style on copperwork also existed during those periods.

The chronology is defined by the relative positions of copper plates found in the primary mound at Lake Jackson in Florida (Calvin Jones, personal communication 1976). This chronology supports James Brown's conviction that the contents of the Great Mortuary at Spiro include examples of material from many periods within Mississippian tradition and were gathered from earlier graves before being deposited there relatively late in the history of the Southeastern Ceremonial Complex. The copperwork found at Spiro included examples in both the early and very latest styles. The earlier tradition includes most of the same symbolic elements as the later one. However, the early style is lifelike and animated while the later expressions are more stylized, stiff and moribund in their overall impression (Compare Plates 1 and 13 and Figs. 37 and 68 with Plate 11 and Fig. 38).

This shift in style and, probably, in ceremonial emphasis is also obvious on a piece of copperwork from Etowah. Engraved heads in a much later style were added to a bi-lobed arrow headdress piece. The original piece is of a type discovered more often in connection with earlier style representations. Many similar pieces have been found at Etowah and other sites. The engraved heads were obviously added some time after the piece was made, probably long afterward, since the engraving is clearly in the later style and the piece itself is little more than a collection of fragments.

Developments in the eastern United States after contact suggest that climatic factors continued to affect ceremonial development. The years from A.D. 1600 to A.D. 1900 have been referred to as a "Little Ice Age." It has been suggested that this sudden cold spell helped trigger the enthusiastic Native American response to the European fur trade and concomitant abandonment of earlier agriculture pursuits (Baerreis and Bryson 1965:214–17). With the introduction of the horse, this shift in climate may also help account for the sudden appearance of the Plains cultures and related ceremonies. Abrupt alteration in ceremonial and especially in burial practices among the Chippewa, documented by Hickerson (1970), may well have been in response to these same phenomena.

Population pressures created by the westward movement of native peoples were due, in turn, to conditions that arose in the wake of European settlement farther east (as well as to the long cold spell). These factors were almost certainly instrumental in the development of ceremonies that involved Post-Mississippian copperwork. Probably the most severe of the responses to these conditions was the virtual destruction of the Huron and other groups by the Iroquois and their consequent mass dispersal to points west in the first half of the seventeenth century. All these developments would have fomented radical shifts in social structure, as well as in demographics and subsistence strategies. Given these circumstances, it is not surprising that the two richest post-contact sites in terms of copperwork and allied ceremonial activity were discovered in the general area settled by these dispersed populations and those they displaced—Dumaw Creek in Michigan and the Anker Site in Illinois. Some time later (between 1760 and 1820), following these individualized responses, a cultural and ceremonial uniformity arose in the western Great Lakes region that certainly rivaled that apparent during Hopewellian and Mississippian times (Quimby 1960:8), although it was less spectacular with regard to the production of ceremonial material. By the end of this period, however, copper was not an important part of such ritual responses.

If climatic- and subsistence-related factors led to the blossoming of important ceremonial movements involving copper, it may be assumed that similar changes or successful adaptation to new social and subsistence modes, could have brought them to an end. The long periods of warm temperatures and related demographic developments that initially gave rise to the ceremonial use of copper among Old Copper Culture peoples, probably also caused its demise—eventually. A gradual loss of interest in the manufacture of copper points on the large scale seen earlier and a shift to smaller ones in areas where they continued to be made suggest a gradual adaptation to the changed ecological situation. Greater expertise was undoubtedly developed in the exploitation of plant resources. Smaller game probably sufficed, with these new foodstuffs as dietary supplements.

Griffin (1960:31) suggests that a cooling of the climate between A.D. 200 and A.D. 700 resulted in the "decline" of Middle Woodland Hopewell-related ceremonial. This, he says, explains why centers farther south did not experience so early a demise. If the foregoing scenario for the development of events surrounding the copper complex is correct, the cooling of the climate probably resulted in a brief *increase* in ceremonial activity, as tensions continued to rise. In fact, the Hopewell type-site, certainly the richest in Ohio, has yielded the most recent radiocarbon date of any Hopewell mound group (*Michigan Archaeological News* 1953:4). Nevertheless, the inability of Hopewell ceremonies and rituals to solve the growing crises caused by the change in climate and related cultural stress could have resulted in a loss of general support for that ceremonial tradition, ending in its rather sudden demise in many areas.

Another important development in increased hunting efficiency probably assured that demise. About the same period, approximately A.D. 500, the bow and arrow replaced the atlatl (Hall 1977:514). This increased efficiency in hunting, combined with what had probably become general agricultural expertise—sufficient to support small groups under ecological conditions at that time, but not to support a large class of nonproductive religious specialists—likely made the return to a simpler lifestyle as easy as it was inevitable. This kind of scenario is roughly similar to the one projected by Willey and Shimkin (1973:470–71) to account for the collapse of

Mayan civilization farther south. Finally, the significant tensions that must obtain in societies shifting from patrilineal to matrilineal social organization may have dissipated as new social structures became the norm.

Developments in Mississippian times could well have been similar. The warming trend that resulted in greatly increased populations and concomitant cultural and ceremonial complexity, set the scene for the first phases of Mississippian ceremonialism. The sudden shift to a colder climate probably resulted initially in heightened ceremonial activity to meet the crises.

Unlike the first stage of the Cult, however, this later ceremonial movement was based upon conditions that arose not from growing prosperity, but rather from a loss of resources. The nature of this difference may account for the distinct shift from a lively and animated art style to a stiff and moribund one that is obvious in the copperwork from these periods. As was probably the case in the later Woodland Periods, these long-term climatic changes almost certainly resulted in a movement away from subsistence modes based primarily upon intensive corn agriculture, to the combined hunting and gathering/agricultural economies described by early European observers (Griffin 1960:27).

A tradition regarding the Delaware Busk festival also hints that the failure of corn crops (probably due to climate) may have been the impetus for the later phases of Mississippian ceremonial. Delaware legend states that the Busk ceremonial, often identified with aspects of the Southeastern Ceremonial Complex, originated during a time when corn "left the people." According to the legend, the entire Busk ceremonial was established at that time as a plea to the Creator and to Corn Mother for its return (Witthoft 1949:14–15).

The question of the complete demise of the copper complex itself remains. It is difficult to see how so pervasive a tradition could have been so completely and so quickly eradicated. With the exception of some ephemeral traditions regarding recent Creek ritual, copper ceased to be important in eastern Native North American ceremonial by Late Historic times. As with so many questions regarding the copper complex, no documentary or archaeological data records precisely why copper ceased to be important in the ceremonial life of Native Americans in eastern North America.

Once again, the answers lie in shreds of evidence available here and there in historical and archaeological records. Much of this evidence simply helps to highlight factors that were probably *not* significant in the rejection of copper as an important ceremonial material. For example, it is certain that the problem was not the result of having forgotten where or how to procure native copper. Information cited earlier indicates that knowledge of some deposits remained current.

The problem was probably not one of closed trade routes either. It has been pointed out above that important ritual material was disseminated personally by religious leaders and their followers in conjunction with the communication of new ceremonies and religious ideas. The extensive travels of Tecumseh and of adherents of the Ghost Dance rituals prove that these traditional avenues of "trade" were still very much in use. Nor did native artists cease to fashion ritual materials from copper because of an inability to work the material. Other evidence presented above indicates that native metallurgists in Historic times continued to exhibit considerable cold-hammering skill in the working of European silver.

Undoubtedly, the reasons for the end of the copper complex can be traced ultimately to the arrival of Europeans on the New World scene. The copper tradition did not cease to be of significance immediately following that arrival, however. As noted above, for some time large amounts of European copper and brass and some native copper continued to be used in many of the same contexts and for the same purposes as earlier (e.g., Quimby 1960:10, 72).

Fairly quickly, however, between Middle and Late Historic times, copper ceased to be of much importance (Quimby 1960:72, 76). According to Howard (1968:13), objects and material culture are "generally the first class of traits to disappear in the acculturation process." Given the almost universal importance of copper in complex ritual tradition throughout the Eastern Woodlands during the preceding millennia, the demise of copper as an important factor within those belief systems must have been as much an integral part of the shock associated with acculturation as it was a result of it.

The loss of so central and so ancient an aspect of culture must have been the result of specific circumstances. Details in the ethnological literature of the period, as well as aspects of the copper complex itself, suggest what those circumstances might have been.

If copper was perceived to be a source and/or validation of power, the amounts of copper possessed by Europeans and their relative nonchalance at giving or trading it away must have greatly impressed Native Americans in the eastern United States. Native models of reality, based upon the reciprocal nature of elemental power and its manipulation, would almost undoubtedly have linked possession of such an abundance of metal to the remarkable characteristics of European weaponry, a link that was obviously more spiritual than technological in nature. That is, the superiority of European weapons was probably interpreted as evidence of spiritual strength, of a properly developed relationship with certain potent supernatural entities. From the native point of view, persons powerful enough to possess and manipulate such large amounts of copper would have been *expected* to have extraordinary weaponry (or some other impressive evidence of spiritual potency to correspond to their possession and manipulation of metals).

Few would argue that different perspectives regarding the nature and ownership of land served to hasten the demise of native political systems. The radical differences between Native Anerican and European models of spiritual and technical reality forged yet another misconception regarding the nature of European culture, one that contributed to the demise of native religious systems in eastern North America, for a time at least.

As copper ceased to be used by Native Americans, its important position in those cultures was almost immediately replaced by silver. European silver is found at Historic sites in many of the same contexts formerly reserved for copperwork.[32] It is likely that Native Americans very quickly became aware of the value Europeans placed upon silver, as opposed to the relatively low position that copper held in European estimation. After contact, the rapid shift in interest from copper to silver, as well as earlier preferences for European copper as opposed to the native variety, suggest that Native Americans may have been trying to tap into the tremendous reservoir of power apparently controlled by Europeans, by accumulating and using European metals. This response was a thoroughly logical and pragmatic one, given the basic ontological and epistemological convictions of the native peoples.

Eventually it must have been painfully clear to Native Americans in eastern North America that copper, traditionally their most powerful agent, could not be successfully manipulated to counter the onslaught of European settlement and domination. Nor could they utilize European metals successfully to counter this threat. It was probably just as devastating to realize that the power believed to be resident in these exotic materials was now under the exclusive control of the newcomers. Not only had they been deprived of a crucial source of power, that potent source was now available to the very group by whom they were threatened. This recognition, however gradual, had to be culturally devastating and probably represents yet another way that contact with Europeans wreaked tremendous cultural havoc among Native North American groups.

This recognition was probably also a factor in the relative ease with which many of the native peoples in the region were dominated. Faced with this perceived loss of efficacy in dealing with their world, these essentially pragmatic peoples undoubtedly looked in new directions for spiritual assistance. Unfortunately, the loss of spiritual power traditionally believed to reside in materials like copper was one for which they could not effectively compensate. Lack of so universally appreciated a symbol and validation of power as copper had been, probably doomed to failure from the outset any late attempts at forming a united Native American front against European incursions. Two poignant bits of historical documentation hint that some groups, at least, were keenly aware of this loss of power, its specific nature and its implications—an awareness that was probably shared, though not recorded, by many others.

The Sioux, greatly repressed by the United States government at the time, forbade the use of any metal in the performance of the Ghost Dance (Mooney 1965:178), although European textiles and other trade materials were often utilized in performances of that ceremony. If metal was consciously eliminated from Ghost Dance ritual simply because of its association with Anglo-American culture, muslin and other trade goods would certainly have been excluded as well. While most European trade goods were deemed harmless enough, perhaps the supernatural powers resident in metals were deemed to have come under the exclusive control of their repressors. Consequently, use of those materials might have rendered the ceremony ineffective.

The other incident was recorded by the Jesuit Allouez (Foster and Whitney 1850:110). He noted the existence of a large copper boulder that protruded from the surface of a certain lake. At some point during his stay in that area it vanished. The native peoples told him that "it was a divinity who had disappeared," although they were unwilling to say why it had gone. Perhaps the loss of that "divinity" confirmed what they were already beginning to feel: the loss of order in the cosmos, that harmony that had supported and perpetuated Native American cultures for at least ten thousand years. In the preceding three millennia, such problems were traditionally dealt with through the accumulation and manipulation of copper. This right and ability had seemed to slip from their grasp into that of the Europeans, leaving the Native Americans of eastern North America powerless to oppose their total domination.

Conclusion

Except for a few examples of copper use in Early Historic times, all the available facts regarding the copper complex are archaeological, the remains of an extraordinarily long and unified prehistoric tradition. Although much archaeological data exists, none of it offers specific information regarding the significance of the copperwork or the motives or intentions of the peoples that used it. Evidence from many other sources must be garnered to accurately reconstruct how copperwork functioned and why it was so important. Ethnological and historical data provide some relevant details. Nevertheless, specific information regarding the significance and use of copper among historic native groups is scant and the facts regarding that use are almost never obvious.

Still, combined with the archaeological data, the implications offered by these shreds of evidence are quite clear. In both Historic and prehistoric contexts, copper was primarily ceremonial in significance, and was possessed, used and manipulated by an hereditary elite. Those individuals who kept and utilized the most spectacular examples were usually religious specialists. Some wielded considerable political and economic influence as well, although the basis for their power and position was primarily spiritual. The prehistoric ceremonial manifestations in which copper played so central a role show a pattern of inception and development that also obtained in Historic religious movements among Native North Americans, although copper was not important in most of the latter. The similarities among major religious developments in Historic times and evidence of them in the prehistoric periods indicate that severe cultural crises gave rise to the major precontact ceremonial developments and the copperwork that was produced in conjunction with them.

The evolution of design and use of copperwork itself presents the most specific information regarding the significance of copperwork, especially when the evolution is viewed in conjunction with the archaeological and historical records. The extraordinary consistency in motif and usage associated with copper during the entire complex suggests that the fundamental concepts associated with copper were established in a very early period, during a time when cultural manifestations and even language were relatively uniform throughout the area. These data indicate that, from the earliest years of the complex to its demise, the production of copper objects was an activity that went far beyond the whimsical or merely aesthetic in its import. For Native Americans, the significance of copper and copperwork apparently also extended well beyond any political or economic importance it may have had.

The motifs used most consistently on copperwork, as well as the methods and modes of its disposition archaeologically and its use historically, indicate that copper was believed to possess special power—a vehicle that provided a link with and potential control of powerful forces. This same consistency in design suggests that the motivations for invoking the powers believed to be resident in copper also remained fairly constant, although the specific conditions requiring such an invocation varied both geographically and temporally. Gradual evolution in the subject matter of these designs reveals a tradition of use and associated motif that coincides with the evolution of subsistence methods throughout the area.

Just as the kinds of objects made of copper and the range of designs applied to it remained similar for thousands of years, the ceremonial structures involving copper throughout the eastern area were also very similar. This fact suggests that peoples throughout the region probably had similar reasons for utilizing copper in these rituals, despite considerable cultural diversity in most other ways. Continual reference to important cosmological concepts in design on copperwork (as well as in ethnological and historical data) indicate that copper played a crucial role in ceremonial movements that were developed to restore and/or maintain harmony within the cosmos.

The manipulation of copper as art, then, was linked to that crucial ritual importance. The aesthetics governing that kind of artistic manipulation must have been rooted in deeply held ontological concepts. Form and design in copperwork, therefore, were not based upon a set of formal requirements established by some school or other: they were the expression of convictions regarding the nature of reality. The beauty and complexity of form, as well as the technical expertise apparent in so much of the copperwork from prehistoric periods, was an outgrowth of the very serious nature of the rituals and ceremonies for which they were created and of the ontological and cosmological convictions they expressed. Prehistoric coppersmiths were most likely engaged in the production of objects that were deemed crucial to their own survival and that of their culture.

Appendix

APPENDIX

Section I—The Analysis: Structure and Process

I.1. METHODOLOGY

To begin analysis of the pre-Columbian Eastern Woodlands copper complex, each piece of copperwork (or, in many cases, group of identical pieces) was classified according to several criteria. This task posed special problems. The specific use of many of the objects is difficult to determine at best, and is often impossible. Labels used in the archaeological literature (gorget, breastplate, button, pendant) generally reflect the locations of the items in individual burials or a guess as to probable use based on shape, the placement of perforations, or other clues. These names are convenient but often misleading labels that may or may not reflect actual use. Continuation here of such essentially arbitrary type designations is regrettable since the actual uses are not known. Still, the conventional designations have meaning for those already familiar with this material, so continuing to use those labels is more efficient than inventing new ones. Other identifications (such as axes, awls, bracelets, and beads) are less arbitrary.

When no use has been assigned to a particular configuration in the literature and none can be determined, the configuration in question was categorized according to the way the copper was shaped. Other pieces defy both abstract formal and functional categorization but have clearly identifiable motifs; these have been used as the basis for their classification. Needless to say, in the resulting system the objects are not always described according to the same parameters.

The system remains consistent, nevertheless, since the use for which each copper artifact was intended was almost certainly determined by both the form of the piece and the motifs applied to it. Once made, those same elements (form and motif) probably served to define the ways in which the object was utilized thereafter. Consequently, categorization according to these two criteria should produce clusters of objects that functioned in similar ways. Since we know so little about the ways in which most of these pieces were used, this kind of variable classification system, based on the physical attributes of the pieces themselves, is more accurate than one that assigns meaning or significance to objects based upon criteria that may or may not have been significant to the groups that produced the copperwork.

I have also avoided arranging the objects into a classification system like the one suggested by Binford (Binford and Binford 1968:23–25) and adopted as a matter of course by many in the field. He proposes the arrangement of archaeological material into three groups:

1. "technomic," objects that "function to articulate man with the natural environment";
2. "socio-technic," objects that "function in the social environment";
3. "ideo-technic," objects "functioning in the ideational environment."

Without a clear perception of the social and ideational environments of prehistoric peoples and of what they would have considered their "natural environment" to be, separation of their material culture into such categories is far too arbitrary. In the absence of documentary evidence, such classification systems must be based on definitions of function that are valid primarily for the definer's culture. Axes and awls would be termed "technomic;" bracelets and ear ornaments, probably "socio-technic;" and more exotic pieces such as copper bear teeth or raccoon penis bones, "ideo-technic."

This approach not only operates in a historical and cultural vacuum; but its usefulness is also all but negated in the face of a phenomenon that has frequently been reported concerning the art of so-called primitive cultures: objects often function simultaneously in all three domains. Thus, to define an object in terms of any one of Binford's three categories to the exclusion of the others, especially without any clear supporting evidence, might well deprive the piece of much of its cultural significance and even obscure rather than elucidate the nature and identity of the people who created it.

Most of the archaeological evidence indicates that precontact copperwork unquestionably did function at several different levels. For example, axes and adzes, while frequently hafted, seldom show signs of use; and many would have been inefficient tools, in any case, because the native copper is so soft. Earpieces, although most often found in or near the ears of burials, are also found grasped in hands, hanging from wrists, in rows along the sides of burials, and in sizeable caches not associated with human remains. Since virtually all the pairs found in single graves are identical and no more than two could have been worn in the ears at any one time, the significance of these pieces must have extended well beyond the merely ornamental.

Furthermore, the remarkable continuity evident in the evolution of object and motif in precontact copperwork suggests that the properties of the material itself were of primary importance, regardless of the shape and nature of the piece. This represents yet another level of significance for every object in the complex that is not allowed for in the kind of classification system Binford proposes and in the kind many other anthropologists and archaeologists utilize. The definition of "applied design" and analysis of the designs themselves pose similar problems.

Examining the copper complex as a whole has been important in working through these difficulties. The same forms and themes appear again and again in copperwork produced throughout much of Eastern North America over thousands of years. Inventory and tabulation of prehistoric copperwork designs confirm this impression. Gradual changes are apparent and preferences within individual cultural units and complexes are distinct. Nevertheless, most of the designs refer to a remarkably limited core of visual ideas, regardless of when or where they were made. The basis for this consistency is apparently the material itself and the important concepts associated directly with native copper.

In order to facilitate analysis of design use, I have divided the corpus into two groups, decorated and undecorated examples. Of the more than fourteen thousand pieces of copperwork analyzed, only about four thousand (20.94 percent) include significant applied design (Table IV). All the copperwork was utilized in essentially the same ways, whether decorated or not. Thus, the preponderance of undecorated examples is significant. It indicates that although the motifs applied to copperwork are certainly important, they probably reflect relatively transient interests and concerns when compared to the larger, persistent, and pervasive complex of meanings which was apparently associated with the material itself.

In fact, the division of the copper corpus into two groups—those items which incorporate elements of applied design and those which do not—creates a distinction that may not have been very significant to those who made and used the objects. Such an approach is instructive, nevertheless, since it allows us to follow the evolution of design in prehistoric copperwork. Defining the nature and direction of that evolution is crucial to reconstruction of the social and conceptual milieux in which the copperwork was produced.

For the purposes of this study, copperwork considered to incorporate significant design elements is defined as any object whose shape and decoration do not appear to have been determined primarily by utilitarian considerations. Thus, axes and adzes, awls and points, as well as simple bracelets and beads—straightforward, unelaborated forms of implements as well as ceremonial paraphernalia—are not considered to include significant design. Copper axe and point shapes that could not have been used as implements *are* included in design totals, however, as are a few examples of more elaborate beads and bracelets. (Of course, it is quite possible that most or all copper implements were themselves symbolic. This is a purely arbitrary distinction to facilitate statistical analysis.)

Unfortunately, the term "functional" is, in many respects, culture-bound. Thus, it may be that several categories of copperwork are assumed to be "non-functional" here, simply because the ways in which they functioned within the societies that made them are unclear. This is almost certainly true of Middle Woodland breastplates and some Mississippian earpieces, for example, whose largely unelaborated forms were almost surely determined by their functions within the societies that used them. As important items of ritual paraphernalia, their forms were undoubtedly determined by their use in important ceremonies. They have been included in the tabulation of design types, nevertheless, because their shapes (consistent in dozens of examples) were probably also of symbolic significance as well as being in some sense functional.

I.1.A. Design Technique

Designs were applied to the copper in four ways:

1. The shape itself—in many instances this is the only design motif involved. The degree of complexity ranges from simple circles or rectangles of sheet copper to the elaborate geometric designs found with the remains of some Hopewell-related peoples (e.g., Plates 2, 3, 6, and 7).
2. Repoussé—the most elaborate and skillful examples of design on copperwork, as well as the most numerous, are worked in a repoussé technique (e.g., Plates 1 and 10–12 and Figs. 5, 21, 47, 48, and 53). Also, a few rather crude examples of the technique consist of little more than rows of punctate dots (e.g., Figs. 13 and 36).
3. Simple engraving—designs were also applied to copperwork with incised lines, although infrequently. Pieces incorporating this method of application are usually rather crude and rudimentary.
4. Copper appliqué—this last method of copper design involved the application of thin sheets or small lumps of copper to objects made primarily of other materials (Figs. 18a and 18b).

The tendency to apply designs to copperwork increased with time. Less than 1 percent of the pieces manufactured in the Archaic Periods was deco-

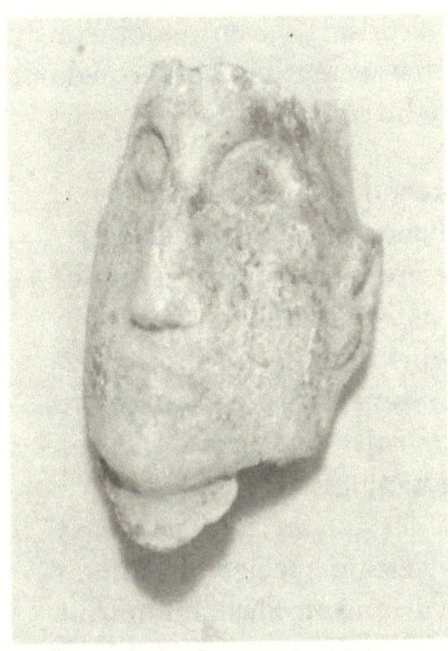

Figure 47. Human Head (with typical Hopewell style features), Middle Woodland. Ohio Historical Society, Columbus, #283/140. Hopewell Mounds, Ross Co., Ohio. Ca. 3" tall.

Figure 48. Repoussé Breastplate, Mississippian. Illinois State Museum, Dickson Mounds, Lewiston. Dickson Mounds, Fulton Co., Illinois. Ca. 5" diameter.

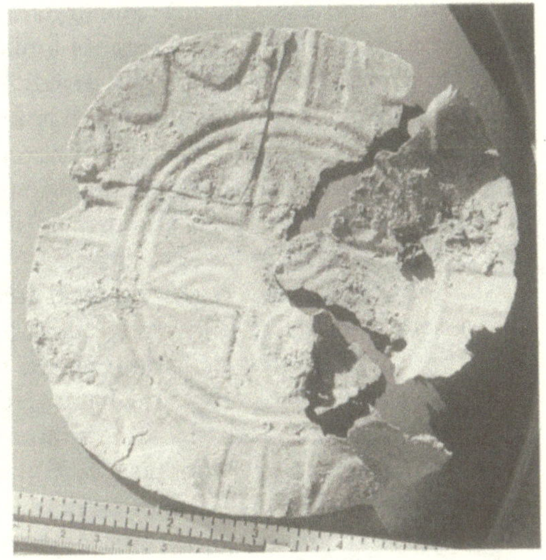

rated. By Mississippian times, a few hundred years before the arrival of Europeans, nearly 50 percent of all copperwork was given some kind of applied decoration. An increase in the relative number of decorated pieces occurs with each successive cultural manifestation of the complex (Table IV).

I.1.B. Designs

The number of designs applied to precontact copperwork was remarkably limited, especially considering the size of the geographical area involved, the centuries spanned by the complex, and the amount of copperwork manufactured.

The narrowness of design parameters is also surprising, given the obviously individualized interpretations and approaches that were exhibited throughout the tradition. The designs fall roughly into three broad categories:

1. *Geometric Forms*—most designs on precontact copperwork consist of variations on a circular form. There are many rectangular designs, but it appears that even they are part of a spectrum of related motifs and symbols whose basis is circular. That is, geometric designs on prehistoric copperwork usually fit into a continuum of designs that ranges from simple circular forms to rectangular ones: circles, crescents, spirals, sunbursts, crosses, swastikas, reel shapes, squares, and rectangles.
2. *Representational Forms*—many of the designs are relatively easy to identify. Human beings, as well as certain species of animals and birds, are quite clearly depicted. Various reptiles and marine univalves are also represented, as well as implement forms. Many other motifs within this category are composite images, combinations of simpler elements from a limited vocabulary of forms, most of which are naturalistically based. Although the specific being or conceptual notion delineated may not be readily identifiable, the elements making up the combination are clear. Of course, the specific significance of these designs may never be known, but unlike motifs in the other two categories of design, at least some aspects of this subject matter are clear.

   Although certain geographical areas and chronological periods were characterized by preferences for certain motifs, essentially the same species were represented throughout most of the five thousand or so years in which the precontact copper complex flourished. Furthermore, the same anatomical features of those species were given special emphasis by coppersmiths in every period.
3. *Composite Forms*—design on many examples of copperwork appears to combine both representational and geometric motifs. The repetition of certain complex designs, produced over long periods of time in widely separated areas and among groups that often shared no common language, suggests not only a body of shared ritual but also a widely shared symbolic vocabulary. Copperwork in this category includes most earpieces and breastplates made in the later periods of the copper complex. Other pieces with this type of design are more complex and appear to represent a distillation of the core concepts that formed the basis of the cultural patterns in the final thousand or so years of the complex. Only a few such pieces exist, but they seem to be very important and are

found only among the products of the most complex of the prehistoric copper-working societies.

Because the categories of design are so limited, it will be useful to introduce each of them along with discussion of their relative frequency of use within the complex as a whole.

I.2. Geometric Forms

I.2.a. Circles

Circles are an important part of the design vocabulary in every major manifestation of the copper complex, excepting Early Woodland Adena groups (Table VI). However, an inordinate proportion of Adena copperwork consists of oval and circular bracelets and rings. These are not included in the design statistics since the form of each is directly related to its function as a ring or a bracelet. However, it is very likely that the form itself was symbolic, representing the same kinds of concepts associated with circular motifs applied to the copperwork of other groups. Overall, circular motifs account for almost 40 percent of the designs in the entire corpus and for an average of more than 30 percent of the designs on copperwork within each major precontact group involved in the complex (Tables VI and VII). Circular designs were applied to copper in all four of the technical processes described above.

I.2.b. Crescents

Crescents were also very important. Their formal relationship to circles is obvious, but crescents represent less that 2 percent of all design elements in the corpus. Most are unelaborated crescent shapes that are used primarily as breastplates, but the design also appears in several other contexts and in all four of the technical processes used.

I.2.c. Spirals

Like crescents, spirals represent less than 2 percent of applied design on the pieces examined. Nevertheless, excepting Middle Woodland Copena peoples, spiral designs were used in all precontact copper-working periods and cultures and include designs worked in all four techniques (Tables VI–VIII). Spirals were used in many of the same contexts as crescents, but they are usually much smaller, whether individually wrought or as applied design.

I.2.d. Sunbursts

The cultural and temporal distribution of sunbursts, another circle-related form, was much more limited. Only Middle Woodland and Mississippian coppersmiths seem to have used this motif (Tables VI–VIII), but it was extremely important to them. Thus, sunbursts are almost as numerous as crescents and spirals in the corpus as a whole, although none were made before Middle Woodland times. Sunburst motifs were also applied to copperwork in all four of the techniques discussed above.

I.2.E. CROSSES

Crosses account for 2.05 percent of the designs. Copper crosses per se were made only occasionally. More often, cross and related swastika forms were used as interior designs on larger pieces of various shapes. These motifs were both incised and depicted in repoussé. Cross shapes on copperwork vary between Greek (equal-armed) and Roman (with one long and one shorter arm) types, depending largely on the overall shape of the piece carrying the motif; those used on circular pieces typically have equal arms and those used on more irregular pieces have one longer arm. Occasionally, the form was set on its side, producing an X.

In purely formal terms, the cross may be regarded as a transitional motif. That is, on the continuum of design types discussed earlier, ranging from circular to rectangular forms, cruciform designs are situated about midway, and are almost as closely related to rectangular motifs as they are to circular ones. The ends of the four arms of a cross may be enclosed in a square or rectangle as readily as they are in a circle. In prehistoric copperwork, however, the cross is consistently found in association with circles, suggesting that an important symbolic relationship may have existed between the two forms, as well as the formal one. This fact also suggests the primacy of circles in the complex as a whole.

The strong relationship between circular designs and cruciform ones on copperwork associated with the Southeastern Ceremonial Complex is also noted by Waring and Holder (1945:4). What they refer to as the "value" of cruciform symbolism on those objects was identical to the "value" of circular motifs—to such a degree that they considered the motifs "interchangeable," even when they were applied to "otherwise rigidly specialized objects." Like sunburst designs, crosses were not used to decorate copperwork until Middle Woodland times, but they continued to be significant in the design vocabulary of Native American metallurgists well into the Historic Periods (Tables VI–VIII).

I.2.F. SWASTIKAS

Again, the close similarity between cross and swastika designs is obvious. The two were apparently used interchangeably in some contexts in Mississippian art, although the swastika is not as important, less than .5 percent of the motifs used. Like the cross, the swastika is also a transitional design, with strong relationships to rectilinear forms as well as circular ones. Swastikas were in use throughout the same chronological periods, as were simpler cross designs, although they are less numerous in the Post-Mississippian material and appear only rarely in Middle Woodland copper (Tables VI–VIII).

I.2.G. RECTANGLES

Rectangles are the second most common (after circles) of the geometric motifs used in precontact copperwork. Although rectangles were used to decorate copper less often than circle-related designs (5.68 percent of rectangular designs were applied, as opposed to 38.22 percent for circles), copperwork of rectangular design was manufactured in every period (Tables VI–VIII). Rectangular and modified rectangular designs were executed in repoussé and through incising or engraving, but in a large majority of cases it is the overall shape, not the interior design that is rectangular. Most rectangular pieces with an identifiable mode of use were breastplates, although many others apparently served as headdresses.

Few pieces are precisely rectangular. In fact, there seems to be a gradual evolution in breastplate forms from the approximately rectangular ones of Archaic groups, through the heavy reel shapes of Adena, to the elongated forms of Middle Woodland Copena peoples (Plate 2). Given this fairly clear development, the essentially trapezoidal Hopewell-related Middle Woodland breastplates, including a few that are almost as rectangular as Archaic ones, seem to represent a bit of a formal regression and show closer links to early Archaic forms than to later Adena ones. Rectangular headdress elements, particularly those of the Middle Woodland Period, were often trapezoidal as well.

I.3. REPRESENTATIONAL FORMS

Identification of specific representational design in much of the copperwork is frequently a matter of calculated conjecture. The complex forms and designs of many pieces make even conjecture difficult. Defining pieces according to geometry is equally problematic, since often pieces do not conform to readily definable shapes. Many other pieces are recognizable in geometric and/or representational terms, but are unique, appropriate to no larger category. This study is primarily an overview of the copper corpus of the prehistoric Eastern Woodlands and is designed to explain the pervasive interest in copper and the consistent use of certain forms throughout prehistoric times. For this reason, most of these very interesting but apparently idiosyncratic forms and designs will not be discussed. The following is one exception to this general rule, however.

I.3.A. MUSHROOMS

Mushroom shapes appear intermittently throughout the history of the copper complex. Although designation of these shapes as mushrooms is rather conjectural in some cases, the identification is unmistakable in others. Since the ceremonial use of psychoactive mushrooms of various types was widespread among native groups throughout the Americas (Schultes 1972:5–6), the inclusion of mushroom shapes in the ritual design vocabulary is not at all anomalous. The shape is found in Archaic as well as in Woodland and Mississippian Period copperwork. Examples are both two and three dimensional and are cut and/or formed from sheet copper. Two Middle Woodland examples are clearly life-sized copper and wood renderings of mature mushrooms, probably of the genus *amanita* that is a highly toxic variety and one used ritually in many parts of the world (Fig. 49).

I.3.B. BIRDS

Birds and bird-related imagery account for 5.17 percent of designs in the copper material examined. Examples have been found at very early sites and the subject continued to be important throughout most periods of prehistory in the Eastern Woodlands. The use of bird motifs increased dramatically in early Mississippian times and continued to be of primary importance well into the early periods of European contact.

The species of bird depicted most frequently is the peregrine falcon or duck hawk (e.g., Plate 4 and Fig. 44). Species identification is not difficult since the artists usually include very specific markings and anatomical characteristics. Circumlocular patterns unique to the peregrine in flight are commonly included, as well as the neck ring and scalloped markings on the tail and wing feathers.[1]

On most copper birds, the hooked beak and talons are also emphasized. Heads and feet are usually enlarged and the perspective is twisted in order to present those aspects of the bird that are most characteristic. On some copper birds the reproductive organs are also emphasized. The head is almost always represented in profile, the body frontally. Wings are usually open and are displayed frontally on each side of the body or as though the bird is in flight.

Other birds are also depicted in precontact copperwork, especially the crow, the vulture and the ivory-billed and/or pileated woodpecker. In all cases, the exaggerated head and shape of the bird's beak clearly identify each species. The wood duck and the bob white quail are also associated with the copper complex. Both appear as stone pipes with copper eyes. None of these species is depicted as consistently as the peregrine falcon, however.

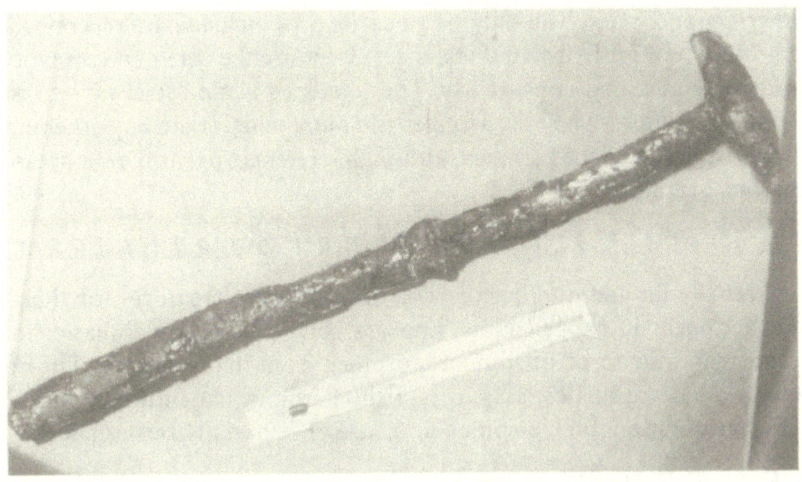

Figure 49. Life-Sized Copper/Wood Mushroom (*amanita muscaria),* Middle Woodland. Ohio Historical Society, Columbus, #260/129. Mound City Mounds, Ross Co., Ohio. Ca. 13" long.

Portions of bird anatomy are at least as common as delineation of entire birds. Parts chosen for use on copperwork include the head, eyes, feet, claws, beak, and tail feathers, features generally enlarged when the entire bird is depicted.

I.3.C. HUMANS

Clear and unequivocal references to humans have come to light only in association with Middle Woodland and Mississippian remains. They amount to just over 3 percent of the motifs tabulated (Table VI–VIII).

I.3.D. MAMMALS

Mammal imagery occurs only a little less frequently than human. Animal subjects appear earlier in the complex but become less important as the use of human imagery increases. Interest in mammalian motifs reaches a peak in the Middle Woodland Period among Hopewell-related cultures. Such motifs are less common in Mississippian times, but they continue to be used.

From the Archaic Periods on, copper design with literal reference to mammals is limited to a few attributes of a few species. Large carnivores, especially the teeth and claws of bears, are represented most often. References to large felines are also found, particularly in the Southeast. Isolated examples of designs that represent mammal canine teeth appear in both Northern and

Southern copperwork. The only other carnivores included are raccoons and otters—in a few, fairly isolated instances. Deer are the sole non-carnivorous mammals represented consistently. The reference is almost always to their antlers. Antler motifs were used longer and more widely than any other mammal-related design in the complex, although references to carnivores are more numerous overall.

I.3.E. Reptiles, Fish, and Other Lower Life Forms

An extremely limited number of depictions of these creatures (or their attributes) appear in copper. None appears before Middle Woodland times, but they continue to be of some importance from that point on. The creatures included are turtles, alligators, fish, a frog (the identification here is somewhat questionable), a spider, and snakes, especially rattlesnakes.

I.3.F. Implements

Copper implement forms that were of no possible utilitarian significance, in conventional terms at least, were made in all prehistoric periods in eastern North America (Table VI–VIII). Implement shapes, especially axes and points, account for more than 4 percent of identifiable motifs in the complex as a whole. These forms must be included in the tabulation of designs because, deprived of a basic utilitarian role due to size and/or fragility of material, it is the form/material nexus itself that becomes significant, beyond conventional utilitarian considerations.

As noted above, even copper implements which have the look and weight of working tools may not have been intended for mundane use. Given the softness of copper, their value for this purpose would have been minimal in many cases. The fact that fewer implements were made as millennia rolled by is also testimony to this fact. If native copper tools were more efficient than their counterparts made of more mundane materials, they would certainly have continued to have been made. Nevertheless, implements of a size and weight that *could* have been functional are not considered to be examples of symbolic implement design since although they might have been used, they would have been only marginally effective.

Some pieces that *are* considered as examples of design—mainly plummets and boatstones—are of a size and weight that could have made them useful as implements. However, they were almost always made from materials other than copper. Because so few copper examples exist, it has been assumed for the purposes of this study that copper versions of these implements were made to look like their functional counterparts, although they operated primarily on a ceremonial level.

Section II—The Objects

II.1. General Information

II.1.a. Awls

Awls are usually pointed at each end and are of round, square, or rectangular section. A few have one spatulate end. More have a point at each end, one of which is thicker and more blunt. Many awls were fitted with handles of wood or some other organic substance.

II.1.b. Breastplates

The term implies a large object, used for protection of the chest. In fact, most copper breastplates within the corpus are quite small, only a few inches long. They are called breastplates in the archaeological literature because many examples were found on the chests of excavated burials. Even this definition appears to have become merely conventional to some extent, however, since many objects designated as "breastplates" in the literature have been found in positions other than on the chests of burials and have been located in non-burial situations.

II.1.c. Headdresses

Like breastplates, headdresses are so designated within this study either because the pieces were obviously worn as headgear in life or because the placement of these objects in burials indicates that they were clearly worn as some sort of headgear at the time of interment. The kinds of items in this category range from large plates that were apparently placed over the head of the deceased, to small repoussé badges attached to bone pins, presumably worn in the hair. Despite the fact that the large plates were probably not actually worn and that the smaller ones almost certainly were, I have avoided subdividing this category based upon what appear to be obvious differences in use. My reasons for this lie in an attempt to focus upon visual and material facts at the outset, at least, rather than making assumptions about use. Focusing on what seem to be obvious parallels between "western" cultures and less complex ones has frequently obscured fundamental differences that would have been more apparent had scholars first examined materials and symbols thoroughly, and *then* looked at probable use and function. What is important for this stage of the study is the fact that all materials and symbols are copper, all are associated with the human head, and all bear specific types of designs.

II.1.D. Miscellaneous

Native American coppersmiths in every precontact period produced pieces that are either unique and virtually impossible to categorize, or that make up groups so small as to render them invalid as categories on their own. Such pieces have been classified as "miscellaneous" in this study. Other items in this category are listed in museum catalogs and/or site reports but are lost, misplaced, or not illustrated. These have occasionally been included in the analysis since many have important contextual data. They are categorized as "miscellaneous" because their precise form is not known. Although few in number, the most frequently found bits of copperwork in this group are pieces of narrow tubing one half to three fourths of an inch in diameter and usually in fragments between one and two inches long. They have been found in sites from every period of copper-working activity. Provenience data is generally poor and most examples are badly deteriorated.

II.2. Old Copper Culture/Archaic Periods

II.2.A. Awls, Axes, and Other Tool Forms

Archaic coppersmiths made a number of variations on the awl form. Some very small double-pointed awls are referred to as "gorges" in the archaeological literature. A groove in the center of a few suggests they could have been used as such, rather like a fish hook except that in this case the fish must swallow bait and gorge entirely in order to be "hooked." Other awls are wide and flat, and still others are shaped like a modern nail with a flat knob on one end and a point at the other. A few exceptionally large awls were also made in Archaic times, essentially identical to smaller versions of the form, but ranging from one to three feet in length and extremely heavy. Some small hooks, apparently fish hooks, were also fashioned of copper during these early periods.

II.2.B. Headdresses

As is so often the case, the unique Late Archaic example of copperwork applied to a headdress is a harbinger of later modes that will become very common.

II.2.C. Miscellaneous

The majority of the miscellaneous pieces from the Archaic Periods are large and heavy. They appear to be implement forms of some kind. Many—harpoons, wedges, and pick shapes—are easily identified. Others seem to be broken or unfinished with less clearly identifiable functions.

II.3. ADENA/EARLY WOODLAND

II.3.A. AWLS, AXES, AND OTHER TOOL FORMS

Adena awls are generally small and carefully wrought. Adena axes, on the other hand, vary considerably in size, shape, and quality of workmanship. Some are only vaguely axe-shaped and may not have been considered implements even on a purely symbolic level. Except for a few small copper hooks and one copper knife, axes and awls make up the entire inventory of tool shapes made by Adena coppersmiths. This represents a radical shift away from the wide variety of implement forms produced by Late Archaic groups.

II.3.B. BEADS

Beads were strung to make bracelets, necklaces, earpieces, and even one ring that is a double strand of tiny globular beads.

II.3.C. BRACELETS

Forty percent of all the bracelets examined in connection with this study were made by Adena-related groups. The precise method of manufacture is difficult to determine through purely visual analysis, but the weight and appearance of the bracelets suggest that they were made of solid copper. Most are round in section, although a few of the more refined ones have an almost square section with four carefully rounded and finished corners.

II.3.D.BREASTPLATES

On some Adena breastplates, the long sides are curved and always concave; on others, the short sides are curved but may be either concave or convex. Almost all Adena breastplates have two perforations arranged along the longitudinal axis, near the center of the piece.

II.3.E. RINGS

Most Adena rings are simple, made of thick copper wire with the ends overlapped slightly. Some may be very thin rolled copper sheet, but are essentially like the others, of a simple and often crude form. The only exceptions to this general rule include a unique example made of tiny beads, as mentioned above, and a few others that were twisted into a spiral form that wound from one and one-third to four and one-half times around the wearer's finger (e.g., Mills 1902:458).

II.4. Hopewell/Middle and Late Woodland

II.4.a. Awls and Knives

A few Middle Woodland groups in what is now Michigan (and apparently not associated with Hopewellian manifestations farther south) made numerous awls of copper, many of which were bent into an angular hook shape. These same peoples also made a few small irregular knives of copper that were remarkably similar to Old Copper Culture forms. Although most archaeologists do not believe that these groups participated in Hopewell ritual traditions, the fact that two examples of these small knives were found at a site assumed to have been occupied by Michigan Hopewell societies implies the existence of a trade relationship if nothing else (Bettarel and Smith 1973:150). Other than these, there do not seem to have been any copper knives made by Hopewell-related peoples.

II.4.b. Axes and Adzes

Middle Woodland axes and adzes are generally refined and carefully worked forms. Some are axe-shaped but without a sharpened blade. A few are very finely finished, except for the absence of a cutting edge. There are also some axe-shaped examples of copperwork that were almost certainly meant to be worn, without any suggestion of utilitarian function. One is the approximate size and weight of a Middle Woodland breastplate. Another is a thin piece of copper worked into a graceful axe shape, carefully polished and perforated near the butt.

II.4.c. Bracelets and Rings

Only a few Hopewell copper bracelets are similar to Adena examples. The majority are entirely different in general shape and method of manufacture. Instead of being solid copper, most are either tubular or have a C-shaped section which may be either rounded or oval. Finished bracelets are both oval and perfectly circular in overall shape. A unique pair was found in Mound 17 of the Hopewell Group in Ohio (Shetrone 1926:46). They are circular bands of copper with a convex inner surface, a flat outer surface and no apparent seams. The sophisticated design of these pieces is typical of much Hopewellian copperwork, both in their craftsmanship and their uniqueness. Hopewellians made only a few copper rings. Those that have been excavated come from sites across the most northern areas under Hopewell influence.

II.4.d. Breastplates

In general, Hopewell breastplates are roughly the same size, although no two are identical. Some examples are very small, however—only 4"–5" long—and a few others are exceptionally large—12"–18" in length. As seams are not evident on these pieces, the size appears to have been determined by the size of the nugget of copper from which each breastplate was hammered.

II.4.E. Buttons and Tinklers

Buttons are small and roughly hemispherical. The solid core of these unique objects has a shallow groove across one diameter of the flat side. This core, including the groove, was covered with an overlay of copper sheeting, as was the hemisphere itself. Two perforations in the copper that are in line with the groove allowed for attachment to clothing or some other foundation. Fiber or sinew passed through the hole at the base of the hemisphere would have anchored each button in two places at the edge of the base. Thus, these objects probably did not function as true buttons, to hold two pieces of fabric together. The workmanship is consistently excellent, to the degree that seams are rarely visible. Nor is the grooving of the core material apparent, unless the piece has been broken.

Distribution patterns of Hopewell copper tinklers are similar to those of buttons. The number of sites in which each has been found is fairly limited, although tinklers and buttons have been discovered in most northern areas where Hopewellian influence was strong. Like the buttons, copper tinklers are also usually sturdy and refined in their construction.

II.4.F. Abstract Two Dimensional Designs

The most complex of these designs are perfectly flat and stencil-like. However, sheet copper worked into simpler designs is often curved. Most examples, whether flat or curved, are perforated. The holes are very small and usually placed near the edges of the piece. Designs range from perfectly circular to ovoid to pear-shaped, with dozens of variations in between, including swastikas and triskel motifs. Other designs seem to be variations on a rectangular theme, from simple rectangles to reel-shaped pieces and axe-shapes. The latter are very decorative in feeling and obviously are not implements. All are refined forms, and often have repoussé accents. Those with curvilinear design are the most decorative in feeling.

Several rectangular pieces were made of heavy copper plate and appear to have served a more utilitarian function by virtue of their size and weight. Other rectangular forms were made from thinner copper sheet, but their designs also appear to be more functional than symbolic or decorative. Important examples of such work are the large trapezoidal pieces from the Turner Mounds. They are completely filled with rows of evenly spaced, perfectly regular, circular holes, eight across and four down, with a tiny

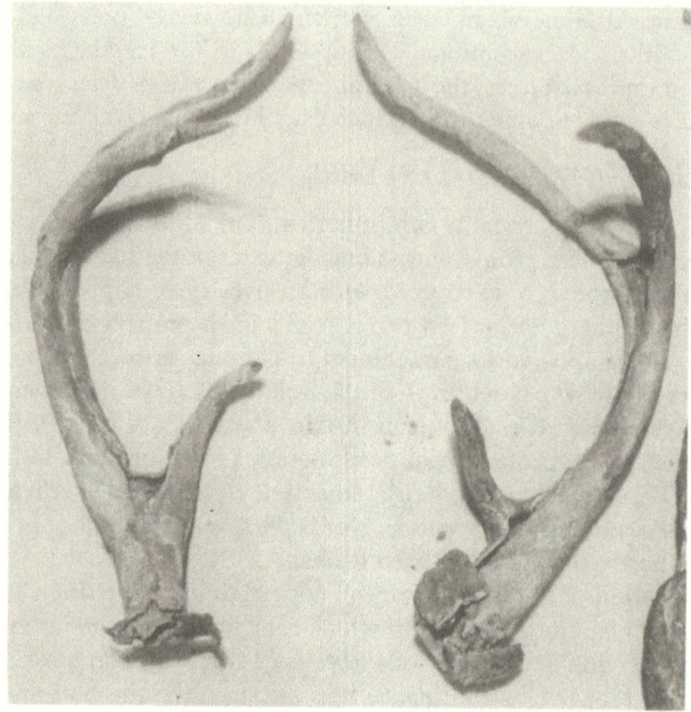

Figure 50. Life-Sized Deer Antlers (with tabs for attachment to a headdress), Middle Woodland. Ohio Historical Society, Columbus, #260/61. Mound City Mounds, Ross Co., Ohio. Ca. 6" tall.

hole just below each larger hole. Still other rectangular pieces appear to have been copper bands that originally wrapped around organic materials of some kind. The actual use for all of these items is unclear.

II.4.G. Earpieces

Several pairs of earpieces from Hopewell-related sites, especially in Georgia and Illinois, are of simpler, less substantial construction than either the standard five-piece Hopewellian form or typical Copena variations. These simpler pieces are made of two thin outer disks that are joined by a single tubular rivet. This approach to construction appears occasionally in Ohio, but usually on exceptionally large earpieces. Several, more typical, Woodland earpieces are also unusual. Each has a thin overlay of silver or meteoric iron on one of the copper disks of the spool. Some areas under Hopewellian influence used only iron when such overlays were applied. Others used only silver. Both types of overlay were important in the core areas of Ohio and Illinois.

II.4.H. Headdresses/Deer

Many examples exist of Hopewellian deer imagery sculpted in copper. Antlers are the most common (Plate 8 and Fig. 50). Some were carved from wood and covered with thin copper sheet. Others were formed of heavy copper sheet in an extremely naturalistic and life-sized reproduction of antlers. Still others are highly stylized and were cut from flat sheet copper. All these antler pairs, regardless of the method of construction, were obviously intended for attachment to a headdress of some sort. A few headplates have wooden stubs and/or copper sockets that were undoubtedly constructed to accommodate such attachments. In one case, antlers made of wood and covered with copper were excavated, still attached to a copper headplate. Other headplates have less easily identifiable protruding elements, and some have moveable parts. Fragments indicate that there were even more elaborate headdresses of copper made during this period, but the specifics of their design are lost to us.[2]

A unique example of deer imagery in three dimensions is a set of deer jaws that is precisely cut from the skull of the animal and covered with sheet copper. That these may have been part of a composite mask worn with an antler headdress seems plausible.

II.4.I. Miscellaneous

There are several examples of Middle Woodland boatstones made from copper. A ground stone version of the form was relatively common in Late Archaic and Early Woodland times. To make Middle Woodland versions, an oval bowl-shaped depression was hammered out in the center of a rectangular strip of heavy sheet copper (about 1"–2" x 4"). This concavo-convex area usually comprises about one-third to one-half the length of the piece. Usually the two flattened ends have perforations. Two examples found in association with small pebbles may have served as rattles, much as the turtle forms discussed below.

Other Woodland Period pieces in this miscellaneous category are curious, irregular pendants, discovered at a few Hopewell-related sites outside the Ohio area. A few strikingly realistic copper mushrooms (Fig. 49) were also discovered. Carefully cut rectangular and trapezoidal pieces of very heavy copper plate were found at some Hopewell-related sites and also belong in this miscellaneous category. Two other unusual examples of Hopewell copperwork have been referred to as "andirons" or "effigies of the praying mantis" (Fig. 51). Probably neither designation is accurate, but a more appropriate one has not been suggested.[3] Still, to make such identifications on the basis of a *very* rough resemblance is inappropriate. Unfortunately, this kind of essentially baseless identification has plagued efforts to interpret much of this material.

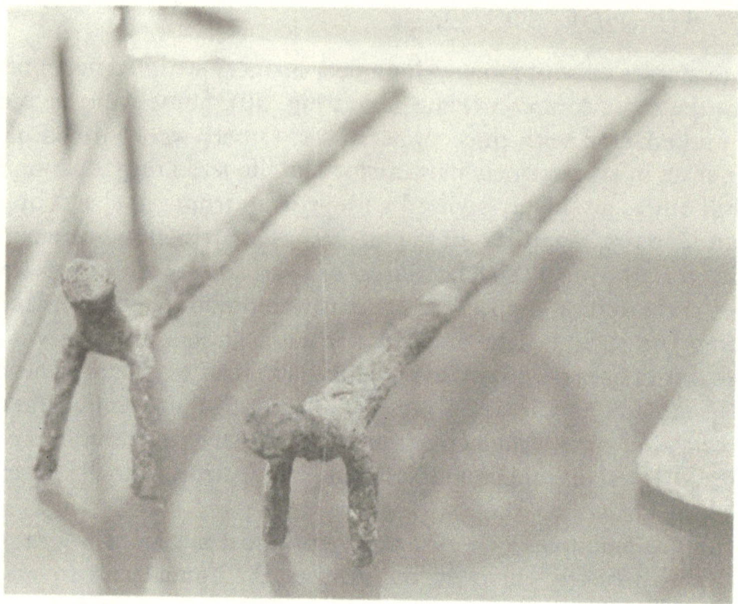

Figure 51. Anomalous Solid Copper Forms, Middle Woodland. Ohio Historical Society, Columbus. Seip Mounds, Ross Co., Ohio. 12 1/2" and 13" long.

Several examples of raw or only slightly worked pieces of copper have also been found at Middle Woodland sites. Unlike many examples of this type from Archaic excavations, they are virtually always found in burial and cremation contexts, frequently with finely crafted and carefully finished (if occasionally fragmentary) objects of copper.

II.4.J. Panpipes

Copper panpipes or, more accurately, copper-sheathed panpipes, are musical instruments constructed of bone or reed tubes of varying lengths (Young 1976:7). (One, from the Hopewell Mound Group in Ohio, has bone instead of reed tubes.) The length of the hollow tube determined the pitch of the sound produced, and each tube was either cut to size or plugged to produce a specific pitch. Most panpipes consisted of three or four tube combinations that were apparently always tuned to play the same three or four notes. Some examples with only one or two tubes may have functioned in a different way. A tubular bone whistle with copper bands at each end from the Bourneville Mound in Ohio may have been used in ritual in much the same way, although it was constructed differently. Instruments with multiple reeds were held together by a wide band of sheet copper. Usually the sheathing

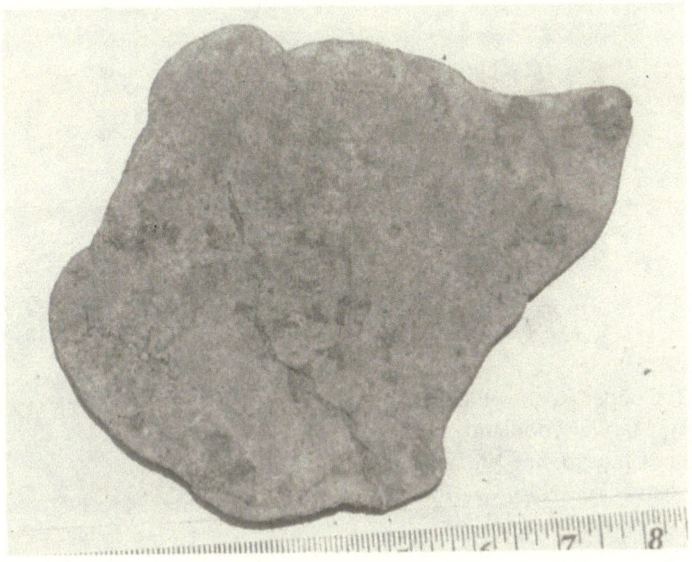

Figure 52. Heavy Copper Plate (cut into the silhouette of a bear's head), Middle Woodland. The Field Museum, Chicago, #56353. Hopewell Mounds, Ross Co., Ohio. Ca. 8" wide.

was curved to the contour of the reeds on the front and was completely flat on the back. On several examples, the copper was overlaid with silver foil, and there are a few with an overlay of meteoric iron.

II.4.K. Bears and Other Carnivores

A spectacular example of bear imagery is the silhouette of a bear's head fashioned from thick sheet copper (Fig. 52). This piece is unique in many ways. It is made of unusually thick—about 1/2"—copper plate. The head, wholly unelaborated yet completely naturalistic, is a formal combination that is rare in Hopewell art.

A pair of objects with bear-related imagery is also unique in several ways. They were excavated at the Hopewell type-site in Ohio. Very few examples of Hopewellian copperwork are decorated in a repoussé technique. This pair of objects is a clear exception to that general rule. Although the identification of the subject matter is generally agreed upon, the precise definition of it is unclear. Each piece includes five elements that may either be miniature claws or canine teeth and are attached to a crescent shape (Fig. 53). Most scholars have referred to the pair as bear paws. They do roughly resemble the form of a bear track left in soft earth, with five claws and the

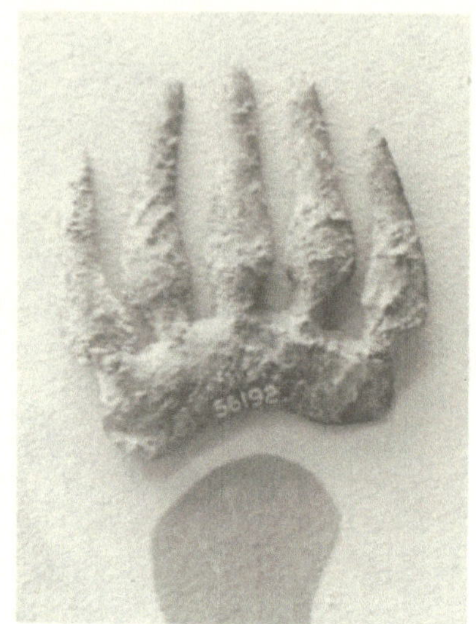

Figure 53. Copper Repoussé Bear Claws (or Teeth), Middle Woodland. The Field Museum, Chicago, #56193. Hopewell Mounds, Ross Co., Ohio. Ca. 4" across.

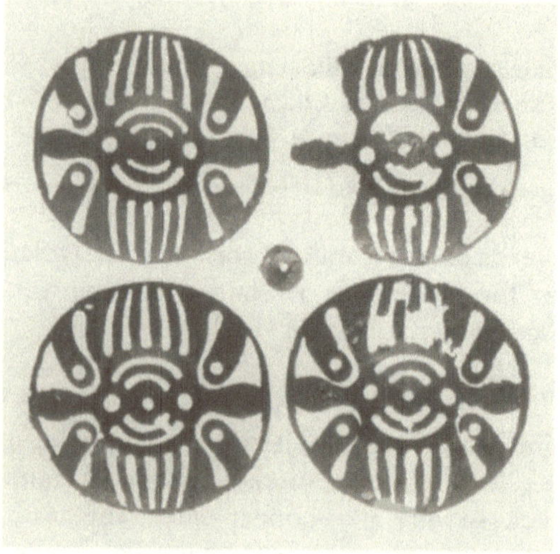

Figure 54. Large Openwork Hopewell Style Earpiece, Middle Woodland. Courtesy, National Museum of the American Indian, Smithsonian Institution, Washington, D.C., #17/0061. Photo by Carmelo Guadagno. Crystal River Site, Citrus Co., Florida. Ca. 3 1/2" diameter.

large front pad of the paw clearly delineated. All six elements of the design have been carefully rounded, a fact that enhances this impression. However, a flat sheet copper ornament with the same combination of elements was discovered in Illinois (Fig. 15). It is a large copper crescent with five pendant elements just like the smaller repoussé piece. However, the pendant elements in the Illinois piece are clearly bear canines, as are so many others found elsewhere.

Precise identification of subject matter may not be important here. It is very possible that claws and teeth were in some sense symbolically equiva-

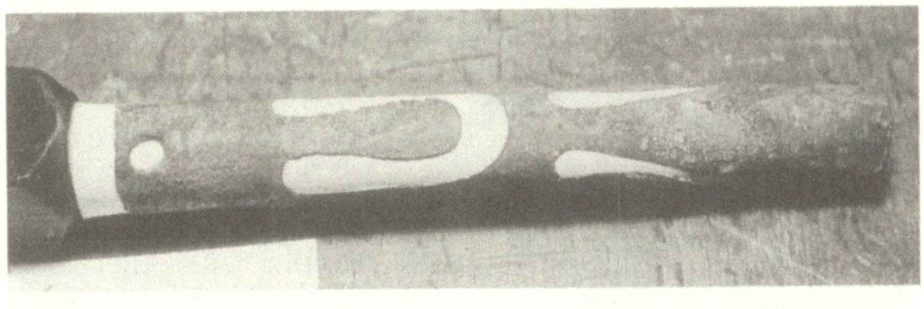

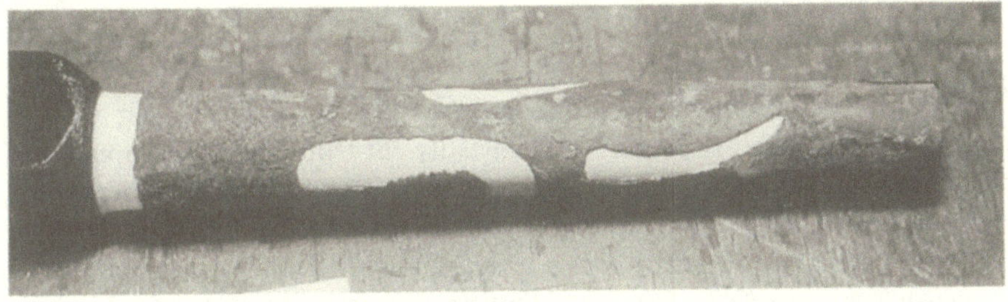

Figure 55a and 55b. A: Openwork Ferule (elaborate end piece for a wooden staff), Middle Woodland. American Museum of Natural History Library, New York, #20.2/6655. Site near Helena, Arkansas. Ca. 9" long. B: Alternate view.

lent, by virtue of their physical similarities. In fact, the visual ambiguity of such pieces may well have been intentional, designed to invoke a broader range of ideas and symbolic references than precise naturalistic representation would have allowed. Whatever the specific interpretation of the design, the same configuration was also excised from the surface of an elaborate pair of earpieces that were found at the Crystal River Mounds in Florida (Fig. 54).

A related design, although clearly more abstract, has four instead of five claws or canine teeth, plus some curved elements and a circle instead of the crescent. This motif was excised from an elegant copper sleeve that apparently formed the end of a staff (Fig. 55). It was found in conjunction with the bundle burial of an elderly female in a mound near Helena, Arkansas. If the design is a reference to paws rather than teeth (or to both, which again is entirely plausible), it may refer to the paw of a puma or other large cat since there are four instead of five claws on its paw. Such references are relatively rare (four, as opposed to five teeth/claws) and, given the provenience of this example, may have been a specific reference to feminine power elements. The geographically widespread yet severely limited use of these designs represents another common pattern in Hopewellian ritual art and is probably indicative of the structure and development of the ritual itself.

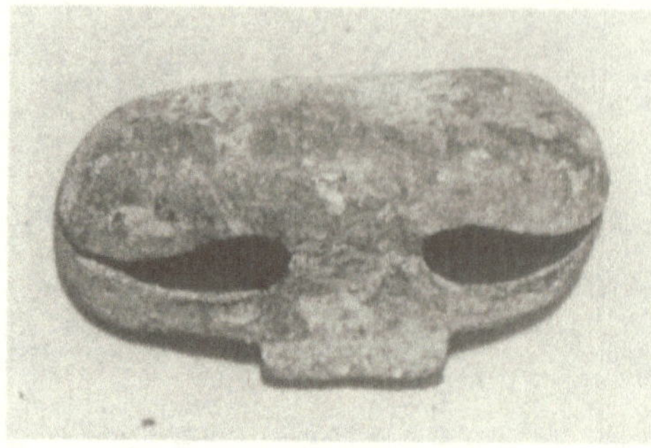

Figure 56. Copper Nose (probably all that remains of what would have been a wooden bear sculpture), Middle Woodland. Ohio Historical Society, Columbus, #957/266. Seip Mounds, Ross Co., Ohio. 2" long.

Examples of three dimensional imagery in Hopewellian copper are limited, but a few exist. Bear teeth were usually cut from flat sheet copper, but some are more realistic and are carved from wood or stone and covered with a thin overlay of copper foil. A unique example of ursine imagery in three-dimensions is a small bear's nose, probably attached originally to a mask or sculpture (Fig. 56). The identification is made on the basis of the design of the piece (as compared to other depictions of bear noses in Hopewell art), the obvious importance of bear imagery in copper and the importance of the bear nose in most northern hemisphere bear ceremonialism.

Another element of mammal anatomy, unique in the corpus, is a small copper raccoon penis bone that was most likely sculpted by a Hopewellian artist. (Unfortunately, data to establish its cultural provenience is lacking.) It is completely realistic in size and shape except that one end is curled around on itself, presumably for use as a pendant of some kind. Although the specific provenience and significance is unclear, the piece was very likely Hopewellian and of some ceremonial importance, since several actual raccoon penis bones decorated with copper bands have been found in Hopewell burial contexts.

Many other forms have been found that could have represented these or other animals, but they are so fragmentary or so stylized as to make positive identification of subject matter impossible. Several forms are probably references to canine teeth or claws, but species identification is not possible in these cases either.

II.4.L. Birds

Three examples of peregrine falcons in copper are included in the Hopewellian corpus, all from the Mound City Site and two from the same grave. The species is indicated by the shape of the bird and by the markings that are suggested by shallow engraving and/or repoussé designs (all are heavily corroded) (Byers 1962:212–13). The two examples found together

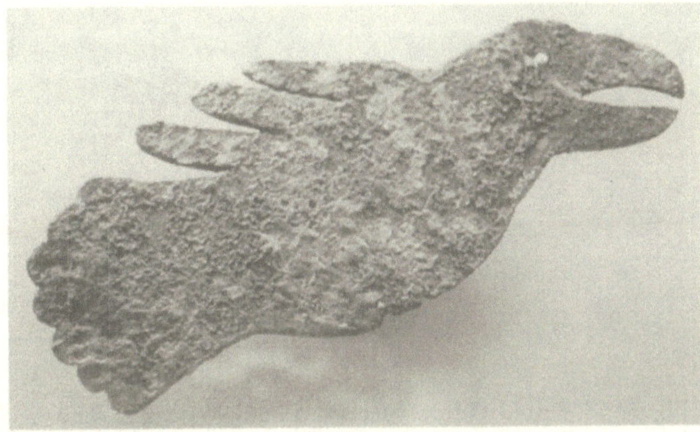

Figure 57. Raven (cut from heavy sheet copper), Middle Woodland. The Field Museum, Chicago, #56356. Hopewell Mounds, Ross Co., Ohio. Ca. 14" long.

depict the entire bird in flight (Plate 15). The perspective is twisted with certain elements enlarged to offer maximum information and, presumably, ritually significant emphasis. The heads, wing, and talons are in profile, but the breast and tail are presented from a frontal view or from below. This latter perspective distortion provides a clear view of the bird's reproductive organ, emphasized by circular engraving. The simple clarity of that emphasis almost certainly has important, albeit obscure, implications in the iconography of the piece and its role in ritual. The third example from this site is more stylized and compacted into an elongated rectangle. Only the distinctive head and circumocular markings of the peregrine identify the species.

Several large bird images were reportedly deposited in a double burial in Mound 25 of the Hopewell Group, but only two representations of a crow or raven (Fig. 57), similar in conception to the Mound City falcons, survived intact (Moorehead 1922:110). Nine other examples of Hopewellian copperwork also refer to birds, but less explicitly. Three examples from another burial at Mound City appear to be two-headed vultures (Fig. 58). They are very similar to several cut sheet copper designs that appear to be purely geometric in both form and motif, except for the clear reference to vultures' heads.

Another Mound City burial included copper versions of the feet of an aquatic bird that was probably a type of duck (Figs. 59a and 59b). These feet have been called bats in earlier literature on Hopewell, but this new interpretation is more consistent with Hopewellian artistic and ritual interest in feet and claws and also conforms more clearly to the actual form of

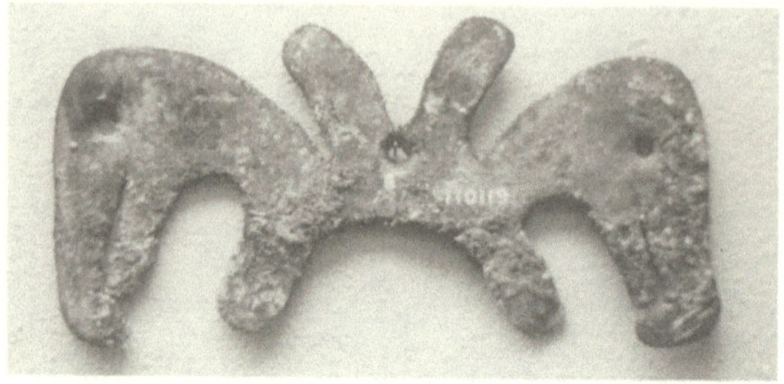

Figure 58. Paired Vulture Heads, Middle Woodland. The Field Museum, Chicago, #110119. Mound City Mounds, Ross Co., Ohio. 4.7" x 2.3".

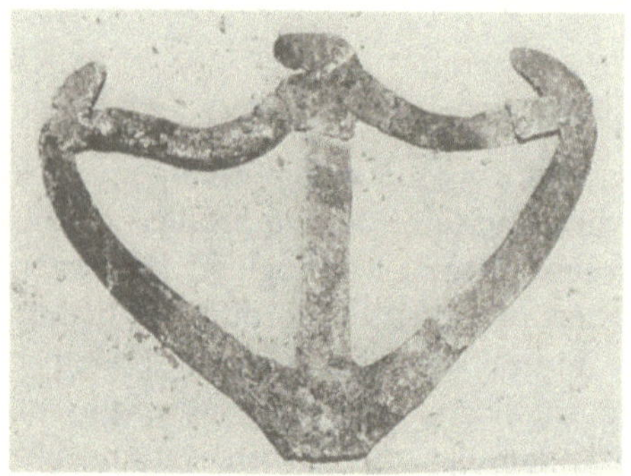

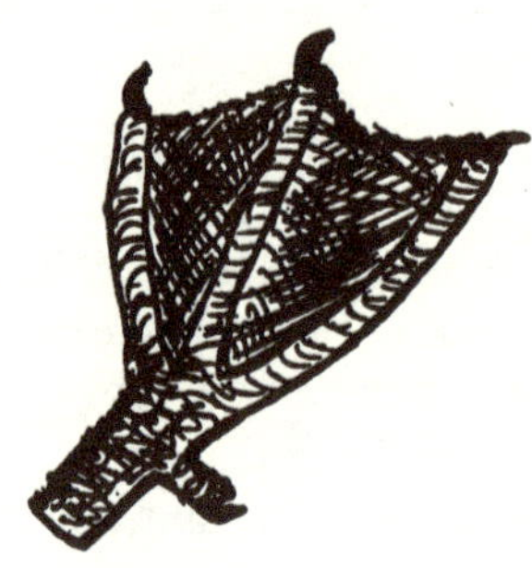

Figures 59a and 59b. A: Openwork Webbed Duck Feet, Middle Woodland. Ohio Historical Society, Columbus, #260/137. Mound City Mounds, Ross Co., Ohio. Ca 6" long; B: Drawing of Duck Foot, A.M. Trevelyan.

the objects. The feet were found in the same grave with the more stylized peregrine falcon. The hunter/prey relationship between the peregrine and ducks (hence the name "duck hawk") may have formed the basis for this combination as it often does in the art of many native groups in North America.

Another pair of cut sheet copper designs probably refers to bird feet as well, the talons of a raptor in this case (Fig. 10). The design is highly stylized and conforms to most objects of this type in its bilaterally symmetrical arrangement. Only the recognizable subject matter distinguishes them from dozens of similar pairs of designs taken from the extensive deposit of copperwork in Mound 25 at the Hopewell Mound group. (Further study will

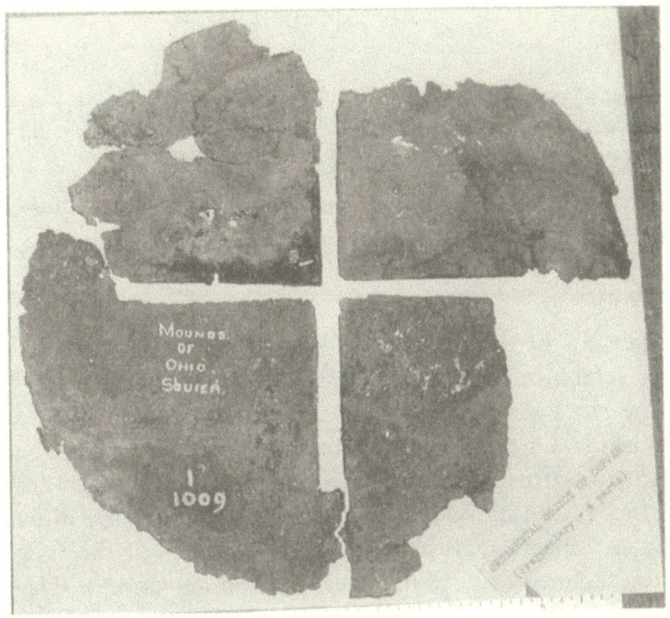

Figure 60. Openwork Cross and Circle, Middle Woodland. American Museum of Natural History Library, New York, #1/1009. Ohio. Ca. 7½" diameter.

probably reveal that many other pieces in this deposit also have naturalistic subject matter, although they are currently assumed to be purely geometric.)

II.4.M. Crescents, Crosses, Sunbursts, and Spirals

Crescent motifs are created both positively, the copper is cut into a crescent shape, and negatively, with the crescent form excised from the main body of the piece. There are also many types of Sunburst and spiral designs. Cruciform motifs are fairly common, although they are more often implied than explicitly rendered. Frequently they are no more than an impression that is created by the negative spaces within a quadripartite design, and usually arranged within a circle (Plate 7).

The only two clearly delineated crosses in the corpus are anomalous and problematic. One is a flat, carved stone covered with sheet copper. Neither its use nor its context are known. It is unique in the Middle Woodland material. The other clearly delineated cross is a fragmentary piece in the collections of the American Museum of Natural History (Fig. 60). The only provenience data indicates that it was part of a very early collection made by Squier and Davis in Ohio. The spare geometric quality of the piece and its lack of any three-dimensional elaboration suggest it was made in Middle Woodland times. This likelihood is reinforced by the fact that most of the sites Squier and Davis explored in Ohio were Hopewell-related. On the other hand, Hopewellian openwork designs usually involve the removal of a larger proportion of the copper ground than is the case here. Furthermore, most Middle Woodland crosses are of the "X" variety, sometimes combined with a "Greek" or equal-arm cross. This is the only example of an unelaborated equal-arm cross in Hopewellian metallurgy.

II.4.N. Humans

Only 1.13 percent of the designs on Hopewellian copperwork have any recognizable reference to human beings. All come from sites in the Ohio core area, the Hopewell and Mound City Mound complexes. Both represent human heads. One is very small and rather stylized, a rare example of Hopewellian sculpture in copper, about three inches tall (Fig. 47). No reference to the sex of the individual is apparent, nor does the individual depicted wear any special paraphernalia. The features of the face are very similar to the features of virtually every human depiction in Hopewellian art. All have a high narrow forehead and aquiline nose, as well as enlarged, almond-shaped eyes.

The other Hopewellian human head in copper has long been misidentified. It was originally reconstructed improperly and assumed to be a grotesque human-insect composite. Careful examination of the fragments and their correct re-assembly reveal that the piece represents a quite normal human, wearing an elaborate headdress (Fig. 11). Although cut from flat sheet copper, the profile reveals the same features that are characteristic of all Hopewell human representations, whether in copper, clay or stone.

Even an anomalous and fairly macabre trio of copper noses seems to conform to this standard treatment of facial features, although none of the noses is truly representational in conception. In fact, all three noses are simply paired cones of heavy copper sheet. The context of their discovery—pushed through the nose cavities of human skulls—makes their identification unmistakable, nonetheless. The relative size of each and the angle of application suggest the treatment of noses in other more anatomically accurate examples.

II.4.O. Turtles and Fish

Miniature versions of its shell are the most common references to the turtle, but several tiny repoussé examples also include the head, legs, and tail. To construct the latter examples, the basic form of the creature was cut from sheet copper. Then the shell area was worked into a convex boss. There are two perforations in the neck of each shell, and a third is at the apex. This third perforation suggests that these examples may have functioned as rattles, with tiny pebbles placed in the cavity before being sewn tightly to some kind of backing.

Several small turtle shells were also sculpted from copper in Middle Woodland times. The detailing on these pieces is very precise and worked into naturalistic patterns. Many are hollow and filled with tiny pebbles. Like their counterparts formed of sheet copper, these undoubtedly functioned as rattles and probably mimicked similar objects made from actual turtle shells, although the copper versions are considerably smaller. Their function as rattles is made more clear by two rows of holes across the back of each in an X form that most likely was intended to enhance the sound. In one instance, several rattles had been attached to a leather strip, probably a belt. Full-sized turtle shells were and continue to be important ritual material among many native peoples from the Eastern Woodlands.

Four copper fish were also excavated from the Hopewell type-site. All were cut from sheet copper with details in repoussé. They are sufficiently accurate in detail to have been identified as *bowfin amia cobra linneaus,* a kind of sucker.

II.5. Southeastern Ceremonial Complex/Mississippian and Post-Mississippian Periods

II.5.a. Awls

Usually Mississippian awls are relatively large. Several from Cahokia in Illinois are the only significant exceptions to this general rule. Small awls, hardly distinguishable from those made in Archaic and Middle Woodland times, make up the largest category of copper objects taken from that site. Larger Mississippian awls come in a variety of forms: flat (rather like a "tongue depressor"), round and square in section, covered in textile, and occasionally bent into a series of serpentine curves. Mississippian sites have also yielded many large wood and bone pins covered in copper. Five such pins were excavated at the Norman Site in Oklahoma, including a few with beads or points fastened to one end and one with a small human masquette.

The practice of bending copper pins into snake-like curves was common among Late Woodland and Post-Mississippian peoples, both before and after the disappearance of most major Mississippian centers. The Late Woodland versions of this form tend to be fairly angular, with four to five bends decreasing in size from a larger, usually blunt, end to a pointed one. In contrast, Mississippian and Post-Mississippian awls of this genre exhibit from four to nine elegant curves, often gradually decreasing in size from the center toward each end. Frequently, one end of these awls is bent tightly back on itself, suggesting the head of a small snake. The opposite end was always left pointed. With the fading of the Southeastern Ceremonial Complex during the Post-Mississippian Period in the South and the Late Woodland in the North, copper awls and pins tended to become less numerous and smaller in size again. Many appear to be miniaturized versions of Mississippian curvilinear awls with one end bent backwards, suggesting the head of a snake.

II.5.B. AXES

In a single cache, a basket at the Spiro Site, over twenty small copper axes were found still attached to hafts that were carved to depict elaborate bird heads (either pileated or ivory-billed woodpeckers) with inlaid eyes of shell. Other Mississippian copper axes appear to have had hafts like those of the monolithic stone axes found at major sites (e.g., Spiro and Etowah) and depicted in shell and ceramic engravings found in the same areas. Occasionally, excavated materials from Mississippian sites have also included finely worked stone axes covered with copper that are more reminiscent of the refined quality of Hopewellian solid copper axes. However, the delicate copper sheathing would immediately have separated had the axes ever been used in any utilitarian way. There are also Mississippian versions of the curious blunt axe-forms that were found at Early and Middle Woodland sites.

No clearly identified examples of Post-Mississippian native copper axes were discovered in the course of this study.

II.5.C. BEADS, BRACELETS, BUTTONS, KNIVES, RINGS, AND TINKLERS

Practically all Mississippian copper beads are tubular or cylindrical. Most were strung to make necklaces and bracelets, often alternating with beads of shell. All but one of the small number of Mississippian globular beads (the typical style in the Middle Woodland Period) examined for this study came from a single grave at the Harlan Site in Oklahoma. These beads are carefully formed, drilled nuggets of solid copper that represent an extremely unusual method of manufacture.

Also, a much larger percentage of Mississippian beads are constructed in copper and wood or copper and shell combinations than was the case earlier. Some of the beads with copper overlay are globular and essentially the same size and shape as Woodland solid copper beads. Others were often quite large, up to 4" long and 1"–1½" in maximum diameter. In some cases, the tapering ends of the beads were elongated into a spindle form. (Like so many precontact copper pieces, the specific functions of these artifacts are unknown, but because all appear to be constructed and pierced like beads, they have been assigned to this category.)

Several specially constructed beads have been found in place near the skulls of elaborately costumed burials. These so-called "forelock beads" had an unusual shape, essentially a flattened hemisphere. A perforation runs through the diameter of the base of the hemisphere (very much like the construction of Middle Woodland copper and stone buttons). Occasionally the path of this perforation is raised slightly and forms a ridge across the base. Sometimes these beads consist only of two concavo-convex copper shells, a dome-shaped one on one side and a saucer-shaped one on the other. The interior of the bead in these cases consists of clay or soft stone and is pierced by a small copper tube.

Leader notes that the costume of the paramount chief of the Calusa was differentiated from others in the group by a similar bead configuration and by special beaded leg bands (Leader 1991:22). Beaded leg bands are also worn by many of the figures with forelock beads that are depicted on Mississippian shell and copper objects. Leader suspects this may represent an aspect of the rather tenuous connections between the Calusa and the Southeastern Ceremonial Complex, connections that may not have developed until after the time of contact.

Most Post-Mississippian copper beads were also tubular. Although frequent in earlier Mississippian Periods, no examples of Post-Mississippian beads made primarily of a substance other than copper with a copper overlay were found in the sample under examination.

Only a few essentially anomalous examples of copper tinklers, button-like objects or rings have been taken from Mississippian sites, and no examples of copper knives or unequivocally provenienced examples of Mississippian copper bracelets were discovered during the course of research for this study. Post-Mississippian contexts have produced more of these categories of objects (except buttons), although whether they were manufactured from native or European copper is often unclear.

Many of these objects are bracelets, and their design is distinctive. All are C-shaped and made of rolled sheet copper. However, instead of being a tight continuous roll, both sides of a long, narrow copper strip were bent inward along the longitudinal axis. The whole was then bent to form an oval bracelet. The resulting piece had a C-shaped section where both ends of the C curled under and formed an abbreviated spiral form. Post-Mississippian and Early Historic metal work in many regions of the Eastern Woodlands shows an increasing interest in the kind of spiral design that results from this technique.

These objects, as well as the method of manufacture, are associated primarily with Oneota peoples who also made a few finger rings constructed in the same way. Some archaeologists believe that the populations that left Cahokia after its demise are one and the same with post-contact Oneota groups and that they were Siouan speakers (Griffin 1978:264). This is certainly plausible, given the ongoing interest of the Oneota groups in copper ritual paraphernalia, although the copper medium used appears to be the only link to earlier ceremonial developments. Post-Mississippian bracelets examined that were not from Oneota sites came from a single burial within the W. Davenport Jones Mound in North Carolina.

Post-Mississippian metallurgists also made several copper knives, although no such objects appear to have been manufactured in Mississippian times. All are small, flat, and often irregular in shape. They resemble small "butter knives" and are referred to as such in the archaeological literature. A single exception to the general characteristics of this form in Post-Mississippian times was found at a Mandan-Arikara Site in South Dakota (catalogue information, Iowa State Historical Museum). It is larger than most and has a leaf-shaped blade.

II.5.D. BREASTPLATES

The definition of Mississippian breastplates is less clear-cut than those of the earlier periods. In fact, a distinctively Mississippian breastplate type has never been identified in the archaeological literature. However, in the course of research on this project, such a definition has emerged. These items have enough in common with Hopewell versions to suggest that small copper breastplates may have functioned in similar ways within the ritual traditions of both groups. Like Middle Woodland versions, Mississippian ones are found most often on the chests of burials and they have the same widespread distribution throughout sites associated with the ritual complex. Also, their use and disposition appears to be consistent between widely distant sites and very different contexts. Most have two perforations, as well, presumably for suspension.

Identical in scale and general decoration to gorgets represented in shell engravings, all but one of the Mississippian copper breastplates in the corpus are circular or roughly so. They are three to four inches in diameter and almost always have concentric circular designs. The one Mississippian breastplate that is not circular was identified as a breastplate by virtue of its position on the chest of a burial at the Etowah Site in Georgia. It was in the grave of a young woman (twenty-seven years of age) and exists only in the form of heavily corroded fragments. Its original shape is not apparent, but it definitely was not circular. The most consistent motifs applied to these objects, in addition to concentric circles, are crosses and "stars" or "sunbursts" (Figs. 24 and 61). A breastplate discovered in a burial in Mississippi County, Arkansas, provides another point of linkage between Mississippian breastplates and Hopewellian ones, and actually appears to be a throwback to those earlier conceptions. Its size and rectangular shape recall Early and Middle Woodland forms, but it carries the repoussé design of a spider found only in Mississippian contexts. This breastplate is illustrated and briefly discussed in *Spiro Mound Copper* but was not available for examination (Hamilton et al 1974:164–65).

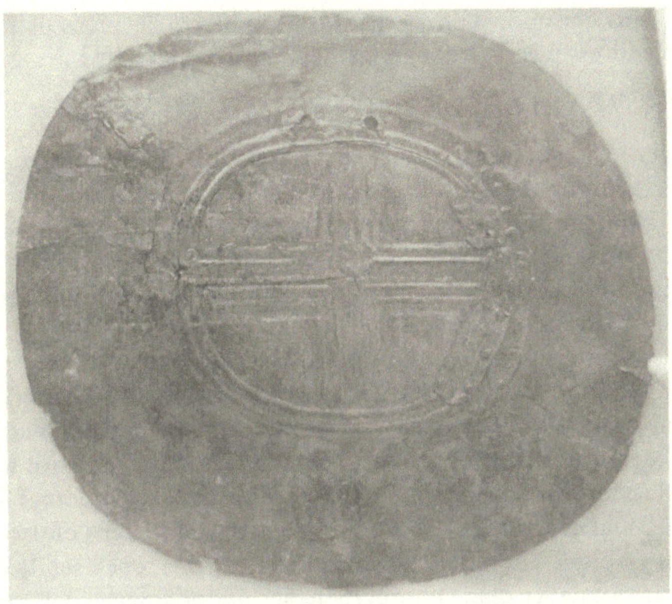

Figure 61. Large Repoussé Breastplate, Mississippian. Etowah Indian Mounds State Historic Site Museum, Cartersville, Georgia, #463. Etowah Mounds, Bartow Co. Georgia. Ca. 6"–7" long dia.

Post-Mississippian breastplates are few in number. Like the Mississippian ones, Post-Mississippian breastplates have not been identified as a specific genre in the archaeological literature. Extant examples seem to conform to a fairly consistent range of sizes and shapes, nevertheless, as was the case with earlier traditions. Once again, these breastplates have been defined as such based upon burial placement and stylistic similarity. Half of those examined are smaller than earlier pieces with similar forms and/or functions (four or five inches long), as is generally typical of copperwork from this period. Their shape resembles a miniature medieval broadsword. Other Post-Mississippian breastplate forms bear no apparent stylistic relationship to the sword-shaped ones. Two are small hook shapes and two are rectangular.

One of the rectangular Post-Mississippian breastplates, like the unique Mississippian example, recalls earlier Woodland Period traditions. It is plain, 6.1" by 5.6" and has two perforations, "Centrally spaced, some distance apart" (Moore 1910:284). (Two copper plates were taken from the same burial. This citation refers to a copper object found on the skull. Moore neither illustrates these two pieces nor specifically describes the perforations of the breastplate, except to say that both pieces were treated in the same way. Thus, the quoted phrase has been applied to the breastplate as well as to the headdress piece, although neither was examined by the author.)

II.5.E. Abstract Two Dimensional Designs

Small copper "badges" are the most characteristic objects of this type in the Mississippian corpus. All are between three and seven inches long and roughly triangular, although the shapes of some examples are more complex. Each is pierced at the larger end with one or two perforations (Figs. 22 and 23). A second group of cut sheet copper pieces consists of small discs (in addition to breastplates and earpieces).

Repoussé designs worked into square and rectangular pieces of copper sheet comprise a third, quite large group of Mississippian pieces in this category. Some or all of these were worked over carved wooden plaques. Several have been found still adhering to bits of wood carved with identical designs. A lack of detailed information regarding the excavation of much of this material makes it difficult to be sure whether this means of production was always employed in repoussé work. Pieces of this type usually come in two basic sizes: smaller than six square inches or one square foot and larger on a side. The majority have elements of concentricity in their designs. All repoussé patterns found on this type of piece are circular, variations on the square, and/or eye shapes. A few have a concentric square pattern, arranged around a central perforation. A number of unique shapes and fragments carefully cut from sheet copper have also been recovered from Mississippian sites.

With few exceptions, Post-Mississippian designs cut from sheet copper are small and limited to four basic shapes: disks, rectangles, triangles, and points. Many of these are elaborated with simple repoussé designs. As is often the case with late examples of copperwork, some confusion exists regarding the source of the copper from which they were made—whether native or European—as well as the time of their manufacture—before or after contact with Europeans. The time depth represented at some of the sites makes it difficult to attribute artifacts to specific periods and often the archaeological literature is unclear. For these reasons, within the statistical data it has occasionally been necessary to assign objects in the category of cut copper designs to the Post-Mississippian Period on the basis of stylistic similarity to positively identified examples.

II.5.F. Earpieces

One category of Mississippian earpiece is small, about the same size as typical Middle Woodland examples. Earpieces in this category consist of a circle of thin sheet copper that was pressed over a base that usually had simple concentric designs carved into it. The base was most commonly made of wood and stone, although horn, shell, bone, and clay were also used. This type of earpiece was apparently attached to the ear with a wood or bone pin. The precise way they were worn is not clear since usually the copper top and a misshapen wooden disk are all that remain in archaeological contexts. Only a few are completely plain and undecorated. Of those with decoration, designs on fewer than half are very simple—a single perforation or small, round concave circle in the center of an otherwise smooth surface. Sometimes a pearl or wooden bead was apparently fastened in the center. With few exceptions, the rest of the decorated examples have a convex boss in the center that is often surrounded by one to three concentric circles in repoussé. The circles are rendered in either continuous bands or tiny punctate bosses. A few exceptional earpieces in this category carry more complex designs that are primarily stars or sunbursts.

The second basic type of Mississippian earpiece is pulley shaped and usually quite large, 2½"–3" in diameter. Several smaller examples exist, however, as well as some variations on the basic pulley wheel shape. Generally both surfaces of these earpieces are circular, but some earpieces have only a small rectangular tab on the back (and were no doubt considerably easier to slip through a slit or hole in the earlobe). On some others, the smaller disk of the pulley is split—probably for ease of attachment as well. Related (small) earpieces resemble old-fashioned collar buttons. The spool shape in these examples is almost eliminated in favor of a broadly pointed arrangement on the back. A narrower ring is carved adjacent to the broad under surface of the large circle and the point was apparently pushed through the opening in the perforated ear.

On all the examples studied, the side of the piece worn closest to the head is plain and smaller than the decorated, copper-covered front side. In most cases, this decorated side is flat, slightly concave and has a simple concentric design. Up to six concentric circles may be engraved into the copper-covered stone face around a single, central boss instead of around a central perforation. In most cases, decoration of this type of earpiece consists simply of a central hole and a flat or beveled surface. There are ten other categories of design found on Mississippian pulley-type earpieces, but only three of those appear on more than a single pair of the examples studied.

Variations on the typical flat pulley form include a few where the concave surface is so exaggerated that the spool becomes almost funnel-shaped. The backs of these earpieces tend to be relatively small, resulting in an overall cup shape. Other variations occur at several sites a considerable distance from Mississippian core areas. Generally these are smaller, simpler versions of the typical earpiece type. Outlying areas also seem to have made greater use of materials other than stone for their earpieces.

As noted above, the existence of smaller pulley-type earpieces emphasizes the important links between Middle Woodland and Mississippian traditions (Figs. 15 and 64). In fact, these earpieces are nearly identical to the four Middle Woodland examples described earlier. Once again, provenience data for two of these is sketchy, but one pair comes from a well-documented site (Wray and MacNeish 1961:8, 18). Such earpieces are completely anomalous in the Middle Woodland corpus but their existence, along with other important parallels in material and design, suggests that the function and symbolism of earpieces used in the elite burials of both traditions were probably similar as well. Other links in earpiece design are provided by another small group of Middle Woodland objects mentioned above that also relates to Mississippian pulley-type earpieces. Again, these earpieces are open rings of either copper or stone with a curved upper surface (Fig. 4). The upper surface of the stone examples has a copper overlay. Similar examples have been found in both Mississippian and Woodland contexts.

Lots of unusual and occasionally unique objects in the Mississippian corpus probably served as earpieces as well. Several nearly identical ones were taken from the Spiro Site. They consist of a thin circle of shell with a small stone disc in the center. The stone discs were ground flat (about the size and shape of a dinner mint) and covered with copper. A pair of fragmentary items from Burial Pit 2 at the Alto-Gahagan Mound, Louisiana, may have been small versions of the same kind of earpiece. Their size, shape, and associated burial data (including the fact that they occur in pairs) indicate that they are earpieces. Other earpieces of wood and shell with central bosses of copper are described by Harrington (1920:86 and Moore 1912:53). These pieces were not available for examination but may be variations of this same type.

Another genre of Mississippian copperwork has been variously described as eagle or bear claw rattles. The shape and size of most examples suggest that they represent bear or puma canines rather than claws. (A pair in the Peabody Museum at Harvard University has been identified as milkweed pods. Their similarity to pieces from other Mississippian sites that clearly represent the canine teeth of large carnivores, as well as the general absence of representational vegetable motifs in any of the precontact copperwork from eastern North America, compromises this theory. Dr. Dwight Moore, an authority on milkweed, has also questioned this identification [McPherson 1962:145].) That these objects are occasionally found at the ears of burials suggests that at least some examples are earpieces. They are carved of wood, partly filled with tiny quartz pebbles and covered with copper.

Three unique pairs of Mississippian earpieces have also been identified. Two pairs, from Spiro, are of the "collar button" variety but were carved to represent the stylized heads of two birds and two bears (Figs. 62 and 63). Another unique example, from Louisiana, is comprised of two thin copper-

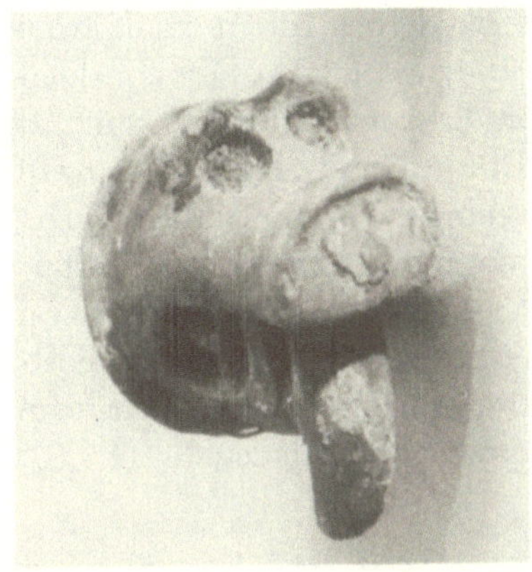

Figure 62. Copper/Wood Bear Earpiece (with shell inlay), Mississippian. Courtesy, National Museum of the American Indian, Smithsonian Institution, Washington, D.C., #21/3861. Spiro Site, LeFlore Co., Oklahoma. Ca. 2" diameter.

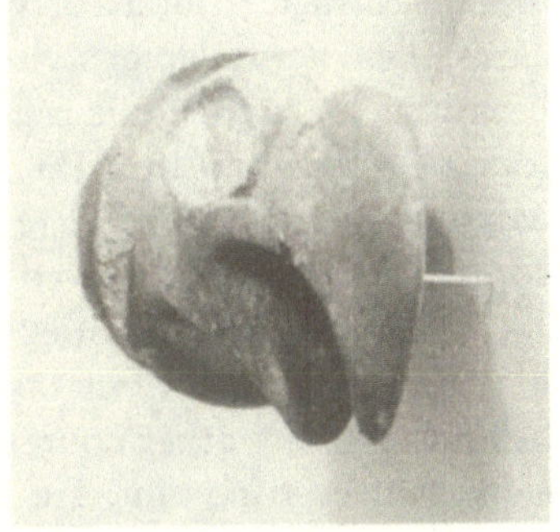

Figure 63. Copper/Wood Bird Earpiece (with shell inlay), Mississippian. Courtesy, National Museum of the American Indian, Smithsonian Institution, Washington, D.C., #22/4942. Spiro Site, LeFlore Co., Oklahoma. Ca. 2" diameter.

covered cedar squares. Each has a concentric circle motif carved into the wood and is worked in repoussé on the copper.

The spool form of copper earpiece gradually disappeared in Post-Mississippian times. Post-Mississippian copper earpieces are rare. All those discovered in the course of research for this study came from a single site in Alabama (Webb 1939:28–29). They bear only a tenuous formal relationship to earlier traditions. All consist of copper wire wound in a spiral, almost like a loose spring. They were worn in a series of holes pierced along the edge of the wearer's ears.

The only apparent relationship between these pieces and earlier ritual use of copper is in the design of a slightly anomalous type of copper artifact that is associated mostly with very northerly, very old sites (Old Copper Culture and others). The latter have strong formal associations with Early Historic spiral earpieces found primarily in sixteenth century Susquehannock and Iroquoian burials (Bradley and Childs 1991) and are made from European trade copper. However, they are almost identical to the earlier ones. Bradley and Childs indicate that all such pieces are from the Historic Periods and occur only within a highly circumscribed area. All are made from European copper. Those examined for this study came from sites considerably farther west than the area defined by Bradley and Childs and some, at least, are from considerably older contexts. Unfortunately, I do not know of any of this type that has been tested to determine the origin of the copper.

Considerable confusion surrounds the dating of some of the Archaic sites in the copper mining areas. Some (if not all) of the flattened spiral pieces assigned to the Archaic Periods may actually date from the Post-Mississippian and Early Historic Periods. If not, the time depth of the form and its use in the Northeast is extremely impressive and unusual.

II.5.G. Headdresses

Mississippian headdress elements included expertly worked sheet copper designs, lashed to bone or wood pins for insertion into the hair. In most cases, these items depict stylized feathers worked singly and in various combinations. A few include representation of the head, tail feathers, and one foot of a raptorial bird (Fig. 30). Many of the large awl forms found in Mississippian contexts were crafted of wood or bone with an overlay of copper, and probably served as pieces of elaborate head gear, as well.

Other objects identified as headdress elements, on the basis of their location in burials, offer no indication as to whether they were worn as headgear in any other contexts. The large copper plates with repoussé designs are a case in point. The headdress on the Big Boy pipe from Spiro (Fig. 28) suggests one way in which such headdresses might have been used. Big Boy wears a large disc-shaped headdress inscribed with an ogee eye form. A large copper sheet found on the head of a burial at Etowah bears the same design and is roughly the same size as the headdress Big Boy wears would have been if the figure were life-sized. (Detail on the Big Boy pipe suggests that it probably represents a specific individual. Both the pipe and the copper headdress are unique in the Mississippian corpus. Thus, it is plausible that the individual buried in the mound at Etowah is either the same one depicted in the pipe or was impersonating that individual.)

Two small examples of copper plates placed in the head area of burials show full length human figures in what appears to be a dancing posture (Plates 1 and 13). They wear various bird attributes and examples of other Mississippian copper headdress elements like those described above. Many similar copper sheets of this size and larger have been discovered, but most were not directly associated with the head of a burial. Another group of ambiguous objects are sizeable rectangular plates with large-scale human heads on them that are usually assumed to be headdresses because of their subject matter. One example differs from all others in that the head has been cut away from the otherwise invariable background sheet. Because this piece came from the commercial excavation at the Spiro Site and because it is almost identical to several others except for this treatment, the head may have been cut from its background after excavation to please the taste of a collector. (In fact, most of the remains from Spiro were removed during the commercial excavation, so nothing is known regarding their actual positions and associations at the site. However, they are sufficiently similar to examples from Alabama and Georgia to warrant the assumption that they served a similar purpose.)

Post-Mississippian headdress elements in copper are very limited and show little consistency in form. Examples from only two of the Post-Mississippian sites included in the study show any significant similarity. In both instances, a pair of small pieces of sheet copper had been cut to resemble rattlesnake rattles and were placed end to end across the cranium of burials in widely separated contexts, one in Alabama and one in Wisconsin (Moore 1900:327 and Collection Catalogue, Milwaukee Public Museum).

II.5.H. Bears and Other Mammals

There are many examples of bear canines in Mississippian copperwork, such as the earpieces described above. The shape of the canines is sometimes quite stylized, unlike Middle Woodland bear teeth, but all examples clearly represent the canine teeth of a large carnivore of some kind. Again, each example is carved from two pieces of wood and has a thin overlay of copper. Size and shape vary somewhat, but all are hollow and most have quartz pebbles inside. They have been discovered through most of the Southeast affected by the Southeastern Ceremonial Complex and are generally found at the ankles or the ears of burials. As noted above, some have referred to these objects as "eagle claw rattles" or even as milkweed pods, but most scholars agree that they probably represent carnivore canine teeth. Only one object in the entire corpus resembles a raptor claw in any way. A few wood and copper bear claws were also made in Mississippian times.

Only two pieces of Mississippian copperwork with bear-related designs depict more than teeth or claws. They are the pair of button-type earpieces found at Spiro and described above as carved from wood in the shape of a bear's head, with eyes and canine teeth of inlaid shell (Fig. 62). Only the wood core and shell decorations remain, but their color and remarkable state of preservation suggest that they were originally sheathed in copper.

Other carnivorous animals are also represented in the Mississippian copper corpus, though rarely. C.B. Moore (1894–1896:32, 153) took the copper-covered jaws of a fox and a second unidentified animal from a burial site in Florida.

In Post-Mississippian times, only two occurrences of copper in mam-

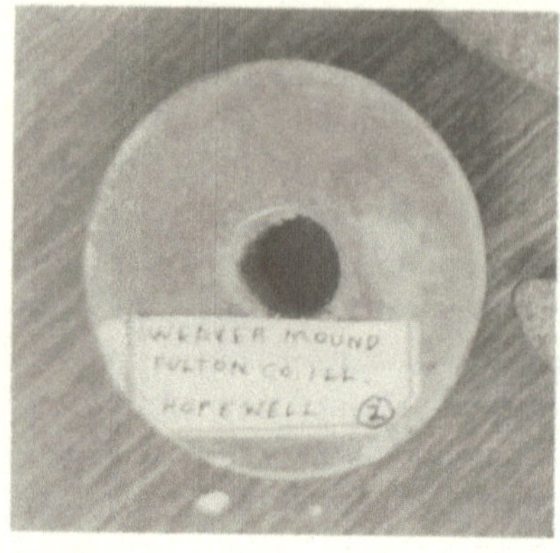

Figure 64. Mississippian Pulley Style Hopewell Earpiece, Middle Woodland. Illinois State Museum, Dickson Mounds, Lewiston. Weaver Site, Fulton Co., Illinois. 1 1/4" diameter.

malian contexts have been identified. Copper eyes that had been inserted in the skulls of an otter and a bobcat were discovered in Oneota-related burials (Bluhm 1961:96).

II.5.I. Birds

At least thirty-eight complete examples of Mississippian copperwork and many fragments represent whole birds. Thirty-four more depict humans with bird attributes including wings, talons, beaks, and tail feathers. The attributes are in different combinations and are worked in repoussé on copper sheet. Anthropomorphic birds are depicted in a wide range of styles and levels of skill. However, all are clearly related, primarily in the details of bird anatomy represented—beaks, wings, and tail markings (e.g., Plates 1 and 11 and Figs. 37 and 64). There is also an example of a wooden bird sculpture sheathed in copper (Harrington 1920:90), and one two-headed bird also exists.

Many copper birds represent the peregrine falcon. Characteristic markings, especially its forked eye, are carefully reproduced and clearly identify the species. Many human depictions also have these characteristics. Other examples of bird imagery, although unique in size and presentation, are also consistent in terms of the depiction of these attributes. In a small, rather crude piece from Tennessee (Fig. 36), the bird imagery is presented piecemeal—in four small sections joined at a single point. The configuration is identical in concept to another important item of copper paraphernalia found at Mississippian sites. Several of the small mace form "badges," or bird beak or point pendants, were very often joined in this way, to form multileafed, fan-like pieces of ceremonial regalia. Even the size and shape of the individual pieces of the Tennessee bird are similar to the triangular bird beak/point badges. Thus, though crude, the piece represents a combination,

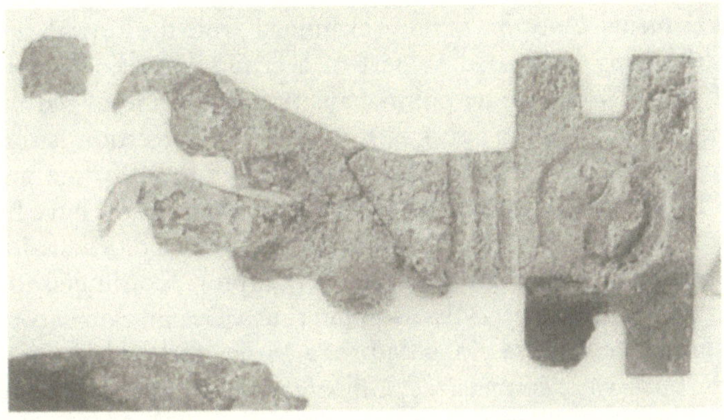

Figure 65. Repoussé Raptor's Claw, Mississippian. Antonio J. Waring, Jr. Archaeological Laboratory, University of West Georgia, Carrollton, #1146. Etowah Mounds, Bartow Co., Georgia. Ca. $3^5/_8$" long.

in extremely reduced form, of two important elements within the Mississippian copper complex, a juxtaposition that can hardly be accidental.

The pileated and/or ivory-billed woodpecker is also represented in copper. The circumocular marking of these birds is a simple band of black. It makes the woodpecker eye look like a perfect circle as opposed to the more oval shape of the peregrine falcon eye. This eye treatment, a simple band rather than the forked eye, also appears on some copper "portrait" plates (Fig. 21). The unusual earpieces discussed above, made of shell rings and small copper-covered stones, may also be references to the eye of the ivory-billed woodpecker.

Other eye-shaped designs are also found on Mississippian copperwork. Several pieces have an eye form that approximates that of the human eye, a kind of double ogee configuration. The rounded eyes of the peregrine falcon and other birds have a very similar shape. The obvious emphasis upon birds and their eyes in Mississippian copperwork suggests that the many unelaborated eye forms within the corpus may well be references to birds.

Other Mississippian pieces that are more specifically avian in subject matter include bird heads cut out of copper sheet with details in repoussé. Like their Middle Woodland counterparts, Mississippian coppersmiths also isolated other parts of bird anatomy for depiction in copper, especially the feet and talons. All were depicted in essentially the same techniques as whole birds (Fig. 65). In a few examples, the head, tail feathers, and one foot of a peregrine falcon are joined in abstract combination (Fig. 30).

Graceful feathers fashioned from copper are some of the most common headdress elements. Only one of those examined (from the Etowah site) lacked evidence of having been used as part of a headdress. Some scholars have identified the sixty-one large, point-shaped objects made of red cedar and copper that were found at Spiro as feathers. The suggestion is that, along with many others, these objects were lashed together to form a quite spectacular, if bulky, copper-feathered cloak. Such a cloak might have been used in impersonating the bird being that is found in so much of Mississippian art.

Bird-related subject matter, particularly raptors, continued to be used on copperwork during Post-Mississippian times. Design elements tended to become simpler and more elongated than earlier forms, but the same aspects of the birds were emphasized. One of the most impressive copperwork pieces is a large, simple one from Amoskeag Falls in New Hampshire. Its simplicity of form recalls Copena breastplates (even to the two central perforations), but it is probably from post-contact times and may have been fashioned from kettle copper (Coe 1976:68). The metal has not been analyzed in order to make a specific determination, however. Six birds made from heavy copper sheet or brass were found in late intrusive burials at the Lake Jackson Site in Florida (Fig. 66). Their feathered head design and the relatively crude metallurgical techniques used in their manufacture are similar to late style and formal changes on reworked copper plates and probably also reflect the upheavals occasioned by European arrival in the region.

Other Post-Mississippian bird forms in metal were found in Arkansas: one at the Scotts Site in Mississippi County and two at the Rose Mound in Cross County (Adams 1972:171). There are also significant shifts in the approach to design in these pieces, although like the brass birds from the Lake Jackson mound, they seem to have functioned in much the same way as much earlier ritual metalwork (Fig. 45). These pieces are so unlike earlier Mississippian material that Moore referred to the Rose Mound pieces as "ceremonial spearhead[s]," but they are clearly stylized birds (1910:292–93). A similar form was also found in an Oneota burial at the Blodeau Farm Site in Wisconsin, but such finds are very unusual. Still, although very few representations of whole birds in copper have been found in Oneota burials, the carcasses of real birds and birds fashioned from other materials were often included and elaborated with bits of copper.[4]

II.5.J. Crescents

Crescent motifs continue to be important in Mississippian times, although more often as stylized elements within other more complex designs, especially within avian depictions and the more abstract bi-lobed arrow design. In this respect, virtually all Mississippian crescent motifs are associated with headdresses of some kind.

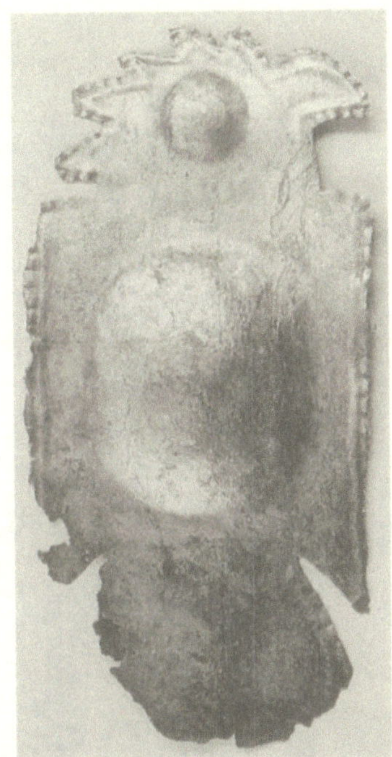

Figure 66. Brass Bird, Post-Mississippian/Historic Period. Florida Division of Natural Resources, Department of State, Tallahassee. Lake Jackson Mounds, Florida. Ca. 14" long.

II.5.K. Crosses

The vast majority of all copperwork with cruciform designs in the entire copper complex was produced during the Mississippian Periods. Crosses are usually joined with circular motifs, and the two designs are most frequently applied to earpieces and breastplates. On the former, the cross design is often negatively expressed amid a series of four nested right angles engraved around a central perforation. Simpler cross forms were also applied to earpieces, including a centralized cross with circles set in each of the four quadrants. A central cross was also the principle motif on Mississippian circular copper breastplates, virtually always in combination with concentric circles either surrounding or superimposed upon it in various ways (Figs. 44, 49, and 50).

Even more crosses appear in repoussé on the small "mace" shapes cut from sheet copper. These shapes are similar to the ones fastened to pins for use as headdresses but are smaller (Fig. 23). Like their larger counterparts, these small ones are apparently miniaturized versions of the large stone maces found at several Mississippian sites and depicted in shell engravings and copper repoussé. The form seems to have evolved through time, becoming more and more elaborate, but the central cross design remained essentially the same through all those changes. The bi-lobed arrow, another piece of copper paraphernalia used primarily as a headdress element, is also essentially cruciform in design (Fig. 31). However, the cross form is not precisely defined on any example; it is just implied in the bilaterally sym-

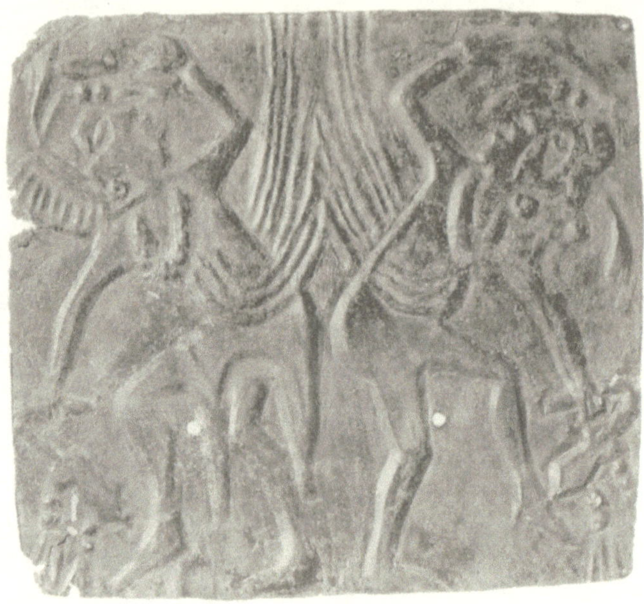

Figure 67. Repoussé Plaque with Two Dancers, Mississippian. Catalogue No. #88142, Department of Anthropology, Smithsonian Institution, Washington, D.C. Bluff Lake area, Union Co., Illinois. Ca. 7 1/2" x 8".

metrical nature of the form. (For that reason, these forms were not included in the statistics for cross designs in this study.)

Copper crosses and cross motifs continued to be important in Post-Mississippian times, although in greatly reduced numbers and in a different form. Most were the small, simple, sword-shaped breastplates cut from thin sheet copper and discussed above.

II.5.L. Humans

References to human beings in copper have been found in most areas where Mississippian remains are found and are usually related to similar designs that represent birds. Even the so-called "portrait" plates generally show individuals that seem to be impersonating birds or exhibit bird-related attributes. Several depict the whole human figure in what appears to be a dancing posture. "Dancer" plates have been found at sites in Alabama, Florida, Illinois, Oklahoma, and South Carolina. Virtually all these plates also include important references to birds, although some do not (Fig. 67). Like bird designs, certain aspects of anatomy are given special emphasis.

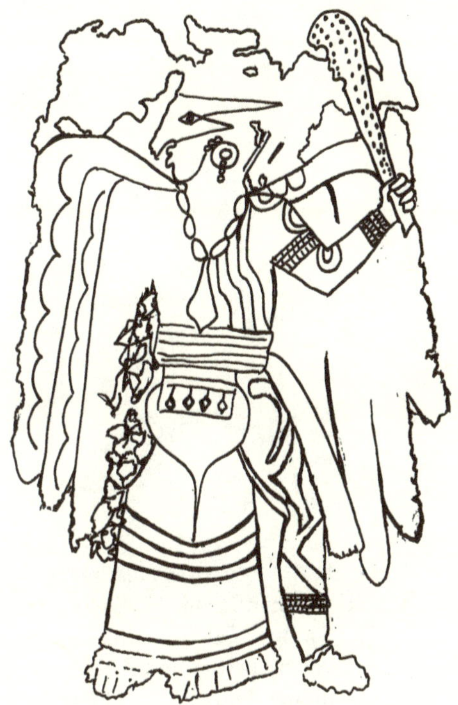

Figure 68. Repoussé Plaque, Mississippian. Florida Division of Historical Resources, Department of State, Tallahassee, #96.115.103.1. Lake Jackson Mounds, Florida. Ca. 17" long. Drawing by A.M. Trevelyan.

The head is usually enlarged and any bird attributes (usually wings and tails) are also disproportionately large (e.g., Plates 1, 11, and 13 and Figs. 37 and 68). The individuals depicted also wear paraphernalia found in many Mississippian burials, much of which is made from copper. One item depicting two dancers represents an approach to the subject matter that is fairly common in shell, but unique in the copper corpus (Fig. 69). As was also the case with bird representations, style and repoussé technique vary regionally, although emphases and specific design elements used are fairly consistent throughout the Mississippian area. Style and design also changed with time. In addition, some examples of Mississippian human representation show few, if any, clear bird attributes. All are quite late and come from only two sites.[5]

Disembodied pieces of human anatomy are also fairly common in the Mississippian copper corpus. Many are the heads delineated in a repoussé technique on large, roughly square sheets of copper (e.g., Plate 16). They are closely related to some types of Mississippian headgear. None has been identified specifically with the head of a burial, however, and one is so small it is unlikely that it could have served as a head covering (illustrated and discussed in Hamilton et al 1974:85). There are two distinct approaches to

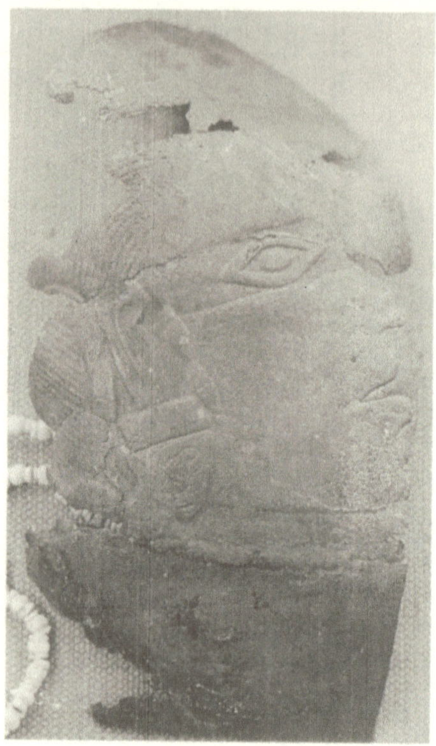

Figure 69. Repoussé Headpiece with Human Head, Mississippian. The Thomas Gilcrease Institute of American History and Art, Tulsa, Oklahoma. Spiro Site, LeFlore Co., Oklahoma. 12" tall.

the subject matter. In one group the neckline is either de-emphasized or not shown at all, and the head fills most of the available space (Figs. 21 and 69). Necks in the other group are clearly delineated by large notches and the head is usually encircled by point or blade-shapes (Plate 16). Perhaps one configuration represents the executioner, and the other represents the executed. There is an interesting correlative alternation in the depiction of individual dancers on smaller copper plates. Circumocular markings on the human head rattles held by some dancers (whose face paint is distinct from their rattles) are almost always the same as the eye decoration on dancers on other plates who do not hold rattles.

The small earpieces dubbed "long-nosed god masks," made entirely of copper, are also essentially human in their attributes, although the shape of the head and treatment of the forehead area are highly schematic (Fig. 27). Construction methods vary slightly from area to area, but these objects were usually made with two pieces of copper sheet. One piece, the face, is a filled in U-shape. The other is a pointed triangle that was inserted in a vertical slit in the face and serves as a much elongated and enlarged nose. Eyes and mouth were worked in repoussé. The mouth is usually de-emphasized

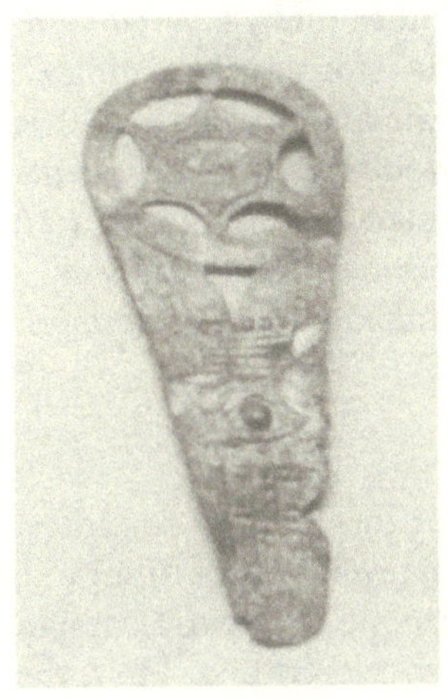

Figure 70. Openwork Repoussé Pendant with Human Hand and Wrist, Mississippian. Courtesy, National Museum of the American Indian, Smithsonian Institution, Washington, D.C., #17/3107. Moundville Site, Alabama. Ca. 5" long.

and small. The eyes are generally circular (as opposed to a more naturalistic oval shape) and disproportionately large. This tendency to enlarge or otherwise emphasize eyes and nasal features is consistent in both bird and human representation throughout most of the copper complex regardless of temporal or geographical factors.

Two more pieces of Mississippian material in this category are strongly reminiscent of copperwork from the Woodland Periods. They are a pair of human hands cut from sheet copper and are unique in the Mississippian corpus (Webb and Dodd 1939:96). Other unique interpretations of human anatomy are in the corpus as well; several other pieces have features that make identification of subject matter ambiguous at best. Many of these images are difficult to identify because the ceremonial impersonation of birdlike beings was apparently such an important part of Mississippian tradition. It is virtually impossible to know whether these represent the eyes of birds, of human beings impersonating birds, or some combination of the two. Waring and Holder (1945:4) suggest another factor that complicates the identification of eye forms in Mississippian art. They argue very convincingly that the eye motif was used interchangeably with a circle and cross combination. Howard (1968:26) comes to the same conclusion.

Two examples, a bird from Etowah and a human hand found at Moundville, as well as the designs applied to both, illustrate the complexity of this issue. The bird claw is depicted with the joints of the foot emphasized and with a tripartite bracelet on the ankle, topped with an encircled cross (Fig. 65). The human hand has the same tripartite bracelet, similar emphasis on the digital joints, and is topped by an encircled sunburst (Fig. 70). It also has an eye in the palm area (or the back) of the hand. The combination of human and bird attributes, plus other multi-layered symbols in both, makes the reading of this iconography enormously complex.

Another problematic form is the "occipital hair knot" (Fig. 34). It is difficult to know whether these copper-covered wood headdress elements depict a formalized hairstyle (and, therefore, human subject matter), an animal attribute (a horn or antler), or some more esoteric configuration.

Examples of Post-Mississippian material with human imagery were not discovered in the course of research.

II.5.M. Implement Forms

Implement forms rendered in a context with other imagery are found on two large repoussé plaques. In both cases, four edgewise views of an axe blade are arranged like a disconnected swastika around the central design element (Fig. 33). This identification is based upon two criteria. First, the cross-sections of many Mississippian stone and copper axes are virtually identical to the shapes depicted. Second, other Mississippian copperwork with a very similar format includes the arrangement of more obviously identifiable implements forms (points) in a similar configuration.

The small mace-shaped objects with repoussé crosses and larger counterparts, used as headdress elements, are obviously instances of the use of implement designs as well. Approximately eighty of them have been discovered (Fig. 23). Details of design vary considerably, but all clearly refer to the large maces carried by dancers pictured in Mississippian shell engravings and on copper repoussé plates. Maces shown in the hands of dancers that are depicted on copper plates have not been included in the statistics for implement motifs since presumably the implement itself, not a design or symbol, is represented. No other actual implements have been included in the design totals either. That is not to say, however, that the full-sized maces were not highly symbolic ceremonial paraphernalia. Most of the small copper ones were found in groups within individual graves. Only three examples of the larger variety that were used as headdress elements have been discovered.

The overwhelming majority of implement motifs appearing on Mississippian copperwork are point shapes. Like the mace motif, most occur as small badges found in groups within individual graves. Since some of these may represent bird beaks rather than points, they are listed within both categories of representational design. Again, the reason for taking this approach is that the objects involved are very similar and seem to have been used in essentially the same ways. The ambiguity in identification may well have been intentional, rendering the two motifs roughly equivalent, like so many designs in the iconography of Mississippian tradition. Other point-shaped designs are found on bi-lobed arrow headdress pieces, as one of the primary elements of

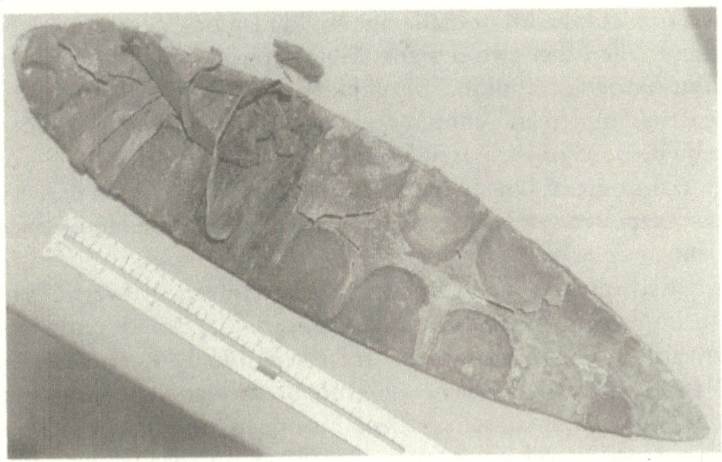

Figure 71. Large Wood/Copper Feather or Point, Mississippian. Ohio Historical Society, Columbus, #3490/253. Spiro Site, LeFlore Co., Oklahoma. 10 1/4" long.

that complex symbol (Fig. 31). A unique example of a point motif was carved at the end of a long wooden pin that was covered with sheet copper. A similar point shape occurs as a design in repoussé on two large copper portrait headplates. The points are arranged around the centralized portrait in much the same way the axe shapes encircle the central motif in Figure 30.

Simpler knife or blade shapes that belong within this category of design are also found in copper at Mississippian sites. Some may have been based on equally symbolic and nonfunctional ceremonial flints that are common in the Mississippian archaeological record. Others are much cruder but may also be knife or blade designs. Probably the most curious examples of Mississippian copperwork that could be non-utilitarian implement forms were found at Spiro. They are the sixty-one large point shapes mentioned above, carved from cedar and covered with copper sheet (Fig. 71). Each has one blunter and one sharper end like many copper awls and most utilitarian points. Once again, there is some ambiguity in their identification. They can be read either as very stylized versions of long leaf-shaped points or as feathers of various configurations. Each has a space about one inch wide that is left undecorated near one end, which is often wrapped with a leather thong. That this space may have been provided for hafting lends weight to the interpretation of the objects as points. Four very different repoussé designs are applied to them. Two can quite easily be read as a stylized rendering of the surface of a chipped flint blade but could also be interpreted to be stylized feathers. The other two designs do not appear to be the result of any known flint-napping technique, but look very much like stylized feathers.

Two actual implements should also be considered more as depictions of implements because of their fragile nature. Neither could have functioned in a utilitarian context. One is an axe so elongated and so thin that it would be useless except in a symbolic context. The other is a small hook fashioned from a delicate tube of rolled copper.

Post-Mississippian coppersmiths produced a few unique versions of non-utilitarian implement forms as well as an occasional piece reminiscent of earlier traditions. Most numerous are the uniquely Post-Mississippian "sword" forms discussed earlier (miniature breastplates cut from thin sheet copper that look like small schematized European broadswords). Like Mississippian mace-shaped badges, all vary somewhat in design but are similar in size and material, and each includes a cross motif. Hook shapes cut from sheet copper are also found at some Post-Mississippian sites, but they are much fatter and flatter than would be suitable for use in fishing.

Perhaps the most intriguing pieces of Post-Mississippian copperwork within this category are a few axe-shaped pieces, finished chunks without a cutting edge. They are intriguing because of their similarity to forms found in much earlier periods of copper-working activity. One of the Post-Mississippian examples is about the size and weight of a classic Middle Woodland breastplate (though axe-shaped, not trapezoidal) and even has the traditional central placement of two perforations. Once again, these recurring forms and themes probably point to fundamental and long-standing structures for exchange as well as to symbolism that was shared to some degree by all the groups that used copper ritually in the Eastern Woodlands in precontact times.

II.5.N. Rectangles

Although copper breastplates are circular instead of rectangular, rectangular formats for other types of copper paraphernalia continue to be important. Most of the portrait-like headplates were rendered on a rectangular format (Plate 16 and Fig. 21). The background for many other repoussé objects with circular designs was also rectangular. Several of the Spiro copper plates featuring dancing figures and similar pieces found elsewhere were also done within a rectangular format (Fig. 67). It is hard to know whether this kind of use for rectangular design had symbolic significance, but it is important to be aware of these shifts in design interest, in any case.

A square motif with loops at each corner was in common use on other Mississippian material, particularly in the Tennessee area, although it appears only once on copper (Fundaburk 1957:Plates 43–47). Reel shapes

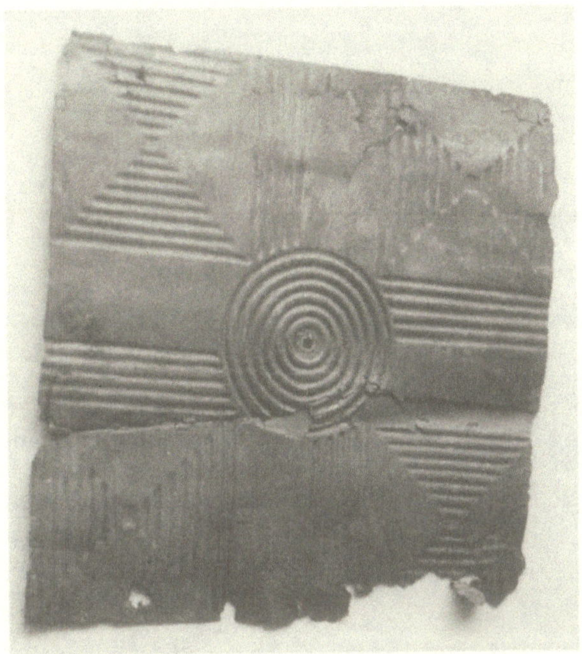

Figure 72. Large Repoussé Headpiece, Mississippian. Courtesy, National Museum of the American Indian, Smithsonian Institution, Washington, D.C., #17/0131. Mount Royale Site, Putnam Co., Florida. Ca. 10" square.

also appear in the Mississippian corpus, but rarely with the flowing grace of Middle Woodland/Copena ones, and always in repoussé. A large square headplate from the Mount Royale Site in Florida has reel shapes arranged in each corner (Fig. 72). These may be read either as individual elements of the design or as elaborations of an implied swastika revolving around a set of concentric circles in the center. The torso area of some copper birds—especially those from Etowah—is rendered in a reel shape as well. A similar shape is also used near the base of some copper repoussé feather headdress pieces from Mississippian sites and on one earpiece.

In Post-Mississippian times, rectangular/trapezoidal copper breastplates reappear (Moore 1911:409). A substantial number of smaller rectangular forms have been recovered from Post-Mississippian sites in the Arkansas area, although the specific use of these pieces is unknown. Each is a small square of rather heavy copper sheet with a large circular boss in the center and a small central perforation.

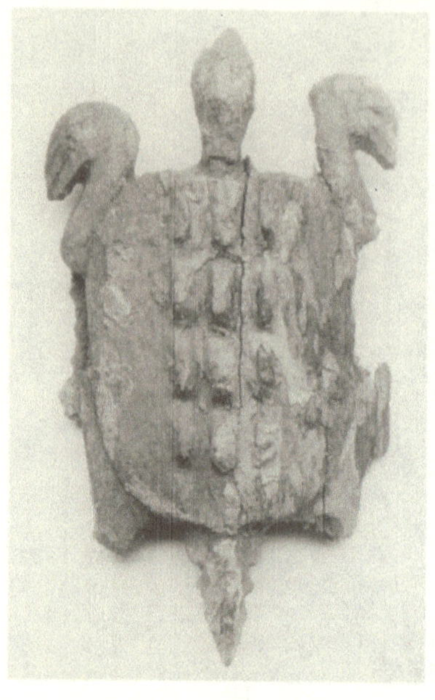

Figure 73. Wood/Copper Turtle Rattle, Mississippian. Courtesy, National Museum of the American Indian, Smithsonian Institution, Washington, D.C., #18/9307. Photo by Carmelo Guadagno. Spiro Site, LeFlore Co., Oklahoma. $6^{7}/_{8}$" long.

II.5.O. Snakes, Turtles, and Spiders

Of the few snakes in the Mississippian copper corpus, the majority are late. Some came from the Charlotte Thompson Place in Alabama (Moore 1900:327). This site included considerable post-contact material. Thus, the pieces are likely to be very late indeed and may even be post-contact. This seems likely since two nearly identical pieces were found at the Walker-Hooper Site in Wisconsin that also had important late prehistoric and early post-contact components (Gibbon 1972).

Only one complete example of a copper turtle was discovered in the corpus. Like most Middle Woodland turtles, it is also a rattle, although it is much larger than Middle Woodland versions. Carved from wood, it depicts the entire animal and exhibits considerable naturalistic detail. The sheet copper overlay that once covered it has almost completely deteriorated (Fig. 73). Another example of copper turtle imagery, a miniature shell, was discovered at a Late Mississippian or Post-Mississippian site explored by C.B. Moore (1894–1896:154, fig. 28).

Only one piece of Mississippian copper that incorporates what might be a fish motif was discovered in the course of research. A number of small fishlike designs were incised rather crudely into a unique piece found in a stack of corroded copper plates from the Spiro Site. Other marine animals are easier to identify. There is a group of copper covered wooden objects in the form of the *busycon perversum*, a marine univalve, from the Etowah Site. Unlike the large shells of this type that figure so importantly in other Southeastern Ceremonial Complex regalia, these are small and represent younger specimens of the species. Some examples depict the entire shell, and others only the spiraling form of the top portion of it.

The spider breastplate mentioned above offers a unique example of this kind of representational imagery. Once again, it is a small rectangular piece with two centrally-placed perforations and is more like traditional Middle Woodland forms than Mississippian ones. The motif that places it in this design category and squarely within the Southeastern Ceremonial Complex iconographical system is a large spider worked in repoussé and filling most of the area of the piece. The spider is a fairly common motif in much of Mississippian art but this is the only example in copper.

Post-Mississippian references to reptiles and other fauna in this category are limited to the depiction of snakes and snake-related motifs. Most examples come from the northern Midwest and are similar to snake references in the Mississippian copper corpus: serpentine awls and small sheet copper rattlesnake rattles.

II.5.P. Spirals

Spirals and spiral-type designs on Mississippian copperwork range from the simple "comma" or curling hook configurations common in the Middle Woodland corpus to fully developed spirals incorporating several turns. Like crescents, spirals appear most often on headdress elements, especially as abstracted feathers and avian circumocular markings. The simple comma-type version of these designs (very similar to Middle Woodland examples) appear in human depictions, though fairly late in the Mississippian corpus. It is also used occasionally on Late Mississippian stone/copper earpieces. The motifs are worked into the circular format of the earpiece in such a way that the spiral designs can also be read as sunbursts or swastikas. This bit of metamorphosis (from spiral to sunburst or swastika, or vice versa) demonstrates the kind of interrelationship typical of most circle-related forms used in Mississippian art.

No examples of Post-Mississippian spiral design have come to light except the spiral-shaped earpieces mentioned earlier.

II.5.Q. Sunbursts

Sunburst designs are almost as numerous as crescents and spirals in the complex as a whole, but they do not appear at all before Middle Woodland times. Although some Mississippian examples look very much like Middle Woodland sunburst designs, this type is not common in the Mississippian

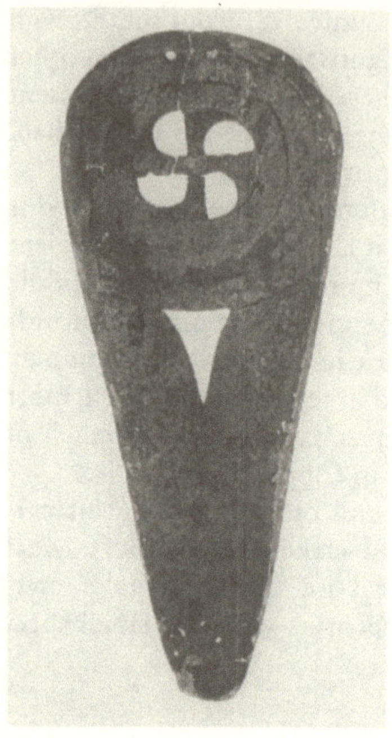

Figure 74. Small Repoussé Pendant, Mississippian. Courtesy, National Museum of the American Indian, Smithsonian Institution, Washington, D.C., #17/0225. Photo by Carmelo Guadagno. Moundville, Alabama. Ca. 4" long.

corpus. The radiating points on Middle Woodland sunbursts tend to be essentially triangular, whereas most Mississippian sunbursts are scalloped. Examples usually have six or eight points, but some have four, five, seven, and even twenty-four.

Sunburst designs are sometimes found at the apex of the small, roughly triangular pendants common in Mississippian copperwork (Fig. 70). They also occur on breastplates and other items of burial regalia, but only occasionally. Naturalistic forms were often conventionalized into a sunburst or a portion of one, as well. Examples include the crest and tail feathers of raptorial birds, and humans with bird attributes, hair roaches on human forms and wrinkles and/or hair on animal representations.

II.5.R. Swastikas

Swastika designs in copper were in use during the same chronological periods as crosses, although they are less numerous in the Post-Mississippian material. Again, like the cross, the swastika is also a transitional form with a strong relationship to rectilinear forms as well as to circular ones. All these formal relationships undoubtedly also had important symbolic implications within the iconography of the period. Mississippian swastikas on earpieces (primarily the stone/copper variety) include a wide range of approaches to the design. Many Mississippian copper breastplates also have a swastika as the main element, surrounded by the typical concentric circles in repoussé. Swastikas sometimes decorate the tops of the more elaborate triangular pendants, as do sunburst designs (Fig. 74). Again, this use may indicate relative iconographic equivalency for the two motifs.

Notes

Introduction

1. E.g., Walthall 1972:146; Quimby 1960:7, 20–22, 522; Sears 1971:324–25; Blakeley 1977:120–22; Bryson and Murray 1977:25–26, 29, 32, 69; Cleland 1976:69–70; Peterson 1984:117–19; Brose 1984:28–29; and Muller 1986:67.

2. E.g., Seeman 1979:406–7 and Perzigian 1977:106.

3. The conditions that gave rise to Hopewell-related ritual and the subsequent dearth of artwork in the Late Woodland Period presents a classic example of this phenomenon. Brose suggests that the art of the late Southeastern Ceremonial Complex functioned in much the same way, although he discusses the phenomenon from an archaeological perspective and in very different terms (Brose 1984:33).

4. Struever and Houart 1972 and Goad 1978.

5. See, for example, Pader 1982:1, Levine 1957:960, and Geertz 1973:127.

Chapter 1. A Long, Consistent History

1. Native copper is almost always more than 99 percent pure, so the percentages of trace elements tend to be very small. Most early attempts at trace element analysis were able to prove that prehistoric objects were fashioned from native copper rather than smelted (and, therefore, European, Meso-, or South American) copper, based on the relative purity of the material. However, the technique was not precise enough to yield positive identification of indigenous sources for the material.

Optical emission spectroscopy and neutron activation analysis are more discriminating. Results of analysis by these methods indicate that numerous sources of copper were exploited in the manufacture of precontact copperwork (Goad 1978); most of the copper used, however, came from a single source area, the Lake Superior region of northern Michigan and southwestern Ontario (Map II).

2. E.g., Trigger 1976:243 and Cartier 1924:170–71.

3. Drier and Du Temple 1961:48–49, Rickard 1934:225–26, and Skinner 1921:279.

4. Goad 1978 and Strachey 1849:26, 33.

5. Drier and Du Temple 1961:21, 42, 144 and Griffin 1961:52.

6. This band of prehistoric mining sites is from two to seven miles in width (Drier and Du Temple 1961:119). The copper was extracted from pits or wide trenches excavated in rows following the veins of copper, though some isolated pits have also been located. One of the trenches was one hundred feet wide in some places. The pits were up

to thirty feet in diameter and ranged from shallow excavations of one or two feet, to sixty feet in depth.

7. One thousand tons of mauls were removed from a single site of mining activity on Isle Royale, and in the Rockland area, "10 wagon loads" of them were carried away (Drier and Du Temple 1961:23). Only a few unused stone mauls have been discovered. Many had one or two grooves to allow for the attachment of handles. The remains of these handles have occasionally been discovered intact in the ancient mines. Some of the mauls with two grooves are so large that they may have been wielded by two miners. Ungrooved mauls have also been found. Many of these have a "polished band," which suggests a different hafting method.

8. Drier and Du Temple 1961:23 and Griffin 1961:58.

9. Drier and Du Temple 1961:6, 7 and Griffin 1961:63, 81.

10. It is probably not merely coincidental that these tools were made of cedar. That particular type of wood has a long association with copper in many traditional cultures (e.g., Jopling 1989:17).

11. Most were purchased from individuals who happened upon them in the countryside of the upper Great Lakes area. They are generally without much in the way of provenience data and were acquired in the early part of this century, especially during the years of the Great Depression. The amounts paid are often noted in museum catalogues—generally very substantial sums.

The weight, texture, and appearance of many of the objects suggest that they might not be made of native copper, although none were metallurgically tested at the time. It is very possible that these examples were made by those who offered them for sale, receiving what probably amounted to a week's wages, at the very least, for a few hours of labor. (Replicating the ancient forms with the copper alloys available at the time would have been fairly easy for farriers and other metal workers who knew how to fashion copper gutter work and the various items made from copper at the time.)

12. In the archaeological literature and various museum catalogues, implements of this type are referred to as "gouges" or "spuds," as well as adzes. Since the precise usage is unknown and most are essentially similar, in this study all such pieces will be called "adzes."

13. Wittry has developed a thorough typology for these copper points (Wittry and Ritzenthaler 1957). Many are socketed, with a folded sleeve, and (usually) have a central ridge on at least one side of the blade. Many socketed points originally had a small copper nail hammered through a perforation in the socket to hold the wooden shaft of the spear in place. Another type of point was cone-shaped and simply fit over the end of the weapon shaft.

Late Old Copper Culture forms are particularly distinctive and tend to be lighter and flatter than earlier examples. According to some archaeologists, Late Archaic Glacial Kame sites contained some Old Copper Culture-type points as well as another distinctive point type, the so-called "ace of spades" point (Baerreis et al 1957:279). Historical evidence suggests that the copper "ace of spades" point was also important well after contact with Europeans, indicating either an almost incredibly long period of use or some mistakes in the dating and/or cultural attribution of these pieces (e.g., Miles 1951:243).

14. Only one example was discovered in material examined from the Archaic Periods. (Copper rings were also found on the fingers of a burial occupant from the Karew Site in Wisconsin. The cultural affiliation of this site is not clear, however, so these rings were not included in the totals for the Archaic Period in this study.)

15. This piece (#55788–21523 at the Milwaukee Public Museum) offers a good example of the wide range of possibilities for the condition of copper objects from the Archaic Periods. It was in such perfect condition that it was assumed to be Historic copperwork initially and was not photographed. The museum number was recorded, however, and double-checked with the catalogue, which listed it as a find from the Old Copper Culture Riverside Site.

16. The latter sometimes have the appearance of miniature crescent knife blades. It has been suggested that some of these are nose ornaments (Robert Hruska, personal communication, 1976).

17. Cultural and chronological attribution for several of these is problematic, since pieces of this genre from sites designated both Archaic and Late Woodland (and even post-contact) appear to be identical.

Stylistic and distributional data for other examples of spirals, also purportedly Archaic (according to archaeological site reports), also seem problematic. Three examples from the "Archaic" Osceola Site in Wisconsin are extremely similar to flattened spirals from Middle Woodland sites in Michigan—Indian Hills, Naomikong Point, and Summer Island (Brose 1970:136). Again, this suggests either an incredibly long and intermittent tradition in copper design, or faulty archaeological identification at one or more of these sites.

18. No scholar has completed a detailed analysis of use-related damage on Old Copper Culture implements in general. The only work done in this area, on a large collection from Wisconsin, cites evidence of use, but never a use related directly to the form of the implement (Penman 1977).

The only signs of wear noted in Penman's analysis were the result of using socketed points as saws or knives. The crafter of a complex and perfectly balanced socketed spear point would be unlikely to ruin it by utilizing it as a knife. I suspect that Penman's examples of implements showing use are, rather, examples of reuse of these objects, and probably not by the original owners. This explanation is highly plausible since most Old Copper Culture implements have been found in isolated contexts along water courses. It would have been just as easy as it is likely that other Native Americans discovered and used examples of Old Copper Culture material, long after the original owner had left it behind. Euro-Americans have been doing so for the last hundred years at least. This kind of secondary and makeshift use corresponds to the kinds of wear Penman identified.

19. In general, the chronology used in this section corresponds to that proposed in Griffin 1976. More recent scholarship has refined these dates somewhat, but scholars continue to disagree about which dates are most accurate. For the purposes of this study, the broad generalized temporal units Griffin proposes are sufficient. Precisely demarcated chronological and cultural designations are always misleading, in any case. They should never be thought of as abrupt boundaries between cultural groups or ideas, all of which developed gradually and continuously. There may be periods of rapid or slow change, but there are few very sudden shifts, particularly in the development of art styles, especially those associated with ritual.

Another area of potential confusion stems from the terms used to describe the various precontact periods in archaeological literature (e.g., Archaic or Early Woodland). These terms usually refer to temporal units, but they may also be use to describe subsistence patterns and often are. For example, although the Early Woodland Period generally predates the development of Hopewell burial traditions (a Middle Woodland phenomenon), some contemporaries of the Hopewellians are considered to be Early

Woodland peoples, based upon cultural criteria, although they lived during the Middle Woodland Period, temporally.

20. One example is a copper "boatstone." Many similar ones were made in the Early Woodland Period, but all were of stone. This copper example was made from a small rectangular piece of thick sheet copper. An oval boss was pressed into the middle so that the edges remained flat with an oval depression in the center. Copper boatstones were far more common in the Middle Woodland Period.

21. Again, there is some disagreement regarding these dates. Jennings pushes the beginning forward to 100 B.C. (1978:297). Quimby, on the other hand, suggests that because Hopewell so dominated the era, the chronological boundary for Middle Woodland should be set as far back as 500 B.C., in order to include the earliest indications of Hopewell development (1960:720).

22. All of the largest and artifactually richest Hopewell-related ceremonial sites were centered in Ohio at six major locations: Hopewell, Mound City, Tremper, Seip, Turner, and Newark. There are also very important Hopewellian sites farther west through much of Illinois and Indiana as well as in Iowa, Arkansas, and Kansas. There are other Hopewell remains in Michigan and Wisconsin, and in Ontario, as well as a number of Hopewell-related sites in the Southeast in Georgia, Alabama, Louisiana, and Florida.

23. For many years, it was assumed that the complex nature of Hopewell-related societies was the result of subsistence surpluses derived from the development of maize agriculture. More recent research has demonstrated that Middle Woodland societies used maize only marginally. There was no substantial change in earlier subsistence strategies with the advent of Hopewell tradition. Hopewellian use of maize may even have been primarily ceremonial (Bender 1985:48).

24. There were actually two important core areas, Ohio Hopewell and the Havana tradition in Illinois. Both begin to be distinguishable from Adena in the third century B.C., but it appears to have happened slightly earlier in Illinois. As noted earlier, there were also important Hopewell-related societies in the Southeast, especially Copena and Marksville. Marksville bears a strong resemblance to the Ohio version of Hopewell. Copena, on the other hand, seems to have had far stronger ties to Adena (hence the name, Copena, a composite formed from the words "copper" and "Adena") and never resembles the Hopewell core areas very closely. Like Copena, many of the regional variations of Hopewell are sufficiently distinct as to suggest all but independent development.

25. Many appear to have been attached to a wooden handle with thongs of some sort, usually from 3/8" to 5/8" wide. This hafting material covered imperfections in the surface of a few examples, otherwise crafted with typical refinement.

26. Several adzes have a large notch in the butt and a few are so asymmetrical as to suggest that they may have been broken and reworked. A few others have been found in pieces within burial mounds, but in those cases the mutilation was almost certainly intentional, not the result of use.

27. E.g., few larger ones (over eight to ten inches long) seem to have been parts of elaborate headdresses rather than tools, like the four copper pins from burial #7, Mound 25, of the Hopewell group in Ohio (Shetrone 1930:212). A few conventionally shaped hooks of copper were also made at this time. They are of a size and shape that could be functional as fish hooks, but are tubular in construction and formed of such thin sheet that they could not have been used for fishing or any other utilitarian activity.

28. Only three (conical) points from the Woodland Periods are mentioned in the archaeological literature surveyed in connection with this study (Cole and Deuel 1937:135 and Crumley 1973:184). None was available for examination. In fact, if these *are*

Hopewell they are probably conical tinklers, not conical points. No other examples of conical points have appeared at Hopewell-related sites, but conical copper tinklers were found at several.

29. In fact, the introduction of special types of copper earpieces into the copper corpus accounts in large part for the dramatic climb in the amount of copper work made in the Middle Woodland Period and again in the Mississippian Periods. From one third to one half of all the decorated copperwork in both periods were circular earpieces. If these items are eliminated from the statistics for applied decoration on copperwork, the pattern of growth in decorative interest for the entire prehistoric complex shows a more gradual and consistent development. On the other hand, the importance of these objects and their circular design points to the tremendous significance of that particular motif in the iconography of the copper complex.

30. Variation in the techniques of copper earpieces do exist, but they are relatively limited. Katherine C. Ruhl (1992) has done a detailed analysis of Hopewellian copper earpieces, identifying eight distinct styles with important chronological implications. In all cases, however, the differences between types are apparent in only the contour of the circular cymbals and a limited number of construction techniques, rather than wide variation in design concept or use.

31. Provenience data for two of them are questionable, so at the outset both were eliminated from serious consideration for this study, particularly because museum catalogue information indicated that they were from Middle Woodland sites. They simply do not look like Hopewellian metal work and are very similar to Mississippian designs. Later in the course of research, however, two more just like them were discovered. The latter are from a well-documented Middle Woodland site, indicating that the two similar ones with less reliable provenience data might have been properly attributed after all (Wray and MacNeish 1961:9, 18). Furthermore, the existence of pairs of nearly identical ritual objects (albeit unique within the corpus—pipes and ceramics, e.g.) found at widely separated Hopewell-related sites is a pattern apparent in several other instances and may be evidence of an important kind of exchange structure within the ritual.

32. There are several other examples of repoussé decoration on otherwise typical Hopewell breastplates found in Ohio.

33. The relative size of the point-shaped piece from Wisconsin and the placement of its two perforations indicate that it is a breastplate, despite its unusual shape. It is quite crude and deteriorated, but the form is unmistakable. (Other very elongated point shapes are reported from the Turner and Hopewell Mound sites, apparently patterned after long, thin ceremonial flints [Willoughby and Hooton 1922:19]. Neither illustrations of these objects nor the objects themselves were available for analysis in the collections examined.)

34. A breastplate from the Crystal River Site in Florida also carries punctate elaboration—similar in technique to the Wisconsin pieces, though more complex in design (Moore 1903:411).

35. Detailed analysis of the symbolism involved and its implications is beyond the scope of this study, however. My purpose here is to identify the copperwork associated with such composite symbolism and probe its significance within the context of the copper complex as a whole.

36. This subject matter accounts for nearly 12 percent of all designs on Middle Woodland copperwork.

37. A conventional copper headplate was elaborated with several pieces of cut mica in rectangular and triangular shapes. A pair of large moveable copper ears decorated

with freshwater pearls were attached to each side (Fig. 14). The result is an elaborated version of the traditional headdress configuration that may have been worn to impersonate the female of the species in much the same way that other headplates were altered to reflect the attributes of a male deer. Along with the limited reference to large felines, this suggests a distinct, if tenuous, pattern of ritual significance that corresponds roughly to other burial evidence. That is, the preponderance of elaborate burials at Hopewellian sites seem to hold the remains of males. However, it is clear that women were not entirely excluded from either elaborate burials or important ritual activity. Thus, what we may have in this particular artifact is another example of paraphernalia designed specifically for female ritual specialists within a tradition whose primary practitioners were men.

38. These copper canines are assumed to be grizzly bear teeth because of their size, much larger than the teeth of *ursus americanus,* the species found in Ohio during Middle Woodland times. The unusual size of these teeth would hardly be sufficient reason to make such an assumption were it not for the fact that dozens of real grizzly bear teeth have been found in Hopewellian graves. Most are perforated in the same way that the copper versions are. The size and shape of the copper teeth match the real ones. In fact, size and shape are so consistent that, at first glance, they would appear to have been cut from a template. However, none is exactly like any other. Variation is even more consistent, so much so that it may be that each is a copper reproduction of a specific grizzly tooth.

39. Most are perfectly flat and often have two perforations located in roughly the same area as the perforations in most breastplates, that is, arranged laterally and centered (Fig. 15).

40. Catalogue information suggests that it includes the cut outline of a bird's open beak and a punctate design that delineates a bird's eye (Coe 1976:62). These design elements were not apparent when the piece was on display in Kansas City in 1977.

41. The piece was taken from the huge deposit in Mound 25 of the Hopewell group and is usually displayed in conjunction with another piece of copper found in the same deposit, a forked design. Together, the two vaguely suggest the head of a serpent with its forked tongue protruding. However, only one "head" was found in the deposit; there were several of the forked pieces. Thus, it is unlikely that the two belonged together originally.

Furthermore, none of the other 250 plus pieces in the deposit suggest any reference to a snake—no tail, no coils, no rattles, nothing. I know of no image in all of the art of the Eastern Woodlands that represents a snake's head in isolation. Serpent imagery in this region inevitably depicts the unique body of the snake and usually refers specifically to the rattlesnake, with emphasis on the tail, for obvious reasons. If this piece does represent a serpent, it is the only example of copperwork from the entire Woodland Period that does. That is not to say that there were not unique examples created. Several have been described above. However, in every case, those pieces are representational in their presentation of subject matter.

42. A roughly similar and equally complex piece from the Rutledge Mound in Ohio is usually called a "frog," but probably has similar ties to Adena design and complex symbolism, as opposed to being a semi-naturalistic reference to a frog (Fig. 17).

43. According to Mills (1922:545–46), the horn was apparently the central element in a complex headdress. It is roughly life-sized and very realistic, either formed by covering an actual horn with copper or one carved of wood or some other material. The conditions of its display at the site make it impossible to distinguish whether it is solid copper, copper overlay on wood, or copper sheet applied to a real mountain goat horn.

44. Several were covered with copper and a few with silver. Like grizzly bear teeth, these originals were also reproduced in wood and covered with sheet copper. There are many of them, although their distribution is limited to only a few sites.

45. E.g., Webb and Baby 1957 and Walthall 1972.

46. Buikstra 1977:73 and Braun 1988:27.

47. Remains of squash (domesticated in Meso-America) dated at 2300 B.C. were found at the Phillips Spring Site in southwestern Missouri and at the Green River Site in Kentucky from about the same period (Chomko and Crawford 1978:406–7).

48. The obvious interaction between southern Copena peoples and those participating in Adena- and Hopewell-related ritual is another important connection. Ritual material from the Marksville Site in Louisiana is so similar to Hopewellian examples in the North that Muller suggests there may even have been a movement of some human population into the area as well as goods from the North (Muller 1978:299).

49. Both Hopewellian and Copena groups used cups made from marine univalves. However, the Hopewellians preferred the *cassis* shell. Copena groups used the *busycon perversum* exclusively, another important marker for later groups associated with the Southeastern Ceremonial Complex (Walthall 1980:125).

50. Much recent scholarship all but rejects the notion that the Complex was a widespread cult, a monolithic development in any sense (e.g., Muller 1978:321, 1984:12). Today it tends to be seen as series of related developments spread throughout the Southeast, all with distinct local traits. Others feel that the reaction against earlier ideas about the complex have gone too far, that there is much (especially in its later manifestations) that is cult-like (e.g., Brose 1984:27–28).

51. Careful examination of the "bird man" motif has led Patricia O'Brien to similar conclusions (1994:24). In many respects the stylistic and symbolic shifts that define the two phases recall some of the differences between the Braden and Craig styles as defined by Philips and Brown (1978). Reuse of Braden-style cups to make Craig-style gorgets suggests that there may have been a temporal division between the two styles (Philips and Brown 1978:38), and that is how it appears within the Mississippian copper corpus. Remains from the Great Mortuary at Spiro suggest this as well, where copper material that was obviously from a much earlier time is combined with blank bird-shaped sheets of copper ready to be made into new paraphernalia of a very different genre stylistically.

52. Many in the field have tended to discount these developments as causal factors in the development of the ceremonial fluorescences that sprung up throughout the Southeast at this time. However, evidence gleaned from a comprehensive look at the copperwork produced in connection with these developments suggests that they were probably very significant.

53. Unfortunately, very few of these Post-Mississippian pieces have been subjected to trace element analysis. This presents a problem since there is some question as to whether copperwork found at the sites was made from native copper or from reworked copper kettles received in trade with Europeans. Other European trade materials have been found at these sites. As a result, archaeologists have often tended to assume that after the arrival of Europeans, Native American groups in eastern North America who continued to practice metallurgy used only European trade copper or brass. This was almost certainly not the case. Since this study has focused exclusively on precontact copperwork and site reports generally assume that metal from these sites is European in origin, objects from these later sites are rarely included in the statistics. Thus, it may be that interest in and use of copper did not fall off as drastically around the time of contact

as statistics developed for this study indicate. In fact, it may be that the use of European trade metals (many of which bore design motifs related to materials manufactured by native coppersmiths) as well as undocumented native copperwork offset much of this apparent decline. Early Historic accounts describe the ongoing significance of copper (both the native metal and that obtained from Europeans) in ritual and ceremony. Details of use and meaning found in these documents offer valuable insights into its prehistoric significance.

54. Post-Mississippian interest in applied decoration falls off considerably, although it never goes much below Middle Woodland levels of interest in that kind of design.

55. Such pieces are referred to as "ear ornaments" in the archaeological literature. The use of the work "ornament" has been avoided throughout this study since it tends to imply that the objects in question were merely decorative in intent—baubles and trinkets, as it were—which they certainly were not.

56. There is a possibility that some of the pieces placed in this category were not earpieces, but a number of factors, including their size, construction, design, and burial provenience suggest that they probably were.

57. I concur with James Brown (1976:297) in the identification of these objects as earpieces. Again, they always occur in pairs, they are constructed in such a way that the two large portions could be separated for placement in an ear, and two were found in position on either side of the skull in one burial.

58. The strong relationship between circular design and cruciform in copperwork associated with the Southeastern Ceremonial Complex was first demonstrated by Waring and Holder (1945:4). What they refer to as the "value" of cruciform symbolism on those objects was identical to that of circular motifs—to the degree that they felt that the two motifs were essentially "interchangeable" when applied to "otherwise rigidly specialized objects."

59. Lewis and Kneberg 1954:45 and Waring and Holder 1945:3.

60. Several examples of this subtler form of swastika motif are essentially identical to others with more precisely outlined swastikas, making clear the design intention of the more ambiguous versions.

61. Waring and Holder (1945:10) describe three kinds of copper plate, associated with material from the Southeastern Ceremonial Complex. The "forked eye" motif appears on all three, in many of the contexts described above. These same eye designs are also found on stone/copper earpieces and worked in repoussé on the small point-shaped badges found in Mississippian sites.

62. The style corresponds roughly with what Philips and Brown (1978) have identified with the Braden style on shell cups.

63. Some of the teeth are so round in section that it has been suggested that could represent feline rather than the flatter ursine teeth (McPherson 1962:145).

64. Antlered figures are so prevalent in the art associated with the Southeastern Ceremonial Complex that Waring and Holder (1945:5) felt that the deer should perhaps be included in their list of "god-animal representations," along with certain birds, rattlesnakes, cats, and humans. Much of their work has since been reinterpreted, but the fact remains that antlered beings are a very important iconographical element in the art of the Complex.

65. The importance of rattlesnakes in other media prompted Waring and Holder (1945:5) to count rattlesnakes in addition to birds, felines, and humans as one of the four major "god-animal representations" within the iconography of the Southeastern Ceremonial Complex. Again, their interpretation of the Complex, particularly the ten-

dency to interpret it as a rather monolithic development, has undergone considerable revision in the fifty years since they developed their theories. Still, the generalized use of certain materials incorporating certain types of motifs throughout much of the Southeast is undeniable and useful for this broad overview of copper use in the Mississippian Periods.

66. E.g., the copper covered stone "lizard" C.B. Moore took from the Foster Place in Lafayette County, Arkansas (Moore 1912:599). It almost certainly represents a turtle.

67. Their hollow form and frequent association with small quartz pebbles also imply that they were rattles.

68. Detailed analysis of this kind of symbolism on copperwork and its implications is beyond the scope of this study. My purpose here is to identify the copperwork associated with such composite symbolism and probe its significance within the context of the copper complex as a whole.

Chapter 2. Meaning and Significance in Design

1. The drive to create such connections and the satisfaction produced by having done so—for both reader and researcher—despite their obviously erroneous character, reflects the power of our own western cultural proclivities, the most significant obstacle to accurate analysis of prehistoric art traditions.

2. E.g., Willoughby 1897:11 and 1932:45; Nuttall 1932:137.

3. This does not, however, invalidate the classification of forms in the analysis of the copper complex—a process necessary to an academic evaluation of the corpus—but it does indicate that the kinds of information generated by that process may suggest a whole range of meanings, most of which do not obtain in traditional western ways of analyzing form.

4. Waring and Holder (1945) came the closest to achieving this kind of approach early on, certainly the primary reason why their study was considered the classic one for interpretation of the Southern Ceremonial Complex for so many years. In general, Phillips and Brown (1978) have utilized similar care in their analysis of Mississippian shellwork. This is also the approach utilized here.

5. E.g., Sandoz 1961 and Niehardt 1961.

6. See, for example, Krickeberg 1968:171, Boas 1928:157, Spier 1921:477, and Wallace 1958:245.

7. Anderson 1979:54.

8. E.g., Swanton 1946:491–497, 519–23.

9. Spier 1921:463, 482; Mooney 1965:179, 185; Witthoft 1949:66, 67; and La Barre 1938:7–8.

10. E.g., Putnam and Willoughby 1896:312 and Willoughby 1897.

11. Swanton 1946:502, 512–13, 520–21; Quimby 1966:9, 92–93; and Griffin 1961:38.

12. Quimby 1943.

13. Holmes 1906:99 and Mooney 1965:185.

14. E.g., Willoughby 1897:10 and 1932:45 and Wilson 1894:894.

15. Swanton 1946:502 and Howard 1968:44.

16. Howard 1968:45 and Witthoft 1949:55.

17. Phillips 1984:23–24 and Skinner 1921:47–48.

18. Swanton 1946:689 and Battle 1922:181.

19. E.g., Hallowell 1926:34, Brannon 1923:41, Spier 1921:469, and Swanton 1946:566–67.

Chapter 3. Meaning and Significance in Material

1. Swanton 1946:499, 526–28 and Bushnell 1916:35.

2. See Emmons, 1908, Mauss 1967:114, and Rickard 1939.

3. E.g., Stelle 1871:414, Webb and DeJarnette 1942:27, and Webb 1939:27.

4. The distinctive characteristics and relative strength of quartz crystals, as opposed to the mineral substances in which they are often found, may also account in part for the special significance accorded these crystals in many Native American cultures.

5. Quimby 1966:76, Rickard 1934:223, and Blue 1894:63.

6. Drier and Du Temple 1961:21, 70 and Griffin 1961:58, pl. xiii, 63.

7. Drier and Du Temple 1961:42 and Griffin 1961:57, 61.

8. Shetrone and Greenman 1931:378, Willoughby and Hooton 1922:47, and Moorehead 1922:128.

9. E.g., Moore 1905a:145–57, 217 and 1907:402.

10. These last comments are not intended to be specifically descriptive of the burial arrangements for a majority of prehistoric native North Americans, but are intended, rather, to give a general impression of the contrast between the individuals buried in mounds or other special burial areas and the average members of the cultures involved.

11. E.g., Moorehead 1922:94, 12 and Shetrone 1930:211.

12. Hariot 1893:30, Smith 1912:162 and 1884:xlix–1, Barlowe 1906:232, and Strachey 1849:57–58.

13. Swanton 1946:501, Percy 1969:137, Squier and Davis 1848:205, Amadas n.d.:125, and Castaneda 1907:337.

14. Smith 1907:114–16 and 1884:cv–cvi.

15. Hariot 1893:385, Smith 1907:104, and Strachey 1849:89.

16. This coincidence of use and probable significance has been noted by a number of scholars, Pickett 1851:85–87 and Howard 1968:68–69, for example.

17. Strachey 1849:103 and Smith 1907:166.

18. Swanton 1946:490–91 and Strachey 1849:113.

19. Apparently brass came to be accorded much the same significance as copper, a likelihood reinforced by the linguistic evidence cited above.

20. It is also significant that, in some cases, items made from copper and brass kettles are common only in the Early and Middle Historic Periods, indicating a loss of interest and/or supply in later times (Quimby 1960:10, 72).

21. E.g., Shetrone 1926:60, Mills 1916:341, Perino 1968:41, and Griffin et al 1969:30.

22. The capacity for this material to spawn beliefs regarding its supernatural powers is apparent even in modern American society. Essentially based on its electrical conductivity, a brisk trade continues in copper bracelets (even gold plated ones) worn to ward off and bring relief from arthritis, despite the repeated debunking of such use by modern medical science.

Chapter 4. Copper: Its Ceremonial Role

1. E.g., Bennett 1968, Caldwell 1968, Goad 1978, Porter 1969, Seeman 1979, Struever and Houart 1972, and Winter 1968.

2. For example, Waring and Holder 1945:30 and Howard 1968:7. On the other hand, Krieger (1945:486) would probably disagree with this interpretation and those that follow.

3. For examples, see Hittman 1973:248, 251; Spier 1921:500, 512–13; and Benedict 1922:3.

4. For examples, see the references in note 3.

5. See, for example, Waring and Holder 1945:56, Shetrone 1926:219, and Moreau 1951:191.

6. According to Wallace, a revitalization movement is the complex response of any society to factors (largely external) that jeopardize the cultural integrity of the group.

7. Perino 1968:40, Duffield 1964:47, Ford and Willey 1940:124, Kellar et al 1962:351, McGregor 1952:52, Gibbon 1972:249, and Weslager 1942:148–49.

8. E.g., La Barre 1938:113, 115 and Mooney 1965:2, 3, 18, 152–53.

9. E.g. Dragoo 1976:5–6 and Seeman 1979:411.

10. Winter 1968:218, Dragoo 1976:3, and Larson 1971:66–67.

11. Many of Waring's observations on the Southeastern Ceremonial Complex were based upon his sense of the complex as a pan-regional development, a position now discounted by most in the field. However, like Wallace's model, Waring's insights remain valid when reduced in scope and applied to fairly circumscribed and primarily regional manifestations.

12. Waring cites other intriguing information in the same passage, a Creek myth that says cult bringers introduced seven plant/medicines, along with other aspects of ritual. Three of these medicines are said to have been forgotten, lost. In myth surrounding the Creek Tuchabachee copper plates, the cult bringer who remained in the town to teach the new converts eventually died, having taken the "wrong medicine" (Howard 1968:71). I suspect that one of these "lost" medicines was the *amanita muscaria* mushroom, an effective hallucinogen, but only if used very carefully. Other members of the genus are deadly poisonous. Convincing likenesses of this mushroom appear in copperwork central to Mississippian ritual headgear.

13. Howard 1968:61, 78, 81, 86–87, 137, 145 and Swanton 1928a:507–8.

14. Slotkin 1952:573, Barber 1941:673–74, and La Barre 1938:111.

15. E.g., Bittle 1954:69 and Hickerson 1970:52.

16. E.g., Waring and Holder 1945:22 and Howard 1968:88.

17. N.B., at the outset in this study, it was assumed that the Old Copper Culture was largely an independent development. Also, since most Old Copper Culture copperwork consisted of unembellished weaponry, its art historical significance seemed limited at best. Consequently, only a small sample of Old Copper Culture implements were actually examined and the numbers recorded in the tables are accordingly small.

18. Wittry and Ritzenthaler 1957:325 and Funk 1978:23.

19. Griffin 1961:56–58 and Drier and Du Temple 1961:23.

20. E.g., Perino 1968:68, McGregor 1952:52, and Gibbon 1970:142.

21. E.g., Miles 1951:243 and Brose 1970:137.

22. Waring 1968:49, Swanton 1928a:645, Boscana 1970:vii, and Rothenberg 1985:542, 547.

23. An intriguing bit of information offered by Bartram and quoted by Squier and Davis (1848:253) indicates that at least some early linguistic patterns apparently remained current, even when migration forced alteration of the precise application of terms. Bartram noted that certain Florida Indians hunted and ate the aquatic manatee and referred to it as the "big beaver," an animal that was still referred to in traditional lore but which virtually none of them had ever seen.

24. Quimby 1960:25 and Yarnell 1964:142.

25. Drier and Du Temple 1961:30 and Quimby 1954:169–70.

26. E.g., Sears 1971:324–25, Seeman 1979:406–7, Walthall 1972:146, Waring 1968:65, Quimby 1960:49, and McPherron 1967:176.

27. Quimby 1960:45 and Griffin 1961:117.

28. Quimby 1960:20 and Binford and Binford 1968:305–8.

29. E.g., Swartz 1971 and Dragoo 1976.

30. Hurst and Larson 1958:179 and Goad 1978:210–12.

31. Morse et al 1961, Henriksen 1965, Kelly and Neitzel 1961, and Gibbon 1970 and 1972.

32. Quimby 1960:92 and Swanton 1946:495–97.

Appendix

1. Byers 1962:212–13 and Howard 1968:37.

2. Mills 1922a:424 and Shetrone 1926:90.

3. Shetrone and Greenman 1931:390 and the Ohio Historical Center Museum Catalog.

4. Bray 1961:16 and Bluhm 1961:90, 97–98.

5. E.g., Kelly and Neitzel 1961:pl. VIII, fig. A.

Maps and Tables

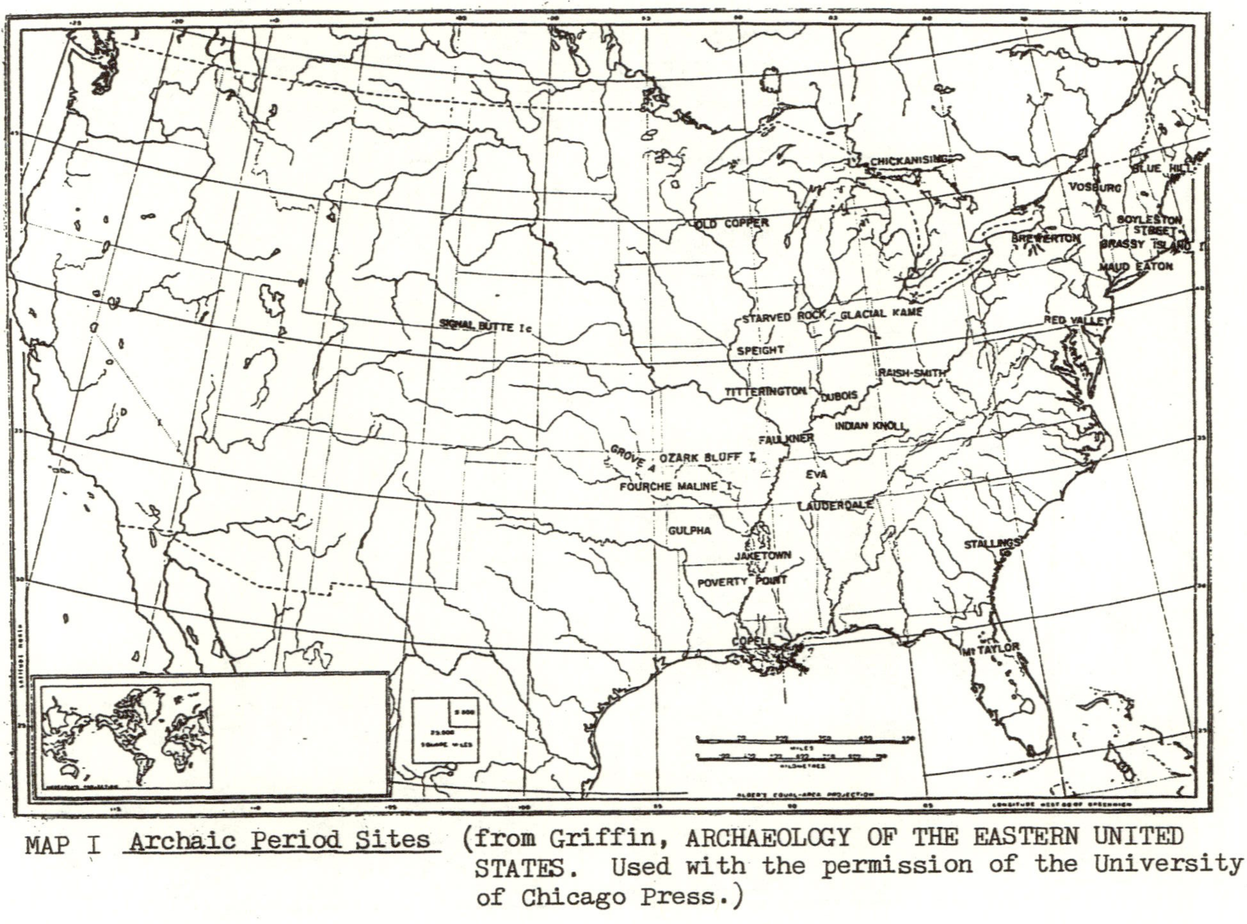

MAP I <u>Archaic Period Sites</u> (from Griffin, ARCHAEOLOGY OF THE EASTERN UNITED STATES. Used with the permission of the University of Chicago Press.)

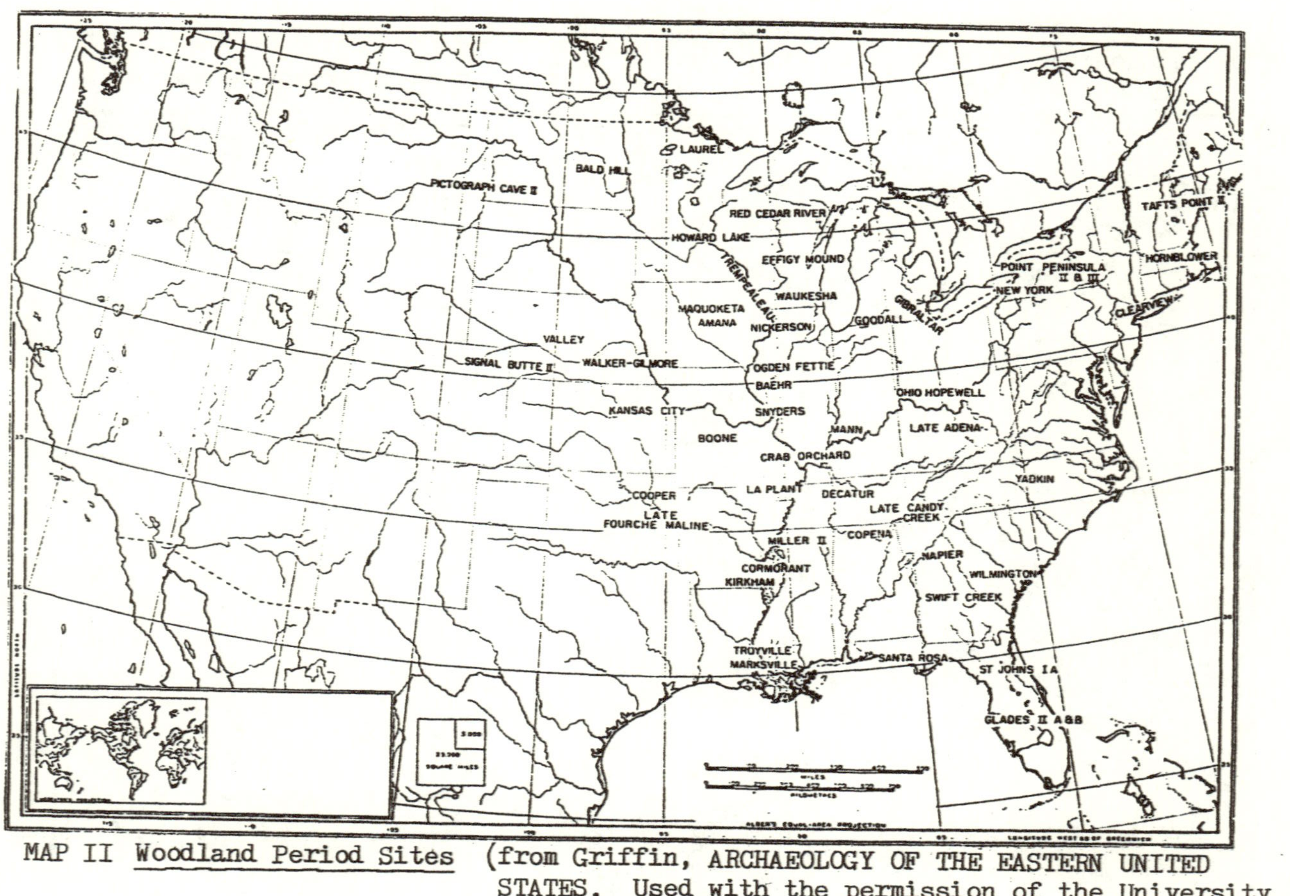

MAP II Woodland Period Sites (from Griffin, ARCHAEOLOGY OF THE EASTERN UNITED STATES. Used with the permission of the University of Chicago Press.)

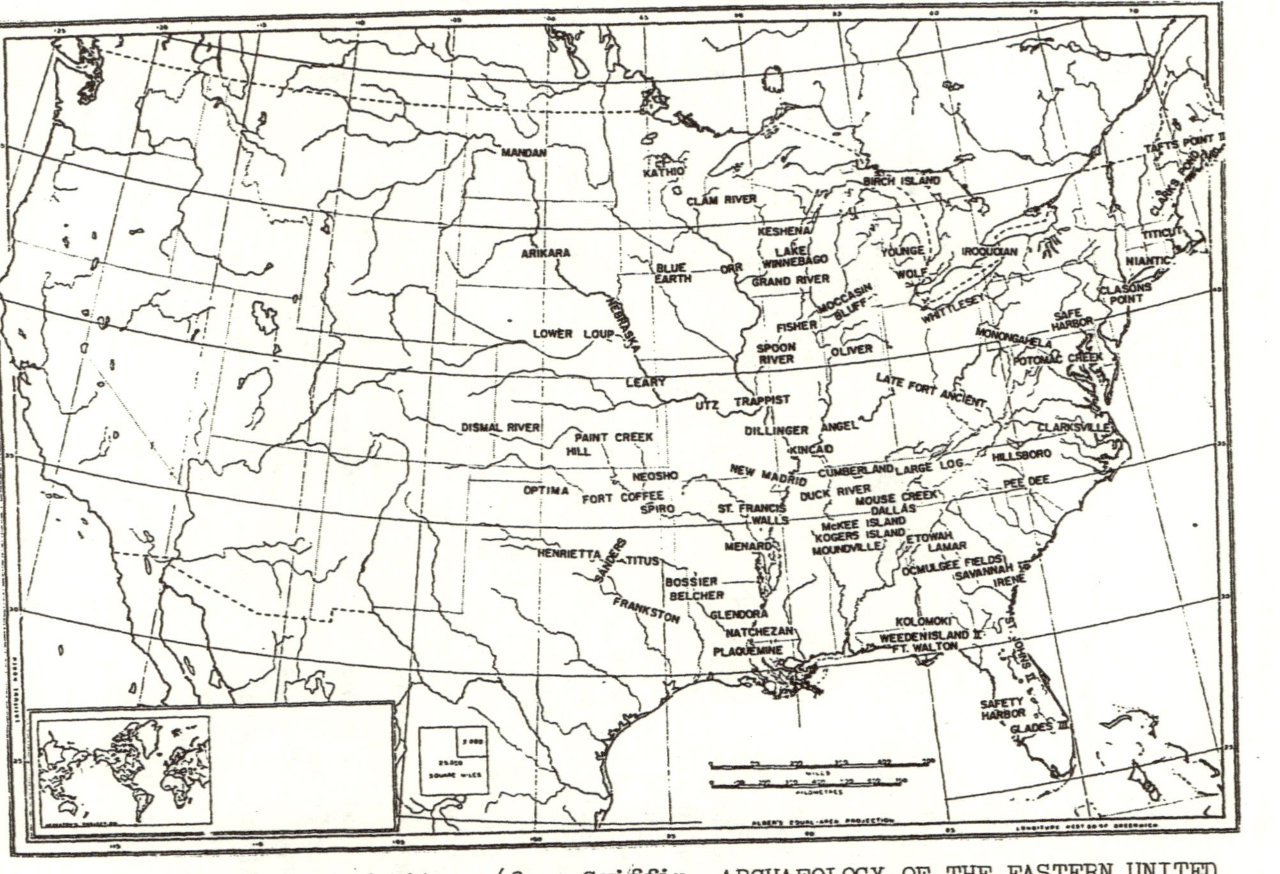

MAP III Mississippian Sites (from Griffin, ARCHAEOLOGY OF THE EASTERN UNITED STATES. Used with the permission of the University of Chicago Press.)

Table I

(Arrangement is according to the size of each group, from the most to the least numerous.)

Object Categories

Category	Number
1. Beads	10,303
2. Points	2,065*
3. Earpieces (Woodland type—all copper)	1,688.5
4. Awls and Pins	923
5. Cut Sheet Copper Designs	556
6. Buttons	457
7. Raw Copper	449
8. Breastplates	382
9. Earpieces (Mississippian type—pulley-shaped)	370
10. Axes	359
11. Bracelets	351
12. Knives	289
13. Adzes	285
14. Headdresses	252
15. Tinklers	176
16. Earpieces (Mississippian type—flat)	170
17. Earpieces (Miscellaneous)	87
18. Applied Copper (other than pipes)	71
19. Panpipes	60
20. Rings	37
21. Applied Copper—Pipes	27
22. Plummets	19

Design Categories

Category	Number
1d. Round, concavo-convex pieces (other than Buttons)	298
2d. Bird Forms	182
3d. Fish, Reptiles, and Marine Univalves	83
4d. Mammal Forms (not human)	67
5d. Human Forms	65
6d. Hook Shapes	65
Miscellaneous Forms and Fragments	1,797

*This number is artificially low. At the outset of the study it was assumed that Old Copper Culture material was not related to later manifestations of the copper complex. Consequently, relatively few examples were examined.

TABLE II

Piece Totals

Arranged Alphabetically and According to Broad Temporal Divisions

	Archaic/ Early Woodland	Middle Woodland	Mississippian to Contact	No Clear Culture or Time Period	Total
Object Categories					
Adzes	146	135	1	3	285
Applied Copper - pipes	---	23	2	2	27
Awls*	689	96	106	32	923
Axes*	117	133	64	45	359
Beads*	3365	5525	417	996	10303
Bracelets	184	67	53	47	351
Breastplates*	11	326	36	9	382
Buttons	---	447	9	1	457
Cut sheet copper forms	30	212	254	60	556
Earpieces: solid copper	4	1683.5	---	1	1688.5
Earpieces: flat with copper overlay	---	---	167	3	170
Earpieces: Pulley type	---	---	368	2	370
Earpieces: miscellaneous	---	6	79	2	87
Fragments	6	196	1204	216	1622
Headdresses	8	50	190	4	252
Knives	257	2	21	9	289
Panpipes	---	60	---	---	60
Plummets	---	15	---	4	19
Points	2050	2	---	12	2064
Raw, unworked copper	353	86	3	7	449
Rings	25	3	3	6	37
Tinklers	1	146	24	5	176
Design Categories					
Bird Forms	1	25	156	---	182
Round, Concavo-convex pieces other than buttons	---	65	222	11	298
Fish, reptile & marine univalve forms	---	75	8	---	83
Hooks	50	4	7	4	65
Human forms	---	4	61	---	65
Mammal forms	---	34	31	2	67
Miscellaneous	69	58	30	18	175
GRAND TOTALS (fragments not included)	7363	9327.5	2333	1287	20310.5
Totals w/beads divided by 10	4334.5	4355	1957.1	390.6	11037.8
Totals, less earpieces	7359	7638	1719	1279	17995
Totals, less earpieces w/beads divided by 10	4330.5	2665.5	1343.1	382.6	8722.3

* Items found in the copper assemblage of every major copperworking group in the prehistory of the eastern United States.

TABLE III

Comparative Copperwork Assemblages by Broad Temporal Divisions

Percentages indicate the relative number of each type of piece found within the total copper assemblage of each division.

	Archaic/Early Woodland		Middle Woodland		Mississippian to Contact	
	% of total pieces	% w/beads divided by 10	% of total pieces	% w/beads divided by 10	% of total pieces	% w/beads divided by 10
Implements (including adzes, awls, axes, hooks, knives, plummets & points):	44.94%	76.34%	4.15%	8.89%	8.53%	10.17%
Copper applied to items made primarily of other materials:	.04%	.07%	6.17%	13.2%	1.37%	1.64%
Simple "ornaments" (beads, bracelets, rings, & tinklers):	48.55%	12.61%	61.55%	17.65%	21.3%	6.22%
Complex "ornaments" (breast-plates, & geometrical or representational designs):	.57%	.97%	7.25%	15.52%	23.4%	27.9%
Earpieces:	.05%	.09%	18.11%	38.79%	26.32%	31.37%
Headdresses:	.11%	.19%	.54%	1.15%	8.14%	9.71%
Miscellaneous:	5.74%	9.73%	2.23%	4.8%	10.94%	12.99%

Bead totals have been divided by 10 since several beads are usually joined to make a single artifact. This division, while arbitrary, brings bead totals into closer and more realistic relationship to totals for other artifacts.

TABLE IV

Number of Pieces with Applied Decoration

			% of Total pieces decorated	% Decorated, less earpieces	% Undecorated
Archaic	40		.68%	.68%	99.32%
Adena	42	(including 4 earpieces; 10 breastplates)	2.63%	2.5%	97.37%
Hopewell	2436	(including 1639 earpieces; 268 breastplates)	29.1%	9.52%	70.9%
Copena	115	(including 46.5* earpieces; 58 breastplates)	9.78%	5.2%	90.22%
Mississippian	1520	(including 602 earpieces; 29 breastplates)	49.56%	29.98%	50.44%
Post-Mississippian	101	(including 5 earpieces; 4 breastplates)	21.49%	21.49%	78.51%
TOTAL	4254	(2296.5 earpieces; 369 breastplates)			

20.94% of all pieces examined include applied decoration.

*Designs, as described in Chapter IV and applied according to criteria listed on pages 140-141.

TABLE V

Number of Pieces with Applied Decoration

Late Archaic/Early Woodland	82	(4 earpieces, 2 breastplates)
Middle Woodland	2551	(1685.5 earpieces, 326 breastplates)
Mississippian to Contact	1621	(607 earpieces, 33 breastplates)

	% of total pieces decorated	% decorated, less beads divided by 10	% decorated less earpieces	% Undecorated
Late Archaic/ Early Woodland	1.11%	1.89%	1.11%	98.89%
Middle Woodland	27.35%	58.58%	9.28%	72.65%
Mississippian to Contact	69.48%	30.35%	43.46%	30.52%

Table VI

DESIGN USE CAVEAT

It should be noted that in order to classify and organize the data for this study, design types were identified and counted with great care. The figures found in the various tables and within the body of the paper are derived from this count. However, because it is clear that many of the motifs probably represent complex concepts with levels of meaning that go well beyond the specific form of the design (even when the subject matter appears to be representational) the precise identification of such motifs is a complex problem. Many fit into more than one category of symbolic identification—composite imagery, for example. To avoid the arbitrary assignment of identity to such forms as bird/human combinations, individual pieces were often categorized under more than one classification. The validity of this approach is supported by the fact that the significance of these representations for the people who made the copperwork was undoubtedly multifaceted as well. As a result of this situation, however, it must be remembered that the percentage figures comparing types of designs are not absolute but, rather, are intended to give a rough idea of the relative importance of each design configuration within the corpus.

Design Usage

Percentages refer to the percent of decorated items that incorporated each type of design within the assemblage of each generalized culture group.

	Late Archaic/ Early Woodland		Middle Woodland		Mississippian to Contact		% of Total
	Archaic	Adena	Hopewell	Copena	Mississippian	Post Mississippian	corpus *
Cross	X	X	1.35%	X	7.37%	3.96%	2.05%
Sunburst	X	X	.9 %	X	3.42%	X	1.02%
Swastika	X	X	.12%	X	2.17%	X	.495%
Spiral	12.5%	16.67%	1.07%	X	2.43%	2.13%	1.29%
Circle	25 %	X	74.1 %	47.75%	58.49%	11.88%	38.22%
Concentric	X	X	68.76%	49.55%	29.74%	21.78%	30.61%
Crescent	25 %	4.76%	1.31%	X	1.84%	X	1.03%
Rectangle	27.5%	50 %	12.52%	2.7 %	2.57%	21.78%	5.68%
Reel	X	19.05%	.78%	50.45%	.46%	X	1.24%
Implement forms	10 %	19.05%	1.72%	X	17.5 %	8.91%	4.63%
Bird forms	2.5 %	X	.41%	X	4.15%	17.82%	5.17%
Fish, reptile & marine univalve forms	X	X	3.28%	X	1.71%	7.92%	1.58%
Human forms	X	X	.37%	X	13.82%	X	3.01%
Mammal forms	2.5 %	4.76%	3.90%	X	4.08%	X	2.27%
Miscellaneous	15 %	2.38%	4.02%	X	1.05%	5.94%	1.87%

* Total instances of design types applied within the corpus - 7272

TABLE VII

Relative Design Type Usages: Percent of Instances of Specific Designs Applied to the Copperwork of Generalized Culture Groups

	Over 50%	30-50%	20-29.99%	10-19.99%	5-9.99%	2-4.99%	up to 2%	None
Archaic			Rectangle Circle Crescent	Misc. Spiral Implement		Bird Mammal		Concentric Cross Human Reel Reptile, etc. Sunburst Swastika
Adena		Rectangle		Implement Reel Spiral		Crescent Mammal Miscellaneous		Bird Circle Concentric Cross Human Reptile, etc. Sunburst Swastika
Hopewell	Circle Concentric			Rectangle		Misc. Mammal Reptile, etc.	Implement Cross Crescent Spiral Sunburst Reel Bird Human Swastika	
Copena	Reel	Concentric Circle				Rectangle		Bird Crescent Cross Human Implement Mammal Miscellaneous Reptile, etc. Spiral Sunburst Swastika

TABLE VII (continued)

Relative Design Type Usages: Percent of Instances of Specific Designs Applied to the Copperwork of Generalized Culture Groups

	Over 50%	30-50%	20-29.99%	10-19.99%	5-9.99%	2-4.99%	up to 2%	None
Mississippian	Circle		Concentric	Implement Human	Cross	Bird Mammal Sunburst Rectangle Spiral Swastika	Crescent Reptile, etc. Miscellaneous Reel	
Post-Mississippian			Concentric Rectangle	Bird Circle	Implement Reptile, etc. Misc.	Cross		Crescent Human Mammal Reel Spiral Sunburst Swastika

* Designs listed in each percentage column in the relative order of numerical importance, most numerous to least numerous instances.

TABLE VIII

Percent of Design Types Found in the Work of Generalized Culture Groups

	Archaic	Adena	Hopewell*	Copena*	Mississippian*	Post-Mississippian
Cross	X	X	4.12%	X	11.93%	3.96%
Sunburst	X	X	2.76%	X	5.53%	X
Swastika	X	X	.38%	X	3.56%	X
Spiral	12.5 %	16.67%	3.26%	X	4 %	X
Circle	25 %	X	20.83%	1.695%	31.26%	11.88%
Concentric	X	X	4.52%	5.09%	10.46%	21.78%
Crescent	25 %	4.76%	4.02%	X	3.05%	21.78%
Rectangle	27.5%	50 %	38.27%	5.09%	4.25%	21.78%
Reel	X	19.05%	2.38%	94.92%	.76%	X
Implement forms	10 %	19.05%	5.27%	X	29.98%	8.91%
Bird forms	2.5 %	X	1.26%	X	6.86%	17.82%
Fish, reptile, marine univalve forms	X	X	10.04%	X	2.38%	7.92%
Human forms	X	X	1.13%	X	22.88%	X
Mammal forms	2.5 %	4.76%	11.92%	X	6.75%	X

Total instances of design (without earpieces designated either circular or concentric): 3274.

X no examples of this design type.

* without earpieces

TABLE IX

Relative Design Type Usages: Percent of Instances of Specific Designs Applied to the Copperwork of Generalized Culture Groups Excluding Circular and Concentric Earpiece Designs*

	Over 50%	30-50%	20-29.99%	10-19.99%	5-9.99%	2-4.99%	up to 2%	None
Archaic			Rectangle Circle Crescent	Misc. Spiral Implement		Bird Mammal		Concentric Cross Human Reel Reptile, etc. Sunburst Swastika
Adena		Rectangle		Implement Reel Spiral		Crescent Mammal Miscellaneous		Bird Circle Concentric Cross Human Reptile, etc. Sunburst Swastika
Hopewell		Rectangle	Circle	Misc. Mammal Reptile, etc.	Implement	Concentric Cross Crescent Spiral Sunburst Reel	Bird Human Swastika	
Copena	Reel				Concentric Rectangle		Circle	Bird Crescent Cross Human Implement Mammal Miscellaneous Reptile, etc. Spiral Sunburst Swastika

TABLE IX (continued)

Relative Design Type Usages: Percent of Instances of Specific Designs Applied to the Copperwork of Generalized Culture Groups Excluding Circular and Concentric Earpiece Designs*

	Over 50%	30-50%	20-29.99%	10-19.99%	5-9.99%	2-4.99%	up to 2%	None
Mississippian	Circle		Implement Human	Cross Concentric	Bird Mammal Sunburst	Rectangle Spiral Swastika Crescent Reptile, etc.	Miscellaneous Reel	
Post-Mississippian			Concentric Rectangle	Bird Circle	Implement Reptile, etc. Misc.	Cross		Crescent Human Mammal Reel Spiral

* Designs listed in each percentage column in the relative order of numerical importance, most numerous to least numerous instances.

Bibliography

Adair, James. 1930. *The History of the American Indians.* Samuel Cole Williams, editor. Johnson City, Tenn.: Wautauga Press.

Adams, C. 1972. The Scott's Site Copper Eagle. *Central States Archaeological Journal,* vol 19, no. 4.

Adams, W.H. 1880. Mounds in the Spoon River Valley Illinois. *Annual Report of the Smithsonian Institution for the Year 1879.* Washington, D.C.

Aitchison, Leslie. 1960. *A History of Metals: Vols. I & II.* New York: Interscience Publishers.

Amadas, Philip and Arthur Barlow. N.d. The First Voyage Made to the Coast of Virginia, 1584. In *Hakluyt's Voyages,* vol. 6. New York: E.P. Dutton and Co.

Anderson, Richard L. 1979. *Art in Primitive Societies.* Englewood Cliffs, New Jersey: Prentice-Hall, Inc.

Baerreis, David A. 1957. The Southern Cult and the Spiro Ceremonial Complex. *Bulletin of the Oklahoma Anthropological Society,* vol. 5. Oklahoma City.

Baerreis, David A., Hiroshi Daifuku, and James E. Fittin. 1957. The Burial Complex of the Reigh Site, Winnebago Co., Wisconsin. *Wisconsin Archaeologist,* vol. 38, no.4.

Baerreis, David A., and Reid A. Bryson. 1965. Climatic Episodes and the Dating of the Mississippian Cultures. *Wisconsin Archaeologist,* vol. 46, no.4.

Bailey, Francis. 1856. *Journal of a Tour in Unsettled Parts of North America in 1796 and 1797.* London: Baily.

Barber, James. 1941. Socio-cultural Interpretation of the Peyote Cult. *American Anthropologist* 43:673.

Barlowe, William. 1906. Early English and French Voyages: 1534–1608. In *Original Narratives of Early Americans History.* Henry S. Barrage, ed., New York.

Bartram, William. 1942. Travels in Georgia and Florida 1773–4, A Report to Dr. John Fothergill. Frances Harper, editor. *Transactions of the American Philosophical Society,* no. 33.

———. 1853. Observations on the Creek and Cherokee Indians. *American Ethnological Society Transactions,* vol. 3, no. 1. New York.

———. 1791. *Travels Through North and South Carolina, Georgia, East and West Florida, The Cherokee Country, The Extensive Territories of the Muscogulges or Creek Confederacy and the Country of the Choctaws.*

Battle, Herbert B. 1922. The Domestic Use of Oil Among the Southern Aborigines. *American Anthropologist,* vol. 24, no. 3.

Beauchamp, W.M. 1903. Metallic Ornaments of the New York Indians. *New York State Museum Bulletin,* vol. 73. New York.

Bell, Robert E. and Robert J. Block. 1972. A Copper Spearhead from Wisconsin in Oklahoma. *Plains Anthropologist,* vol. 17, no. 55.

Benedict, Ruth Fulton. 1922. The Vision in Plains Culture. *American Anthropologist,* vol. 24, no. 1.

Bennett, J.W. 1968. Reciprocal Economic Exchanges Among North American Agricultural Operators. *Southwestern Journal of Anthropology,* vol. 4, no. 3.

Bettarel, Robert Louis, and Hale G. Smith. 1973. The Moccasin Bluff Site and the Woodland Cultures of Southwestern Michigan. *Anthropological Papers,* no. 49. Museum of Anthropology, University of Michigan, Ann Arbor.

Binford, Sally R., and Lewis R. Binford. 1968. *New Perspectives in Archaeology.* Chicago: Aldine Publishing Co.

Bittle, William E. 1954. The Peyote Ritual: Kiowa-Apache. *Bulletin of the Oklahoma Anthropological Society,* vol. 2.

Blakely, Robert L., ed. 1977. *Biocultural Adaptation in Prehistoric America.* Southern Anthropological Society Proceedings, no. 11. Athens, Ga.: University of Georgia Press.

Blue, A. 1894. Mine Report. *Third Report of the Bureau of Mines, 1893.* Toronto.

Bluhm, Elaine A. 1961. The Anker Site in Chicago Area Archaeology. *Illinois Archaeological Survey Bulletin,* vol. 3. Urbana.

———. 1960. The Excavation of Three Hopewell Mounds at the Caterpillar Tractor Company in *Indian Mounds and Villages in Illinois, Illinois Archaeological Survey Bulletin,* vol. 2. Urbana.

Boas, Franz. 1940. *Race, Language and Culture.* New York: Free Press.

———. 1928. *Primitive Art.* Cambridge: Howard University Press.

Boscana, Geronimo. 1970. *Chinigchinich.* Andrew Rolle, translator. Santa Barbara, Calif.: Peregrine Smith, Inc.

Bradley, James W., and S. Terry Childs. 1991. Basque Earrings and Panther's Tails: The Form of Cross-Cultural Contact in 16th Century Iroquoia. *Metals in Society: Theory Beyond Analysis.* Robert M. Ehrenreich, ed. MASCA Research Papers in Science and Archaeology, vol. 8, part 3. Philadelphia: The University Museum, University of Pennsylvania.

Bradley, Kenneth. 1952. *Copper Venture.* London: Max Parrish and Co., Ltd.

Brandon, William. 1965. American Indians and American History. *The American West,* vol. 2, no. 2.

Brannon, Peter A. 1923. The Tuckabatchee Plates. *Arrowpoints,* vol. 7, no. 3. Montgomery, Alabama.

Braun, David P. 1988. Midwestern Hopewellian Exchange and Supralocal Interaction. In *Peer Polity Interaction and Sociopolitical Change,* Colin Renfrew and John F. Cherry, ed. Cambridge University Press.

Bray, Robert T. 1961. The Flynn Cemetery: an Orr Focus Oneota Burial Site in Allamakee County, Iowa. *Journal of the Iowa Archaeological Society,* vol. 10, no. 4. Iowa City.

Brose, David S. 1984. Mississippian Period Cultures in Northwestern Florida. *Perspectives in Gulf Coast Prehistory.* Dave D. Davis, ed. Gainesville: University Presses of Florida.

———. 1984a. From the Southeastern Ceremonial Complex to the Southern Cult: You Can't Tell the Players Without a Program. *The Southeastern Ceremonial Complex: Artifacts and Analysis,* Patricia Galloway, ed. Lincoln: University of Nebraska Press.

———. 1970. The Archaeology of Summer Island: Changing Settlement Systems in Northern Lake Michigan. *Museum of Anthropology, University of Michigan, Anthropological Papers,* vol. 41.

Brown, James A. 1976. The Southern Cult Reconsidered. *Midcontinental Journal of Archaeology*, vol. 1, no. 2. Kent, Ohio: Kent State University.

———. 1976a. The Artifacts. *Spiro Studies*, vol. 4. Norman, Okla.: Stovall Museum of Science and History, University of Oklahoma.

———. 1971. Approaches to the Social Dimensions of Mortuary Practices. *Memoirs of the Society for American Archaeology*, vol. 25.

Bryson, Reid A., and Thomas J. Murray. 1977. *Climates of Hunger: Mankind and the World's Changing Weather.* Madison: University of Wisconsin Press.

Buikstra, Jane E. 1977. Biocultural Dimensions of Archaeological Study: A Regional Perspective. *Biocultural Adaptation in Prehistoric America.* Southern Anthropological Society Proceedings, no. 11. Athens, Ga.: University of Georgia Press.

Bullen, Ripley P. 1951. The Terra Ceia Site, Manatee County, Florida. *Florida Anthropological Society Publications*, no. 3. Gainesville.

Burnett, E.K., and Forrest Clements. 1945. The Spiro Mound Collection in the Museum. *Contributions of the Museum of the American Indian-Heye Foundation*, vol. 14.

Bushnell, David I. Jr. 1920. Native Ceremonies and Forms of Burial East of the Mississippi. *Bureau of American Ethnology*, bulletin 71.

———. 1916. Aboriginal Forms of Burial in the Eastern United States. In *Holmes Anniversary Volume: Anthropological Essays.* Washington, D.C.

Byers, Douglas S. 1962. The Restoration and Preservation of Some Objects from Etowah. *American Antiquity*, vol. 28. no. 2.

Byington, Cyrus. 1915. A Dictionary of the Chocktaw Language. *U.S. Bureau of American Ethnology*, Bulletin 46. Washington, D.C.

Caldwell, Joseph R. 1968. Interaction Spheres in Prehistory in Hopewellian Studies. Joseph R. Caldwell and Robert L. Hall, editors. *Illinois State Museum Scientific Papers*, vol. 12. Springfield.

Cartier, Jacques. 1924. The Voyages. *Publications of the Public Archives of Canada*, no. 11. H.P. Biggar, editor. Ottawa.

Castaneda, Pedro de. 1907. The Narrative of the Expedition of Coronado. In *Spanish Explorers in the Southern United States.* F.W. Hodge and T.H. Lewis, editors. New York.

Chapman, Jefferson. 1985. *Tellico Archaeology: 12,000 Years of Native American Archaeology.* Report of Investigations no. 43, Department of Anthropology. University of Tennessee, Knoxville.

Charles, Douglas K., Steven R. Leigh, and Jane E. Buikstra, eds. 1988. *The Archaic and Woodland Cemeteries at the Elizabeth Site in the Lower Illinois Valley.* Center for American Archaeology, Kampsville Archaeological Center, Kampsville, Illinois.

Childs, S. Terry. 1991. Iron as Utility or Expression: Reforging Function in Africa. *Metals in Society: Theory Beyond Analysis.* Robert M. Ehrenreich, ed. MASCA Research Papers in Science and Archaeology, vol. 8, part 3. Philadelphia: The University Museum, University of Pennsylvania.

Chomko, Stephen A., and Gary W. Crawford. 1978. Plant Husbandry in Prehistoric Eastern North America: New Evidence for Its Development. *American Antiquity*, vol. 43. Menasha, Wisconsin.

Cleland, Charles E. 1976. The Focal-Diffuse Model: An Evolutionary Perspective on the Prehistoric Cultural Adaptations of the Eastern United States. *Midcontinental Journal of Archaeology*, vol. 1 no. 1. Kent, Ohio: Kent State University Press.

Clifton, James A. 1978. Potowatomi. In *Handbook of North American Indians: Northeast*, vol. 15. Bruce Trigger, vol. ed. Washington, D.C.: Smithsonian Institution.

Coe, Ralph T. 1976. *Sacred Circles: Two Thousand Years of North American Indian Art.* Arts Council of Great Britain.

Cole, Fay-Cooper, and Thorne Deuel. 1937. *Rediscovering Illinois: Archaeological Explorations In and Around Fulton County.* Chicago, Ill.: University of Chicago Press.

Crumley, Carole S. 1973. The Kantzler Site (20 By 30): A Multi-component Woodland Site in Bay County, Michigan. *The Michigan Archaeologist,* vol. 19, nos. 3 and 4.

Douglas, Frederic H., and Rene d'Harnoncourt. 1941. *Indian Art of the United States.* New York: The Museum of Modern Art.

Downing, A. 1895. The Cherokee Indians and Their Neighbors. *American Antiquarian and Oriental Journal,* vol. 17. Chicago.

Dragoo, Donald W. 1976. Adena and the Eastern Burial Cult. *Archaeology of Eastern North America,* vol. 4. Eastern States Archaeological Federation.

———. 1963. Mounds for the Dead: An Analysis of the Adena Culture. *Annals of the Carnegie Museum,* vol. 37. Pittsburgh.

Drier, Roy W. 1961. The Michigan College of Mining and Technology Isle Royale Excavations, 1953–1954 in *Lake Superior Copper: Miscellaneous Studies of Great Lakes Prehistory,* James B. Griffin, editor. *Anthropological Papers,* no. 17, Museum of Anthropology, University of Michigan, Ann Arbor.

Drier, Roy W., and Octave J. Du Temple. 1961. *Prehistoric Copper Mining in the Lake Superior Region: A Collection of Reference Articles.* Drier and Du Temple.

Duffield, Lathal F. 1964. Engraved Shells from the Craig Mound at Spiro, LeFlore County, Oklahoma. *Oklahoma Archaeological Society, Memoir no. 1.*

Edmunds, R. David. 1983. *The Shawnee Prophet.* Lincoln, Nebr.: University of Nebraska Press.

Emmons, George T. 1908. Copper Neck Rings of Southern Alaska. *American Anthropologist,* vol. 10.

Emmons, W.H., and F.B. Lanery. 1926. Geology and Ore Deposits of the Ducktown Mining District, Tennessee. *U.S. Geological Survey Professional Paper 139.* Washington, D.C.

Fairbanks, Charles H. 1956. Archaeology of the Funeral Mound, Ocmulgee National Monument, Georgia. *U.S. National Park Service Archaeological Research Series,* no. 3.

Farquharson, R.J. 1875. Recent Archaeological Discoveries at Davenport, Iowa of Copper Axes, Cloth, etc. *Proceedings of the Davenport Academy of Natural Science.*

Finkelstein, J.J. 1940. The Norman Site Near Wagoner, Oklahoma. *The Oklahoma Prehistorian,* vol. 3, no. 3.

Firth, Raymond. 1966. The Social Framework of Primitive Art. In *The Many Faces of Primitive Art,* Douglas Fraser, editor. Englewood Cliffs, N.J.: Prentice-Hall.

Fogel, Ira L. 1963. The Dispersal of Copper Artifacts in the Late Archaic Period of Prehistoric North America. *Wisconsin Archaeologist,* vol. 44, no. 3. Milwaukee.

———. 1952. Measurements of Some Prehistoric Design Elements in the Southeastern United States. *Anthropological Papers of the American Museum of Natural History,* vol. 44, part 3.

Ford, James A., and Clarence H. Webb. 1956. Poverty Point, A Late Archaic Site in Louisiana. *Anthropological Papers of the American Museum of Natural History.* vol. 46, part 1. New York.

Ford, James A. and Gordon R. Willey. 1941. An Interpretation of the Prehistory of the Eastern United States. *American Anthropologist,* vol. 43.

———. 1940. The Crooks Site, a Mardsville Period Burial Mound in LaSalle Parish,

Louisiana. *Anthropological Study Number 5,* Department of Conversation, Louisiana Ecological Survey, New Orleans.

Foster, J.W., and J.S. Whitney. 1850. Report on the Geology and Topography of a Portion of the Lake Superior Land District in the State of Michigan. *Executive Document 69, House of Representatives.* 1st Congress, 1st Session. Washington, D.C.

Fowler, Melvin L. 1957. Rutherford Mound, Hardin County, Illinois. *Illinois State Museum Scientific Papers,* vol. 7, no. 1. Springfield.

Fundaburk, Emma Lila, and M.D.F. Foreman. 1957. *Sun Circles and Human Hands.* Luverne, Ala.: Fundaburk.

Funk, Robert E. 1978. Post-Pleistocene Adaptations. In *Handbook of North American Indians: Northeast,* vol. 15. Bruce Trigger, vol. ed. Washington, D.C.

Furst, Peter T., and Jill L. Furst. 1982. *North American Indian Art.* New York: Rizzoli International Publications, Inc.

Galloway, Patricia, ed. 1984. *The Southeastern Ceremonial Complex: Artifacts and Analysis, The Cottonlandia Conference.* Lincoln, Nebr.: University of Nebraska Press.

Geertz, Clifford. 1973. *The Interpretation of Cultures.* New York: Basic Books.

Gibbon, Guy. 1972. The Walker-Hooper Site: A Grand River Phase Oneota Site in Green Lake County. *Wisconsin Archaeologist,* vol. 53, no. 4.

Gibbon, Guy. 1970. The Midway Village Site: An Orr Phase Oneota Site in the Upper Mississippi River Valley. *Wisconsin Archaeologist,* vol. 51, no. 3.

Gibson, Edmond P. 1954. Ancient Mounds near Grand Rapids in the Lower Grand River Valley in Southwestern Michigan. *Michigan Archaeological Society News,* vol. 1, no. 3.

Goad, Sharon I. 1980. Patterns of Late Archaic Exchange. *Tennessee Archaeologist,* vol. 5, no. 1, pp. 1–16.

Goad, Sharon. 1978. *Exchange Networks in the Prehistoric Eastern United States.* Unpublished Ph.D. dissertation. Department of Anthropology. University of Georgia.

Greenlee, Robert F. 1944. Medicine and Curing Practices of the Modern Florida Seminoles. *American Anthropologist,* vol. 46, no. 3.

Griffin, James B. 1978. The Midlands and Northeastern United States. *Ancient Native Americans,* Jesse D. Jennings, ed. San Francisco: W.H. Freeman and Co.

———. 1976. The Ancient Midwest—Twelve Thousand Years. In *Art of the First Americans.* Cincinnati Art Museum.

———. 1965. Hopewell and the Dark Black Glass. *The Michigan Archaeologist,* vol. 11, nos. 3–4, Ann Arbor.

———. 1961. Contributions on Isle Royale Prehistory. In *Prehistoric Copper Mining in the Lake Superior Region: A Collection of Reference Articles.* Roy W. Drier and Octave J. Du Temple, editors. Drier and Du Temple. Calumet, Michigan.

______. 1960. Climatic Change: A Contributory Cause of Growth and Decline of Northern Hopewell Culture. *Wisconsin Archaeologist,* vol. 41, no. 2.

______. 1949. Meso-America and the Southeast: A Commentary. *The Florida Indian and His Neighbors,* J.B. Griffin, ed. Inter-American Center, Rollins College, Winter Park, Florida.

______. 1944. The de Luna Expedition and the "Buzzard Cult" in the Southeast. *Journal of the Washington Academy of Sciences,* vol. 34.

Griffin, James B., editor. 1961. Lake Superior Copper and the Indians: Miscellaneous Studies of Great Lakes Prehistory. *Anthropological Papers, Museum of Anthropology,* University of Michigan, Ann Arbor.

Griffin, James B., A.A. Gordus, and G.A. Wright. 1969. Identification of the Sources of Hopewellian Obsidian in the Middle-West. *American Antiquity,* vol. 34. no. 1.

Grosvenor, A.W., editor. 1962. *Basic Metallurgy Vol. I: Principles.* American Society for Metals. Metals Park, Ohio.

Haberland, Wolfgang. 1964. *The Art of North America.* New York: Crown Publishers, Inc.

Hall, Robert L. 1991. Cahokia Identity and Interaction Models of Cahokia Mississippians. *Cahokia and the Hinterlands: Middle Mississippian Cultures of the Midwest.* Thomas E. Emerson and R. Barry Lewis, eds. Urbana: University of Illinois Press.

———. 1977. An Anthropocentric Perspective for Eastern United States Prehistory. *American Antiquity,* vol. 42, no. 4.

Hallowell, A. Irving. 1975. Ojibwa Ontology, Behavior and World View. In *Teachings from the American Earth.* Dennis and Barbara Tedlock, editors. New York: Liverwright.

———. 1926. Bear Ceremonialism in the Western Hemisphere. *American Anthropology,* vol. 28.

Hamilton, Henry W. 1952. The Spiro Mound. *The Missouri Archaeologist,* vol. 14.

Hamilton, Henry W., et al. 1974. Spiro Mound Copper. *Missouri Archaeological Society,* no. 11.

Hariot, Thomas. 1893. *Narrative of the First English Plantation of Virginia.* Reprint. London.

Harn, Alan D. 1971. The Prehistory of Dickson Mounds: A Preliminary Report. *Dickson Mounds Museum Anthropological Studies,* no. 1. Springfield.

Harrington, M.R. 1920. An Archaic Iowa Tomahawk. *Indian Notes and Monographs.* New York: Museum of the American Indian-Heye Foundation.

Henriksen, Harry C. 1965. Utica Hopewell, A Study of Early Hopewellian Occupation in the Illinois River Valley. *Middle Woodland Sites in Illinois,* Bulletin 5. Urbana: Illinois Archaeological Society.

Hickerson, Harold. 1970. *The Chippewa and Their Neighbors: A Study in Ethnology.* New York: Holt, Rinehart and Winston, Inc.

Hittman, M. 1973. 1870 Ghost Dance at the Walker River Reservation. *Ethnohistory,* vol. 20.

Holmes, William H. 1906. On the Origin of the Cross Symbol. *Proceedings of the American Antiquarian Society.*

Howard, James H. 1968. The Southeastern Ceremonial Complex and Its Interpretation. *Missouri Archaeological Society,* Memoir, no. 6. Columbia.

Howard, James H. 1960. When They Worship the Underwater Panther: A Prairie Potowatomi Bundle Ceremony. *Southwestern Journal of Anthropology,* vol 16, no. 2.

Hurst, V.S. and L.H. Larson Jr. 1958. On the Source of Copper at the Etowah Site, Georgia. *American Anthropologist,* vol. 24, no. 2.

Jeffries, Richard W. 1976. The Tunacunnhee Site: Evidence of Hopewell Interaction in Northwest Georgia. *Anthropological Papers of the University of Georgia,* no. 1.

Jennings, Jesse D. 1978. *Ancient Native Americans.* San Francisco: W.H. Freeman and Co.

Jones, B. Calvin. 1982. Southern Cult Manifestations at the Lake Jackson Site, Leon County, Florida: Salvage Excavation of Mound 3. *Midcontinental Journal of Archaeology,* vol. 7, no. 1.

Jopling, Carol F. 1989. *The Coppers of the Northwest Coast Indians.* Transactions of the American Philosophical Society, vol.79, part 1.

Juet, Robert. 1841. Journal of the Voyage of the Half-Moon. In *Collection of the New York Historical Society,* 2nd series, vol. 1.

Kavolis, V.M. 1972. *History on Art's Side: Social Dynamics of Artistic Efflorescences.* Ithaca, N.Y.: Cornell University Press.

Kellar, James H., A.R. Kelly, and Edward V. McMichael. 1962. The Mandeville Site in Southwest Georgia. *American Antiquity,* vol. 27, no. 3, Salt Lake City.

Kelly, A.R. 1954. Etowah, An Ancient Culture Center in Georgia. *Archaeology,* vol. 7, no. 1.

Kelly, A.R., and R.S. Neitzel. 1961. The Chauga Site in Oconee County, South Carolina. *University of Georgia Laboratory of Archaeology Series,* Report no. 3. Athens.

Kelly, A.R., and Lewis H. Larson Jr. 1957. Explorations at Etowah, Georgia 1954–1956. *Archaeology,* vol. 10, no. 1. Brattleboro, Vermont.

Kneberg, Madeline. 1959. Engraved Shell Gorgets and Their Associations. *Tennessee Archaeologist,* vol. 15, no. 1.

Krickeberg, Walter. 1968. *Pre-Columbian American Religions.* Holt, Rinehart and Winston. New York.

Krieger, A.D. 1945. An Inquiry into Supposed Mexican Influences on a Prehistoric Cult in the Southeastern United States. *American Anthropologist,* vol. 47, no. 4, Menasha.

La Barre, Weston. 1938. The Peyote Cult. *Yale University Publication in Anthropology,* no. 19. Yale University Press.

Lane, Ralph. 1965. An Account of the Particularities of the employments of the Englishmen left in Virginia by Sir Richard Greeneuill under the charge of Master Ralfe Lane, General of the same, from the 17. of August, 1585, until the 18. of June 1586. In *The Principal Navigations, Voyages and Discoveries of the English Nation.* Richard Hakluyt. Cambridge, Eng.: Cambridge University Press.

Larson, Lewis H., Jr. 1971. Archaeological Implications of Social Stratification at the Etowah Site, Georgia in Approaches to the Social Dimensions of Mortuary Practices. J.A. Brown, editor. *Memoirs of the Society for American Archaeology,* no. 25.

———. 1959. A Mississippian Headdress from Etowah, Georgia. *American Antiquity,* vol. 25, no. 1.

———. 1954. Georgia Historical Commission Excavations at the Etowah Site—Summer 1954. *Early Georgia,* vol. 1, no. 3. Cochran, Georgia.

Lawson, John. 1860. *History of Carolina, containing the exact description and natural history of that country.* Raleigh, N.C.

Leach, Edmund. 1973. Levels of Communication and Problems of Taboo in the Appreciation of Primitive Art. In *Primitive Art and Society.* Anthony Forge, editor. The Wenner-Gren Foundation for Anthropological Research, Inc. Oxford University Press.

Leader, Jonathan. 1991. The South Florida Metal Complex: A Preliminary Discussion of the Effects of the Introduction of an Elite Metal on a Contact Period Native American Society. *Metals in Society: Theory Beyond Analysis.* Robert M. Ehrenreich, ed. MASCA Research Papers In Science and Archaeology, vol. 8, part 3. Philadelphia: The University Museum, University of Pennsylvania.

———. 1988. Technological Continuities and Specialization in Prehistoric Metalwork in the Eastern United States. Unpublished Ph.D. dissertation, University of Florida.

Lee, Dorothy. 1960. Linguistic Reflection of Wintu Thought in *Explorations in Communication.* Boston, Mass.: Beacon Press.

Levine, Morton H. 1957. Prehistoric Art and Ideology. *American Anthropologist,* vol. 59, no. 6.

Lewis, T.M.N. 1946. Editor's note. *Tennessee Archaeologist,* vol. 3, no. 1.

Lewis, T.M.N., and Madeline Kneberg. 1954. The Cross Symbol on Artifacts. *Ten Years of the Tennessee Archaeologist.*

Linton, Ralph. 1943. Nativistic Movements. *American Anthropologist,* vol. 45.

Lurie, Nancy. 1959. Indian Cultural Adjustment to European Civilization. In *Seventeenth Century America.* James M. Smith, editor. Chapel Hill: University of North Carolina Press.

Magrath, Willis H. 1945. The North Benton Mound: A Hopewell Site in Ohio. *American Antiquity,* vol. 11, no. 1. Menasha.

Malinowski, Bronislaw. 1936. Science, Religion and Reality. In *The Riddell Memorial Lectures.* J. Needham, editor.

Maringer, Johannes. 1976. Blood in Cult and Belief of Prehistoric Man. *Anthropos,* vol. 71, nos. 1 and 2.

Mason, Ronald J. 1981. *Great Lakes Archaeology.* New York: Academic Press.

Mathews, Zena Pearlstone. 1982. Of Man and Beast: Effigy Pipe Chronology of the Ontario Iroquois. In *Native North American Art History.* Mathews and Jonaitis, editors. Palo Alto, Calif.: Peek Publications.

Mauss, Marcel. 1967. *The Gift: Forms of Exchange in Archaic Societies.* New York: Norton.

McAdams, William Jr. 1884. Mounds of the Mississippi Bottom, Illinois. *Annual Report of the Smithsonian Institution for 1882.* Washington, D.C.

———. 1880. Ancient Mounds of Illinois. *Proceedings of the American Association for the Advancement of Science,* vol. 29. Salem.

McDonald, S. Edgar. 1950. The Crable Site, Fulton County, Illinois. *Journal of the Illinois State Archaeological Society,* vol. 7, no. 4.

McGregor, John C. 1958. *The Pool and Irving Villages: A Study of Hopewell Occupation in the Illinois Valley.* Urbana: University of Illinois.

———. 1952. The Havana Site in Hopewellian Communities in Illinois. Thorne Deuel, editor. *Illinois State Museum Scientific Papers,* vol. 5, no. 1. Springfield.

McKenzie, Douglas H. 1965. The Burial Complex of the Moundville Phase, Alabama. *The Florida Anthropologist,* vol. 18, no. 3, part 1.

McKern, W.C. 1937. A Hypothesis for the Asiatic Origin of the Woodland Culture Pattern. *American Antiquity,* vol. 3, no. 2.

———. 1931. A Wisconsin Variant of the Hopewell Culture. *Bulletin of the Public Museum of the City of Milwaukee,* vol. 10, no. 2. Milwaukee.

McPherron, Alan. 1967. The Juntenan Site and the Late Woodland Prehistory of the Upper Great Lakes Region. *Anthropological Papers,* no. 30. Museum of Anthropology, University of Michigan, Ann Arbor.

McPherson, H.R. 1962. Copper Covered Objects of Wood from an Arkansas Mound. *Central States Archaeological Journal,* vol. 9, no. 4.

Michigan Archaeological Society News [no author named]. 1953. Vol. 1, no. 1.

Milanich, Jerald T., and Charles H. Fairbanks. 1980. *Florida Archaeology.* New York: Academic Press/Harcourt, Brace, Jovanovich Publishers.

Miles, Suzanne W. 1951. A Revaluation of the Old Copper Industry. *American Antiquity,* vol. 16, no. 3. Menasha.

Miller, Samuel, Rev. D.P. via Rev. John Heckewelder. 1841. Indian tradition of the first arrival of the Dutch on Manhattan. In *Collections of the New York Historical Society,* 2nd series, vol. 1. New York.

Mills, William C. 1922. Exploration of the Mound City Group. *Ohio Archaeological and Historical Society Publications,* vol. 31, nos. 1–3. Columbus.

———. 1922a. The Exploration of the Mound City, Ross County, Ohio. *American Anthropologist,* vol. 24, no. 4.

———. 1916. Exploration of the Tremper Mound in Scioto County, Ohio. In *Holmes Anniversary Album, Anthropological Essays.* Washington, D.C.

———. 1909. The Seip Mound in *Putnam Anniversary Volume.* New York: G.E. Stechert and Company.

———. 1902. Excavations of the Adena Mound. *Ohio Archaeological and Historical Society Publications,* vol. 10, no. 4.

Mooney, James. 1965. *The Ghost Dance Religion and the Sioux Outbreak of 1890.* Chicago, Ill.: University of Chicago Press.

Moore, C.B. 1912. Some Aboriginal Sites on Red River. *Journal of the Academy of Natural Sciences of Philadelphia,* 2nd series, vol. 14, part 4.

———. 1911. Some Aboriginal Sites on Mississippi River. *Journal of the Academy of Natural Sciences of Philadelphia,* 2nd series, vol. 14, part 3.

———. 1910. Antiquities of the St. Francis, White, and Black Rivers, Arkansas. *Journal of the Academy of Natural Sciences of Philadelphia,* 2nd series, vol. 14, part 2.

———. 1907. Moundville Revisited. *Journal of the Academy of Natural Sciences of Philadelphia,* 2nd series, vol. 13, part 3.

———. 1905. Certain Aboriginal remains of Mobile Bay and Mississippi Sound. *Journal of the Academy of Natural Sciences of Philadelphia,* 2nd series, Vol. ?, part 2.

———. 1905a. Certain Aboriginal Remains of the Black Warrior River. *Journal of the Academy of Natural Sciences of Philadelphia,* 2nd series, vol. 12, part 2.

———. 1903. Certain Aboriginal Mounds of the Florida Central West-Coast. *Journal of the Academy of Natural Sciences of Philadelphia,* 2nd series, vol. 12, part 3.

———. 1900. Certain Aboriginal Remains of the Alabama River. *Journal of the Academy of Natural Sciences of Philadelphia,* 2nd series, vol. 11, part 3.

———. 1894–96. Certain Sand Mounds of the St. Johns River, Florida. *Journal of the Academy of Natural Sciences of Philadelphia,* 2nd series, vol. 10.

Moorehead, Warren K. 1932. *Etowah Papers.* New Haven, Conn.: Yale University Press.

———. 1922. The Hopewell Mound Group of Ohio. *Field Museum of Natural Histroy Publication 211,* Anthropological Series, vol. 6, no. 5.

Moreau, Maxwell. 1951. The Woodland Cultures of Southern Illinois. *Logan Museum Bulletin,* no. 7, Beloit College, Beloit, Wisconsin.

Morse, Phyllis, Dan Morse, and Merrill Emmons. 1961. The Southern Cult: The Emmons Site, Fulton County, Illinois. *Central States Archaeological Journal,* vol. 8, no. 4. Springdale, Arkansas.

Muller, Jon. 1986. *Archaeology of the Lower Ohio River Valley.* Orlando, Fla.: Academic Press, Inc.

———. 1986a. Pans and a Grain of Salt: Mississippian Specialization Revisited. *American Antiquity,* vol. 51, no. 2.

———. 1984. The Southern Cult. *The Southeastern Ceremonial Complex: Artifacts and Analysis,* Patricia Galloway, ed. Lincoln: University of Nebraska Press.

———. 1978. The Southeast. *Ancient Native Americans.* Jesse D. Jennings, ed. San Francisco: W.H. Freeman and Co.

Myer, William E. 1924. Indian Trails of the Southeast. *Forty-Second Annual Report.* Washington, D.C.: Bureau of American Ethnology.

Myron, Robert E. 1954. Hopewellian Three-Dimensional Sculpture: Part 1. *Illinois State Archaeological Society Journal.*

———. 1954a. Hopwellian Three-Dimensional Sculpture: Part 2. *Illinois State Archaeological Society Journal,* vol. 1, no. 1.

Newman, George K., and Melvin Fowler. 1952. Hopewellian Sites in the Lower Wabash Valley. In *Hopewellian Communities in Illinois.* Thorne Deuel, editor. *Scientific Papers, Illinois State Museum,* vol. 5, no. 1. Springfield.

Newport, Christopher. 1969. Letter, the Original Voyage. In *The Jamestown Voyages Under the First Charter 1606–1609,* vol. 1. Works issued by the Hakluyt Society, no. 136.

Niehardt, John G. 1961. *Black Elk Speaks: Being the Life Story of a Holy Man of the Oglala Sioux.* University of Nebraska Press, Lincoln.

Nuñez Cabeza de Vaca, Alvar. 1951. *The Journey and Route of the First European to Cross the Continent of North America: 1534–1536.* Cleve Hallenbeck, editor. Port Washington, N.Y.: Kennikat Press.

Nuttal, Zelia. 1932. Some Comparisons Between Etowah, Mexican and Mayan Designs. *Etowah Papers.* New Haven.

O'Brien, Patricia J. 1994. The Bird-Man There in the Southeastern Ceremonial Complex. Paper presented at the Second Southeastern Ceremonial Complex conference, Austin, Texas.

Pader, Ellen-Jane. 1982. *Symbolism, Social Relations and the Interpretation of Mortuary Remains.* British Archaeological Reports International Series 130.

Painter, Floyd. 1971. Concentric Rectangles: A Recurring Decorative Motif Having Possible Magico-Religious Significance. *The Chesopiean,* vol. 9, nos. 5–6.

Pasztory, Esther. 1982. Shamanism in North American Indian Art. In *Native North American Art History.* Mathews and Jonaitis, editors. Palo Alto, Calif.: Peek Publications.

Peebles, Christopher S. 1971. Moundville and Surrounding Sites: Some Structural Considerations of Mortuary Practices (II). In *Approaches to the Social Dimensions of Mortuary Practices.* J.A. Brown, editor. *Memoirs of the Society for American Archaeology,* no. 25.

Penman, John T. 1977. The Old Copper Culture: An Analysis of Old Copper Artifacts. *The Wisconsin Archaeologist,* vol 58, no. 1.

Percy, George. 1969. George Percy's Discourse. In *The Jamestown Voyages Under the First Charter 1606–1609,* vol. 1. Works issued by the Hakluyt Society, no. 136.

Perino, Gregory H. 1968. The Pete Klunk Mound Group, Calhoun County, Illinois: The Archaic and Hopewell Occupations in Hopewell and Woodland Site Archaeology in Illinois. *Illinois Archaeological Society Bulletin,* No. 6. Urbana.

———. 1962. Hopewellian Art: The Gilcrease Raven Pipe. *Central States Archaeological Journal,* vol. 9, no. 1. Springdale, Arkansas.

Perzigian, Anthony J. 1977. Biocultural Adaptation in Prehistoric America. *Biocultural Adaptation in Prehistoric America.* Robert L. Blakeley, ed. Southern Anthropological Society Proceedings no. 11. Athens, Ga.: University of Georgia Press.

Peterson, Dennis, A. 1984. A History of Excavations and Interpretations of Artifacts from the Spiro Mounds Site. *The Southeastern Ceremonial Complex: Artifacts and Analysis.* Patricia Galloway, ed. Lincoln: University of Nebraska Press.

Phillips, Philip and James A. Brown. 1978. *Pre-Columbian Shell Engravings from the Craig Mound at Spiro, Oklahoma,* vols. 1–6. Cambridge, Mass.: Peabody Museum Press, Harvard University.

Phillips, Ruth B. 1984. *Patterns of Power.* Government of Ontario. Ottawa.

Pickett, Albert. 1851. *History of Alabama and Incidentally of Georgia and Mississippi from the Earliest Period,* 3rd ed., 2 vols. Charleston: Walker and James.

Porter, James W. 1969. The Mitchell Site and Prehistoric Exchange Systems at Cahokia. *Explorations into Cahokia Archaeology.* Illinois Archaeological Survey, Urbana.

Price, T. Douglas, and James A. Brown, eds. 1985. *Prehistoric Hunter-Gatherers: The Emergence of Cultural Complexity.* New York: Academic Press, Inc.

Putnam, F.W. and Charles C. Willoughby. 1896. Symbolism in Ancient American Art. *Proceedings of the American Association for the Advancement of Science,* vol XLIV.

Quimby, George I. 1966. *Indian Culture and European Trade Goods.* Madison: University of Wisconsin Press.

———. 1963. Late Period Copper Artifacts in the Upper Great Lakes Region. *Wisconsin Archaeologist,* vol. 44, no. 4.

———. 1960. *Indian Life in the Upper Great Lakes: 11,000 b.c. to a.d. 1800.* Chicago: University of Chicago Press.

———. 1954. The Old Copper Assemblage and Extinct Animals. *American Antiquity,* vol. XX, no. 2.

———. 1943. A Subjective Interpretation of Some Design Similarities Between Hopewell and Northern Algonkian. *American Anthropologist,* vol. 45. Menasha.

Rands, R.L. 1957. Comparative Notes on the Hand-Eye Motif. *American Antiquity,* vol. 22, no. 3.

———. 1954. Horned Serpent Stories. *Journal of American Folklore,* vol. 67.

Rickard, T.A. 1939. The Use of Iron and Copper by the Indians of British Columbia. *British Columbia Historical Quarterly,* vol. 3.

———. 1934. The Use of Native Copper by the Indigenes of North America. *Journal of the Royal Anthropological Institute,* vol. 64, nos. 7–9.

———. 1932. *A History of American Mining.* New York: McGraw-Hill Book Co., Inc.

Rothenberg, Jerome. 1985. *Technicians of the Sacred.* Los Angeles: University of California Press.

Ritzenthaler, Robert, et al. 1957. "Reigh Site Report." *Wisconsin Archaeologist,* vol 38, no. 4. Madison.

Ruhl, Katherine C. 1992. Copper Earspools from Ohio Hopewell Sites. *Midcontinental Journal of Archaeology,* vol. 17, no. 1.

Salzer, Robert J. 1974. Bear-Walking: A Shamanisitic Phenomenon Among the Potowatomi Indians of Wisconsin. *Wisconsin Archaeologist,* vol. 53, no. 3.

Sampson, Kevin, and Duane Esarey. 1993. A Survey of Elaborate Mississippian Copper Artifacts from Illinois. *Illinois Archaeology: Journal of the Illinois Anthropological Society,* vol. 5, nos. 1 and 2.

Sandoz, Mari. 1961. *Crazy Horse: The Strange Man of the Oglalas.* University of Nebraska Press, Lincoln.

Sassman, Kenneth E. 1995. The Social Contradictions of Traditional and Innovative Cooking Technologies in the Prehistoric American Southeast. *The Emergence of Pottery,* William K. Barnett and John W. Hoopes, eds. Washington, D.C.: Smithsonian Institution Press.

Schultes, Richard Evans. 1972. Hallucinogens in the Western Hemisphere. In *The Flesh of the Gods: The Ritual Use of Hallucinogens.* Peter Furst, editor. New York: Praeger.

Sears, William H. 1971. Food Production and Village Life in the Prehistoric Southeastern United States. *Archaeology,* vol. 24, no. 4.

Seeman, Mark F. 1979. The Hopewell Interaction Sphere: The Evidence for Interregional Trade and Structural Complexity. *Indiana Historical Society Prehistoric Research Series,* vol. 5, no. 2. Indianapolis.

Shetrone, H.C. 1930. *The Mound-Builders.* New York: D. Appleton and Company.

———. 1926. Explorations of the Hopewell Group, *Ohio Archaeological and Historical Quarterly,* vol. 35, no. 1. Columbus.

Shetrone, H.C., and E.F. Greenman. 1931. Explorations of the Seip Group of Prehistoric Earthworks. *Ohio Archaeological and Historical Quarterly*, vol. 40, no. 3. Columbus.

Skinner, Alanson. 1921. Material Culture of the Menominee. *Indian Notes and Monographs*, no. 20, Museum of the American Indian-Heye Foundation, New York.

Slotkin, James Sydney. 1952. Menomini Peyotism. *Transactions of the American Philosophical Society*, n.s., vol. 42, part 4.

Smith, John. 1912. *"Works" in First Explorations of the Trans-Allegheney Region by Virginians: 1650–1674*. Clarence W. Alvord and Lee Bidgood, eds. Cleveland.

———. 1907. Works: 1608–1631. In *Original Narratives of Early American History: 1605–1625*. J. Franklin Jameson, editor. New York: Charles Scribner's Sons.

———. 1907a. Works: 1608–1631. In *Narratives of Early Virginia: 1606–1625*. Lyon Gardiner Tyler, editor. New York.

———. 1884. Works 1608–1631. Edward Arber, editor. *English Scholar's Library*, no. 16. Birmingham.

Speck, Frank G. 1914. The Double-Curve Motive in Northeastern Algonkian Art. *Anthropological Series, Geological Survey of Canada, Memoir 42*. Ottawa.

Spier, Leslie. 1921. The Sun Dance of the Plains Indians: Its Development and Diffusion. *Anthropological Papers of the American Museum of Natural History*, vol. 16, part 7. New York.

Spier, Leslie, A. Irving Hallowell, and Stanley S. Newman. 1941. *Language, Culture and Personality*. Sapir Memorial Publication Fund. Menasha, Wisconsin.

Squier, E.G., and E.H. Davis. 1848. Ancient Monuments of the Mississippian Valley. *Southern Contributions to Knowledge*, vol. 1. Washington, D.C.

Stelle, J. Parish. 1871. Account of Aboriginal Ruins at Savannah. *Annual Report of the Smithsonian Institution*. Washington, D.C.

Stirling, M.W. 1934. Smithsonian Archaeological Projects Conducted Under the Federal Emergency Relief Administration, 1933–34. *Annual Report of the Smithsonian Institution, 1934*. Washington, D.C.

Strachey, William. 1849. *The historie of travaile into Virginia Britannia*. Hakluyt Society Publication, vol. 6. London.

Struever, Stuart and Gail Houart. 1972. An Analysis of the Hopewell Interaction Sphere. In Social Exchange and Interaction, E. Wilmsen, ed. *Anthropological Papers*, no. 46. Museum of Anthropology, University of Michigan, Ann Arbor.

Swanton, John R. 1946. Indians of the Southeastern United States. *Smithsonian Institution Bureau of American Ethnology*, bulletin 137. Washington, D.C.

———. 1929. Myths and Tales of the Southeastern Indians. *Smithsonian Institution Bureau of American Ethnology*, bulletin 88. Washington, D.C.

———. 1928a. Aboriginal Culture of the Southeast. *Forty-second Annual Report of the Smithsonian Institution Bureau of American Ethnology*. Washington, D.C.

———. 1928b. Religious Beliefs and Medical Practices of the Creek Indians. *Forty-second Annual Report of the Smithsonian Institution Bureau of American Ethnology*. Washington, D.C.

Swartz, B.K. Jr., ed. 1971. *Adena: The Seeking of an Identity*. Ball State University Press.

Taxay, Don. 1970. *Money of the American Indians and Other Primitive Cultures of the Americans*. New York: Nummus Press.

Thomas, Cyrus. 1890. *Twelfth Annual Report of the Smithsonian Institution Bureau of American Ethnology*. Washington, D.C.

———. 1884. The Etowah Mounds. *Science*, vol. 3, no. 73. Cambridge, Massachusetts.

Thwaites, Ruben Gold, editor. 1896–1901. *Jesuit Relations and Allied Documents: Travels and Explorations of the Jesuit Missionaries in New France, 1610–1791.* Cleveland.

Trevelyan, Amelia M. 1976. *Linguistic Relationships Regarding Words for Copper in Native American Language.* Unpublished Paper.

Trigger, Bruce. 1976. *The Children of the Aataentsic: A History of the Huron People to 1660.* McGill-Queens University Press, Kingston and Montreal.

Tuck, James A. 1978. Regional Cultural Development 3000–300 B.C. In *Handbook of North American Indians: Northeast,* vol. 15. Bruce Trigger, vol. ed. Washington, D.C.

Verazzano, John. 1841. Voyage. In *Collections of the New York Historical Society,* 2nd series, vol. 1. New York.

Walker, J.R. 1975. Oglala Metaphysics. In *Teachings from the American Earth.* Dennis Tedlock and Barbara Tedlock, editors. New York: Liveright.

Wallace, Anthony F.C. 1969. *The Death and Rebirth of the Seneca.* New York: Random House.

———. 1958. The Dekanawidah Myth Analyzed as the Record of a Revitalization Movement. *Ethnohistory,* vol. V.

———. 1956. Revitalization Movements: Some Theoretical Considerations for their Comparative Study. *American Anthropologist,* vol. 58.

———. 1952. Handsome Lake and the Great Revival in the West. *American Antiquity.* Summer.

Walthall, John A. 1980. *Prehistoric Indians of the Southeast: Archaeology of Alabama and the Middle South.* University of Alabama Press.

———. 1972. The Chronological Position of Copena in Eastern States Archaeology. *Journal of Alabama Archaeology,* vol. 18, no. 2.

Waring, Antonio J. Jr. 1968. An Engraved Monolithic Axe of Georgia. *The Waring Papers,* S. Williams, editor. *Papers of the Peabody Museum of Archaeology and Ethnology,* vol. 58. Harvard University.

———. 1968a. The Southern Cult and Muskogena Ceremonial, (1940, 1945). In *The Waring Papers.* S. Williams, editor. *Papers of the Peabody Museum of Archaeology and Ethnology,* vol. 58. Harvard University.

———. 1968b. The Striped Pole and Terrace Motif. In *The Waring Papers.* S. Williams, editor. *Papers of the Peabody Museum of Archaeology and Ethnology,* vol. 58. Harvard University.

Waring, Antonio J. Jr., and Preston Holder. 1945. A Prehistoric Ceremonial Complex in the Southeastern United States. *American Anthropologist,* vol. 47, no. 1.

Webb, Clarence H., and Monroe Dodd Jr. 1939. Further Excavations of the Gahagan Mound; Connections with a Florida Culture. *Bulletin of the Texas Archaeological and Palaeontological Society,* vol. 11. Abilene.

Webb, William S. 1941. Mount Horeb Earthworks, Site 1, and The Drake Mound, Site 11, Fayette County, Kentucky. *The University of Kentucky Reports in Anthropology and Archaeology,* vol. 10, no. 2. Lexington.

———. 1940. Ricketts Site Revisited, Site 3, Montgomery County, Kentucky. *University of Kentucky Reports in Anthropology and Archaeology,* vol. 3, no. 6.

———. 1939. Archaeological Survey of the Wheeler Basin. *Smithsonian Institution Bureau of American Ethnology,* bulletin 122. Washington, D.C.

Webb, William S., and David L. DeJarnette. 1942. An Archaeological Survey of Pickwick Basin in the Adjacent Portions of the States of Alabama, Mississippi and Tennessee. *Smithsonian Institution Bureau of American Ethnology,* Bulletin 129, Washington, D.C.

Webb, William S., and Raymond S. Baby. 1957. *The Adena People,* no. 2. Ohio Historical Society. Columbus.

Webb, William S., and Charles G. Wilder. 1951. *An Archaeological Survey of the Guntersville Basin in Northern Alabama.* University of Kentucky. Lexington.

Webb, William S., and William G. Haag. 1947. Archaic Sites in McLean County, Kentucky. *University of Kentucky Reports in Anthropology and Archaeology,* vol. 7, no. 2. Lexington.

———. 1947a. The Fisher Site, Fayette County, Kentucky. *University of Kentucky Reports in Anthropology and Archaeology,* vol. 8, no. 2. Lexington.

Wedel, Mildred Mott. 1959. Oneota Sites on the Upper Iowa River. *The Missouri Archaeologist,* vol. 21, nos. 2–4. Columbia.

Weiss, K.M. 1972. On the Systematic Bias in Skeletal Sexing. *American Journal of Physical Anthropology,* vol. 37, no. 2.

Weissner, Polly. 1989. Style and Changing Relations Between the Individual and Society. *The Meanings of Things: Material Culture and Symbolic Expression.* Ian Hodder, ed. London: Unwin Hymann.

Weslager, C.A. 1942. Ossuaries on the Delmarka Peninsula and Exotic Influences in the Coastal Aspect of the Woodland Pattern. *American Antiquity,* vol. 8, no. 2.

Whittlesey, Charles. 1872. The Great Mound on the Etowah River, Georgia. *Proceedings of the American Association for the Advancement of Science,* vol. 20. Cambridge.

Whorf, Benjamin L. 1941. The Relation of Habitual Thought and Behavior to Language. In *Language, Culture and Personality.* Menasha, Wisc.: Sapir Memorial Publication Fund.

Willey, Gordon R., and Demitri B. Shimkin. 1973. The Maya Collapse: A Summary View. In *The Classic Maya Collapse.* T. Patrick Culbert, editor. Albuquerque: University of New Mexico Press.

Willimas, Stephen, and John M. Goggin. 1956. The Long-Nosed God Mask in the Eastern United States. *The Missouri Archaeologist,* vol. 18, no. 3.

Willoughby, Charles. 1932. Notes on the History and Symbolism of the Muskhogeans and the People of Etowah. In *Etowah Papers I: Exploration of the Etowah Site in Georgia,* W.K. Moorehead, editor. Phillips Academy, Yale University Press.

———. 1897. An Analysis of the Decorations upon Pottery from the Mississippi Valley. *Journal of American Folklore,* vol. 10.

Willoughby, Charles C., and E.A. Hooton. 1922. The Turner Group of Earthworks. *Peabody Museum of Archaeology and Ethnology,* vol. 8, no. 3.

Wilson, Thomas. 1894. The Swastika. *Report of the United States National Museum,* 1894.

Wintemberg, W.J. 1923. Certain Eye Designs on the Archaeological Artifacts from North America. *Transactions of the Royal Society of Canada,* vol. 17, 3rd series.

Winter, Howard D. 1968. Value Systems and Trade Cycles of the Late Archaic in the Midwest in *New Perspectives in Archaeology.* Sally R. and Lewis R. Binford, editors. Chicago, Ill.: Aldine Publishing Company.

Witthoft, John. 1949. Green Corn Ceremonialism in the Eastern Woodland. *Occasional Contributions from the Museum of Anthropology of the University of Michigan.* Ann Arbor, Mich.: University of Michigan Press.

Wittry, Warren L., and Robert E. Ritzenthaler. 1957. The Old Copper Culture: An Archaic Manifestation in Wisconsin. *Wisconsin Archaeologist,* vol. 38, no. 4.

Wray, Donald E., and Richard S. MacNeish. 1961. The Hopewellian and Weaver Occupations of the Weaver Site, Fulton county, Illinois. *Illinois State Museum Scientific Papers,* vol. 7, no. 2. Springfield.

Wright, Gary A. 1967. Some Aspects of Early and Mid-Seventeenth Century Exchange Networks in the Western Great Lakes. *Michigan Archaeologist,* vol. 13, no. 4

———. 1964. Aboriginal Relationships Between Culture and Plant Life in the Upper Great Lakes Region. *Anthropological Papers,* no. 23, Museum of Anthropology, University of Michigan. Ann Arbor.

Yarnell, Richard Asa. 1976. Early Plant Husbandry in Eastern North America in Cultural Change and Continuity. In *Essays in Honor of James Bennett Griffin,* Charles E. Cleland, ed. Academic Press, New York.

———. 1964. Aboriginal Relationships Between Culture and Plant Life in the Upper Great Lakes Region. *Anthropological Papers,* no. 23. Museum of Anthropology, University of Michigan, Ann Arbor.

Young, Gloria H. 1976. Structural Analysis of Panpipe Burials. *Tennessee Archaeologist,* vol. 32, nos. 1 and 2.

Index

Bold numbers refer to plates; *italic* to figures; upper case Roman numerals to tables; and maps are referred to as MI, MII, and MIII

www.ingramcontent.com/pod-product-compliance
Lightning Source LLC
LaVergne TN
LVHW050147080826
844660LV00002B/108

* 9 7 8 0 8 1 3 1 2 2 7 2 4 *